Intervention and Transnationalism in Africa
Global–Local Networks of Power

As the concept of globalization emerged in late twentieth century social science, understanding how external forces and phenomena shape the politics of nation-states and communities became an even greater imperative. This volume calls attention to "transboundary formations" – intersections of cross-border, national, and local forces that produce, destroy, or transform local order and political authority, significantly impacting on ordinary people's lives. It analyzes the intervention of external forces in political life, both deepening and broadening the concept of international "intervention" and the complex contexts within which it unfolds. While transboundary formations can emerge anywhere, they have a particular salience in sub-Saharan Africa where the limits to state power make them especially pervasive and consequential. Including conceptual contributions and theoretically informed case studies, the volume considers global–local connections, taking a fresh perspective on contemporary Africa's political contraints and possibilities, with important implications for other parts of the world.

THOMAS M. CALLAGHY is Professor of Political Science at the University of Pennsylvania. His publications include *The State-Society Struggle: Zaire in Comparative Perspective* (1984) and *Hemmed In: Responses to Africa's Economic Decline* (1994).

RONALD KASSIMIR is Program Director of the International Dissertation Field Research and Africa Programs. He has published on issues related to African politics in journals such as *Commonwealth and Comparative Politics*, *African Affairs*, and *Africa Today*. He is co-author (with Mark Pires and Mesky Brhane) of the study *Investing in Return: Rates of Return of African Ph.D.s Trained in North America* (1999).

ROBERT LATHAM serves as Director of the Social Science Research Council Program on Information Technology, International Cooperation and Global Security. He is also Adjunct Assistant Professor of International and Public Affairs at Columbia University. His publications include *The Liberal Moment: Modernity, Security, and the Making of Postwar International Order* (1997) and *Cooperation and Conflict in a Connected World: Information Technology and Global Politics* (in preparation).

Intervention and Transnationalism in Africa

Global–Local Networks of Power

edited by

Thomas M. Callaghy

University of Pennsylvania

Ronald Kassimir

Social Science Research Council

Robert Latham

Social Science Research Council

CAMBRIDGE
UNIVERSITY PRESS

PUBLISHED BY THE PRESS SYNDICATE OF THE UNIVERSITY OF CAMBRIDGE
The Pitt Building, Trumpington Street, Cambridge, United Kingdom

CAMBRIDGE UNIVERSITY PRESS
The Edinburgh Building, Cambridge CB2 2RU, UK
40 West 20th Street, New York, NY 10011-4211, USA
477 Williamstown Road, Port Melbourne, VIC 3207, Australia
Ruiz de Alarcón 13, 28014 Madrid, Spain
Dock House, The Waterfront, Cape Town 8001, South Africa

http://www.cambridge.org

First published 2001

Printed in the United Kingdom at the University Press, Cambridge

Typeface Plantin 10/12 pt.   *System* LaTeX 2_ε [TB]

This volume is the product of a joint initiative of the Africa Program
and the International Peace and Security Program of the Social Science
Research Council.

A catalogue record for this book is available from the British Library.

Library of Congress Cataloguing in Publication Data
Intervention and transnationalism in Africa : global–local networks of power /
[edited by] Thomas M. Callaghy, Robert Latham, Ronald Kassimir.
    p.   cm.
Includes bibliographical references and index.
ISBN 0 521 80666 6 – ISBN 0 521 00141 2 (pb.)
1. Africa – Politics and government – 20th century.   2. Power (Social sciences) –
Africa.   3. Social sciences – Network analysis.   I. Callaghy, Thomas M.
II. Kassimir, Ronald, –   III. Latham, Robert.
JQ1875 .I68   2001
320.96 – dc21   2001025912

ISBN 0 521 80666 6 (hardback)
ISBN 0 521 00141 2 (paperback)

Contents

Contributors

MICHAEL BARNETT Department of Political Science, University of Wisconsin

THOMAS M. CALLAGHY Department of Political Science, University of Pennsylvania

FREDERICK COOPER Departments of Afro-American Studies and History, University of Michigan

RONALD KASSIMIR Africa Program and International Dissertation Field Research Fellowship Program, Social Science Research Council

ROBERT LATHAM Program of Information Technology, International Co-operation and Global Security, Social Science Research Council

CAROLYN NORDSTROM Department of Anthropology, University of Notre Dame

CYRIL I. OBI Nigerian Institute of International Affairs Lagos

WILLIAM RENO Department of Political Science, Northwestern University

JANET ROITMAN Centre National de la Recherche Scientifique

HANS PETER SCHMITZ Post-Doctoral Fellow at the Human Rights Program, University of Chicago

Preface

This volume started with a belief that global–local connections were poorly understood by both scholars and practitioners in general, and in Africa in particular. We felt some of these gaps could be addressed by bringing different perspectives into creative interaction with each other, both within disciplines (e.g. comparative politics and international relations within the discipline of political science) and across them (e.g. history, political science, and anthropology). Our entry into these issues was via what is usually termed international "intervention" and the question of how "networks" that form between global, state, and local forces channel these interventions in ways that often produce unintended outcomes. Our notion of intervention was expansive: we included not just peacekeeping forces or structural adjustment packages (i.e. the activities of juridical international institutions) but a wide range of practices by "external" institutions that shaped political processes in Africa – commercial circuits, NGOs, mercenaries, and missionaries, for example.

Although we began with an expansive view of intervention, we soon discovered that it was not adequate for examining these processes as they involved the production of authority and order "on the ground." It became clear that we needed to focus on how networks, and the goods, power, and ideas that flow within them, "bumped into" broad political and economic structures, global discourses, and local socio-economic and political practices. Networks obviously matter on a variety of levels, but we recognized that the contribution of this project would be, in part, to show that networks are but one of a number of formations involved in translocal constructions of authority and order. The focus of the book thus became *transboundary formations*, which include what is conventionally called intervention as well as global, national, and local networks, institutions, and discourses.

We also reflected on the framing of these issues in terms of the duality "global–local." While many of the authors in the volume (including the editors in their own chapters) wrestle with bringing specificity to this phrase, we came to understand that the weight carried by the terms "global" and "local," and the sometimes invigorating, sometimes stodgy debates that surround them, made it ever more difficult to identify and analyze existing empirical examples of political phenomena that connected different levels of analysis and troubled the presumed separation of them. Once again the notion of transboundary formations appeared to have more potential of capturing the rich empirical manifestations of "global–local" intersections without having to make sweeping pronouncements about globalization or unsubstantiated generalizations about Africa's insertion into global political, economic, and cultural structures and flows.

Along the way, we were constructively prodded by the contributors to this volume. While they may have questioned the formulation of specific questions, all helped us shape the project and pushed us and each other to think about the transboundary production of authority and order in ways that go beyond current emphases on intervention, global governance, regime transition, civil society, or "the coming anarchy." In good dialectical fashion, we asked them to revise their chapters to meet these shifts in emphasis. These chapters do not share a full consensus (which would surely be premature) on how to approach the transboundary production of order and authority. But they do share a commitment that an understanding of these phenomena is critical at the current political juncture for Africa and other parts of the world, as well as for conceptual work in the social sciences and humanities. Their methods of treating what many of them see as transboundary formation innovations and adaptations are themselves innovative and adaptive.

This project had a relatively complex genesis. It began as a joint endeavor between the SSRC's Africa Program and its MacArthur Foundation-funded International Peace and Security Program in early 1996. A planning meeting was held in March of that year at the School of Advanced International Studies in Washington, DC. The MacArthur Foundation also supported a workshop in Guatemala on "States in Crisis, States in Flux: Processes of Reconfiguration," which produced ideas that helped to shape this project. With the support of the Research Council of Norway and the European University Institute (EUI), a conference was held in March 1998 at EUI in Florence, where papers were first presented and discussed. In order to hone the volume's chapters as well as further develop its thematic thrust, a follow-up workshop was held at the University of Pennsylvania in December 1998, hosted by Penn's African Studies Center and the Christopher H. Browne Center for International Politics.

As a result of the unfolding of this process, we have many people to thank. Our appreciation goes out to William Zartman, who hosted the School of Advanced International Studies meeting, and all of those who participated in it (too many to name here). We thank Jonathan Friedman and Kajsa Eckholm-Friedman for connecting us with the Research Council of Norway, and to Council representatives Øyvind Hansen and Karin Dokken. At EUI, Thomas Risse graciously hosted the conference and contributed to local costs. He also contributed productive intellectual guidance to the project. Eckholm-Friedman, Hansen, and Dokken, as well as Risse, all attended the conference and contributed substantively to the discussions. In addition to them and to the authors of the chapters in the book, we also want to acknowledge the contributions of other participants at the Florence conference: Musa Abutudu, Gilbert Khadiagala, Audie Klotz, Peter Otim, Paul Richards, Hildegard Scheu, and several students at EUI. We especially appreciate the subsequent insights and criticisms offered by Richards throughout the development of the project.

Thanks also go to Sandra Barnes and Leigh Swigart of Penn's African Studies Center and to Avery Goldstein and Vikash Yadav of the Center for International Politics for making arrangements for the workshop and to both Centers for supporting some of the costs of the meeting.

Two final expressions of gratitude are in order. First, a number of wonderful SSRC program assistants contributed vital administrative support over the course of the project: Alison Lichter, Amini Kajunju, Mark Shoffner, Missy McNally, and especially Funmi Vogt. Second, the editors wish to thank all of the authors of this volume. They suffered our prodding with great intellectual engagement, sometimes in the face of tight deadlines. We learned a great deal along the way.

THOMAS CALLAGHY
RONALD KASSIMIR
ROBERT LATHAM
Swarthmore and New York

Abbreviations

ADB	African Development Bank
Afrodad	African Network on Debt and Development
CBO	community-based organizations
CM	Chikoko Movement
COSED	Coalition for Self-Determination
CRS	Catholic Relief Services
DCF	District Consultative Forum
DRC	Democratic Republic of the Congo
ERA	Environmental Rights Action
Eurodad	European Network on Debt and Development
FORD	Forum for the Restoration of Democracy
HIPC	heavily indebted poor country
IDB	Inter-American Development Bank
IFI	international financial institution
IMF	International Monetary Fund
INGO	international non-governmental organization
IPG	Inter-Parties Group
IPPG	Inter-Parties Parliamentary Group
IYC	Ijaw Youth Council
KADU	Kenya African Democratic Union
KANU	Kenya African National Union
KHRC	Kenya Human Rights Commission
MNOC	multinational oil corporation
MOSOP	Movement for the Survival of Ogoni People
MSF	Médecins Sans Frontières
NCCF	National Constitutional Consultative Forum
NCCK	National Council of Churches in Kenya
NCEC	National Convention for Constitutional Reform
NGO	non-governmental organization
PEAP	Poverty Eradication Action Plan
PRSP	Poverty Reduction Strategy Paper
RPF	Rwandan Patriotic Front

RPP	Release Political Prisoners
TD	transterritorial deployment
TNC	transnational corporation
UMDF	Uganda Multilateral Debt Fund
UN-UCAH	United Nations Humanitarian Assistance Coordination Unit
UNDP	United Nations Development Program
USAID	United States Agency for International Development
WB	World Bank
WFP	World Food Programme
WHO	World Health Organization

1 Introduction: transboundary formations, intervention, order, and authority

Robert Latham, Ronald Kassimir, and Thomas M. Callaghy

A tale of two countries

What is this book about? Rather than jumping directly into key conceptual matters, perhaps it would be useful to start with a vivid tale that illustrates many of the issues, themes, and questions raised in this volume – ones of order and authority, war and peace, intervention, and the structures, networks, and discourses that shape these outcomes. Hence this tale of two countries whose destinies seem to be closely interrelated and the varied, multi-textured forces that are shaping them.

In the 1970s, Uganda under the tyranny of Idi Amin became the early prototype of the failing post-colonial state as its economy and capacity to govern seemed to melt away while violence and uncertainty spread. Despite external help, the Ugandan governments of the early 1980s were unable to put Humpty-Dumpty back together again, as conflict ravaged many parts of the county. Yoweri Museveni formed a guerrilla army that eventually took power, and he became president in early 1986. To the surprise of most observers, Museveni managed for the most part to put Uganda back together again in the waning years of the Cold War. He had a great deal of external support from Western governments, the International Monetary Fund, the World Bank, agencies of the United Nations (UN), the Catholic Church and other religious groups, and a whole host of non-governmental organizations (NGOs). This help was reinforced and influenced by dominant international discourses about economic reform, political liberalization, human rights, poverty reduction, and development more generally. Complex regional, international, and diaspora trading networks provided additional assistance. Despite this unexpected renaissance, by the mid-1990s Uganda was still not completely free of violence as armed conflict flared in the north and the west with the support of neighboring countries.

The terrible genocide that erupted in Rwanda in April 1994 led to a renewed invasion of that country by the Tutsi Rwandan Patriotic Front (RPF), many of whose fighters had helped Museveni seize power and then invaded Rwanda from Uganda in 1990. The combined events resulted in over a million deaths and nearly two million refugees in surrounding countries, most of them in the Kivu region of Zaire (now the Congo). The UN, major Western states, and the international community proved to be totally ineffective in coping with these events, while a number of NGOs struggled mightily to alleviate the horror.

Zaire (now the Democratic Republic of the Congo [DRC]), in the 1990s, like Uganda in the 1970s, was a failing state under the brutal tyranny of Mobutu Sese Seko. The state no longer performed basic services, especially education, health care, and the maintenance of basic infrastructure. Its people were worse off than at any time since independence. The army brutalized many Zaireans while Mobutu and his generals auctioned off the country's vast resources to an unseemly set of international business actors.

Continuing turmoil in Rwanda and neighboring Burundi expanded the population in the refugee camps as the United Nations and various NGOs intervened to stabilize the situation. At the same time, the overthrown Hutu government of Rwanda reassembled itself and its army in eastern Zaire with the help of Mobutu, international arms merchants, and mercenaries. This massive social trauma reinvigorated longstanding tensions in Kivu, leading to the reemergence of local militia groups that tried to defend a complex set of local interests, mostly regarding land. Tutsi long resident in Zaire were increasingly in jeopardy, and in October 1996 they launched a rebellion. To the surprise of many, it quickly became a full-fledged effort to overthrow Mobutu, one with striking parallels to events in the early and mid-1960s.

In the post-Cold War context, Mobutu did not receive his usual assistance from major Western governments, while the rebels enjoyed the support of Rwanda, Uganda, Burundi, and Angola. The rebels were a strange mix of regular and irregular forces that overwhelmed Mobutu's retreating and looting army. Led by Laurent Kabila, a rebel leader from the 1960s turned minor warlord, they took Shaba (Katanga) and other mineral rich regions. In order to finance the ongoing uprising, Kabila, as the presumptive new leader of the country, hurriedly made deals with an odd assortment of international mining companies and other firms. His forces entered Kinshasa in May 1997 to the rejoicing of almost everybody. Mobutu fled and died in exile several months later.

During Kabila's march to power, the international community had sung its hymns of democratization, economic liberalization, and human rights, but to little if any avail. Zaire was rebaptized as the DRC and became a much bigger and vastly more complex Humpty-Dumpty than Uganda. The tasks that Kabila faced were staggering, and the record of his government in dealing with them proved to be weak indeed. In addition, he kept the United Nations and most of the NGOs from operating in much of the country, while unseemly business deals continued unabated. The Rwandans and Ugandans at first believed that they had solved their rebel and border security problems by helping put Kabila in power. This proved not to be the case, however, and in August 1998 the war was reignited as Rwandan and Ugandan forces moved against their erstwhile ally. Kabila received last-minute, regime-saving help from Angola, Zimbabwe, and Namibia, later reinforced by assistance from Chad and the Sudan.

Regional and international efforts to mediate what was being called Africa's "first world war" had little impact until an agreement was reached in Lusaka in July 1999. It was, however, characterized mostly by its constant violation by all sides. In the meantime, the rebel forces became ever more fragmented, especially with a split in the main rebel group and the addition of a militia force headed by a former Congolese businessman with major backing from Uganda. While the rebels and their allies held much of the north and east of the country, Ugandan and Rwandan forces began battling each other deep in the Congo, largely over the economic spoils of the conquered territory, as well as their mainly Congolese and Zimbabwean opponents. In return for their part in the struggle, Kabila allowed senior Zimbabwean military officers and politicians to engage in a wide range of lucrative economic activities. Under the terms of the Lusaka agreement, the United Nations was to place a peacekeeping force in the Congo, and many NGOs were anxious to get access to the beleaguered populations. By late 2000, this still proved impossible to do. As a result, war continued to rage, more refugees were created, economic resources were pillaged, and social life remained in turmoil as old local orders shattered and new ones emerged. The few coherent organizations that remained, such as the Catholic Church, did what they could to ameliorate the suffering of this terrible regional war. The International Monetary Fund and the World Bank tried to assist Kabila's "sovereign" government, but they too proved to be relatively ineffective. One of the many ironies of this situation is that Uganda, the rebuilt failed state of the 1970s, was one of the major players in the collapse of the Congo in the 1990s.[1]

One thing that stands out in this story is the role of "external" forces in its unfolding, the way they intersect with "internal" forces, and the pluralization of the kinds of forces involved over time. Museveni's

---

[1] Kabila was assassinated by one of his bodyguards on January 6, 2001 and was replaced by his son Joseph Kabila. The effect of this event on the hostilities, and on politics more generally, in the Congo remains very unclear at this time.

successful rebellion in the mid-1980s was unusual in the degree to which external actors were not involved. Taking place in the waning days of the Cold War and at a time when African states still largely followed norms of non-intervention (the major exception being, ironically, Tanzania's 1979 invasion of Uganda to oust Amin), both Western powers and Uganda's neighbors remained on the sidelines. As we chronicled above, this situation changed once Museveni captured the state. Through a combination of genuine goodwill, the desire of international financial institutions (IFIs) to find a willing partner in its structural adjustment prescriptions, and Western fears of the so-called "rogue state" of Sudan looming on its northern border, Uganda became the recipient of huge amounts of aid and the site of much NGO activity. It then became a major actor across its borders, beginning with its tacit support of the RPF invasion of Rwanda (the trigger event in the Great Lakes conflagration) and leading to its military support and adventurism in the Congo.

The Great Lakes conflicts, and especially the wars in the Congo, are thus impossible to make sense of without accounting for the role of regional and transnational forces. From the failure of French and United Nations peacekeeping efforts and the naivete of the NGO community in pre-genocide Rwanda[2] to the establishment of refugee camps in eastern Zaire, from the use of mercenaries to the presence of a range of foreign militaries, and from the influx of multinational firms to the mediation of the United Nations, external forces powerfully shaped the Congo's fate in the last decade of the twentieth century. They were neither peripheral nor determinative in the political trajectories of Uganda, the Congo, and the Great Lakes region in general. They were, and are, constitutive.

Indeed, the central challenge of this volume is to begin to develop ways of understanding this constitutive effect in general, and in Africa in particular. Both the resurrection of Uganda under Museveni and the disintegration of the Congo, first under Mobutu, then under Kabila, thus illustrate many of the key issues central to this volume. How do state and non-state, local and external forces interact to produce order and authority in various different kinds of social and political space? What kinds of actors are involved? What strategies are used? How stable, extensive, and productive are various forms of order and authority? How do different types of order and authority relate to each other? Whose voices and claims are heard and whose are silenced?

Unlike most standard accounts that employ the normal lenses of international relations and comparative politics, where "internal" and

---

[2] Superbly chronicled in Uvin (1998).

"external" forces are separated for analytical purposes, this volume conceptualizes and analyzes what we call transboundary formations of considerable diversity. They link global, regional, national, and local forces through structures, networks, and discourses that have wideranging impact, both benign and malign, on Africa, as well as on the international community itself. Above all, they play a major role in creating, transforming, and destroying forms of order and authority.

We now turn to more conceptual matters. This introduction will first discuss the nature and importance of transboundary formations and their relationship to recent discussions of "global" phenomena, then their role and impact in Africa, followed by their relationship to processes of "extraversion," and, lastly, their considerable institutional variety.

Transboundary formations, orders, and authorities

It is still too early to tell what kind of ultimate impact the surge of interest in things "global" will have on the social sciences. Despite the widespread hum of concern with "globalization," it is far from clear that work across the disciplines would be seriously undermined if the term were to disappear tomorrow. The analysis of phenomena and processes closely associated with the term – lightning financial exchanges or widely diffused cultural icons, for example – could be carried on under their own rubrics. And while the designation "global" may seem ubiquitous to some, a great deal of research is being conducted with no gesture toward it at all.

It may be some time before the designation "global" gains the kind of theoretical and empirical thickness and richness that terms such as state and society have. Until, or if ever, it does, we should not overlook a closely allied but more general development – the growing concern among social scientists and practitioners with processes and relationships that spill across national boundaries. Increasingly it is being taken for granted that there can be significant crossboundary dimensions to almost any object of study – village, identity group, class, NGO, or political party.

However, a division of labor, sometimes explicit, generally exists within and across the social science disciplines. Analyses can focus on phenomena that are by definition transboundary in nature (such as trade, migration, and diplomacy) or that are only influenced by cross-boundary forces (such as a national economy or local activism). US political science offers the most blatant form of division with its sub-field of international relations that stands apart from comparative politics, political theory, and the study of its own polity (American government). In sociology and anthropology there are less formal divisions, but the relatively recent attention to transnational cultural flows, and in the past to dependency theory, stands out against the tradition of studying societies and communities as though they were self-contained. The recent challenge to that self-containedness has come in numerous forms: from research into the ways that external forces such as multinational media or foreign-owned factories become integrated into a place or community, to the analysis of domestic political responses to international institutional pressures (Stallings 1995) produced, for example, by the IMF or international human rights organizations.

The distinction between objects of study that are by definition cross-boundary and those that are not overlaps with a number of binary oppositions that became quite fashionable in the 1990s – global/local, space of flows/space of places, external/internal, and outside/inside (Castells 1996; Hannerz 1996; Massey and Jess 1995; Robertson 1992; Walker 1993). Of all of these, the opposition global/local has had the greatest resonance in the social sciences. Not only have the terms global and local enjoyed incredibly stellar careers inside and outside the academy, but the two terms have conveniently subsumed an unusually wide band of referents (including flows, places, integration, fragmentation, regions, cities, systems, and sites). Opposing global with local is quite intuitive since the former term ultimately refers to some kind of claim about the range of forces operating across space. Typically, the local is either a discrete element within that global range or simply a site or phenomenon subject to global forces that are external to it.

This volume starts from the assumption that what is compelling about the opposition global/local is what lies silently between: the structures and relations that emerge through the intersection of social phenomena that vary in range, as well as form. The point is to pull back the global/local as though it were a husk comprising conceptual claims about what the global and the local are, or about how they shape one another. What should be exposed are the rich kernels of specific junctures joining diverse structures, actors, ideas, practices, and institutions with varying ranges in a common social and political frame. As the chapters in this volume show, these frames can involve civil war, the generation of wealth, or the protection of human rights.

As implied above, applying the label global, external, or foreign to something makes sense to us only if it is contrasted with phenomena that we might label local or national. Even in analyses of existentially cross-boundary processes, such as transnational migrations, it is the relationship to some place left or arrived at that is central.[3] What is unique

---

[3] See, for example, a recent edited volume on "transnationalism" and migrant communities,

about this collection is that each chapter strives to identify specifically how intersections form and operate; how they draw in and are shaped by institutions as diverse as states, international organizations, NGOs, transnational corporations, and national and local polities. These transboundary formations defy simple classification as existing at one level of analysis or another (local, national, or global). Sometimes they involve networks reaching around the world from diamond mines in Angola to the boards of trade in Antwerp. Other times they involve international arenas of discourse (for example, around human rights, the environment, and development) within which various actors, local and global, vie to set agendas, contest policies, and garner support. And at still other times they involve systems of rule – often violent and exploitative – over enclaves of territory involving state and private militias and transnational corporations. Occasionally, there may be direct intervention by external military forces that may be sanctified by the norms advanced by international organizations such as the UN. Some transboundary formations are seen as instances of "intervention" while others are perceived to be the natural outgrowth of regular socio-economic and political interaction. This volume deals with both and with the blurred line between them. The central concern in this effort is to show how cross-boundary forces become directly involved in the constitution of forms of order and authority in various social and political contexts that can range from the local, translocal, and national to the regional and transnational. The chapters seek to address the question of how orders and authorities that shape social existence form and operate at specific sites within societies or across multiple territories (in transboundary distribution systems, political alliances, or social organizations). It is important to assess how cross-boundary forces enter into these sites and contexts and with what consequences. These orders and authorities – which are not necessarily based on legitimate force or voluntary compliance – are not merely a function of activities of central state governments. Competition and conflict between and among both international and local NGOs are treated with the same seriousness as the politics of concerted pressure by or on state officials. The drawing up of life in towns into informal, sometimes illicit webs of distribution is taken as seriously as formal, national markets. Connections between nongovernmental and state institutions, and between informal and formal realms, are central to the kinds of orders that concern us in this volume.

whose editors state that their guiding concern is "to discern how this process (transnationalism) affects power relations, cultural constructions, economic interactions, and more generally, social organization at the level of the locality." Thus, one of the volume's main analytical themes is "the centrality of 'locality' in a historicized sense" (Guarnizo and Smith 1998, 6).

There is actually very little organized knowledge about how forms of order and authority operating in specific contexts are shaped by and in these junctures. Certainly there is no body of theory to turn to automatically or a language to rely on to describe transboundary units of analysis, besides general and often arbitrarily defined terms such as "transnational," "international," or "global." A related body of work, which is applied to historical contexts, is contemporary (post-) colonial studies, where the concern has been to understand the role of imperial power in the construction of the order and authority of colonial states of one form or another (Comaroff and Comaroff 1991; Mamdani 1996; Young 1994).

Questions about transboundary constructions of order and authority in the post-colonial period have received less attention. The chapters in this volume by Barnett, Cooper, and Latham deal in different ways with some of the intellectual fallout from this gap. Post-colonial studies have focused on the enduring, especially cultural, legacy of colonialism for contemporary politics and society. While the problem of authority – understood as Michael Barnett shows below, borrowing from Bruce Lincoln (1994), to be a matter of who or what is able to establish a presumptive right to speak or act – has figured meaningfully in post-colonial studies, the problem of order itself has taken a less prominent place. When it comes to the post-colonial period, authority, if anything, is generally treated as though it has been unhinged from order.[4] Authority is now often seen as being embedded in discursive webs and the micro-practices of particular agents. Order has become something of a dirty word, associated with the Hobbesian (and, later, Huntingtonian) sense in which order seemed to stand as an end in itself rather than as a means to justice or what is now called human security or human development. Order of this sort was understood as a stable system, national in reach and conservative by design.[5] We need not assume, however, that order is by definition a territory-wide or national phenomenon. As this volume will show, order can also be a transboundary phenomenon, though not necessarily in a zero-sum relation to the national state. At the same time, order can be situated in a locale or anchored in a particular domain such as religion or finance. In all of these cases, it can also be transitory and provisional. It is our contention that the term "order" should be used to denote what is produced when groups and institutions attempt to establish reproducible boundaries to what they do in the world, involving

---

[4] Akhil Gupta and James Ferguson have recently examined the question of "cultural order," but are quick to dismiss its analytical utility (Gupta and Ferguson 1997a, 4).

[5] The term "political order" developed by Samuel Huntington has recently been revived in the literature on Africa, without such biases but as yet without much specificity. See Goran Hyden (1999).

specific people and places, social relations and practices, and mechanisms and methods (violence, law, command, redistribution, etc.). When the UN High Commission for Refugees establishes a refugee camp in some locale it must establish who is a refugee and who is not, what it will do for them and what it will not, and how it will do it or what the effects will be if it does not.

Thus, the right to pronounce and act – to be authoritative – is not just a function of circuits of discursive reproduction. It is inseparable from order-making, however contingent or provisional. The chapters in this volume treat authorities and orders not only as things to be discovered, announced, or imposed, but as things that can be pursued, produced, and contested in often novel ways. Orders can emerge not only as overt programs but as corollaries of the search for security, survival, or wealth.

That order, especially local order, had dropped more or less from analytical sight owes something as well to the post-World War II assumption that it is whole sovereign states and societies that are drawn into transboundary and external orders and authorities. Thus was born dependency theory. External – or if you like global – forces were typically understood in the dependency framework either to emasculate the possibility of real politics, of real sovereign leadership and governance, or to render indigenous, authentic, or natural economic and social relations inoperative. Ministries and presidents do not "really" rule, and markets are shot through with outside goods and extractions. One version of the dependency perspective underscored that "real" politics and authenticity were illusions from the start, not least because they were constituted from the very start by external forces. In this extreme version, real agency and autonomy on the part of local actors (politicians, "comprador" capitalists, and the masses) become impossible because of global capitalism.[6]

Cardoso and Faletto (1979) offered a correction to the strand of dependency analysis that focused on how local economic life was drawn up into international capitalist structures. They insisted that analysis also needed to be thrown into reverse, with a focus on the specific dynamics and history of local political-economic relations.[7] This call was heeded, but far too infrequently.[8]

---

[6] For a recent and critical reflection on underdevelopment and dependency theory by an influential contributor to the approach as it was applied to Africa, see Leys (1996).

[7] The parallel within colonial studies was the emphasis, associated with John Gallagher and Ronald Robinson (1953), on what happened outside of metropoles and cores.

[8] One important example of doing so regarding Africa is Bayart (1993) whose concept of "extraversion" is discussed below. Other examples from Latin America include Bergquist (1986) and Coronil (1997).

While it is true that external forces have received increasing attention in the social sciences and humanities, they often serve only as a background context from which a scholar can select the actors of interest to him or her (merchant, missionary, soldier, or diplomat). In such analyses, cross-boundary relations and processes are merely drawn from external contexts (see for example, Buell 1994). This volume seeks to help rectify this situation by focusing on transboundary formations. However, it does not start from any single perspective fixing the types of transboundary formations that are the most crucial to investigate. The authors instead center their chapters on the particular configurations of forces and processes relevant to their cases. The resulting diversity of transboundary phenomena examined in this volume – for example, illicit networks, social movements, intervening states, international financial institutions, NGOs, militias, and multinational corporations – have received varying degrees of attention in international relations, history, and the fields that have been central to area studies (see the chapters by Barnett, Cooper, and Kassimir this volume). However, questions about how they produce order and authority have generally been overlooked. Consider the well-studied subject of local and transnational social movements, which are seen as central to the politics of globalization (Smith et al. 1997; and Obi this volume). Numerous studies exist of how groups organize on a worldwide basis to contest state and international policies, or of how organizations can emerge, even just locally, in reaction to practices and pressures from forces identified as global.[9] However, serious questions have not even been raised yet about whether or how such movements actually shape and produce order and authority not simply in the international realm but in communities and political institutions within and across a variety of territories. The chapters in this book should prompt readers to consider why these questions matter.

Transboundary formations and Africa

While this volume's authors focus on African examples, the relevance of these questions is not limited to the region of the globe often labeled as the most extreme in lacking "political order" and which stands as the exemplar of a new form of global "disorder" (Kaplan 1994). We witness various permutations from Central Asia to Southeast Asia, from the Balkans to the druglord-dominated regions of Latin America. There are, however, several advantages to examining transboundary formations in

---

[9] For a recent survey, see Keck and Sikkink (1998).

Africa. Since the end of the Cold War, many African countries, especially in Central Africa as described above and parts of West Africa, are viewed as "failing" or "collapsed" states (Zartman 1995). As with the Congo, they have become sites for external intervention, refugee "management," armed conflict, economic extraction, and political engineering. Following on earlier models of relief aid, development assistance, and structural adjustment, there is now a diverse set of mechanisms for intervention by the "international community" in the continent – peacekeeping, post-conflict reconstruction, democratization, building of civil societies, environmental preservation, and coping with special diseases, for example. Beyond the international community, there has been a proliferation of a variety of institutions, many of them new, others reconfigured – private security companies and arms dealers, missionary organizations, NGOs, and multinational firms that operate under different logics and in different contexts than their predecessors. Longstanding trading networks now not only cross national borders, but reach into diaspora communities in New York, Paris, and elsewhere.

The scope and diversity of these forms of intervention and connection make Africa a particularly trenchant place not only for viewing the intersection of "the global and the local," but also for revealing the assumptions and folk theories that various international actors have with regard to the way orders and authorities "work" in Africa. The region thus provides an arena for recording and analyzing how these institutions and networks become insinuated in political structures and relations "on the ground."

Political analysis of Africa has typically treated the kinds of linkages, formations, and processes that this book highlights in one of two ways. First, large parts of the academic literature have either ignored transboundary phenomena or treated them as residual to the states and populations that are affected by them, help to create them, or use them for their own purposes. Ironically, this is particularly true for parts of the literature that focus on various "transitions" that are presumed to be under way in Africa, such as economic liberalization, democratization, and the growth of civil society.[10] The approach advanced in this volume seeks to problematize the implication that the links between international and local realms can only be encompassed through the lens of international relations theory or the classic dualism of state and civil society. We are

---

[10] For exceptions, see Aina (1997), van de Walle (1999), and Mkandawire (1999). In an influential volume on the role of civil society in state reform and political transition (Harbeson et al. 1994), only the chapters by Guyer and Callaghy treat the international dimensions of, and constraints upon, African civil societies as central to the latter's political role.

suggesting that these linkages cannot be automatically subsumed by the macro-categories of state, civil society, and international community.

Second, in other parts of the literature which have been more attuned to transboundary phenomena, states appear to fade rapidly into a pale background – seen as actors no longer relevant to African realities, accounted for by failure or sheer lack of presence (e.g. Forrest 1998). Undergirding this perspective is the observation that African states have never been very close to the model of the Weberian, "modern" state assumed by much of the literature, especially in international relations. The general conclusion reached is that African post-colonial states have been long on juridical sovereignty and weak on empirical sovereignty (Jackson 1990). This gap in authority and presence is typically assumed to be filled by either patrimonial networks or communal leadership and not the variety of transboundary formations discussed in this volume. This volume underscores that it is important not to overlook the range of actors, processes, and forces that are driving political realities in Africa;[11] or to underestimate the degree to which states are bound up in transboundary formations along with a wide variety of non-state actors.

Transboundary formations, states, and the global context of "extraversion"

One way to understand how states have been bound up in transboundary formations is through what Jean-François Bayart (1993) has called strategies of "extraversion." Rulers build relationships largely with non-African states, transnational corporations, and international organizations as ways of surviving and compensating for their weak empirical stateness. These extraversions have altered over time as African and external conditions have changed. Individual states have used them in different ways: first, to stabilize or strengthen themselves, sometimes after serious decline (Uganda, Mozambique); second, to slow decline by deflecting certain kinds of challenges, often from non-state transboundary formations (Nigeria, Kenya); or third, to manage decline (Angola, Cameroon, both Congos, Chad, and Sierra Leone) while attempting to carve out new orders that might benefit those who control the increasingly hollow state.

Extraversion is a strategic disposition of state leaders in relation to both their domestic spaces and their international realm. When this strategy produces specific structures of order and authority, a transboundary

---

[11] An excellent, recent study of those processes and forces that overcomes that risk is Clapham (1996).

formation of one form or another is likely in operation. As Reno's chapter shows, for example, where empirical stateness has significantly weakened, certain types of transboundary formations that may create quite violent forms of order and extraction enter into play. Yet we know from the chapters by Schmitz and Callaghy that occasionally more benign outcomes can be seen in the formations that coalesce in areas such as human rights and debt relief.

The chapters in this volume also demonstrate that, over the course of the post-colonial period, extraversion strategies have increasingly spread to non-state actors and social movements.[12] This happens in a conjuncture where processes of state decline occur at the same time that international organizations and NGOs assert or respond to perceived new needs in Africa that they claim they can do something about – human rights, refugees, debt, environmental concerns, and the spread of various diseases. As Kassimir and others illustrate, African non-state, "societal" actors have turned increasingly to extraversion strategies as a way of managing their fraying socio-economic situations and asserting new claims on resources, claims to authority, and claims for representation.

The volume's chapters quite vividly demonstrate that relations between states and non-state institutions should not be presumed as zero-sum in nature, although, under certain circumstances, this may be the case. Transboundary formations initiated by non-state actors can coexist with weakening states, possibly leading to slower decline or, conversely, to partial stabilization (see Roitman this volume). As Reno shows, they may also help to determine winners in "countries" that face major factional struggles or civil wars. This may produce significant overlapping and intermingling of various forms of order that result from even quite narrow and temporary transboundary interactions, as Latham illustrates. State as well as non-state organizations may operate in more than one transboundary formation in quite effective, if often not benign, ways (see chapters by Nordstrom and Roitman this volume).

In this sense, both African and non-African states, or parts of them, can be drawn into transboundary formations in ways that are unexpected and have unintended consequences. With regard to the latter, many non-African states are now much more leery of becoming part of certain types of transterritorial deployments described by Latham – mostly interventionist, order-oriented ones – while continuing to be involved in others, such as those relating to economic reform, democratization, and "building" civil societies. In some cases, state-oriented transboundary

---

[12] For discussions on extraversion and religious institutions in Africa, see Bayart (1989a), Gifford (1998, ch. 7), and Kassimir's contribution to this volume.

formations have succeeded in strengthening the capabilities of some states (Ghana, Uganda, Mozambique), especially on the economic side. Even here, however, "donor fatigue" continues to takes its toll as these cases remain relatively few in number.

In thinking through the origins and consequences of transboundary formations in Africa, we must take care not to get too carried away with a focus on purely "global – local" interactions. As several of the chapters show, transboundary formations do not have to be primarily composed of external (non-African) institutions or actors. They can also be the result of largely transnational regional adaptations, which may then develop external ties (see Roitman, Reno, and Nordstrom in this volume). Especially on the non-state side, the tendency is to view transboundary formations as being generated largely externally. But several of the chapters underscore the point that regional transboundary formations emerge out of local institutions. At first they may be transboundary within the regional context, but eventually they may develop a variety of external linkages – to transnational religious movements or international market networks in weapons, drugs, and people, for example. Many of the emerging order-creating regional transboundary formations may be forged initially by the intersection of non-state institutions. In some cases (Liberia, Somalia, Sierra Leone, for example), the "order" they impose has a distinctly malign character and no developmental potential.

But in other emergent regional transboundary formations, African states play a major role. This is most dramatically apparent in several overlapping transboundary formations that may be emerging from Africa's first major inter-state war unfolding in Central Africa, with which we started this chapter. While this war originated in local and regional conflicts in the Great Lakes region, most of the actors have increasingly developed external linkages to states, international organizations, firms, and global markets (Reno this volume, and Callaghy forthcoming).

New transboundary formations may not be, as Roitman argues, sovereign in any traditional sense, certainly juridical or even ideational, but they often constitute quite viable "regulatory authorities." They may overlap relatively comfortably with existing states, but, as they become more coherent and are able to approach higher levels of control over resources, people, and territory, their status may take on a zero-sum quality in regard to the juridical states on whose territory they operate. But the potential zero-sum quality of these new regulatory authorities may pertain for some domains of what are conventionally seen as state functions (provision of security, economic management), but not others.

The institutional diversity within transboundary formations

As we have noted, transboundary formations, and the institutions that shape them, have grown in number and type. A point of departure for this volume is the recognition of the wide range of institutions shaping order and exercising authority in Africa.

Institutional diversity has, of course, been a hallmark of Western theories of pluralism that highlight the role of civil society in the political realm. Foucault – by building on the kinds of insights provided by Max Weber and Antonio Gramsci, and by undertaking specific histories – made clear that in modernity institutions such as professional associations could also be authoritative shapers of social orders. However, both the pluralists and Foucault took for granted that a formal, neo-Weberian state would be central to politics and governance, serving as the predominant, authoritative underwriter of order (for Foucault, through law, knowledge, and violence). The authors of this volume are forced to relax this assumption and thereby treat the myriad of institutions they study in Africa as producers of forms of order and authority that involve states in uneven and often problematic ways.

The diversity of institutions drawn into analysis across the chapters of this book vary along two basic dimensions. On the one side, there is the classic distinction between those institutions that are part of, or directly (re)produced by, the state and those that are not. On the other, we introduce a less conventional distinction: juridical and non-juridical institutions. We use the term juridical to designate that an institution's existence rests on some form of legal expression, such as a constitution or charter that is accorded recognition by other institutions and groups operating as legal entities. Put together, these two dimensions produce the following institutional map presented in Figure 1.1.

Figure 1.1 is meant to underscore that the four institutional fields are quite proximate to and apt to intersect with one another in the ways mentioned throughout this introduction and the chapters that follow. This emphasis is important, since all too often we have been faced with the assumption either that the juridical dimensions of states are the only places to look when analyzing structures of order and authority, or that when states are apparently incapable of living up to the Weberian ideal type, "real" authority lies in other institutions. While there may be empirical examples that approximate either of these extremes, patterns of authority in Africa and elsewhere for the most part feature dense inter-connections of institutions and hybrid formations. These institutions may have their own relatively autonomous (even if contradictory)

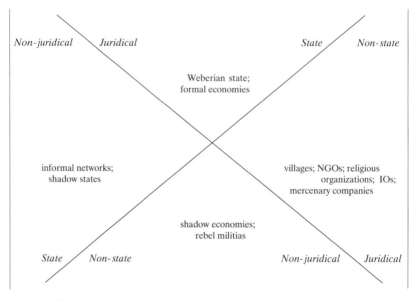

Figure 1.1 Mapping institutional diversity.

logics, but it is only through the juncture points that we can understand how people's everyday lives are or are not ordered, how local security is constructed or ruptured, and what possibilities exist for the representation of identities and interests when the audiences for such claims are often fragmented, opaque, or unaccountable. It is precisely because so many institutions are drawn up into global, transnational, or other cross-border webs of activities that we refer to these juncture points as transboundary formations.

The introduction of the juridical/non-juridical distinction is critical in capturing the complexities of order and authority. Indeed, while much scholarship recognizes the existence of non-juridical arenas and institutions (e.g. "parallel" or "informal" economies), most studies of African politics continue to treat states and civil societies in the juridical realm as discrete units of analysis. Institutional innovations in the non-juridical realm are often dismissed as unfortunate pathologies, or alternatively celebrated as examples of local invention, while the connections between them and juridical institutions are considered, if at all, in an *ad hoc* manner. For example, and as some observers and the chapters in this volume point out, state institutions and the actors populating them are embedded not only in the juridical realm, but also in a wide range of non-juridical informal or illegal political and economic arenas and practices (e.g. Reno

1995). A customs official in a lonely border outpost may also be a central node in a smuggling network; a member of parliament may be the most public face in a gray zone of patron – client ties; a defense ministry official may be a principal mobilizer of a private militia. "State power," to the degree it exists, might sometimes best be understood from a vantage point that encompasses the intersection of juridical and non-juridical realms (see Obi, Reno, and Roitman this volume).

The juridical/non-juridical distinction also provides much greater depth to our understanding of the political possibilities of non-state institutions. Non-state, juridical institutions include those organizations that much conventional analysis labels as "civil society" (see Kassimir this volume). The international equivalent would involve entities such as international NGOs and advocacy networks and is sometimes labeled "global civil society" (see Callaghy and Schmitz this volume). Yet, as Schmitz shows, these institutions are quite often connected to non-juridical realms, patronage systems, ethnic networks, or "non-civil" protest movements. In Kenya, the most visible (juridical) human rights organizations are linked (and, perhaps even more critically, are perceived to be linked) to those (non-juridical) ethnic groups that have been denied access to state power. A similar connection between social movements that make rights claims and ethnic-based mobilization can be observed in the conflict over oil extraction in the Niger Delta. In addition, as Obi demonstrates in his chapter, peaceful protests, secessionist claims, and violent acts of sabotage against Western oil companies and the Nigerian state cannot be neatly compartmentalized into discrete "civil" and "uncivil" components of local resistance, not to mention the obvious connections between "private" transnational corporations and the juridical and non-juridical arms of the Nigerian state.

The volume's chapters analyze how domestic institutions that are either juridical (Callaghy, Obi, Schmitz) or non-juridical (Reno, Roitman, Nordstrom) are enmeshed in translocal and transnational networks through which ideas about human rights, neo-liberal economic theories, diamonds, arms, and foreign aid flow. In his contribution, Latham makes a distinction between such networks and transterritorial deployments where "external" forces are physically present within a domestic setting. These deployments can take either juridical or non-juridical form. Juridical forms include transnational corporations, development agencies, and peacekeeping troops. Non-juridical forms include syndicates and trading diaspora conducting illegal commerce and rebel forces penetrating neighboring territories. What is unique about the chapters here is not only their concern with exploring how these networks and deployments are imbricated with one another, with communities, and with other locally based institutions such as towns, but also their concern with how states figure into this mix. In this conjuncture, forms of social existence are shaped in often transitory orders, and more formal modes of authority are exercised by institutions such as the UN and international financial institutions (see Barnett, Latham, Callaghy).

Our chapters show in rich detail the diversity of processes that cross boundaries. For instance, international financial institution policies on debt are revised by coalitions of debt forgiveness movements and economic experts (Callaghy); diamonds are traded both for weapons that fuel civil wars and for contraband which then figures into the survival strategies of street children (Nordstrom, Reno). International norms and discourses are appropriated in local political struggles – e.g. human rights and environmentalism (Obi); invoked in order to gain access to juridical and economic resources – e.g. sovereignty (Reno, Callaghy); and repudiated in the face of civil conflict – e.g., rules of war (Nordstrom, Reno). At each of these points of intersection, configurations of power emerge that are at once "global" and "local." None of the chapters offers anything like a model for comparing across specific instances, but by focusing on transboundary formations they help create an analytical basis for comparison. Many of the authors argue, implicitly or explicitly, that formal institutional changes in regime (democratization) and economy (marketization) occur in the shadow of these structures, and thus efforts to promote juridical reforms ignore these chains of political and social intersection at their peril.

Around these intersections, the themes of violence and representation recur throughout the volume. The monopoly of legitimate violence that is seen as a critical marker of the juridical Weberian state appears as a chimera in most of the cases offered here. Vigilante groups and civil defense forces emerge to provide local order in the context of civil war, while external peacekeeping missions may attempt the same on a national level (Barnett this volume; Herbst 1996; Richards 1996); paramilitary groups, private security firms, and mercenary armies provide protection for mineral extraction and forge military-commercial networks (Roitman, Nordstrom, Reno); militias encouraged by state officials engage in ethnic cleansing and in attempts to derail political reform (Schmitz); and national armies provide security to multinational firms, acting against their own citizens in the process (Obi). Violence, both legitimate and illegitimate, and order, both brutal and just, are imposed by a wide range of "local" institutions, but rarely without connections to state officials and transboundary forces. Again, this points to the overlaps between the state and non-state, juridical and non-juridical. Vigilante groups and militias (that are non-state and non-juridical) are typically linked to components of the state apparatus. And these linkages change over time, as Roitman and Reno demonstrate.

How are local identities and interests voiced and represented under such conditions? Again, here we must relax the assumption, handed down to us by the juridical state model, that representational claims are made to a state which provides order, promulgates and implements rules for the allocation of resources, and asserts a national purpose. In addition, and as Kassimir argues in his chapter, many non-state, juridical institutions can be seen not only as "representers" of societal interests to the state, but also as authority-claiming and order-making agents in their own right. Many of our chapters show the multiple faces of the institutions making representational claims and the increasing diversity of the audiences toward whom such claims are directed. International financial institutions (Callaghy) and NGOs (Callaghy, Schmitz, Obi) are drawn up into local politics of representation, especially in the cases where state officials are deaf to many representational claims. Latham, Barnett, and Callaghy discuss the problems of accountability of international institutions that emerge in such interactions. More broadly, if non-state institutions are themselves not simply representing societal groups but also part of the construction of order and authority, we need to understand how these organizations and their leaders become the targets for appeals by various social forces (Kassimir, Barnett, Obi). But in those localities where state and/or non-state forces either provide a brutal form of order or have interests in maintaining disorder, representation becomes increasingly problematic (Nordstrom, Obi) or infinitely more complex (Roitman). In the cases presented by Reno and Nordstrom, questions of who represents which social groups are virtually erased under the weight of violent collective institutions (state and non-state) with no stake in accountability, while Roitman, in discussing paramilitary commercial networks in the Chad Basin, suggests that certain forms of reciprocity can develop between such networks and at least some parts of local populations. In all cases, even when the state is no longer a major presence, as an imagined force or a reference point it does not disappear from representational politics.

We started this introduction with the vivid tale of two countries in Central Africa, which raises many of the themes and questions central to this volume. After assessing the intellectual context in which these issues are typically discussed, we laid out the conceptual basis for investigating them using the notion of transboundary formations. The rest of the volume will expand on this discussion. It is divided into five parts, the first of which focuses on "Historical Dimensions and Intellectual Context," with chapters by Fred Cooper and Michael Barnett. A second part explores "Theoretical Frameworks" through chapters by Robert Latham and Ronald Kassimir. Parts III and IV examine empirical manifestations of transboundary formations in Africa: Part III, "Transboundary Networks, International Institutions, States, and Civil Societies," has chapters by Thomas Callaghy, Hans Peter Schmitz, and Cyril Obi, while Part IV, on "Political Economies of Violence and Authority," contains chapters by William Reno, Carolyn Nordstrom, and Janet Roitman. The volume ends with a chapter by Kassimir and Latham, which reviews where we have been and where we might go in analyzing transboundary formations and their relationship to order and authority in Africa and beyond.

Part I

Historical dimensions and intellectual context

2 Networks, moral discourse, and history

Frederick Cooper

This chapter is a historian's reflection on connections across time and space and on the relationship of those connections to what is imaginable politically. Fifty years ago, to take one example, a colony was a perfectly ordinary political structure. Before the nineteenth century, slavery was a normal social category. Colonization and slavery are no longer politically imaginable; they have been consigned to the past. It took a great deal of work over many decades to make it that way, not least the mobilization of geographically dispersed movements. Colonized people and slaves certainly played crucial roles in their own liberation, but not simply by acting within their categories. And if the movements involved elite emancipators seeking to keep their privileges while purifying their societies of well-defined evils, they did not have the power to define issues as they would, or to maintain the boundaries of debate across time and space. Antislavery and anticolonial movements were not organizations of the already like-minded, but rather intersections of different sorts of people with different sorts of motivations and interests, whose overlapping viewpoints crystallized around particular ways of framing an issue. But if slavery or colonialism became unimaginable, other forms of exploitation, humiliation, and abuse did not. These movements were extensive, but not global, and if they developed moralistic discourses in universalistic language, the universe was in fact particular, with its own set of inclusions and exclusions.

How does one analyze changes in what is imaginable and possible over a long period of time and across a large space? This chapter approaches that question by juxtaposing, over time, the relationship of structures to networks to discourses. Structures such as states and empires, networks such as commodity chains and transnational human rights mobilizing efforts, and discourses such as free labor ideology and human rights doctrines shape each other. Over time – sometimes long periods of time – these intersections have consequences which cannot be understood by an analysis that limits itself to one of these dimensions. But these relationships are complex. How do mobilizations create networks and shape discourses that in turn redefine norms, perceptions of commonality and difference, and visions of what is politically possible? How do discourses give cohesion to networks and how do networks influence institutions that can make and enforce policy? Whose voices influence discourses and are supported by networks? How do networks establish inclusions and exclusions and what sorts of discourses reinforce those patterns?[1]

Studying transnational networks, arenas, and deployments – to use Robert Latham's terminology – offers possibilities for getting beyond some of the conceptual difficulties in much scholarship today. First is a widely used distinction between a "global" that is far more global in talk than it is in actuality and a "local" that is not nearly so local in reality as it is in the texts of social scientists. Second is the assertion that the era of "globalization" is the present one – the last quarter or third of the twentieth century onwards. It does not help to assume a dichotomous choice between studying "flows" that link everything with everything and neatly bounded structures or between a past of territories and a present of deterritorialization; scholars need to analyze long-distance connections over long periods of time with more precision (Cooper 2001).

I will, later in this chapter, look at a related series of shifts that occurred over a very long time, involving transnational issue networks (Keck and Sikkink 1998) which succeeded in making slavery, colonialism, and apartheid into debatable issues when they once had been taken for granted. This contestation took place within a transcontinental space that was neither global nor local and which was marked by the intersection of institutions, networks, and discourses – the Atlantic economy and the

---

[1] I am using network in a loose sense, although I am aware that this word is used in a highly formalized way. My interest is in forms of affiliation and association that are less defined than a "structure" but more than just a collection of individuals engaging in transactions. Networks are organizations which stress voluntary and reciprocal patterns of communication and exchange, which if not necessarily "horizontal" are not fully controlled by vertical systems of authority. A network could be a collection of diverse people who agree enough about a single issue to act collectively, or it could be a set of people – with or without prior affiliation – who develop linkages across space, for a common purpose (trading), to follow for a time a particular leader (a gang). Networks produce commonality as much as they reflect it. There was discussion at the Florence workshop of the relationship of networks to social movements, but I would argue that each term has its place. The social movement concept assumes a "social" around which a movement develops. That may not be the case with a network, although a network may well turn into a social movement if its members become convinced that they constitute a collectivity. A network may or may not have ideological contents; it may consist of people with a set of strong commitments, or it may deepen and reconfigure the commitments participants have; it may be built around a set of norms, yet as its interactions work out areas of commonality and disagreement, it may define and redefine a normative framework. I have less at stake in the term network than in an effort to explore forms of connection, especially their relationship to institutions and to discourses.

colonial empires created out of European expansion from the fifteenth century onward.

Elusive connections

Social scientists of many stripes have trouble dealing with connections. History is organized around particular places and times, anthropology around particular peoples, political science around institutions and states, economics around transactions, sociology around population groups. The concept of "network" has flitted into and out of social science, and other linking concepts – such as diaspora – have been evoked more than they have been theorized.

The network concept has certainly been an available one in the social sciences. Anthropologists such as J. Clyde Mitchell, whose work grew out of the "situational" school of the 1950s and 1960s, realized that African migrants to cities moved between one set of structures and another and that the process of using and forging connections required as much analysis as the situations found at either end (Mitchell 1969; Mitchell and Boissevain 1973). Sociologists trace personal linkages within particular settings and how "identities" crystallize at certain nodes within networks (White 1992). Studies of diasporas have become fashionable, in Jewish and African American Studies for example, and there is now even a journal of that title, along with several devoted to the study of migration.

But if one can easily grasp the importance of the analysis of spatial connections, why have they not been better institutionalized in different disciplines? Let me start with my own – history. In the United States, at least, history departments function by a kind of tacit agreement that divides the world by place and time, acknowledging the legitimacy of each unit. Such a division allows for the main business at hand – allocating jobs – to be conducted in relative peace and it allows for considerable theoretical variety, as long as each historian has plenty of footnotes to primary sources, although it does not necessarily encourage a great deal of critical interchange across the lines. This treaty system even allows for a degree of change, so that a field such as African history could be absorbed relatively easily into departments, perhaps after disputes at the margins, but without forcing everybody to rethink his or her disciplinary position. Historians are well aware that history does not actually fit these compartments – that some of the most interesting questions are to be asked about connections across space as well as time – but that recognition has affected the hiring process least of all. If a historian has the temerity to study both ends of a migratory process or a phenomenon such as a transoceanic trade route or comparisons of similar processes in different places, it is wise to have a regional base, and preferably tenure.

Economics in the United States is at the other extreme of theoretical conformacy, but the theory in question conceives of the "global" as an aggregation of individual transactions rather than as a phenomenon of networks, and it encourages research into data sets defined by units which habitually collect them, so that individuals are typically aggregated by state. There is no such thing as "field economics" that could uncover how diasporic trading communities or executives of international banks actually operate. Anthropologists helped to open network analysis, but – despite some strong pleas to the contrary (Gupta 1992; Malkki 1994) – the discipline values context-rich, site-specific research, which makes the following of people over space (on time schedules acceptable to Ph.D. committees) a risky endeavor. Anthropology has of late been seduced by evocations of "the global" (Appadurai 1996), but much less by actual investigation into the long-distance but none the less bounded processes that cut across space. Political science has an entire wing devoted to international relations, but it tends to take its name literally and treat nation-states as units of analysis, making it harder to see the varying forms in which connections are made.[2] It is far from clear whether the profession would value the kind of empirical study necessary to unravel a long-distance network or show how linguistic frameworks through which people perceive and articulate interests are shaped and reshaped.

Neither economics' ultra-modernist emphasis on individual choice nor postmodernist anthropology's vision of constructions, flows, and indeterminacies gets very far in examining the specificities of connections. All the social sciences are much better at positing different units – individuals, transactions, and states – in relation to some kind of totality, the world in a geographic sense or a more abstract container for universalistic propositions. The elusive area is between unitizing and totalizing levels, in forms of connection that are spatially spread out but still spatially bounded, in linkages that embrace many people – including people who differ in language, citizenship, or other fundamental characteristics – but which are none the less particularistic in membership.

The second difficulty in today's thinking about the "local" and the "global" has to do with its time dimension. There has been a great deal

[2] Sociology has a more consistent record of interest in networks (Granovetter 1973; Powell 1990), but it is not clear, to an outsider, at least, whether such work rivals the influence of that which emphasizes "solidarities" of various sorts: class, ethnicity, race, nationality, or more inclusively and more problematically "identity." On the problems of the latter construct, see Brubaker and Cooper (2000).

of talk about the late twentieth century as the age of globalization – an era of rapid movement across the globe, in which territorially defined states have less and less place, in which the connections of individuals and institutions are fragmented, in which commodities, money, and ideas circulate independently of each other. There is no question that much has happened in recent decades along these lines, but a historian is bound to wonder whether this is really a unique period in world history for any reason other than the fact that those currently writing happen to live in it. Electronic communication is fast and wonderful, but is the break which the Internet and the Web have brought about anything like as revolutionary as the invention of the telegraph, which for the first time made it possible for a message to move over long distances instantly and independently of a messenger? Boundary crossing in its many forms is as old as boundaries, and as *The Economist* never tires of reporting, the period in world history when state budgets represented the largest proportion of world GNP is right now. Not surprisingly, globalization talk is by now producing reactions, some making the quite sane proposition that territorial structures have long been defined and redefined in relation to changing patterns of transnational economic relations and political structures (e.g. Brenner 1997; Hirst and Thompson 1996).

The peculiar history of global interaction: slavery and antislavery

In the late fifteenth and sixteenth centuries, Iberian navigators and traders brought Asia, Africa, and the Americas into relation with Europe and with each other. The slave trade was central to the transformation of both productive and commercial relations. These relationships did more than exchange surplus production – as did other long-distance exchange networks – but changed the ways in which production was constituted. This violent and horrific commerce also became the focus of what might well be the world's first transnational issue network – the antislavery movement. The world became not only a unit of economic ambition and quests for political domination, but a unit of moral discourse.

The kind of exercise that supposedly reveals how interactive patterns of consumption and production are in the late twentieth century works quite nicely for eighteenth-century Jamaica. A Jamaican slave would have been bought on the west coast of Africa in exchange for iron bars produced in England; these bars would have moved along African trade routes far inland in the continent, serving as a form of money in a long-distance commercial system as well as entering into the production of iron tools and encouraging war machines that would produce more slaves. African slave traders on the west coast might become Christian and take up parts of European material culture, while in the interior or on the east coast they might become Muslim, make the pilgrimage to Mecca, and support networks of religious scholars. Meanwhile, the Jamaican slave would consume dried fish from a wide network of Caribbean and Atlantic fishermen and agricultural commodities from North America, while producing sugar. The slave's owner would live amidst European-produced luxury items and regard himself as part of European civilization – and indeed might well live in London while entrusting supervision of the estate to hired Europeans and mixed-race supervisors. The sugar would be consumed in England, as part of the intake of calories and stimulants necessary to keep a budding industrial labor force at work for long hours at low cost (Mintz 1985). Those wage workers would transform cotton grown by slaves in North America into textiles, affecting Anglo-American social and political relations as well as economic ones. Industrial products would contribute to the possibilities for a European working class to live via purchased commodities and would enter colonial markets in India as well as Africa. The capital generated in this process would deepen the circuits described here and allow for the development of new ones.

One need not buy the argument of Eric Williams (1944) – that the slave trade financed the industrial revolution – to accept the simpler point that capitalist development in England and slavery in the colonies grew up together and were deeply intertwined. One should accept the point of C.L.R. James (1938) that the organizational innovations of capitalist production – massed laborers working as gangs under supervision, clearly defined time-discipline in agriculture and processing, year-round planning of tasks, control over residential as well as productive space – were pioneered on Caribbean sugar estates as much as in English factories.

Slavery was not new. What was new was the scale, and what made that possible was the interrelationship of Africa, Europe, and the Americas. African rulers, slave traders on the Atlantic, merchants in the West Indies, planters in the Americas, and industrialists in England were caught in a relentless logic that drove expansion of the system into the nineteenth century. This connected world was not literally global: China was at the center of another set of commercial linkages, and in many parts of the world, other networks retained considerable autonomy, even if they were connected at certain nodal points to the Atlantic one that had developed from European expansion (Pomeranz 2000). Such interfaces would remain points of tension; some still are in the sense that total incorporation or subordination to a "global" world economy has not quite happened.[3] But a combination of money and connections created enormously wide sets of linkages in Africa, Asia, Europe, and the Americas by the eighteenth century.

One could pursue the argument to examine the ways in which geographic and cultural difference was defined and redefined as the voracious Atlantic system encountered and exploited people who came from different places. Such discourses were an important part of this history. But let us turn instead to the end of the eighteenth century and the beginning of the nineteenth, when slavery, which since the time of the Ancient Greeks had given rise to unease and misgivings, finally became the object of coherent and organized critique, when an antislavery movement began. One might argue that this was the ancestor of the movements we are talking about today – using a universalistic language, making an appeal about the humanity of people who are "different," acknowledging the moral implication of people in one place in the fate befalling people in another. The antislavery movement was a precedent of another sort: a universalistic moral discourse is used to tell other people how to behave, not acknowledging the particularistic uses to which universality is being put. Antislavery is part of the history of European imperialism in Africa as well as of European self-criticism.

The history of antislavery movements is a long story, but it is worth looking at its relationship to issues of power, space, and cultural particularity. David Brion Davis (1975) has complicated the argument of Eric Williams that slavery was discarded when it no longer served capitalism by showing that it was the ideological incompatibility of slavery and capitalism – not an economic contradiction – that gave rise to a powerful movement to rid British capitalism of its evil twin. The moral superiority of wage labor was very much in question in England itself in the late eighteenth century, where wage laborers were not convinced they should be left to the mercies of the market. British elites could hardly make a case for why market discipline was more virtuous than community and paternalism when their compatriots were insisting that slavery was just as good economically and morally. English antislavery movements had working-class as well as upper-class support, but the version of antislavery which triumphed with the ending of the British slave trade in 1807 and slavery in British colonies in 1834 was a relatively conservative one,

---

[3] Much as world system theory calls attention to the development at a particular time of such interactions, it tends to assume that they actually spanned the world and then bases its analysis on the presumed functionality of this presumedly world system. See the critical reflections in Cooper et al. (1993).

which defined a sharply bounded evil, slavery, and implicitly legitimated other forms of labor discipline.

We need to pause to make clear the connection of structures, networks, and discourses in the development of antislavery. The argument depends on thinking of capitalism as a complex, "thick," institutionally developed system. Concepts such as private property and institutions such as courts were vital to its continued functioning, and elites devoted much energy to thinking how coherent, how natural, how legitimate capitalist social relations appeared to be. It was in the course of thickening this institutional nexus that issue networks developed which tried to push discourse in certain directions – some to defend concepts of community under assault by an increasingly harsh market, some to justify the workings of the impersonal market, some to emphasize the continued legitimacy of a landed elite, some to bring subtly shifting religious norms into harmony with changing social relations. These conflicting mobilizations and discourses were contested and sorted out over a long period of time and through very complex processes. The near-simultaneous passage of the New Poor Law – which escalated official control over the marginal working class – and the emancipation of colonial slaves in the early 1830s marked the triumph of a discourse that emphasized both free labor and labor discipline, reinforced through institutions in the metropole (poor houses, labor market regulations) and in the colonies (rural magistrates, naval patrols interdicting slaving vessels).

The antislavery movement took off in the United States in the 1830s, but it was at this time a largely Anglo-American affair. Attempts to mobilize in France, Spain, and elsewhere found support among people who saw themselves as part of a pan-European bourgeoisie, but the second-tier capitalist powers had more at stake in their colonies, less in a purified vision of capitalism (Drescher 1987; Schmidt-Nowara 1999). The extension of this issue network was thus uneven, the encounters with countervailing forces even more so.

In France, slavery and other colonial questions were caught up – with little delay – in the question of what would be the universe within which the broadly inclusive rhetoric of the Revolution of 1789 would apply. The authors of the Declaration of the Rights of Man had not quite thought through the implications of their universalistic language, but colonials reminded them: first planters who wanted their voice heard in the governance of France's Caribbean islands, then "gens de couleur," property-owning people of mixed ancestry, who wanted equivalent citizenship status, then slaves, who insisted that the rights of man concerned them as well. In France, the field of application was a hotly debated concern, while in Haiti, the ferment of these debates and the uncertainties of power relations spiraled into the second major revolution of the 1790s. This revolution was actually a many-sided affair, in which complicated positions and alliances arose amidst a confused armed struggle, which epitomized both the difficulty which the elites of "France" had in containing their revolution within metropolitan boundaries and the multiple possibilities which civil war created for slave mobilization outside the rights framework as well as within it. The revolution ended with both the destruction of slavery in Haiti and the destruction of colonization. Out of context, one can imagine that Haiti could have been portrayed in the "Age of Revolution" as the vanguard of liberation. It was not. The fledgling nation-state, liberated at the wrong time by the wrong people, was treated as a pariah, shunned by many proponents of slave emancipation for making the end of slavery appear dangerous to order. Indeed, within the Caribbean – Atlantic world black sailors and other voyagers spread word of what had happened to other African American collectivities.[4]

In France's other colonies, slavery was abolished in 1794 in the midst of revolutionary fervor – and fear of further colonial rebellion – and restored by Napoleon in 1802. Both the proponents of abolition and defenders of Napoleon's restoration of slavery used sociological arguments about the nature of the population to whom the language of rights and citizenship should apply: whether a category of people could be described in empathetic terms was crucial to arguments over whether such a category should be included within a right-bearing collectivity.[5] Meanwhile, England, which forbade its own subjects from engaging in the slave trade in 1807, used state power – especially its navy – to internationalize the slave trade question, bringing the normative issues raised by the growing transnational issue network into the arena of diplomacy and geopolitics. After Napoleon's defeat, the British government pressured other European powers to agree in the Treaty of Vienna in 1815 to a formal condemnation of the slave trade as against the norms of civilization and to acquiesce to naval intervention against slave-carrying ships. By around 1850 such measures were having an effect. More slowly, the continued efforts by the antislavery movement to emphasize the incompatibility of slavery with international norms resonated with political processes in the French and Spanish empires, in the United States, and in Brazil. Slavery was definitively abolished in British colonies in

---

[4] On African American seafarers and communications within the Afro-Caribbean – Atlantic world, see Julius Scott (1986). The Haitian revolution is told in many versions, among them James (1938), Fick (1990), and Trouillot (1995).

[5] Tessiu Liu's current research is shedding considerable light on the terms in which such debates were conducted in France's revolutionary years. On citizenship and slavery in post-revolutionary France, see also Dubois (1999).

1834, in French colonies in 1848, in the United States during its Civil War, in remaining Spanish colonies in 1886, and finally in Brazil in 1888.

The Haitian revolution is a remarkable instance – for the time when it occurred – of a discourse "from above" being seized "from below," with long-term and hard-to-predict implications. A century and a half later, when anticolonial movements were gathering steam, C.L.R. James wrote a book about this revolution, *The Black Jacobins* (1938), which emphasized Haiti as part of a universal struggle for emancipation, an attempt to reverse the pariah status in which Haiti had since the 1790s been regarded and install it at the vanguard of a new movement. In so doing, James emphasized the citizenship side of the revolution, but not the aspect that Michel-Rolph Trouillot many years later (1995) called the "war within the war," a revolt of African-born slaves against the rebel leaders they had once supported, entailing a rejection of private property, labor discipline, and compromise via a rebellion as deeply rooted in African imagery as the original rebellion was in Jacobinism. In James' rewriting of Haitian history one sees another important dimension of transnational social movements: he was writing about quite specific mobilizations in a quite specific locality, but he was also writing a universal history, a liberation narrative whose beginning he saw in Haiti in 1791 and whose end he was trying to bring about throughout the colonized world in the 1930s. But in James' time as well, the language of emancipation would be only part of what would make anticolonial movements work. They too were built on the grievances and aspirations of people located in particular contexts and on connections that gave rise to broader – but still bounded – issue networks.[6]

There is another important lesson here too: the actual unraveling of slavery first occurred in Haiti via the action of slaves, even as the antislavery movement was only beginning to get going. In Jamaica and Martinique in 1831 and 1848, slave revolts preceded emancipation: both reflected rumors that had crossed the oceans that emancipation might be on the cards, and both revolts may well have precipitated the emancipation acts. The resonance of a transnational movement and the actions of a specific group were thus an important question – it was also that way in Cuba and Brazil (Blackburn 1988).

Emancipation in the British West Indies was accompanied by a concerted effort of officials and missionaries to instill new forms of work discipline. This did not resonate so well, nor did it work out as planned. British parliamentary reports from the eve of emancipation reveal an

---

[6] For a pioneering study of transatlantic connections, see Von Eschen (1997).

interesting openness to the possibility that slaves of African descent might transform themselves into "rational" economic men. They did not end up that way, at least not within officials' understanding of economic rationality or in regard to the data that were most relevant to them. Sugar production fell drastically. Ex-slaves sought to combine periods of wage labor on sugar estates with family cultivation on small plots and small-scale marketing – much to officials' resentment. Their vision – family-centered, refusing subordination to the singular demands of plantation production in order to forge a linkage of the small farms on which families grew food, town markets, and periods of wage labor on plantations – stood at an oblique angle to the universalistic conception of British officials, economic theorists, and at least some of the humanitarian lobby. To an increasingly influential segment of the British ruling class, the decline of plantation-based, wage-labor agriculture meant that the laws of economic behavior had a racial exception (Holt 1990). Here again is a point that one sees echoed in more recent times: frustration and anger at the recipients of humanitarian assistance for not performing prescribed roles and a willingness to label people who didn't act as desired as backward, lazy, and otherwise peculiar. The particular had reared its head in the face of universalistic conceptions of market behavior and of social morality.

Empire and progress

Applied to slavery within Africa itself, the parallels to intervention in the name of "Western" norms in today's world become stronger. From the 1860s, missionaries – the nineteenth-century equivalents of NGOs and human rights groups – began to articulate within Europe a sharp portrait of Africa as a continent ridden by tyrants and slavers, crying out for the intervention of Christians. The causes of the late nineteenth-century scramble for Africa were of course complex, but the case for action – made to increasingly democratic polities in France and England after the 1870s – depended on associating a European idea of progress with the conquest and remaking of Africa. Here we have an instance of a reformulation of large-scale structures in the light of new discourses about states and human progress. The antislavery campaign had rendered untenable the slash–grab–enslave colonization of an earlier era; the "new imperialism" of the 1860s and thereafter was the imperialism of the "civilizing mission," something acceptable to civic-minded voting publics in France and Britain and a public bent on national progress in Germany. Erecting such empires required considerable efforts at structural design and entailed considerable frustration as these countries quickly discovered the limits of their own power and the inadequacy of their vision in distant lands (Conklin 1997). There were even attempts at internationalizing an ideology of colonization: the Berlin conference of 1884 and the Brussels conference of 1889–1890 set out rules of the game for preventing European rivalries from leading to messy intrigues with African leaders and for setting minimum standards for what a civilized government should do – including ending the slave trade.

But the reality of colonial conquest and administration was very different from the world of the treaties and soon led to situations that were both brutal and contradictory – and criticized by much the same people in much the same terms as African slave traders had been. The attempt to define standards would continue: the campaign against the outrages of King Leopold of Belgium, international criticism of Portuguese and Liberian round-ups of coerced laborers, the League of Nations resolution against slavery in 1926, and the International Labor Office's convention against forced labor in 1930 (Cooper et al. 2000).

How can one understand this kind of do-good imperialism? In its time, and to a limited extent since, one tendency was to take it at face value, to insist that the "civilizing mission" was for real, perhaps unfulfilled because of greed and racism, but none the less a genuine thread of principled action against tyranny and violence, whether perpetrated by Europeans or Africans. Since the 1960s, a more likely tendency is to ignore this entire argument and to insist that mild-mannered criticism from Europe had little to do with reforming or ending colonialism. Another perspective takes the humanitarian colonial edifice more seriously, but uses it as a wedge to get at something deeper in the nature of "progressive" European ideologies themselves. Rather than play a "bad" colonialism off against a "good" reformism, this argument finds in European rejection of certain kinds of social practices – whether by other Europeans or other peoples – proof of the long-term intertwining of liberal reformism with imperialism. The ultimate arrogance lies in asserting the universal validity of principles that come from a particular history and serve particular interests.

The latter line of argument has been developed by scholars from India, including but not limited to those associated with the journal *Subaltern Studies*. The nineteenth-century missionary attack on sati (widow burning), for example, has been analyzed as a way in which white men inscribed on brown men the label of backward for the way they treated brown women (Mani 1990). The late nineteenth-century attack on African slavery fits this picture too: a particular practice is extracted from its social context and labeled as evil, then this precisely defined evil can be abolished, and the abolitionists take credit for their contribution to civilization, having firmly associated Africans with primitive and inhumane practices.[7]

Some scholars have argued that the ability of colonial liberals to play this game – even against themselves – allowed them to define the very forms of opposition, setting out a realm of citizenship in which political action could take place, while excluding any form of political mobilization that didn't fit this picture (Chakrabarty 1992; Chatterjee 1986, 1993). One could easily fit contemporary human rights discourse into such a framework: particular practices of African societies – such as clitoridectomy – or of African regimes – imprisonment without trial, torture – are identified and labeled. The evildoers are clearly demarcated, leaving an aura of their evil attached not only to themselves but also to everything around them. At one level, the distinctions are overly precise – a particular act is detached from its context – while at another, they are so imprecise that victims as well as perpetrators are blended in a singular portrait of Africa as the heart of darkness, as in the Conradian writing of Robert Kaplan (1994).

The critique of colonial liberalism, and its modern variants, should be taken seriously, but not necessarily accepted as it is. It misses the extent to which humanitarian discourses, however arrogant in intent, only transformed social relations if they resonated with something on the ground. However narrowly European officials wanted to define African slavery so that they could eradicate a bounded evil without endangering commerce and social order, African slaves might seize the opportunity to bring about more radical changes. Thomas Holt (1990) argues something like this for Jamaica, and I have previously shown this in the case of Zanzibar and coastal Kenya: ex-slaves perceived the waning power of their masters and used geographic mobility, kinship relations, access to marginal land, moving in and out of wage labor, and other strategies to give "freedom" a different and deeper meaning than its colonial advocates intended (Cooper 1980; Cooper et al. 2000). Whereas colonial emancipators often wanted to sustain large-scale production units, emancipation often had the effect of shaping dispersed peasantries, using market relations while avoiding too much dependence on them, and sometimes resulted in the creation of new productive structures, as in the growth of peanut cultivation organized by Islamic leaders in Senegal after the collapse of slavery in a wide region of Senegambia and Mali (Klein 1997).

This critique also misses the extent to which concepts such as "citizenship," "equality," and "liberalism," within Europe and beyond, changed

---

[7] Such an argument about slavery had already been rehearsed in British India (Prakash 1990). For a collection of studies on the abolition of slavery in Africa, see Miers and Roberts (1988).

when different people applied them to themselves. That the citizen, in liberal theory, was supposed to meet a certain "anthropological minimum" in level of civilization – seen in terms of race, gender, property, literacy, etc. – was a *sine qua none* since Locke. Uday Mehta (1990) has argued that this minimum hardened in early nineteenth-century India – as British liberals faced the actuality of a colonial society. But the anthropological minimum was torn wide open by the political mobilization that ensued. A discourse about turning black slaves into citizens in the West Indies and the United States opened the door to arguments that voting was a universal right (Fredrickson 1995; Holt 1990). Claims for the rights of all individuals to vote or to share in certain social resources are not a universal essence of "liberalism" but an argument confronting alternative conceptions of liberalism. And the people who made use of such arguments did not necessarily dissolve their constituencies into a sea of unmarked individuals, but often mobilized along particular social networks and used the status they gained to assert the place of particular collectivities in a social order.[8]

The spaces of ideological innovation: between empire and humanity

In its early days, antislavery discourse addressed the question of action on the level of the empire. Were the "rights of man" to apply on the French island of Saint Domingue as well as in Paris? Should the British Parliament abolish the right of British citizens in British overseas territory to hold other people as property? The universality of French and British variants of rights-centered arguments – and the international mechanisms of the trades in slaves and slave-produced commodities – meant that a question in one empire necessarily raised questions about other empires, but the immediate object of antislavery mobilization was to change imperial policy. That meant considering the empire as a whole as both a unit of authoritative action and a moral entity – "slavery under the British flag" was a favorite target of antislavery reformers in the late nineteenth and early twentieth centuries (Cooper 1980). This implies that there was a certain moral ambiguity about the status of a colonial subject – not a citizen, but not a mere subject to be manipulated, exploited, or destroyed at

---

[8] Tensions between individual membership in political bodies and conceptions of communities and collectivities are and have long been important and often fraught. But one should think of them as tensions rather than neat oppositions. It does not help to *begin* an analysis of such tensions with a dichotomy of a citizenship of unmarked, acultural, asocial individuals versus the cultural solidarity of groups. The latter is as problematic as the former is ahistorical.

will. The idea of empire defined an imaginable space, an area where the exercise of power was echoed by the necessity to think of people as somehow British or French. The conflicts over implementing emancipation, as I have argued above, in some ways reemphasized the distinctiveness of ex-slaves within imperial society, an exercise made necessary precisely because the distinction between ex-slave and ex-master was not in itself self-evident.

Empires are peculiar kinds of spaces, and recent work in "postcolonial theory" often misses the unevenness of imperial space via an overly sweeping conception of "coloniality" or "otherness" (Stoler and Cooper 1996). Nor indeed do nineteenth- and twentieth-century empires fit into a picture of this era as that of the nation-state, for the empire-state featured long debates over degrees of inclusion and exclusion and was thus more complicated than the projection of national power over subordinated subjects overseas. An empire such as the British empire included zones of white settlement where something like British life were to be replicated (even if this meant imagining large populations out of existence); zones of extraction and exploitation, where intensive economic transformation and exploitation were to take place; zones of supervised appropriation, where indigenous people were allowed to organize social life and production more or less as they could, with the colonial state appropriating some of the surplus; catchment zones, where laborers might be recruited to service either plantations or indigenous farming units, their economies being hemmed in and restricted but not directly exploited; and zones of marginal control, where the colonial state could do little except deny the sovereignty claims of indigenous rulers or other colonizing powers. Empires included commercial diasporas organized along ethnic lines, such as Indians in East Africa or Chinese in Southeast Asia, or Hausa or Dyula in large regions of West Africa – instances of networks with particular cultural, religious, and ideological frameworks of their own, allowed to exist within imperial structures. Prior political units – kingdoms, chiefdoms, segmentary polities – might be smashed or co-opted, or something in between. But the empire as a whole raised the awkward possibility that some people among the "colonizers" (such as a missionary) might raise awkward questions about concepts of rights, citizenship, or humanity that might apply to the entire unit, or that actions by the "colonized" might call into question the tacit arrangements that made things work.

One cannot understand nineteenth-century empires without coming to grips with the uneasy relationship between grandiose imperial claims and highly circumscribed realities. The ideas of civilizing backward peoples, of bringing new areas under the rational control of European states, of turning empire into a large-scale system for producing wealth – these had appeal in France or England. But what empires could actually do was quite different – resulting in islands of "civilization," islands of productive exploitation, amidst seas in which imperial control was shallow, in which colonial regimes survived only because they worked within narrow limits and made deals with the very indigenous rulers whose primitiveness or brutality had been invoked to justify conquest. David Edwards (1989) has invoked this pathos in relation to British conquest in Afghanistan – a seemingly glorious conquest that unwittingly revealed the limits of colonizing power. Unable to turn colonies into *either* zones of rational exploitation or zones of civilization, colonizers singled out particular traits of the colonized population that they could actually claim to transform: hence the emphasis, in Afghanistan, on "mad mullahs" whose fanatic Islamicist practices had to be tamed, on African slavers whose cruelty had to be checked, on backward Indians whose superstitious tendencies to burn widows or mistreat people of lower castes had to be countered. The imperial structure – and the ambiguity of where concepts of humanity, rights, and citizenship were to be located – implied that someone would worry about whether these isolated symbols of the civilizing mission went far enough, whether empires were not subverting their progressive missions through short-term greed, whether British or French values were being respected. These were arguments only – and these arguments were sometimes rooted in the fact that missions, merchants, planters, and officials had interests in different sorts of arrangements with indigenous peoples – but the uneven structure of empire in the era of bourgeois European culture assured that they would be made. And there was always the possibility that some elements within colonized communities might mobilize around issues that resonated in the metropole as well.

So the empire was an ambiguous structure in relation to networks and discourses – possibly too big, too hard to control, too ambiguous in its moral constitution to be immune from widespread mobilization. The empire needed functioning trading diasporas; it needed the collaboration of indigenous leaders and literate subordinates; it needed peasants and indigenous traders whose economic activities were valuable but whose collective ideas and organizations might be dangerous. In the twentieth century, empire tried to exclude some forms of cross-regional networking – pan-Arabism, for instance – while allowing others, such as Indian traders in East Africa. Around the time of World War I, imperial needs made it possible for French and British Africans to demand more recognition for their place in the imperial order – as soldiers, workers, and citizens – and the 1920s witnessed an imperial reaction against this – a retraditionalization of Africa and a withdrawal from efforts at what was beginning to be called "development" for fear that Africans were beginning to act as if they were citizens. The depression encouraged this retreat into conservatism, stagnation, and traditionalism. The hints at recovery in the mid-1930s in British – and somewhat later in French – Africa led to recognition that the world of tribes colonial officials were trying to imagine did not contain important and necessary categories of colonial subjects, including urban wage workers, who were making their presence increasingly felt. But as soon as colonial governments began – hesitatingly before World War II, hastily afterward – to extend to Africans concepts of social inclusion and social control based on the experience of class conflict and accommodation in Europe, the possibilities for new networks and new discourses sharply expanded (Conklin 1997; Cooper 1996).

The resonance of claims to self-determination politically and to equal treatment socially and economically in the post-war world upset the stability of empire as a unit. Or more precisely, the universalistic discourses gave imperial rulers a choice between taking seriously their rhetoric of empires as real units of citizenship and belonging – meaning enormous expenditures – or accepting that this unit no longer made sense. The latter choice became increasingly attractive as France and Britain saw Europe as an increasingly useful zone of economic and political action compared with their empires. The post-war era witnessed the opening up of worldwide debates about the equivalence of all human beings – in the shadow of the war against Nazism, in the face of mobilizations in colonies, in regard to national minorities who were the victims of discrimination, and in the context of fears that opposed sides in the Cold War might hook up with mobilizations in the colonies. Meanwhile, the very effort to reimagine a post-war world in which social conflict could be managed – expressed in the consolidation of European welfare states after 1945 – carried implications to the colonies too, that all humanity could be included in the "modern" world.

There was something slightly desperate about this fantasy, but it was an important one in allowing French and British governments to respond to colonial pressures in ways other than stubborn resistance: they could see a world in which they could profitably interact with Africans without having to command them at every instance. Imperial rulers, by the end of the 1950s, wanted to believe this, whether there was much basis or not, for the alternative was worse: giving into demands for equality – pushed by social movements and international organizations such as the ILO – within empires (Cooper 1996). A combination of connections and discourses had exploded a set of structures.

The peculiar history of national sovereignty

This brings us back to another aspect of the Subaltern Studies critique: did the movement of colonized people for "self-determination" represent the triumph of a universal vision of political freedom? Or was this vision itself enfolded within a constricting discourse on the limits of politics that was part of the imperial project itself? Did colonialism determine the conditions of its demise?

There is no question that movements within colonies are at the center of the story of decolonization. One reason they were able to succeed, however, was that they convinced people elsewhere that colonialism no longer made sense. That the Gold Coast or Indonesia or India could exercise "self-determination" became imaginable only because of the visibility of political organizations there capable of organizing popular support. In the process, what citizenship, equality, or participation actually meant changed profoundly, precisely because certain people claimed these constructs applied to them. At the same time, it was particular meanings of those constructs that were imaginable, not just any one.

Partha Chatterjee (1986) has argued that such a process excluded a wide variety of forms of political action and focused on one, which was itself of European extraction and linked to a wider conception of just what constituted political rationality – the state. As such, nationalism could only be a "derivative discourse," bounding people to a particular form of institution and particular ways in which those institutions connect to subject-citizens. He is right to a significant extent: the nation-state has since the 1960s been normalized as the only relevant unit of political activity and the idea of a nation-state acting via organizations such as schools, prisons, health facilities, censuses, etc. to bring "docile bodies" into relationship to it has had powerful effects throughout the world. But focus on what the state is or on what it does may underplay all the ambiguities which surround it: the embeddedness of state actors in different networks and discourses within and outside the territory. In that sense, states are continuously reinvented even if the idea of *the state* has become a modular element of world history.

The relationship between mobilization at "local," "national," and "transnational" levels is indeed complex and one of the most remarkable features of campaigns against slavery in the early nineteenth century, colonialism in the mid-twentieth, and apartheid in the late twentieth. To take one example, William Beinart and Colin Bundy (1987) have tellingly described the kinds of mobilization that took place in one area of the Eastern

Cape region of South Africa during the early twentieth century: some people were organizing around an issue of reforming chieftaincy within the region, talking in a local idiom about kinship and power relations; Africans with mission education and involvement in Christian churches were organizing among themselves and making use of religious language to assert their worth as human beings; a constitutionalist argument was being heard from educated Africans, using the language of rights and citizenship to make a case that resonated with South Africans involved in the creation of the African National Congress and with sympathizers abroad; pan-Africanists connected with movements among African Americans, first in the African Methodist Episocopal Church, later in the Garvey movement. The politics of a particular locality thus took place in ways that involved regional, national, and transcontinental linkages as well as ideological frameworks that ranged from highly specific to the most universalistic.[9]

Movement along these axes varied greatly in colonial Africa – regionalist groupings, such as the National Congress of British West Africa in the 1920s or the Rassemblement Démocratique Africaine in French Africa in the late 1940s, had their moments, as did movements demanding the appointment of a paramount chief in western Kenya in the 1930s or labor movements claiming "equal pay for equal work" and allied to the French communist trade union federation in the late 1940s and 1950s in French West Africa, or the specifically antimodern movement rich in Kikuyu symbolism that became known as Mau Mau in the 1950s. The ability of key figures in political mobilization to move among different networks and different mobilizing discourses was crucial in the 1940s and 1950s to enable the building of coalitions and political machines in highly differentiated political contexts.

What is most important for our purposes is that some of these mobilizing strategies were connected to European networks and ideologies via networks formed by African students and intellectuals (such as Léopold Senghor and Jomo Kenyatta), especially to leftist movements in Europe, civil rights organizations in the United States, and world or regional trade union federations (Cooper 1996; Von Eschen 1997). The kind of phenomenon that James Scott (1990) writes about – a movement that develops its "hidden transcript" in isolation from colonial forces and then

---

[9] South Africans' religious connections at the beginning of the twentieth century were closely linked to those of African Americans (James T. Campbell 1995), while antiapartheid mobilization within South Africa in the late twentieth century had a powerful international component (Klotz 1995). The "local," meanwhile, turns out to be full of linkages, as Guyer (1994) has argued.

bursts forth in a sudden challenge to the colonial order – perhaps existed at certain moments and in certain places, but that was rarely more than one dimension of a more multiplex, more interactive pattern of mobilization. Frantz Fanon's (1966) vision of a pure anticolonial struggle rooted in the authenticity of a peasantry and a lumpen proletariat – rejecting the sociologically determined, inalterably compromised categories of a petty bourgeois or labor aristocracy – has little to do with how the Algerian revolution, or any other, actually was organized (Stora 1991).

The retreat of colonial regimes in Africa during the 1950s had much to do with the juxtaposition of movements such as the one British officials called Mau Mau, which entirely rejected colonial categories, and opposition that came in understandable forms. African leaders such as Tom Mboya became skilled at manipulating officials' fears of the unfathomable as much as their hopes to find Africans with whom they could negotiate. The possibility of international action against slavery, colonialism, or apartheid made it possible for opponents within any given territory to imagine their opposition in wider – and more optimistic – terms that would otherwise be the case. These connections made it possible for officials to imagine alternatives to the *status quo* in palatable forms. White settlers in Kenya and later in Rhodesia and South Africa, who imagined themselves to be part of a global "civilization" – sharing a middle-class view of life and possibilities for global exchange and travel – discovered that they had become isolated and had lost the battle of connections and external legitimization.

None of this is to deny that the process of turning mobilization into a political victory involved discarding part of any collectivity's program and pushing others that could be understood elsewhere. The power to shape categories of struggle is not equally distributed. But it would be wrong to think of the process as entirely one-sided: what has been seen as "universal values" have changed in particular ways. To line up capitalism, colonialism, liberalism, and universality on one side and locality, authenticity, community, culture, and particularity on the other does not get either side right.

What this historical sketch has shown is both the possibility of mobilization across borders, across conceptual frameworks, across interests, and the possibility that discourses can be changed: that what is imaginable in one period can become inconceivable in another, and what cannot be hoped for at one moment can become what is expected at another. Mobilizations have changed discourses; new discourses have made it possible to imagine changing structures. But the question of the limits of discourses, networks, and structures remains.

The sovereign, the global, and the local

Sovereignty could cover up many sins. The new – very shaky – system of the decolonized world required considerable mythologizing and wishful thinking, for states to "pretend in many cases that the criteria for legitimate statehood were met, regardless of how evidently fictitious this pretence may have been" (Clapham 1996: 15). This fiction in turn created the possibility for other actors – sometimes the same ones now transformed into chiefs of state – to make claims on richer states or international organizations, citing the need to make sovereignties work. African states have been termed "monopoly states" (Clapham 1996) or "shadow states" (Reno 1995) or "gatekeeper states" (Cooper forthcoming), all terms to suggest the weakness of bonds between the state and the people within its territory and the reliance of state rulers on the very idea of the state, on resources deriving solely from its position within a global structure of sovereignties. Not only did this have particular implications about the kinds of networks (client states of major powers, Third World blocs, development institutions) in which African states participated, but it shaped the discourses that were effective, stressing above all else sovereignty, nation-building, and development. Those were the terms in which state-based actors could appeal for resources. The cross-territorial discourses which had been so important in the 1940s and 1950s – about equality, about the rights of labor – were repressed at the national level and discouraged at the international level, as states and international organizations all sought to play the "family of nations" game (Ferguson 1997; Malkki 1994).

At the climax of the anticolonial movements, discourses about what states should do implied a "thick" conception of citizenship: the population should be mobilized and it should demand accountability; the state should provide social services and define the space for a truly national economy; people should aspire to mobility within a national social system. The collapse of the dreams of the 1950s and 1960s has often left the inhabitants of African states with a citizenship that is very thin – providing little accountability, few services, and meager security – while ruling elites use sovereignty to gain a degree of leverage among international and national networks, licit or otherwise (see the other chapters in this volume).

One can trace the ups and downs of sovereignty-centered discourses and sovereignty-crossing discourses from the 1960s to the 1990s: the sovereignty regime never quite killed off the universalizing implications of all the earlier talk about equal pay for equal work, about minimum standards of living, about human rights for all citizens of the world. The recent emphasis on "human rights," "democratization," "good governance," and "sustainable development" thus appears within a deeper temporal context. It is debatable, in today's context, whether such discourses encourage a thick notion of social citizenship and political accountability within or among nation-states, or whether they imply a thin notion of the individual as an economic actor or rights-bearing entity, with weak reinforcement by sovereign governments and piecemeal intervention by international organizations against the most publicized violations.

Rights talk or sustainability talk may come from well-intentioned lobby groups in rich countries, or they may come from on-the-ground mobilizations in poor ones; the question of origins may be less important than the question of resonances. What kind of movement gets sustenance abroad? What kind of global campaign makes sense to people in their daily lives and fosters activism? In the nineteenth and early twentieth centuries, empire constituted a unit on which such arguments focused – forced labor or freedom of association was debated in relation to imperial policy. Since the 1960s, the nation-state has become the accepted container for policy debates – but it is a porous one, as was the empire before it, for the language of universality and issue networks link different parts of the world.

One should not assume that transnational networks are all warm and fuzzy. Some can be quite nasty – diamond- and arms-trading networks in Sierra Leone or Angola (sometimes calling themselves rebels, sometimes linked to state institutions), highly personal connections between the French government and unsavory leaders in certain African countries, mining companies with hired armies. Cross-border networks may not have any ideological content at all; they may in more senses than one be mercenary. But they can still have lasting effects, even after the conditions (civil war, for example) that gave rise to them pass, for linkages that cross space become vested interests in maintaining network-dominated relations of power. If the strength of such networks is a sign that a state is "weak," it is not a sign that the state is absent: official leaders may be active in the "parallel" economy, and sovereign states may prefer to use linkages to "security" firms and multinationals to undertake governmental activities, especially in the realm of force (see Nordstrom and Reno this volume, as well as Bayart et al. 1997). And such networks may hook up at the other end to "respectable" actors on the "global" scene – arms manufacturers, oil and mining companies. But the more private firms or shady mafias perform "state" tasks, the less accountability can be fixed on such a state.

Such a situation is itself subject to transformation and eventually formalization of authority in a renewed state structure – the example of Uganda stands out. But there are disturbing lessons to be had in the recent history of Africa: just as linkages of national, local, and transnational mobilizations eroded the authority of colonial regimes and gave rise to a crystallization of legitimate authority around the nation-state, the development of shadow states and illicit networks makes it difficult for citizens to see how they can obtain accountable government, debate crucial issues, and obtain predictable behavior from institutions visible to them.[10]

For better or worse, particular forms of transnational connection have specific implications – even with organizations deeply committed to principles they regard as universal. Certain humanitarian NGOs – with their discourses of helping people in danger of starvation – find ways of working with states or with organizations in civil society in endangered regions of Africa, but they propagate worldwide an image of Africa as famine-ridden and dependent. When NGOs moved in to assist people fleeing from Rwanda to the camps in eastern Zaire in 1994, most of them insisted that their mission was simply to provide food and medical care to people defined as "refugees," not to deal with politics (the presence of armed militias in the camps) or justice (that those militias were responsible for genocide). The effect of this framing of the problem was not neutral: it helped to turn the camps into centers in which many "refugees" were coerced into playing the politics of the militia leaders and to staging raids and murders – and the conflict over the camps in turn had enormous consequences throughout Central Africa, going way beyond anything the NGOs had been willing to talk about. At the same time, the possibility that activists within African countries might link up with NGOs has brought about widespread debates on such issues as gender relations, political oppression, and the environment, which neither African states nor Western states – with their geopolitical concerns – wanted to take seriously. It is thus not necessarily the case that the actions of transnational issue networks and aid organizations undermine accountability – they may open up issues of responsibility in contexts where states have tried to cut off any such discussion – but it is nevertheless unclear where that accountability lies.

Looking at the relationship of structures, connections, and discourses will not tell us whether virtue or vice will triumph. It does help us to see how what is possible and impossible in the world changes, and forces us to ask what kinds of organizational and discursive developments might lead to what kinds of possibilities. Such an approach is more fruitful than

---

[10] Efforts – from external or internal pressure – to downsize governments and privatize economies may do less to create a market system in which individual actors enter into transactions, but increase the importance of personal networks, as happened to a significant extent in post-Soviet Russia (Lonkila 2000).

an effort to search for "authentic" African political values or languages on the one hand and "Western" ones on the other.

A "local" actor can make use of particularistic authority and at the same time find resonance between his/her mobilizing ideology and moral discourse that claims to be "universal." And organizations that come to Africa with universalistic ideals in mind will likely find people to whom those ideals are relevant and useful in obtaining support and in associating one cause with a more widely shared one. One need not fall into a dichotomy of global and local, between allegedly universal principles and supposedly particular communities, for the historical record is filled with networking and discursive formations situated in between. The analyst needs to follow these linkages and their limits, and that is not easy. Networks operate in different ways in different places – a subtle understanding of one end of the system (links of an NGO to community activists) does not necessarily help understand what happens at another end (lobbying in Paris).

The power to shape discourse is not evenly distributed, but it is not uniquely located in a single region either. If looking backward in time is of any use in the present, it should be to remind us that the present is but a moment in history, not necessarily any more important than any other. But we know that minds and structures do change. It has happened before.

Authority, intervention, and the outer
      limits of international relations theory

Michael Barnett[1]

The social sciences and the humanities are presently littered with various
concepts, phrases, vocabularies, idioms, and slogans that are intended
to resituate how scholars think about the "global" and its relationship
to a reconceptualized "local." The utility of these concepts and frameworks is to be found not in their ability to be all things to all scholars, but
rather in their capacity to highlight newly emergent structures in global
politics, how those structures are created by and are responsible for new
networks of actors, and the development of new discourses and practices
that collapse and telescope the local and the global. In the search to better understand the relationships between these emergent properties and
their relationship to global and local outcomes, there is no substitute for
careful, grounded, and historically rich studies. Abstract theorizing and
master structural concepts have an important place in theory development and in guiding empirical research, but arguably the best strategy
for the purposes of teasing out new insights into global – local relations is
one that, following Glaser and Strauss (1967), accepts the methodological value of "grounded theory." Closely observed and chronicled cases
are the media for more generalizable claims.

This volume follows these orthodox admonitions, and, in doing so,
arrives at some heterodox observations for theorists of international relations. I have in mind two important and related observations that form
the basis of this chapter. The first is the need to move beyond the statist
ontology that defines the discipline of international relations. This ontology tells us about how the world is carved up, the defining actors of
that global polity and what structures and guides their interactions, and
on what basis they make authoritative claims in global politics and thus
influence outcomes and defend their territorialized space. In contrast to
the reigning statist ontology, this volume (and other statements) invites
us to examine how this conceptual apparatus can become a debilitating

[1] I would like to thank the editors, Ian Hurd, and the reviewers of the manuscript for their
helpful comments.

crutch. Following this claim, the first part of this chapter explores the tendency in IR theory to collapse state, authority, and territory, how that bundling makes it more difficult to understand complex global relationships and processes that defy and flirt with the neat boundaries between the systemic and the domestic, and recent contributions that unbundle these concepts and thus generate new insights into the organization and practice of global politics.

An important payoff of this conceptual exhuming is that the isolation and consideration of a concept that is currently camouflaged in the thicket of IR theory becomes telescoped: authority. As recent scholarship and the chapters in this volume have reconsidered the relationship between global and local forces, they have explicitly and implicitly observed how authority is invested in non-state actors because of transnational processes and global developments, problematized the concept of sovereignty and questioned whether states are authoritative and how and over what domains, and become eyewitnesses to a local that has a cast of characters that claim authority over different domains and according to different legitimation criteria. Building on these observations, the second part of the chapter focuses attention on that woolly concept of authority with the goal of providing greater evidence that doing so presses important foundational and empirical issues for global politics. In the interest of demonstrating the utility of unpacking this concept and forwarding some specific items for future research, I begin with a brief discussion of the concept and then animate that discussion through the chapters in this volume and a relatively recent statement by UN Secretary-General Kofi Annan regarding UN intervention.

The status of the global in international relations theory

In recent years many scholars of international relations have been struggling with alternative conceptualizations of the relationship between the "global" and the "local," but have found themselves hamstrung by the same conceptual architecture that has served them reasonably well for so long in so many areas. The reason for this intellectual glaucoma is because of the statecentrism of the discipline. International relations as an academic discipline, or at least as an American social science, formed around the study of enduring relations and patterns between states, the anarchy problem and how states can establish order given the absence of a supranational authority, and lately by the possible role of international institutions in helping states manage their relations, overcome problems associated with interdependent choice, and limit the consequences of growing interdependence.

Statecentrism's extreme form is embodied in what John Agnew (1994) calls the "territorial trap." This trap has several features. First, International Relations carves up the world into mutually exclusive territorial states. In fact, the study of international relations is about the relationship between these units. At the extreme the image is of "billiard-ball" like states, but even when this imagery is relaxed and transnationalism and interdependence processes are allowed, the territorial imperative of the discipline remains. Second, states are assumed to have authority over their political space. How that authority is understood and defined can vary from scholar to scholar, but the common thread is that state officials radiate power that is derived from centralized authority (and a monopoly of the means of coercion) from the center to the territorial border where it comes to a dead halt. This authority over a geographically defined and (mainly) contiguous space is reinforced and underscored by the principle of sovereignty, in which states recognize each other's authority over that space and deny any authoritative claims made by those outside the state. Such matters inform the classic differentiation in IR theory between anarchy on the outside and hierarchy on the inside, where coercion reigns in the former and law and authority in the latter. Third, the territorial trap generates a rigid domestic/foreign distinction, which, according to the IR theorist R.B.J. Walker (1993), constitutes an "inside/outside" image of global politics. This inside/outside distinction, in turn, shapes a host of other dichotomies: the state is a source of security for those on the inside and against the anarchy that exists on the outside; society exists within the territorial container of the state, and there is no meaningful society outside; and the community within the state can aspire to universal values, while particularism runs rampant outside. State, territory, and authority are forever married in IR theory.

Contributing to an air of overdetermination, additional reasons for this territorial trap and statecentrism deserve mention. International relations theory has largely been interested in systemic patterns, that is, enduring patterns between states, and a widely accepted methodological claim is that one cannot understand the workings of the whole by examining the individual units in isolation. Ken Waltz (1979) is most famously associated with this position, though the same point has been made in a less polemical manner by other scholars drawing on different theoretical traditions and methodological informants (also see Jervis 1997; Wendt 1999). This injunction concerning how to explain satisfactorily and parsimoniously the workings of the state system spills over into an epistemological claim that the principal constraints on – that is, the primary cause of – the state's foreign policy behavior derive from systemic properties (Keohane 1987). By no means do all international relations scholars hold that system-level variables provide an exhaustive explanation of the state's foreign policy, but many do subscribe to the more modest claim that the system properly represents the first cut into the problem and that domestic and individual level factors are the source of (sometimes considerable) residual variance.[2] Alongside and buttressing this view is the claim that there exist different "levels" that can be distinguished by the nature of the units and how these levels are organized internally and *vis-à-vis* one another.[3]

These commitments and dispositions are produced and reproduced by the discipline of political science, which in the United States is the departmental home for the academic study of international relations. Here the important distinction is between comparative politics and international relations: processes within the state are studied by scholars of "comparative politics" and processes that cross state boundaries or that occur between states are studied by scholars of "international relations." Scholars of comparative politics and international relations have been equally vigilant at policing their territorial and disciplinary boundaries. Of course, frequently those from each camp will deliver well-received speeches that observe the artificiality of these disciplinary boundaries and assert that many of the most pressing and interesting research questions bridge, blur, and mock the borders. After the applause, however, scholars retreat to their respective base camps. The institutionalization of these divisions can be most readily observed when they are challenged not by boilerplate statements but by important funding agencies that are perceived to be trying to break down these barriers through new spending protocols. At such moments, cheers for theoretical pluralism yield to panicked shrieks coming from disciplinary police. For these and other reasons IR has maintained a fairly tight distinction between the systemic and the domestic.

The manner by which IR scholarship has historically attempted to "integrate" the domestic and the global reflects this territorial trap, for such integration has generally included not a consideration of the boundaries between these realms that are understood as ontologically distinct (or even their very relevance) but rather the interactive relationship between these pre-given realms. In many respects, James Rosenau (1969) inaugurated thinking on these matters in his seminal studies on

---

[2] Though recently there has been an effort by IR scholars to change this dance and introduce a "two-step" that begins with domestic politics as sources of variation in state preferences and then examines the interactions of state interests in an international context. See Moravsik (1997) and Legro (1996).

[3] For the literature on levels of analysis, see Buzan (1995); Hollis and Smith (1990); Moul (1973); Onuf (1995); and Singer (1961).

domestic – international linkages. Several years later Joseph Nye and Robert Keohane's massively influential *Power and Interdependence* (1977) recognized that the boundaries between states were becoming increasingly permeated by transnational interactions, shaping the nature of domestic politics and the pressures and constraints on states from above and below; but they couched their views as calling attention to the permeability and not the ontological standing of the state, a point reaffirmed by their later essays that emphasized an anarchy-centered starting point and the state as the most fundamental unit in global politics. The following year Peter Gourevitch (1978) introduced the concept of "second-image reversed," noting how systemic processes shape domestic political and economic arrangements. Robert Putnam's concept of "two-level games" has spawned a cottage industry of scholars interested in how state officials, who are at one and the same time foreign policy officials and domestic political creatures, are constrained by the international and the domestic environment, and play games on both levels as they try to achieve their various foreign policy goals (Putnam 1988). The editors' introduction to the fiftieth anniversary issue of *International Organization* makes fairly consistent claims and observations (Keohane et al. 1998).

These conceptual compasses are joined by other studies that have examined how the international political economy shaped domestic political and economic relations, and vice versa (Keohane and Milner 1996), how war and conflict have altered state – society relations, and vice versa (Barnett 1992; Tilly 1990), and so on.[4] These studies have led to knowledge accumulation concerning how systemic processes and patterns shape domestic outcomes, and how domestic processes and patterns shape foreign policy behavior and systemic outcomes. It must be noted that intelligible and knowledgeable state and non-state actors engage in practices and utter discourses that draw from and help to reconstitute the domestic and the international as separate and distinct realms; in short, IR's research agenda and conceptual architecture are not driven by misplaced postulates that have a tenuous grasp on social reality. Whatever the cause(s), IR is a discipline whose research agendas, ontology, and epistemology are constituted by an understanding of the domestic and the international as existing in separate and discrete realms or as constituting different levels.[5]

---

[4] For a very thorough and excellent survey of the relationship between the domestic and international politics, see Moravsik (1995). For more recent efforts at "integration," see Moravsik (1997) and Sterling-Folker (1997).

[5] IR scholars are not necessarily any more myopic than are scholars in other disciplines when it comes to thinking creatively about the relationship between the global and the local. Anthropologists have long defined their enterprise as the "local" and absented the "global"

Over the past decade, however, IR theorists have become more aware of the limitations imposed by this territorial trap and the bundling of the state, territory, and authority. This development is informed by critiques of neo-realism and statism; the introduction of new theoretical traditions from outside political science; a willingness to problematize sovereignty and historicize the Westphalian state system and to exhume its origins and investigate closely its rumored decline; and a shifting research agenda owing to the disappearance of the Cold War and the related appearance of once marginalized topics.

Scholars have recently debated the various ways in which territory, authority, and the state can be "bundled" (Ruggie 1993: 165). The concept of sovereignty has been the central motivating vehicle for this discussion. Consider the debate over the nature of the medieval European states system and how it compares with the Westphalian model. John Ruggie (1983) pointed the way in his famous review of Kenneth Waltz's *Theory of International Politics* (1979), faulting him for failing to recognize that different types of international systems have been organized according to very different principles, and contrasting the organizing principles of the medieval states system, with its overlapping spheres of authority, heteronomous principles, and absence of fixed territorial boundaries, with the Westphalian states system and its constitutive principle of state sovereignty. Many IR scholars have been highly engrossed by the medieval states system precisely because it represents a non-Westphalian bundling of state, authority, and territory. Indeed, others have suggested that perhaps the best predictor of Europe's future is its past, looking to pre-Westphalian Europe for hints regarding a post-Westphalian Europe (Bull 1979: ch. 10; Slaughter 1997; Spruyt 1994: ch. 9).

IR scholars also have had to confront the possibility that territoriality, authority, and the state might be bundled in different ways in present-day Europe. Here the debate is over what *is* the European Union. At one extreme is the claim that the EU is nothing more than an institution established by states to further their interests and overcome their collective action problems; in this reading, state sovereignty and all its entitlements

---

from their purview. As Gupta and Ferguson (1997a) note, anthropologists have been reluctant to go anywhere beyond rural communities in "Third World" societies. Shore and Wright (1997: 13) also note that anthropology has its own dichotomies that are made into ontological categories: "One central problem for anthropology was how to move away from a conceptualization of the local and the nation, or the villages and the state, as two separate polities with 'relations' mediating between them." For an attempt, see Appadurai (1996) and Kearney (1995). Sociologists, too, have paid remarkably little attention to the relationship between the "global" and the "local," largely because "society" is defined by the state's territorial boundaries. For an important exception, see the work under the world polity school and especially Boli and Thomas (1999).

and duties remain snugly secure and unchanged. At the other end is the claim that the EU represents a step on the road to a supranational state; in this reading, European states are yielding their authority and their sovereignty to a suprastate. Recognizing, however, that for all their differences, both readings have the state, territory, and authority bundled in exactly the same way, the critical difference between the two is the geographical domain. Statist thinking defines the limits of both approaches.

Not all scholars have limited their analysis to this "territorial trap," for many have begun to imagine different ways in which European states are related authoritatively, politically, and constitutionally. John Ruggie (1993) calls Europe a "multiperspective polity," by which he means that "it is increasingly difficult to imagine the conduct of international politics among community members, and, to a considerable measure even domestic politics, as though it took place from a starting point of twelve separate, single fixed view points."[6] Ole Waever (1998) argues that Europe is a political entity that stands between a pluralistic and an amalgamated security community – that is, a post-sovereignty community of states that has managed to establish dependable expectations of peaceful change. James Caporaso (1997) has claimed that it is a place where "constitutionalism" has been internationalized, and has urged IR theorists to see hierarchy and anarchy as ideal types that bookend a continuum. And finally, there is a debate over the European Court of Justice, specifically, regarding its source of authority, the reasons why sovereign European states have largely honored its decisions, and how to characterize its jurisdiction over "domestic" space (Alter 1998; Mattli and Slaughter 1998). The debate over the past, present, and future shape of the European architecture provides vivid testimony to the necessity of rethinking the relationship between the state, authority, and territoriality.[7]

Other emergent research domains also have escaped the territorial trap. Although there always has existed an extensive literature on non-state actors in world politics, most famously in the case of multinational corporations, the recent focus on NGOs and transnational actors has demonstrated their capacity to shape outcomes even though they are absent the material bases of power and rely on persuasion, communication, and information (Keck and Sikkink 1998; Price 1998; Smith et al. 1997). Theorists of globalization have debated long and hard whether the various and nearly always ill-defined processes lumped under its heading are eroding

---

[6] Also note the important functionalist and neo-functionalist literatures, which explicitly recognize transnational linkages and the possible transformation of the units (Deutsch 1968; Mitrany 1966).

[7] Indeed, many of these scholars have noted that what is occurring in Europe might also be true elsewhere (Caporaso 1997: 580; Ruggie 1993: 172–174).

the state's authority, autonomy, or sovereignty; in doing so, they have been forced to address what are the new connections and networks that structure interactions between state and non-state actors and generate new spheres of authority.[8] Other scholars ruminate about the emergence of a global civil society, hypothesizing a structure of interaction among various non-state actors that are responsible for producing new normative arrangements and expectations that can be binding on states.[9] Scholars of epistemic communities examine how individuals claiming expertise and authority over particular issue areas are able to create the demand for and the possibility of new forms of interstate cooperation (Adler and Haas 1992; Johnstone 1991; Litfin 1994). IR's recent interest in international law also has introduced a reconsideration of the relationship between international and domestic institutions (Goldstein et al. 2000). And, finally, critical examinations of the international political economy, particularly those that are interested in historicizing globalization, have also located authority in bodies other than states (Cutler 1999; Cutler et al. 1999).

Arguably scholars of non-European regions have been less seduced by the territorial trap. While many scholars of Third World politics have mechanistically applied European-driven models of international relations, others recognized that the Third World state as an ideal type is distant from the European and Westphalian state as an ideal type. As a consequence, they have turned various ontological assumptions into empirical questions, as they have explored the different international forms that can exist, chronicling how state actors work hard to unify state, territory, and authority; the fictional boundaries of authority that are drawn between the domestic and the international; how non-state actors, including missionaries and multinational corporations, have penetrated local space and claimed authority and imposed control, and how their activities have reverberated through other functional and geographic spaces; the networks that are the chains of resource exchange and appropriation from the local to the global (though rarely in reverse because of the gross asymmetries of power between the former and the latter); how external pressures shaped new societal arrangements and created a demand for sharper legal, political, and economic boundaries between the "local" and the "global"; and how domestic actors have confronted external pressures through symbolic means and appropriated universalizing discourses as a weapon of the weak, using them on international stages.

[8] See, for instance, Albrow (1996); Armstrong (1998); Clark (1998); Shaw (1998).
[9] See Clark et al. (1998); Lipschutz (1992); *Millennium* (1994); Wapner (1995).

The entry point for these claims has been the palpable "weakness" of the Third World state. The Third World state is a "shadow state," a "shell state," a "weak" state, an "alien" state, and an "artificial" state. Such metaphors are intended to convey the existence of a state that has very little legitimacy and authority in domestic politics, has little control over its territory, and does not have a magnetic hold over its population and economy. Thus, politics and exchange take place outside the state's purview and transcends its highly porous borders. The scholars in this volume also climb through the window of the weak African state to consider alternative ontological grids, the networks of actors that congregate and span those grids, and the overlapping and complex relationship between the various "levels" of politics that mock the neat categories of the "global" and the "local." The territorial trap is easily eluded for these scholars, though arguably it is the empirical and historical state of affairs that drives the demand to rethink the global architecture. Necessity is the mother of invention.

Authority in global politics

The contributions to this volume raise the concept of authority in various ways, confer that social attribute to a multiplicity of actors, and suggest that these actors are conferred authority because of new structures, networks, and discourses. In this section I want to focus attention on this concept of authority, and forward a set of provisional claims concerning why we should care about the concept, when actors are likely to be authoritative and thus shape outcomes, and the sorts of effects that authorities have.

What is meant by authority? By no means has an avalanche of writings on the subject led to a consensus position. For my purposes here, the following claims are useful for thinking about authority in global politics in ways that cease to automatically bundle it with the state and begin to imagine how non-state actors might be accorded authority.[10] To begin, the interest in authority stems from its relationship to the central issue of social control; in this regard, it is part of the family of concepts that include domination, power, manipulation, persuasion, coercion, and force. There is general agreement, however, that authority is somewhere between domination and persuasion. Weber's (1978) famous discussion of authority links it to domination that has been legitimized, and the effect is that an actor's commands that are emitted are obeyed for reasons other

---

[10] For treatments of authority, see Arendt (1968); Lincoln (1994); Raz (1990a); Weber (1978).

than overt coercion. Others, however, argue that it is less about domination *per se* and more about actors that are given a presumptive right to speak and to act because of their position or standing (Lincoln 1994). In this second view, the claim is that some actors, because of their standing in the community and polity and the roles that they occupy, are conferred the right to speak.

Such matters obviously relate to the conditions under which an actor is likely to be conferred authority. For the purposes of considering authority in global politics, three issues stand out. First, many scholars ritualistically begin with Weber's famous three ideal types of authority, charismatic, traditional, and rational-legal, but then quickly offer that the latter is the most relevant for discussions of authority in the modern world system. A second point concerns the critical distinction between those who are "in authority" and those who are "an authority." Actors whose authority derives from the institutional roles that they occupy can be said to be "in authority." The classic example here is actors occupying positions in the state apparatus; their authority derives from a particular institutional role. Those who are "an authority" derive their standing from the presumption that they are experts owing to credentials, education, training, and experience. We frequently recognize that some people are "authorities" owing to their accomplishments and thus are given a presumptive right to speak. Actors who are an authority and in authority are presumed to have the right to speak and act, though there are distinct mechanisms that generate that presumption.

Third, authority suggests compliance that is secured through an appeal to reason, prior cultural beliefs, and community standards. The appeals and reasons given by an authority must be grounded in the beliefs, aspirations, and interests of the community. In this way, "authority is only justified to the extent that it serves the needs and interests" of the community and its members (Raz 1990a: 5). Blending normative theory and definitional claims, the insinuation is that authority only operates as a legitimate force and can be sustained when claims are grounded in established values of the community. A community can be said to exist wherever there are multisided interactions between actors, a shared identity, and a sense of obligation. Although there are good reasons to presuppose that community is more likely to exist within the state than outside it because of these conditional propositions, we must also allow for the possibility that a community might exist below the state or transcend it. Networks emergent in functional and geographic spaces might generate a thin version of community, and in doing so allow particular actors to be conferred authority by those within that network (Adler and Barnett 1998). In short, many discussions of authority implicitly assume that the referent community is exhausted by the territorial state, but this must be understood as a contingent and not as a categorical claim.

Identifying the conditions under which an actor is likely to be conferred authority is critical for linking that recognition to outcomes. The ideal type of rational-legal authority, the distinction between in authority and of authority, and the appeal to interests and beliefs of the community arguably help narrow the conditions under which an actor is likely to be understood as an authority and thus have the capacity to influence outcomes by virtue of that authority. But careful empirical studies have documented how actors that have been conferred authority escape these conditions, and that actors that have seemingly fulfilled every imaginable social structural and cultural category have had their authority challenged. Such typological shortcomings have led many scholars to look for more contextual and climatized features. For instance, for Bruce Lincoln (1994) authority is highly dependent on the "right speaker, the right speech, the right staging and props, the right time and place, and an audience historically and culturally conditioned to judge what is right in all these instances and to respond with trust, reverence, and respect." Lincoln's formulation suffers from being so contextualized and historicized that it can admit only *ex poste ante* discussions and precludes an a priori assessment of the conditions under which an actor is likely to be conferred authority by a particular audience. Yet this approach's vice also contains a virtue in that it has an easier time recognizing actors who are "in authority" and whose claim to authority is highly dependent on the cultural backdrop and the stage on which those claims are made.

What do authorities do? An enduring line in legal theory is that a function of authority is to help resolve coordination problems (Raz 1990a: 6–11). There are two key aspects here. One is that authorities help to determine when a coordination problem exists. There are various sorts of "games" in social life, and only some of them can be properly defined as coordination games. It is not immediately apparent, however, when actors are in a game of coordination or in some other game. The challenge for actors in authority is "to get people to realize that they are confronting a coordination problem . . ." (Raz 1990a: 9). In short, coordination games are not part of objective reality that stands outside experience but rather are subjectively defined and constituted within social experience, and authorities help to create that subjective reality. The other way that authorities help solve coordination problems is by suggesting particular mechanisms to accomplish coordination. There are potentially many different institutional forms available to solve coordination problems, some of which are viewed as more efficient and normatively desirable than are others. In this important respect, authorities not only are involved in regulating the activities and interests of actors but also are fundamental to the constitution and construction of the social world.

Sociologists, anthropologists, political scientists, and legal theorists have spilled rivers of ink over the concept of authority because they have not presumed that one and only one actor has it, and that once it has it, it has it forever and under all and any circumstances. Instead, they have debated long and hard about what it is, about the conditions under which an actor is conferred authority, and what authoritative actors do with it and with what effects. To highlight how central are these issues for IR theory, I want to draw from the issues raised by this volume and by a speech by Secretary-General Kofi Annan. Let me begin with the speech.

In June 1998, UN Secretary-General Kofi Annan traveled to Ditchley Park in the United Kingdom to deliver an address on "intervention." He opened by predicting that his audience was probably expecting him to warn of the dangers of intervention. Yes, he confirmed, intervention was to be condemned when the strong intrude upon the weak; under such circumstances, "intervention" is tantamount to "invasion." But, he continued, intervention can have a "benign" side:

We all applaud when the policeman intervenes to stop a fight, or the teacher prevents big boys from bullying a smaller one. And medicine uses the word "intervention" to describe the act of the surgeon, who saves lives by "intervening" to remove a malignant growth, or to repair damaged organs. Of course, the most intrusive methods of treatment are not always to be recommended. A wise doctor knows when to let nature take its course. But a doctor who never intervened would have few admirers, and probably even fewer patients.

Annan's rhetorical question is easily anticipated: "Why was the United Nations established, if not to act as a benign policeman or doctor?" Only the UN, he argued, has the authority to act in this "benign" capacity, an authority that comes from decisions of the Security Council, whose own authority comes from the Charter of the United Nations, a document that has legal standing among its signatories and is a constitutional expression of the international community.[11]

Annan's relatively brief autobiographical statement on UN intervention, an instance of what Robert Latham (this volume) calls a transboundary deployment, joins with the chapters in this volume to raise a series of interesting answers to the following questions. From where does authority derive? How does authority collapse the space between the global and the local? How are the effects of authority not merely

[11] Cited from http://www.un.org/NEWS/Press/docs/1998/19980626.sgsm66.hmtl.

regulative but also constitutive? And how are those constitutive effects bound up with power and amendable to critical analysis?

The first issue to be addressed concerns the conditions under which an actor is likely to be conferred authority. How might we best understand the source of the UN's authority? At a rudimentary level its authority is delegated authority (Sarooshi 1999). The UN's authority comes from the mandate given to it by the Security Council. The Security Council's authority derives from the Charter of the United Nations. The Charter of the UN is a legal document codified by states. In this respect, we are in the domain of principal-agent analysis and the view that the agent's authority is contingent on the delegation of that authority from the principals in whose name it acts.

But we also can think of the UN's authority as linked to its standing as a modern bureaucracy. Modern bureaucracies, according to the Weberian view, contain legal-rational authority.[12] In contrast to earlier forms of authority that were invested in a leader, legitimate modern authority is invested in legalities, procedures, and rules, and thus rendered impersonal. This authority is "rational" in that it deploys socially recognized relevant knowledge to create rules that help determine the means that should be selected to pursue already identified ends. The very fact that they embody rationality is what makes bureaucracies powerful and makes people willing to submit to this kind of authority. According to Weber,

in legal authority, submission does not rest upon the belief and devotion to charismatically gifted persons ... or upon piety toward a personal lord and master who is defined by an ordered tradition ... Rather submission under legal authority is based upon an *impersonal* bond to the generally defined and functional "duty of office." The official duty – like the corresponding right to exercise authority: the "jurisdictional competency" – is fixed by *rationally established* norms, by enactments, decrees, and regulations in such a matter that the legitimacy of the authority becomes the legality of the general rule, which is purposely thought out, enacted, and announced with formal correctness. (Gerth and Mills 1978: 299, emphasis in original)

In addition, a bureaucracy's power derives from specialized knowledge that is technical, originating from training and professionalized criteria and control over information. Weber stressed that while such technical rationality might enable the bureaucracy to be more efficient for carrying out the directives of politicians, its own claim to authoritative knowledge represented an important source of its ability to command

---

[12] This discussion on international organizations and legal-rational authority derives from work I am doing with Martha Finnemore. See Barnett and Finnemore (1999).

compliance with its directives (Gerth and Mills 1978: 233). These features of authority combine to make bureaucracies powerful precisely by creating the appearance of depoliticization. The power of bureaucracies is that they present themselves as impersonal, technocratic, and neutral – *not* as exercising power but instead as serving others; the presentation and acceptance of these claims is critical to their legitimacy and authority (Burley and Mattli 1993; Ferguson 1990; Fisher 1997; Shore and Wright 1997).

These observations of the modern state have relevance for thinking about international organizations. The UN's authority can be seen as deriving from its embodiment of rational-legal authority and its claim to expertise over issues. UNHCR claims to be the "lead agency" on refugee matters, an authoritative claim that it makes based on its decades of experience handling refugee flows. The World Bank prides itself on being the foremost development expert, an authority it arrogates to itself by virtue of its possession of technical expertise and years of involvement in such matters. This is not merely information that is not available to other international organizations (IOs) or NGOs but rather information that is given the veneer of legitimacy because of its relationship to organizations that are accorded rational-legal authority.[13] Moreover, the UN can be viewed as a self-deprecating actor, denying and asserting its authority at one and the same time. Throughout the speech Annan reaffirms what all UN documents authored by the Secretariat loudly proclaim: that the UN is merely a technical and apolitical organization whose authority comes from member states. In this respect, the UN is nothing more than the sum of its parts. Yet nearly in the same breath that UN officials erase any sense of independence, they resuscitate it in several ways: by asserting an authority based on learned practices and decades of experience, that is, on rational-legal criteria and expertise; and by employing a discourse of the international community that refers not simply to states but also to peoples who are linked by transnational values, and that forwards the UN as the symbolic and organizational expression of that community. The UN's authority is delegated, layered, and textured, generated from organizational capacities and from discursive linkages to the community, and effectively asserted and denied at the same moment.

But many of the chapters in this volume highlight how authority can be conferred on those in different social situations and because of additional conditions, most importantly on those who are viewed as "an authority." Thomas Callaghy's "consultants" and Hans Peter Schmitz's

---

[13] Price (1998), however, balks at thinking of these actors as authoritative.

"activists" are actors that have authority because of their expertise and credentials. Other chapters in this volume similarly claim that what grants local and non-state actors authority is their relationship to global networks and emergent discourses. In addition to being viewed as "an authority," Cooper and others in this volume note how various global discourses that have a moral and normative content also are a source of authority for non-state actors in global and local spaces. Provocatively, these contributions also suggest that these actors are well aware that their authority is dependent on their claims being situated within a particular network and discursive space, and so work to strengthen those properties as a way to increase their authority and power.

Authority to do what? Here the distinction between regulative and constitutive effects is key. Annan bundles his authority to various social roles that have various sorts of effects. As a doctor, teacher, and police officer the UN has many roles in the international community, though all build on the desire to create and maintain the community's aspirations. Sometimes this involves helping states manage the peace among themselves and regulate their relations. But more interesting in the context of this volume is that the UN intends to intervene to help states find internal peace. Specifically, Annan is preaching intervention in domestic space to alter the political and economic landscape in order to help states better manage their internal and external relations. Consider the following statement. In response to a September 1997 request by the Security Council to examine the past and future prospects for promoting peace and security in Africa, in spring 1998 UN Secretary-General Kofi Annan presented his *The Causes of Conflict and the Promotion of Durable Peace and Sustainable Development in Africa*. In that document, Annan identifies the sources of ethnic conflict and civil wars in Africa – largely the legacies of colonialism and how acutely self-interested and power-seeking African leaders had dealt with and exploited those legacies; ways to prevent and address those conflicts – largely through new practices on the ground and intervention from above; and how to lay the foundations for a durable peace and economic growth – largely through African states' acceptance of democracy and markets and renunciation of violence as an arbiter of political disagreements and of the state as an allocator of resources. Authorities such as the UN, therefore, are attempting to convince individuals that the dilemmas and conflicts that they confront are not zero-sum games but rather coordination games that are much more amenable to solutions.

But Annan's report also is significant in that it spends less time suggesting how the UN can help states regulate their relations with other states and their societies and more time discussing how it can help states reconstitute and recreate themselves. The UN espouses that democracy (however ill-defined) and markets (however ill-defined) are not only the most efficient but also the most desirable of all social institutions. The UN is not alone in this project, a point clearly articulated by Annan as he submits his report on the future of Africa to the Security Council, the "General Assembly, and other components of the United Nations system that have responsibilities in Africa, including other Bretton Woods institutions." Similarly, the chapters in this volume note how IOs and NGOs are involved in constituting the social world and African states, advocating a particular model of social, economic, and political organization adhering to not only efficiency criteria but also to legitimacy and symbolic criteria.

Being "an authority" and "in authority" gives IOs and other actors the opportunity and the legitimacy to intervene in local affairs to help regulate what already exists and to help constitute something new. Several points should be made concerning the distinction between "in authority" and "an authority." First, being "an authority" is not limited to so-called technical and scientific issues. The boundary lines between scientific and non-scientific matters is a blurry one (where do we put economics?). Arturo Escobar and Jim Ferguson suggest how development in the Third World came to be defined in a scientific way and thus susceptible to manipulation and control by IOs and other governors (Escobar 1995; Ferguson 1990). Schmitz (this volume) observes how various human rights "experts" are able to meddle in local affairs because of their "expertise." Second, taking these categories as given ignores the tremendous work that actors do to try and maintain them for precisely the purpose of shoring up their authority. Development experts attempt to use various criteria to demonstrate the technical nature of their enterprise and are thus amenable to intervention only by certain classes of actors. Callaghy's consultants are interesting for precisely their ability to challenge the IMF's authority claims. Obi's chapter suggests how international NGOs are able to use their authority in environmental affairs to challenge the political, economic, and environmental consequences of multinational involvement in oil exploration and exploitation. Third, once an issue is defined as "technical" and solvable through more "scientific" methods, it is more likely to be governed by outside experts (who are involved in portraying the issue as technical and thus amenable to manipulation and control). Ron Kassimir's study of civil society is suggestive of this process. The general point here is that non-state actors are increasingly involved in Third World affairs because they are viewed as being "an authority" and "in authority" over an increasing expanse of social, political, and economic life. And they are employing that authority not simply to help regulate and coordinate already existing activities but also to alter the domestic topography in ways that make it more consistent with already existing and legitimated models of political, economic, and social organization.

This growing involvement by IOs and other non-state actors need not imply that local and state authorities are undermined. IR theory tends to operate with a zero-sum view of authority: there is a finite amount of authority, and if the authority of some actors is increasing then the authority of other actors is decreasing (Rosenau 1990). UN activities suggest, and the chapter in this volume by Janet Roitman explicitly notes, that this zero-sum myopia fails to recognize that authoritative activities can have additive and not subtractive properties. Sometimes this is by design. The UN employs its authority to reinforce rather than diminish the authority of local and state agents. IOs, for instance, have been involved in strengthening the autonomy and capacity of grassroots and indigenous movements, and these movements, in turn, are using the legitimacy provided by IOs to strengthen their legitimacy and authority over certain realms. Many UN peacekeeping interventions are intended to strengthen local authorities precisely because of the view that their involvement was necessary in the first place because of the breakdown of local authority structures. James Ferguson provocatively suggests that World Bank development failures must be treated as a success in a particular way: they have strengthened the power, control, and authority of the state over local actors (Ferguson 1990). The chapters by Schmitz and Roitman in this volume testify to how external interventions and new global discourses empower and grant authority to local actors. The point here is to move away from a zero-sum conception of authority; to imagine the various ways in which different authority structures interact and combine to produce different constellations of authority.

Such considerations lead to a further issue: although IOs and non-state actors present their interventions as symbols of progress and by definition as good things, we should not be so gullible. Annan instructs his audience that the UN's intervention is, by definition, a good thing. The UN is a combination of doctor, rescuer, and teacher. An agent of progress when the conditions are right and when states are wise enough to allow the UN to operate, the image is less that of a benign agent than of a heroic actor. Part of the discursive move is to juxtapose the practices, interests, and category of IOs (and other non-state actors) to the practices, interests, and category of states. States have particularistic interests, and their transnational activities are by definition forms of intervention that are intended to assert those interests over the countervailing interests of other states. The UN's interests derive from the broader community, and its transnational activities are designed to heal (doctor), to instruct (teacher), and to help the weak (police). Without question Annan sees the UN as Dr. Kildare and not as Dr. Kervorkian; this doctor is not part of a managed care complex but instead carries a leather satchel and makes house calls.[14]

But this discourse erases the possibility that the UN is an organization that might have interests that are distinct, self-interested, and perhaps contrary to the demands and wishes of those for whom it is authorized to assist. Scholars must be ready to unmask the vested interests that can lie behind the cosmopolitan reasons IOs give for their actions. Critical approaches to intervention have begun to do just that, questioning the motivations, consequences, and benefits of intervention by IOs and NGOs (Keen 1994; Malkki 1995, 1996).

Once we ask ourselves "who benefits?" from an intervention and from global discourses that make possible and direct that intervention, we become more naturally inclined to raise issues of distributive justice. How do these interventions change people's life chances, income streams, political opportunities, and cultural creativity and autonomy? The UN portrays its peacekeeping interventions as representing a progressive and democratic force in local politics, opening up space for the downtrodden and outside the power elite. But such peacekeeping interventions also have tended to reinforce the *status quo* because of a desire to forge an agreement between contending rivals for power. Students of the World Bank and the IMF have made similar observations for years, calling into question how liberalizing forces are in fact agents of inequality (Hurrell and Woods 1995). International actors will nearly always portray their interventions as producing progress, equality, and protection for the weak; sometimes that might be the result, sometimes not. Global discourses and networks can confer power and authority to local actors in all sorts of insidious ways, as Roitman and Reno (this volume) note in the context of shadow networks.

Once IR theorists operate with a view that the state and authority are not forever chained, it becomes possible to imagine other actors that might be authoritative, it becomes important to consider the conditions under which these actors are conferred authority, and it becomes necessary to ask what these actors do with that authority. These considerations lead to a reconceptualization of the global and the local, and, as the chapters in this volume suggest, closely watched developments in local circumstances can lead to global conclusions.

---

[14] For the discourse of intervention and the projection of "doing good," see Fisher (1997).

Conclusion

Scholars from a variety of disciplines are searching and stretching to create the proper metaphor and model for thinking about the relationship between the global and the local. Each discipline struggles to overcome its own history and baggage. For IR that baggage is tightly encapsulated in the territorial trap, a tendency to bundle the state, territory, and authority, and to view the systemic and the domestic not simply as convenient starting points for carving up the social world but as real and ontologically given realms. Although there have been some important changes as of late, change comes slowly.

IR theorists, like all scholars, will face the daunting task of trying to discern how to study connections that exist at different levels, sites, and political spaces. The one matter that is becoming settled is the need to avoid seeing one particular location as the natural starting point for analysis and for tracing the causal chains. Consider the following statement by two anthropologists:

The key is to grasp the interactions (and disjunctions) between different sites or levels in policy processes. Thus "studying through" [that is, tracing ways in which power creates webs and relations between actors, institutions and discourses across time and space] entails multi-site ethnographies which trace policy connections between different organizational and everyday worlds, even where actors in different sites do not know each other or share a moral universe. (Shore and Wright 1997: 14)[15]

Without too much slippage, this statement is fairly consistent with the plea offered by Keck and Sikkink (1998: 199) as they urge IR scholars to "grapple with the multiple interactions of domestic and international politics as sources of change in the international system."

The chapters in this book further provide the important methodological reminder that scholars interested in global transformations would do well to start at the local rather than at the global. The authors have begun at the local level to understand global transformations and connections, begun inductively as the first step toward more generalizable and transportable findings, and have found the importance of making multisited and multisided connections between actors at different locales. Starting at the global and abstract level might help comprehend the broad changes that are taking place in organizing principles and structures, but oftentimes the first hint of those changes comes from new sorts of effects and practices that can only be understood on the ground and at the micro-level.

[15] Shore and Wright (1997: 14); also see Fisher (1997: 450).

Part II

Theoretical frameworks

4　Identifying the contours of transboundary political life

Robert Latham

The transboundary formations discussed in this volume involve a broad array of activities and practices. They range from the transmission of ideas and commodities to the signing of international agreements and the deployment of armies. An increasing number of scholars outside International Relations in a variety of fields and disciplines the world over are making such phenomena central to their research. The breadth involved is impressive enough to make one wonder whether the identification of overall structures among such phenomena is a hopeless task.

The reason to bother with this task is not to rein in interests and analysis that have become too diffuse and scattered. Rather, it is to see whether common analytical languages can be forged which might help draw connections among the many lines of analysis emerging from an increasingly varied range of fields. Opportunities will be missed if the study of transboundary forces becomes entrenched in analytical ghettos populated by discrete sets of phenomena – ranging from transnational relations and global cultural flows to regional integration.

One starting point for thinking about structure is to focus on the ways in which intersecting fields of international, global, or transnational forces directly bump up against seemingly concrete political and social life "on the ground." This life can include the well-known social forms of the state and the market. It can also include, as the authors in this volume show, the ethnic group, social movement, militia, political party, town, and village.[1]

This approach, however, does not produce any road maps. We can point to such organizational ensembles as the UN or such institutional configurations as an international financial regime and show how these directly shape the politics of places around the world. But this would

---

[1] However much these social forms, on the ground, are shot through with international or global dimensions and can themselves shape international or global phenomena, the point is that they are not reducible to one another. This is one of the useful points to be derived from a level-of-analysis perspective.

not indicate whether these or other entities are structures basic to the global realm in the way that the state is in relation to a national context.

Thinking about political life at the level of the state is, of course, girded by a baseline recognition of some common features – there are forms of demarcated territory, functional administration, organized systems of coercion, and political claims involving citizenship (it, of course, took centuries for that baseline identity to emerge). The standard answer to the question of why there have been no parallel constructions at the global or international level is that it was exactly the commitment to the state as the central political form that impoverished the other levels. Thickness at one level, so it goes, yields thinness at others.[2]

As scholars such as Barrington Moore (1966) have underscored for us, states have had powerfully organized constituencies vying to shape their contours and purposes. However diffuse in comparison, the shaping of international and global life has also involved powerful pressures, from merchants pursuing trade routes and statesmen organizing world war to the myriad purveyors of predominant norms and practices, imperial and liberal. Thus, we end up with a global realm that is thin, fluid, and lacking an accountable center, and yet in its diffusion is rich with varied forms, political projects, and discourses.[3]

The existence of obstacles to identifying structure for this realm has not deterred a few theorists from the task. Most famous of all structural endeavors has been Immanuel Wallerstein's (1974) capitalist world systems theory. John Meyer (1987) also uses the language of world system, albeit differently. He has posited the existence of a world polity to describe the ensemble of knowledge and norms circulating among elites in state capitals and international bureaucracies about how to organize states and societies. Robert Cox (1987) has suggested that we may be in the early stages of the formation of an "international state" that can govern fields of political, social, and economic relations on an international basis. And Susan Strange (1988) contends there are four fundamental international structures of power (organized around security, production, finance, and knowledge) that affect political and social life across the planet.

---

[2] Traditional and non-traditional approaches to international relations share this observation. For traditionalists it is the international anarchy flowing from a plurality of states that limits the international. For critical theorists or post-structuralists it is a form of modernity wherein the political is contained in the state form.

[3] The extent to which the relatively limited dimensions of collective claim-making constitute an important difference is an issue that is beyond the scope of this chapter. Standing out as notable exceptions are movements to end European colonization and South African apartheid, and to limit weapons in Europe.

In these approaches a configuration of power and institutions is identified as an essential structure of governance, shaping the seasons and tides of international and transnational relations. These configurations entail specialized sets of functions operating at the international level (constituting nation-states in Meyer's case, shaping political and economic relations in Cox and Strange's case). The underlying attitude from which these structures are proffered is decidedly top-down, perched at the heights of planetary existence.

I want to take a more bottom-up approach to structure by focusing on differences in the nature of interactions occurring across boundaries. I will argue that interactions across the boundaries of social spaces can take form as international arenas, translocal networks, or transterritorial deployments. I will explore the third form in detail. Transterritorial deployments are associated with interactions that are often considered interventions, broadly conceived. That is, intervention understood to include not just humanitarian aid, international development work, or military incursions, however important these are, but also imperialism, international economic advisory teams, and the economic penetration of merchants and capitalist practices. As should become clear, however, the range of issues and dynamics surrounding transterritorial deployments moves far beyond the intellectual and political legacy surrounding the term intervention.

Transterritorial deployments are central to many of the chapters in this volume (as are arenas and networks, which will be briefly described for that reason and in order to underscore what is unique about deployments). Deployments are hinges joining global and local forces around the exercise of power and responsibility and the pursuit of political projects across boundaries. As I will suggest, these hinges set serious limits to the nature of transboundary social encounters. These limits help explain the sometimes tragic nature of transboundary politics considered in this volume.

Dimensions of transboundary interaction: arenas and networks

There are three options that individuals, groups, and institutions in one place (e.g. a city or headquarters) have for interacting with agents in another place to, for example, communicate, act in concert, or exchange with them. They can convoke in some common arena; they can transmit something from one point to another; or they can dispatch or deploy themselves or a representative from their place to another place.

Convocation, transmission, and deployment are genetic logics of inter-action in international and global life.

Convocations have actually been the most longstanding objects of study in the field of International Relations. In one international arena or an-other states have met to hammer out treaties, conventions, war settle-ments, alliances, regimes, and NGOs have attempted to influence those activities and define new ones by public lobbying and advocacy cam-paigns. In these arenas intangible social forms and practices such as international law or worldwide conventions share the characteristic of populating a sort of spaceless "international realm" which is everywhere and nowhere. It is in these arenas that international norms are articu-lated and disseminated through the documents and discourse of the UN and its officials and diplomats, and through the reports, campaigns, and statements of activists.

These arenas can be thought of as "international" exactly because they rest on the recognition – by the actors within them and the various publics around the world that constitute their audiences – that states and societies can convene over one issue or another. These issues typically bear directly on the activity of states, even though the actors involved are often not state representatives themselves. Together, a multitude of arenas overlap and intersect to constitute what is often perceived to be the more singular "international realm."

Diplomatic conventions and meetings, NGO forums, and international court proceedings are examples of activities in arenas. But arenas are not merely international public events.[4] They can persist as long as there are actors, issues, discourses, and audiences. Actors need not literally come together, face-to-face. All that is necessary is some common forum where practices and discourses have immediate and direct amplification beyond the point from which they are produced.[5]

---

[4] By public I do not mean to imply that all the activities carried out in an international arena are accessible or open to general view (as they are not, for example, in "private diplomacy"), but only that at least there is a "public" to which the business of the arena is directed.

[5] It is for this reason that the media and their coverage of international news is so central to international arenas. In the mid-1880s, in his famous *Gemeinschaft and Gesellschaft* (1957), Ferdinand Tönnies wrote about the media as an organ of pub-lic opinion that "is comparable and, in some respects, superior to the material power which the states possess through their armies, their treasuries, and their bureaucratic civil service. Unlike those, the press is not confined within natural borders ... it is definitely international, thus comparable to the power of a permanent or tempo-rary alliance of states. It can, therefore, be conceived as its ultimate aim to abol-ish the multiplicity of states and substitute for it a single world republic, coextensive with the world market, which would be ruled by thinkers, scholars, and writers and could dispense with means of coercion other than those of a psychological nature" (p. 221).

Even when a highly diverse range of individuals and institutions is joined by a set of broad-reaching issues, such as the environment, the arena formed remains particular and bounded. Each arena can be thought of as possessing its own "culturally specific institutions" (Fraser 1992: 126) from the scheduled meetings of the G8 to the reports circulated by activists worldwide about human rights violations in Tibet or East Timor.

Although arenas operate in a sort of spaceless realm, they can have profound effects on social spaces, local, regional, or national. These effects surface throughout this volume around issues such as debt (Callaghy), human rights (Schmitz), environmental degradation (Obi), and sovereignty (Reno). All the authors are careful to emphasize that the direct relationships between arenas and specific political and social contexts are uneven dialectical processes. The tensions, limits, and pressures involved in the politics of local and national contexts can undermine or contradict the often too neat categories and logics that populate discourses in international arenas.

It is not just local conditions that can shape discourses, norms, and practices in international arenas. Networks of various forms that populate the pages of this volume are often crucial factors in the politics of arenas. These networks transmit values across political boundaries and social spaces. Since the 1960s and 1970s they have received increasingly concentrated attention in a variety of disciplines.

While network activity can surely shape activities in international arenas – and become relevant to decisions and discussions in them – it remains a fundamentally different dimension of interaction. In an international arena actors – state and non-state "come together" in a sort of international public sphere. Networks rest on the transmission of one form of capital (political, symbolic, informational, financial, etc.) from one node (populated by individuals or organizations, including those of a state) in one place to another node and place. The constituents of these networks remain emplaced in their various local contexts, propelling flows of symbols and materials to one another from those positions.[6]

Of course, an international arena can be shot through with networks and can, if one likes, be identified itself as one large network or web of networks. Likewise, networks can be viewed as types of arenas, as celebrants of virtual communities like to point out. These are, however,

---

[6] Translocal networks are a distinct species of the wider network genus. If translocal networks are on one end of a hypothetical continuum, then on the other end are networks based on "elective affinity," composed of nodes in close, everyday proximity to one another (such as a network of support among immigrants in an urban neighborhood).

reductive views that fail to acknowledge the distinct public character of international arenas (spaces where not only diplomats convene, but such things as international law and universal declarations are written, ratified, coded, and stored). Translocal networks stand out from arenas as specialized pathways of flows of messages, knowledge, and goods from one "place" to another along a channel or trajectory that is not typically open to the view of a public.

Indeed, the relationship between networks and arenas is not just about how comparatively narrow networks shape the arguments and regulative contours of public arenas (or how a "network of networks" can publicize an issue through its accumulative reach – see Keck and Sikkink 1998). From the other direction, the discourses of international arenas, as Cooper shows, can enter the narrower circuits of networks defined by exclusive memberships according to claims to professionalism (e.g. NGOs), privilege (e.g. financial access), and faith (e.g. religious "brotherhoods"). As Obi and others show (Wilson 1997), local NGOs caught up in specific struggles adopt "global idioms" of rights-talk to frame their political claims.

The diversity of activities pursued by the variety of institutions and individuals that populate networks and arenas is on its face seemingly overwhelming. Moreover, the boundaries between networks and arenas are often not automatically self-evident, especially when the network exchanges of an organization such as Greenpeace can spill over into an arena as an ever wider circle is exposed to its activities and information. Any organization can operate in both networks and arenas and they face fundamental strategic and tactical choices as to how and when they do so. One way to move toward mapping differences in the nature, range, and impact of activities across networks and arenas is to identify how widely amplified activities and practices are. Internationally circulating publications, treaties, or press releases are far more widely amplified than the internal memorandums of a given network.

A second basis of distinction is the degree to which the activities and practices of an institution, organization, or network of individuals have "sway" over those of other institutions, organizations, or individuals. The activities of the networks described by Carolyn Nordstrom and Janet Roitman are relatively narrowly amplified and effectively private. Nonetheless, such networks do impact deeply the lives touched by the activities and practices carried on within them in the various towns and villages across countries such as Angola and regions such as the Chad Basin. They have sway over individual lives, communities, and institutions that are not operatives or members of the networks.

Transterritorial deployments

Besides arenas and networks there is a third dimension that is associated with the logic of dispatch and it is populated by what can be called "transterritorial deployments." They have received no real explicit theoretical attention – and yet are relatively easily recognized and historically prevalent. A transterritorial deployment (TD) is an installation in a local context of agents from outside that context. The place from which they are deployed is typically some kind of organizational platform (e.g. the headquarters of an international agency such as the UNHCR, a transnational corporation [TNC], or even the capital of a Western state).[7] I will focus on TDs because they are the least understood of the three forms of interaction and yet are critical to many of the chapters in this volume.

I am using the word "transterritorial" to describe simply the movement of a social entity across the boundaries of a territory from some external place, where the entity retains in that territory its identity as external.[8] That entity could be an invading army, a scientific expedition, a charitable aid organization, a caravan of merchants, or a group of technocratic international financial institution advisors. More extreme versions include "stateless" refugees shunted from one transit point to another or even air traffic that literally cuts across territory.[9]

The starkest ideological manifestation of transterritoriality is the designation of a place entered into as "empty" or "vacant" space. Such designation requires neglect of existing socio-political organizations of people

[7] The reader might want to argue that a given system of deployment is nothing but a network. However, in the way I am using the term network here this makes no sense, as we shall see, because what is unique about deployments is the connection of that which is deployed (e.g. a temporary field office) and the organizational platform from which it is deployed (e.g. an international agency headquarters), rather than its more autonomous links to nodes situated in other local or national contexts.

[8] By using the term transterritorial in this specialized way I am clearly distancing myself from the more common use of it to describe all the interactions and institutions that are not rooted in territorially bounded organization. Ruggie (1993) sees these interactions as anchored in "nonterritorial functional space." I am arguing that such interactions and institutions appear in all of the three dimensions outlined above (the international arena, the translocal network, and the deployment). I am saving the term transterritorial for the last dimension because the movement of an entity across territory is what distinguishes it from the "nonterritorial" arena. In contrast, what is distinctive about the transborder network is the rootedness of its nodes in territorial organization, from which capital (monetary or informational) can thereupon be transmitted across borders or territory if you like.

[9] Externality is naturally a tricky status in that, for some readers, any external force by definition becomes "internalized" by its presence. But that is a reductive standpoint that fails to recognize as legitimate the designation or organization of a social entity as external and ignores the interesting tensions generated by that status in a local context. It is the negotiation of the terms of that externality between local and non-local forces that is exactly what is interesting.

and places. Whereas this designation justified property claims over lands in the name of effective use in the European colonization of the Americas and Africa (Tully 1995: 93), more recently it provided theorists of modernization with a way to characterize so-called pre-modern, under-developed rural lands (LaPalombara 1971: 230).

Something is external when it has relatively thick organic links back to some outside point of origin. However, not all transterritorial phenomena involve deployment. The transterritorial movement of refugees or air traffic, despite retaining an external point of reference, does not in any meaningful sense involve deployment. Deployment entails the purposeful forward placement of a unit, division, or representative of an organization or institution in some local context, such that the entity deployed stands as a component of that deploying organization (which I labeled above a platform). An army sent into a territory from some command center is a prime example. But so is a team of World Bank experts or the field operations of the Red Cross.

Transterritorial deployments are by definition specialized in relation to any local social order they enter since they rest on the forward placement of a defined and delimited organization from outside. In other words, they move along relatively narrow bands of intervention or engagement with local order. An organization, individual, or institution could never carry with it the range of culture, politics, and social relations that are encountered in a given locale. The most extreme form of this external movement is extra-territorial, where the deployed organizational form (e.g. military or consular) carries its own culture, laws, and juridical authority (or in the case of a "factory," its own system of economic extraction and trade). Extra-territorial status is mirrored today in the near immunity possessed by some humanitarian workers who increasingly employ their own security forces (de Waal 1997: 190). It is also too closely mirrored in the "camp havens" for traders profiting from war described by Nordstrom in chapter 10, which resemble the merchant compounds from centuries past, as well as in Roitman's contemporary regional trading entrepôts. Reno suggests in chapter 9 that whole new forms of extra-territoriality are emerging for some African rulers operating in zones outside their formally recognized state boundaries.

We can contrast this with a political authority such as a municipal administration that, in principle, has general responsibility for a local polity. Yet we know that a deployed army can take on such general responsibility in an occupation of enemy territory, as the US Army did in Japan after World War II. Armies conveniently carry their own system of order on their backs in the shape of strict hierarchies and circumscribed missions. They also are unlikely to be dependent on local security forces. Despite being relatively self-contained, armies cannot help confronting the problem of local order if for no other reason than that they so often disrupt the orders that fall in their pathway. Occupation duty and colonial glory are, in this respect, two sides of the same coin. What to do in the aftermath of conquest is never automatically clear even within earshot of the imperial trumpet.[10] An army's presence in a place forces it to confront, reluctantly or not, the question of post-conflict order. As General Eisenhower put it in 1942 regarding the US Army in French North Africa: "[T]he sooner I can get rid of all these questions that are outside the military scope, the happier I will be! Sometimes I think I live ten years each week, of which at least nine are absorbed in political and economic matters" (cited in Benvenisti, 1993: 82).

If deployments are (in principle) limited, then how are the boundaries of their specialization enacted "on the ground" and defined or identified by planners, practitioners, and local recipients of the deployment? This is really a question about the *scope* of the involvement of the organization deployed – how much of political and social life "on the ground" is drawn up into its purview and range of self-defined responsibility.

Besides scope, another dimension that is basic to the identity of a transterritorial deployment is its *status* as temporary or permanent. What distinguishes a military occupation in formal terms from a colonization or political incorporation is its status as temporary. This is not a mere function of duration since how long a (temporary) deployment lasts is often quite variable, sometimes continuing for a seemingly indefinite period, as in the Israeli occupation of Palestine.

Status, like scope, has a bearing on the question of responsibility for local order. It also serves as a marker for what an outside agent thinks it has a right to do in some place and is another basis for keeping a deployment along narrow, delimited channels within a local context. With temporary status there is no acknowledgment that what is deployed is present to serve as the ultimate and lasting authority over a local order (which is a claim the state makes within its territory). Whether something is recognized as permanent or temporary will likely change the terms of interaction between transterritorial and local actors. For example, in calculating whether it is worth cooperating with an international aid effort, local actors need not do so when they know that withdrawal is near at hand. This was understood to be part of the logic of interaction between Somali warlords and international interveners in the early 1990s.

---

[10] Conklin (1997: 52, 95) describes the uneasy relationship between a conquering French army in Africa and its limited capacity to construct new orders in places over which it achieves dominance.

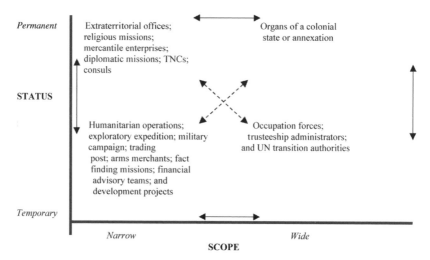

Figure 4.1 Dimensions of transterritorial deployment.

Although the variety of deployed forms that can operate across social or political boundaries is considerable, the dimensions of scope and status allow us to begin to map out some differences and help us identify where transterritoriality begins and ends (recognizing that these differences are not discrete but form a continuum), as shown in Figure 4.1.

At one extreme are deployments so narrow and temporary that their imprint on a social space is questionable. Historian Owen Lattimore (1962: 132) aptly described the self-containedness of an air traffic system *vis-à-vis* the material life of Central Asia:

[A] few airplanes more or less flying in from distant industrial lands cannot themselves change the structure of Central Asia. The real question is whether air traffic in that region – and throughout Asia – is to be merely a kind of air-borne colonial enterprise, or whether the full fabric of a modern industrialism can be created to "naturalize" the use of the air and make it part of an inclusive social command over the environment.

We could just as easily substitute for "air traffic," air-borne humanitarian aid and for "social command over the environment," local social and political order.

Even if deployments have the same scope and status they can vary in terms of their sway over people and places. The narrow and temporary fact-finding missions by human rights organizations and UN agencies described by Obi and Schmitz have little direct influence over the lives of people in the countries they visit. The highly circumscribed nature of their mission precludes greater influence. In contrast, when a development organization such as UNDP sets up a project in a given locale, it may remain a temporary effort that is narrowly focused on some aspect of economic life. But its sway over the lives drawn into that project can be considerable (especially when project budgets can match or exceed government budgets in the relevant locale).

On the opposite end of the continuum are phenomena that are permanent and broad. Political forms such as colonial states and annexations represent the outer boundary of TDs. That is, whatever the original scope and status of an organ deployed from a metropole or state capital, once moves toward annexation, political incorporation, or state-formation emerge the external quality of a deployment evaporates. The move from a military occupation (temporary but likely to be relatively broad) to the permanent claims of a colonial regime to order a social space implies an internalization of the conqueror's presence within the territory in question. (Decolonization can be understood as exactly the attempt to externalize colonial regimes.)

But we also have to be careful about assuming all imperialisms were broad in scope. Dutch imperial strategy only drew up into its net what was essential to profitable commercial relations (Braudel 1984: 202; see also Arrighi, 1994: 201). Territorial responsibility was avoided where possible in the pursuit of "secure retreats" for merchants (Fieldhouse 1966: 50–51). With time this changed as the scope of activity widened (especially with settlers following on the heels of merchants and explorers in southern Africa or the East Indies). Even with the acquisition of colonies in the Americas these were generally treated by the Dutch "as if they were mere factories or estates" (p. 52).

In general, a given form of deployment, such as trusteeship, can change its status and scope, especially from temporary to permanent and from narrow to wide (or exhibit more than one type of status or scope). This implies that across the various types of deployments – ranging across differences in scope and status – there are sometimes significant connections. In the historical development of various imperial relations, there was often a starting point where missionaries, merchant adventurers, or soldiers were deployed along narrow channels of relations. In time the scope of these penetrations expanded along with a clear definition of permanent status, leading to full-fledged colonization.

Why and how these transformations occur are among the more interesting sets of questions associated with transterritorial deployments. With the exception of the activities of the Spanish in the Americas, formal and outright acquisition of relatively large aggregations of land and peoples was not the typical process of colonial development. Not only was there explicit interest sometimes in expansion providing it could be achieved through strategic points and key monopolies (the Dutch minimal approach), but initial penetrations into Africa and elsewhere were often undertaken by mercantile companies that sought to contain their scope of responsibility (in social, political, and territorial terms) to that which was judged profitable. Narrowly defined scope to serve privately defined purposes was often not a viable basis upon which to build a self-sustaining presence even along a coast, prompting aid from and often acquisition by states from home.

Quite often, one transterritorial deployment can invite in another, typically to bolster or advance its position in some locale. Missionaries were not immune from inviting European armies into Africa in the name of order and security. These invitations often ended in the establishment of protectorates, which in turn transformed into formal colonies. Even though missions, traders, explorers, or adventurers may be forms of micro-deployments, their activities have often forced the question of what kind of relationship their home states have to a penetrated place, promoting changes in status and scope (see Fieldhouse 1966: 84–85, 97, 179; and Doyle 1986: 179).

Relatedly, many of the narrow, African coastal enclaves established before the last decades of the nineteenth century became platforms for further deployments inland in places such as the Gold Coast, Sierra Leone, and Nigeria. Initial, narrow-based deployments typically developed into permanent acquisitions along coasts. Pre-port settlements were transformed into Portuguese towns in Mozambique. Elmina started as a fort and then acquired a municipal charter. Enclaves such as these, as has often been recounted, provided the basis for military expeditions and trading circuits nearby and became stepping stones toward the formation of more full-blown protectorates and colonial annexations.

It should not be assumed that the only type of relevant transformation of a deployment is toward permanent and broad forms associated with colonialism. A deployment such as a church mission, a transnational oil corporation installation, or an international NGO office can also become a node in a translocal network. The organizational form in this case is no longer simply an external entity: a mission becomes a diocese, a company affiliate becomes "domesticated" (Obi's term), and a factory becomes a town. Connections to platforms such as headquarters may take on both network and deployment qualities.

Finally, with the delegitimation of colonialism in the second half of the twentieth century, the most likely fate for a transterritorial deployment is not some transformation to a permanent and broad political form but some sort of termination. Rather than rendering TDs irrelevant, in the age we have entered it *seems* that narrow and temporary deployments are proliferating in form, if not also in number. Even the classic occupation model (e.g. post-WWII) has fallen out of favor. Recent UN peacekeeping missions rest on relatively loose coordination between multilateral organs, individually deployed in the short-term, rather than centralized political authority.[11]

Situational power

In contrast to international arenas, which rest on the expansive possibilities of widely amplified discourses and practices, transterritorial deployments are defined by limits. The more limited a deployment (the more narrow its scope and provisional its status), the more transterritorial it is. The most transterritorial of deployments, in principle, would draw hardly any of the social and political life occurring in a territory into its web of relations.

But even the lightest of deployments can affect considerably life within the locale it enters. This forces the question of why, if TDs are generally defined by their limits in scope and status, they are so closely linked with some of the most excessive exercises of power in human history. It is natural to look to uneven capabilities associated with technology, social organization, and wealth (Headrick 1981). While certainly this is part of the answer, it cannot be the whole story, especially since quite often deployments (limited by their very nature) were out-manned and out-resourced by the political communities they encountered (such as other empires or states). I think there is something uniquely powerful about the narrowness of deployments that works to their advantage in local contexts.

The relationship between limits and power is usually viewed in terms of constraints, those imposed on someone or something (or power understood as the construction and imposition of constraints that shape outcomes – see Lukes 1974). What I have in mind is different: how (self-imposed) constraints shape the actions and character of the producers of such limits.[12] The constraints I am interested in are those of the limited mission of a UN-led aid effort, the minimal engagement of a TNC with problems of local governance, the lack of public authority of an international NGO, or the disregard for existing political relations in a locale by a mercantile company. Transterritorial deployments, being narrow in

---

[11] The attempt to resurrect something like the occupation model to organize and authorize broader-based UN-led interventions is outlined in Chopra (1996).

[12] An abstract discussion of power as negativity more broadly is in Dyrberg (1997: 133–37).

character, define a delimited range of concerns and interactions within which they will be engaged. That delimited range can be thought of as a "situation." It might be a refugee crisis, a famine, an ethnic conflict, a security threat, or an opportunity to extract primary resources. Power first operates in the emergence of a bounded definition of a situation – a crisis, conflict, or opportunity. The power – understood as shaping outcomes – comes from the keeping out of other issues – those associated with the broader political and social implications of a situation.[13] With a boundary, a TD is able to locate a range of operation: thus, the constraints may open the way to capability within a narrow channel of practices and discourses.

In the past couple of decades, inspired by leftist critiques and Foucault, we have become used to thinking of power outside the classic Weberian "power over another's choices" as a matter of having power over or within the structures that constitute social existence. The more constitutive capacity, the more power. Situational power, in contrast, is a power within which this constitutional role is delimited: it refracts people, discourses, and resources into a contained situation, by coding them and bringing them into a bounded, temporary space, ranging from the refugee camp to the makeshift factory. This is not power that can be hegemonic. That is, it is quite different from the intensive power over and extensive power within society and social space of some states as described by Michael Mann (1984). It is the power not to have to take on the responsibility entailed by these powers over and within society. It is the power to enter and withdraw relatively flexibly from situations. The SWAT team analogy, as drawn by one UNHCR spokesman to describe the agency's growing emergency relief operations, is quite apt (cited in Barutciski 1996).

The relationship between situational power and flexibility is interesting. Flexibility has often been thought of as flowing from the strength and depth of an institution – its ability to adapt to changing circumstances without decaying (Huntington 1968: 13–17). But when it comes to TDs, flexibility should be seen as a function of constraint and narrowness. It reflects an ability to move along narrow channels without being overly constrained by the broader social and political environment in a local context. We are familiar these days with this relationship because

---

[13] In one example of an explicit recognition of how important situational power has become to an agency such as the UNHCR, and how it displaces broader political approaches, a recent anonymous staff member contrasted "situational approaches" to those that focused on the politics of an entire region by engaging "with regional institutions such as OAS, OSCE, OAU, and CIS in order to address asylum practices and forced migration patterns on a regional basis" (Takahashi 1997: 271).

of its economic manifestations, however much they may be exaggerated. Capital is "footloose" and production is flexibly configured.

However, when deployments that start out transterritorial become more deeply embedded in their social contexts – evident most typically in the assumption of responsibility for constituting forms of social existence – they become less flexible. As a result, a deployment loses latitude over movement and withdrawal. This happens, for example, when a trading post becomes a town or a seat of colonial administration.[14]

What does it mean to have a lot or a little situational power? Being powerful in this context means being flexible and contained. It means having the ability to remain highly specialized and ready to channel flows of resources, meanings, and bodies in and out of a "situation" according to its defined logic. The ideal level of this power is perhaps only approached by TNCs in free trade zones around the world or investment houses channeling capital in and out of markets. But even such supposedly "footloose" actors are quite dependent on and vulnerable to the regulatory and constitutive actions of states within which they operate. All TDs are vulnerable to pressures and "manipulation" by local forces, state and non-state (just as those local forces remain vulnerable to manipulation by TDs). One pointed example is the use of UNHCR refugee camps as safety and concentration zones by rebel or counter-rebel forces in Central Africa, or as sources of cheap labor for local enterprises.

From one angle it may seem contradictory to posit a form of power so closely tied to vulnerability and the effectiveness of outside agents. But the point is that self-contained forms of power abdicate to varying degrees responsibility for organizing and securing their external environments. They therefore remain subject to organization by – and threats from – others. When the Portuguese built their sea-borne empire mostly on the control of key points (factories, trading posts, and bases) they assembled a remarkable web of power that was, however, highly vulnerable to manipulation and capture by others exactly because of its minimal presence in various places. Indeed, quite often factories and forts were established through negotiation with local powers rather than force. Likewise, today a great many humanitarian deployments rest on "negotiated access" or the promise of "peace corridors" for their operation. Once deployed, they can have considerable sway over people's lives because of the relatively abundant resources circulating within their zones of operation.

---

[14] The Huntingtonian notions of adaptability and situational flexibility are related, in that what gives a thick institution the ability to flexibly adapt is its capacity to set boundaries around past, outdated practices, around too many demands on those and current ones, etc. In effect, within its world it narrows and re-channels itself.

Power viewed not as a singly dominating and secure force, but as something by its very nature accompanied by vulnerability, is consistent with the rather tragic co-dependency analyzed by William Reno between rulers and corporations, both of which remain narrowly contained within their own delimited range of operations. The presence of TDs not only alters the social and political landscape; it can, in so doing, open up options for rulers, who can build alliances with TDs on narrow terms. As a result, they can better avoid more broad-based political alliances which might subject such rulers to political claims associated with the operation of a moral community.[15]

One reason for the contemporary vulnerability of TDs is that there are various relevant networks and arenas of which local actors can be a part. Access to these networks and arenas can change their relationship to TDs. When, for example, UNDP deploys a field team to a district, it interacts not only with "locals" but with some locals who are part of regional or translocal networks exchanging information about development with international NGOs that in turn can be applied in negotiations with UNDP. Likewise a team deployed by the World Bank to a capital, as Callaghy shows, is likely to confront quite a few experts who are part of translocal networks. And we can also count on these experts and other officials to be participants in activities at the UN or other sites. The point is that the local must always be understood to be a juncture point between arenas, networks, and deployments.[16] The problem is that the politics of those junctures rarely unfold on equal terms, as capacities to shape images in international arenas or the terms and currency of network exchanges have been historically uneven.

Local governance, supralocal rule, and the state

The question of power has taken us close to what lies at the heart of TDs: their interface with actors and forces in the places where they operate. Deployed entities can traverse territory to approach some particular place

---

[15] Migdal (1988: 266) points to the additional fear that political alliances might simply strengthen local political forces that could compete with forces in the state capital (as a result, it is better to deal with an international mining company).

[16] This juncture is one of two ways in which intersections can occur between the dimensions. The other is from within one of the dimensions. For example, representatives of a group of states convening in the international arena can be recipients of information or money from networks whether they are lobbying NGOs or corporate contributors. In general, in order for an intersection to take place there needs to be some kind of a "space" (or more accurately point in space) that serves as the juncture point. A local context, where there is likely to be a mixing of actors and institutions operating in the different dimensions (often any given actor can operate in all three dimensions), is especially propitious for such intersections.

within it (a town or state capital). Key here is the way in which "what is deployed" intersects with a specific range of what is "happening on the ground."

Intersections of this sort can be viewed most easily in geographical terms (the village, town, or district). But we should not overlook whether the space of intersection can be functional rather than simply geographical. That is, organs deployed somewhere can engage with a specialized range of political operations and practices within a territory. For example, when an IFI advisory unit is deployed to a state capital to help shape national policy it typically does not confront the range of communities in that city or territory or the problems of governance associated with them, but a narrow range of technical specialists. (In contrast, a civil administration unit of a military occupation can confront a wide range of interests and governance issues.) Indeed, the kind of intervention we associate with "structural adjustment" efforts would hardly have been possible without that sort of functional specialization. (Of course, functionally localized intersections of this sort can have considerable sway over people's lives.)[17]

Since TDs are narrow in scope and often temporary in status they are unlikely to be very good candidates as constitutors of order, even if they sought to be so. There is, of course, order constituted within the relatively self-contained spaces of a deployment. But we have to be cautious about attributing governance capacity (as Kassimir uses the term, this volume) to TDs based on this internal ordering and governance. Consider two types of examples. The first is the company compound – equivalent to company towns – that arose in different parts of colonial Africa. As long as these compounds remained effectively cordoned off from the social space within which they entered, they remained external entities ordering their own domain. (However, when company compounds became towns they no longer retained the external quality that distinguishes a deployment as transterritorial.)

A second type of example is the refugee camp present in Africa today. These camps, in contrast to company compounds, do not typically change their status and become a permanent part of the geographical landscape. They can be viewed as an ordered social space for this population of refugees, since sometimes quite some effort goes into governing a

---

[17] It is important to avoid seeing the local everywhere, since there will always be a limit as to who and what an organization can engage. Recognizing the trap of this reductivism, I none the less feel comfortable contrasting an organization that takes broad (read "non-local") responsibility for (or authority over) the provision of social and political order with an organization that seeks to intervene in that order only at key entry points (read "local").

camp's internal domain. Even so, they tell us something different than the compounds do about the limited relationship between TDs and locales. Refugee camps are far less able to be cordoned off from the contexts in which they are installed. They are usually installed in some identifiable *and recognized* locale, whether it is on the outskirts of a town or in a district or region. It is telling that a great deal of UNHCR effort goes into negotiating the terms of the establishment of a camp (especially security and access) with local authorities or "local power groups" (Kirby et al., 1997: 182). So we would have to be cautious about attributing local order to an organization such as the UNHCR. True to their form as TDs, UNHCR field operations have had severely limited capacity to directly shape local order and have found themselves, as mentioned above, quite often subject to penetration from outside forces, including militias. It is their situational power that allows them to construct a refugee domain in a local context – and an order within it – without being hegemonic over the local context itself.[18] Their presence affects that local context, but does not order it.

A consideration of the relationship between TDs and locales cannot proceed as though these two forms directly intersect on their own terms. There are also questions about which fields of order – with wider geographical reach – can lay claim to a locale and what type of relationship a relevant TD has to those fields. (I am using the term order here to denote some form of bounded political association rather than to denote an arrangement or system of relations as is typically meant by terms such as "international order.") The two master fields are the state and empire. It is not possible to think seriously about the relationship between local life and non-local forces without making processes of state-formation, colonial or not, central.

Constituting an order of this sort entails making claims of responsibility, on a supralocal basis, over one or more locales. These locales can aggregate into a contiguous territory as in the case of a state or a

---

[18] It can be argued that ultimately there is no single force that is responsible for constituting local or any other form of order (and that it is always a matter of multiple forces and actors). I am quite sympathetic to that view and argue for it elsewhere regarding sovereignty – see Latham (2000b). However, my concern is not with any one actor, institution, or configuration of forces constituting order. Rather, it is with the relationship between a field of order constituted – meanings, codes, legitimate practices – and a set of agents establishing or maintaining that field. My argument is that a TD can contribute to a part of such a field of order through its presence and the domain it works within or creates, but it need not be one of the forces directly constituting the general fabric of order in a given locale. For example, while UNHCR may constitute a refugee camp that shapes order near a small city, it does not constitute the municipal order (even though that order rests on a varied array of actors and institutions in government, the economy, and society).

land-based empire, or remain relatively isolated and dispersed islands of incorporation and colonization within other geographical spaces (the sea-borne fort and outpost-based empire – e.g. early Dutch model). The pursuit of supralocal claims over locales is something that – in the history of social science theory – rulers do, whether they are imperial metropoles or just state institutions in national capitals.[19] How and why supralocal claims are made depends on the types of political projects rulers are caught up in: the type of state-formation or empire-building being pursued. As Cooper (this volume) reminds us, the fifteenth and sixteenth centuries witnessed the emergence of new political projects associated with European expansion that altered the possibilities of supralocal rule across distances and the relationship of deployments to those possibilities. These projects changed since that time as various "civilizing missions" and humanitarianisms arose while others fell away.

Supralocal rule emerges when an ensemble of institutions and agents, organized hierarchically and coordinated around some common identity, can project itself into a set of geographical and social spaces. The construction of such rule has, as argued above, generated a considerable number of TDs. Rulers have often been quite capable of constituting platforms for deployments as the history of imperialism makes clear.[20] Expeditions to explore and map spaces, to develop trade monopolies, and to convert to a religion are pointed examples. Whatever the initial motives of encounter, a ruler in principle has a choice as to whether a deployment

---

[19] The term supralocal rule is being used instead of political center. The term political or societal center (see Shils 1975) has been with us for some time and is not without problems. Most of all, the concept, as an ideal type, automatically accords the status of center to a configuration of agency such as a state in relation to some typically formal social field such as a territory and its inhabitants, when this status may be in the least questionable. Of course, problems with the power and status of centers *vis-à-vis* a territory were exactly what theorists such as Edward Shils were concerned with. But in the intellectual spirit of modernization theory they allow an idealized theoretical vision of centrality *per se* to guide their analysis (challenged by dependency theory's peripheralization of centers). Note that the concept is also wholly internalistic, with no suggestion of dynamics between internal and external forces (however much the impact of colonialism was recognized in modernization theory). The point is not to throw out terms such as center, or even related ones such as core and metropole since they usefully suggest structures of hierarchy. But we need to qualify and contextualize our use of such terms by recognizing, on the one hand, that the status of centrality is a function of a political project rather than being an inherent condition and, on the other hand, that there are internal and external dimensions to the boundaries or social spaces a center applies to that also are a function of a political project. Supralocal rule supplies an analytical vantage point from which to make those qualifications.

[20] The interesting question is what kind of field of power comprises contemporary international organizational deployments, NGO networks, and international arena activities. So far the catch-all phrase for it is either international order or more recently "global governance."

will entail claims over a locale to incorporation within a wider order or remain transterritorial. The possibility of choice becomes constrained when a given project, such as an imperialist one, by its nature more or less maps what the relationship between a ruler and an encountered locale should become.[21]

The project of a supralocal rule that perhaps offers the least latitude over relations with locales is the construction of national territory. States can adopt two basic attitudes toward geographical spaces and the locales within them. One attitude is that of territorial incorporation. Obviously, incorporation can involve internal territorialization (adding national territory) or external incorporation (adding colonies). Both entail claims to embed locales in wider supralocal orders.

The second attitude is the development of some external relationship, short of incorporation, which can be labeled interventionary. The interventionist approach of a state depends on TDs sent from platforms floated by the state (e.g. in the US case the Pentagon and its Southern Command). Interventionary deployments by states typically are transterritorial and do not involve taking responsibility for local order or embedding a locale in a wider order, however much such interventions impact local life. The activities of USAID stand out as exactly this type of intervention.

There has been no real effort to draw out how the actions of states operating in their internal and external realms correspond and differ. We have on one side the study of the foreign policy operations of powerful states such as the USA and on the other the longstanding study of state-formation and development *vis-à-vis* political and social life inside national boundaries. I have attempted elsewhere to draw attention to this problem by unbundling the state into a state center that can face inward as an "internal state" toward the locales and orders inside its territory and outward as an "external state" toward societies and orders outside its borders.[22]

Might the same sets of logic regarding scope and status carry over to the internal sphere? Certainly we know that in the long history of European state-formation there have been some very narrow deployments (e.g. taxes, courts, and sheriffs) relative to the twentieth-century

---

[21] This does not preclude arguments over whether a locale is to be subject to colonization (leading, when answered in the negative, to potentially informal imperialistic relations).

[22] See Latham (1997a: ch. 2) regarding the post-World War II US state. Notable exceptions to this include the theoretical tradition that treats state formation as a form of colonization as in the work of Michael Hechter (1975) or Eugene Weber (1976). There is also the dependencia concept of the periphery that is inside a core.

experience in the West with the comprehensively ordering state (or as Foucault would have it, the "governing" state).[23] There is a great deal at stake in this question. And those stakes are not just about the sometimes noted potential parallels between the history of European state-formation and the development of states in regions such as Africa. Rather, they are about viewing such parallels in terms of internal and external patterns of formation, moving to the point where taking the separation of the internal and external for granted as a starting point of analysis ought to be questioned (see Bayart 1993: 20–32).

This turn of view is especially relevant for the African region, where supralocal rule is considered weak – barely able to penetrate national territory to govern and construct an order. And, so it goes, those who cannot penetrate are condemned to be penetrated. African state "weakness" emerged as the primary element anchoring understandings of international order changed from empires and colonies to sovereign states. New African rulers could use these new norms to legitimate claims over territory and resources (Jackson 1990). However, an imperial legacy remained in that African leaders were forced to derive their standing from a translocal project: this time not empire but international liberal order. In so doing, African rulers legitimated (to former colonial rulers and the UN) an order that was also unaccountable to their nations. As a result, merchants, missionaries, and humanitarians, in their transterritorial deployments, could confront Africans as subjects of international order rather than as guardians of their own robust national projects.[24] When intervening in some place outsiders need not concern themselves with the existence of a national moral community. That place essentially is treated as one big internal frontier. Deploying to Africa, and directly intervening in local contexts, remains a very viable option (exercised according to the interests of the agents involved). African rulers must share their internationally constituted national territories – or claims on the locales within – with organizational platforms ranging from NGOs and IOs to states in the West. Reno's discussion (this volume) of the reach of US courts over the practices of Firestone in Africa is a pointed example of this.

[23] Likewise, a national sphere is laced with networks, some of which reach out beyond national borders. And it is not so far-fetched to imagine that a nation-state is composed in part of an overlapping set of national arenas, which have many of the characteristics of international arenas.

[24] In effect, African states are viewed as unable to constitute robust national "arenas" where systems of law, norms, and bodies of representation and deliberation operate in processes of constituting and reconstituting broad civic projects associated with the provision of public welfare and the regulation of economic and social life. We should not accept at face value the implication in Jackson's framework that domestic thinness means that African political figures are more "extraverted" (Bayart's [1993] term) *vis-à-vis* forces and resources coming from outside Africa.

This perspective rests on the assumption that states in the West enjoy far greater control over the terms of penetration within their national territories. UNHCR does not set up refugee camps in Western Europe or North America. Yet we know that Western national territories are viewed as being notably vulnerable to transborder networks of intra-firm trade, currency transactions, capital movements, and transnational mafias. Western countries typically have a robust array of translocal networks (associated with international civil society) reaching out across international space.[25] When we consider some of the local implications – the formation of "global cities" somewhat disarticulated from national centers and territories and local claims to some autonomy against state centers within wider configurations of order such as the European Union – we also need to loosen the internal/external dichotomy for the West.

In Africa and elsewhere, as Roitman and Reno (this volume) show, supralocal rule is not necessarily undermined by the power of local and transboundary forces. The ability of locales to order and integrate themselves into translocal webs of networks or broad systems of transborder order decreases the pressure on rulers to have to do the ordering themselves, providing there does not emerge any untenable costly conflict between the ruler's interest and those external networks and orders or challenges to national territorial claims. This point has a parallel in the long history of empires founded on forms of indirect rule, where it was in the interests of metropoles to let locales govern locally so that the imperial power would not have to take responsibility itself for governance all the way down. The precarious balance suggested by this prospect may be leaving states with far greater latitude over when, where, and how they might intervene in local contexts. While states might retain claims to order the spaces and places of a national territory to varying degrees – based, for instance, on the robustness of national systems of law and policing – locales would informally be tied into networks via the activities of their residents. This is not necessarily a happy prospect because responsibility devolves away from a supralocal ruler (or is never really lodged there when the ruler is weak). States that can deploy themselves into local contexts along narrow

---

[25] We could view these networks as operating at the behest of the state as informal charters (arguing that they could be shut down at any time by Western states that construct the space for them – see Latham 1997b). This would require some very complicated and confusing counterfactual reasoning that is likely to exaggerate the import of the observation that Western states have been complicit in the construction of these networks and underplay the observation that states are quite dependent on them and unable to maneuver in the web of interests involved in their operation.

channels when and where they choose based on their own self-defined interests are not necessarily desirable.[26]

Conclusion: transterritorial deployments and responsibility

This chapter began as an exercise in identifying structures of interaction across boundaries. As analysis progressed, a rather disturbing side to transboundary interaction came into focus: the narrow, circumscribed, and temporary character that dominates much of it, especially those parts that are labeled humanitarian (De Waal 1997). This aspect of transboundary interaction bears directly on the problem of establishing responsibility across boundaries.

Political theorist John Dunn (1994) points to the "perils" posed by the "temporary empire" of humanitarian military intervention when interveners come close to the assumption of "the responsibilities of dominion" without a developed understanding of the aims and reasons for intervention. I believe this condition exists because today the array of intervening deployments available to the international community outflanks the development of political projects to guide them. The age of imperialism, differently, allowed for a uniquely powerful reconciliation of unfortunately robust transboundary political projects (empires) with self-contained and self-defined limits of responsibility for the social life that was reached into. The history of the past few centuries teaches us that we ought to be suspicious of general calls for more responsibility, especially if they do not take seriously the questions of responsibility for whom and on what terms. Moving beyond Dunn, we ought also to be troubled by interventions where the issue of responsibility – in the pursuit of the temporary and the narrow – is avoided. Clearly, something is missing in our understanding of responsibility across boundaries when we are tempted to condemn both too much and too little responsibility (see Latham 2000a).

Any serious development of our understanding of responsibility requires that we avoid formulaic, abstract prescriptions for lodging responsibility in one place or level or another (local, national, international) and instead make sure that concepts of responsibility flow from

[26] Anthropologist Charles Hale (personal communication) informs me that the Guatemalan state is taking on exactly this type of relationship to the local contexts in its national territory. Despite having a relatively powerful army and other resources at its command it has in places strategically withdrawn from local responsibility, choosing when, where, and how to intervene in local situations.

the substance of a given political project. In this respect it matters who the actors involved are. The long history of involvement of private actors (e.g. companies, mercenaries, and NGOs) in deployments of all forms (from mercantile to humanitarian) is hard to overlook. Their involvement, through mechanisms such as private charters and missions, leaves little room for the exercise of public authority across boundaries. I have underscored above, however, that even the narrowest and most temporary of deployments can transform into broader and more permanent ones.

We may need to look more closely at the history of capitalism – not just of empire and intervention – to understand better the dialectics between constricted and expansionary forms of responsibility. At times capitalism (in both its mercantilist and post-Fordist forms) has depended on narrow, penetrating deployments, the containment of responsibility, and the flexibility of temporary entries and exits across the fabric of local contexts around the world. This contrasts with the far broader and deeper forms of responsibility and penetration associated with capitalist systems of industrial production, which hold sway over work, consumption, and technology in societies. The question is, how and to what degree is this same dialectic shaping forms of political and social intervention around the world, inside and across states and societies, such as those discussed in this volume?

5   Producing local politics: governance, representation, and non-state organizations in Africa[1]

Ronald Kassimir

> The representative is, typically, both special pleader and judge, an agent of his locality as well as a governor of the nation. His duty is to pursue both local and national interest, the one because he is a representative, the other because his job as representative is governing the nation. That dual task is difficult, but it is neither practically nor theoretically impossible.
>
> (Pitkin 1967: 218)

> ... practices of government are, on the one hand, multifarious and concern many kinds of people: the head of a family, the superior of a convent, the teacher or tutor of a child or pupil; so that there are several forms of government among which the prince's relation to his state is only one particular mode; while, on the other hand, all these other kinds of government are internal to the state or society. It is within the state that the father will rule the family, the superior the convent, etc. Thus, we find at once a plurality of forms of government and their immanence to the state ...
>
> (Foucault 1991: 91)

Introduction

In the first quotation above, Hanna Pitkin writes of the dual role of politicians representing a locality to the political center. She also hints at the potential tensions between the tasks of "representing" and "governing." In this chapter, I explore this tension, but shift the analytical lens from the state and legislators to non-state organizations and their leaders. These leaders also make representational claims on behalf of their members and beneficiaries. While they are not "governor(s) of the nation," they do attempt to "govern" some spheres of social life in the localities in which they are embedded and which they claim to represent. In focusing on this tension, I characterize the relationship between governance and

---

[1] The various iterations of the chapter have benefited from the comments of the participants in this project. Special thanks go to Robert Latham, who commented extensively on several versions, as well as Deborah Avant, Thomas Callaghy, and Frederick Cooper.

93

representation in non-state organizations as a dialectical one. In other words, the leaders of non-state organizations typically combine attempts to influence powerful others (the state, the international community) *on behalf of* a particular identity and the exercise of authority within the organization. Representation and governance, as dimensions of non-state political authority, constitute critical analytical categories for an understanding of local politics.

This rather abstract point is deployed for a more concrete aim. At a time when great expectations have been touted for the role of non-governmental organizations and civil society institutions in Africa, it is important to emphasize that these organizations are themselves vehicles for access to power and resources. That these organizations have their own internal political dynamics is often acknowledged, but the consequences of these dynamics are rarely analyzed. The ways in which the representational and governing practices of non-state organizations intersect, overlap, and contradict each other may have serious consequences for their own performance and legitimacy. The point is not that some internal governance practices of non-state organizations make for distorted representations of the "real" interests of their members – although some members of the group may find their interests ignored or misrepresented. Rather, the making of effective representational claims presupposes some kind of governing process that both impacts upon organizational efficacy and inevitably creates mixed motives for organizational leaders. These leaders are likely to frame representational claims in a way that validates their own position as an interlocutor (i.e. representative) and as a "governor." Thus, in addition to examining the effects of non-state organizations on the state via their representational claims and practices, I propose that we also consider how they influence the construction of local political orders via their governing practices.

In a sense, seeing non-governmental organizations in this way resonates with how we talk about states: as "externally" representing a society to the international system while governing that society "internally." Whether or not one characterizes the activities of non-state entities as "state-like," these organizations are, in some sense, "polities" that engage in "governing".[2] However, it is clear that different non-state organizations balance the imperatives of representing and governing in diverse ways.

---

[2] "A polity (or political authority) has a distinct identity; a capacity to mobilize persons and their resources for political purposes, that is for value satisfaction; and a degree of institutionalization and hierarchy (leaders and constituents)" (Ferguson and Mansbach 1996: 34). The equation of political purposes with value satisfaction is off-base in this definition, begging the question of whose values within the "polity" are being satisfied and who defines what values are worth pursuing.

Women's groups and religious institutions both seek to represent the identity and interests of their members, but the latter are typically more intensively engaged in the "governing" of their members than the former.

A second purpose in examining the dual face of non-state organizations is to call attention to the ways in which non-state organizations intersect with international and global forces in Africa and elsewhere. While, in the quote above, Foucault argues that all forms of non-state governance are immanent to the state, the extent and nature of state encapsulation of these forms of governance varies across local contexts and world historical moments. Much contemporary analysis emphasizes processes of the privatization, localization, and globalization of authority at the expense of the state. We need not assume that such processes are necessarily in a zero-sum relationship with sovereign states. For the moment, suffice it to say that in sub-Saharan Africa such processes are present and expanding. The sources and agents of non-state governance, and the audiences and agents for non-state representation, have become increasingly transnational. International NGOs provide resources and training for local development organizations and peacekeepers, and international arms dealers and private security firms provide weapons and training for local warlords. Some international non-state organizations directly exercise governance – transnational corporations, mercenary forces, refugee camps, and large-scale development projects are all examples of what Latham terms "transterritorial deployments."[3] Similarly, international institutions are often the audiences for local non-state organizations claiming to represent various groups and communities ignored or repressed by state forces. Vertical networks forged between local and international organizations sometimes attempt to give voice to these claims.[4] At times, international organizations directly take on representational practices even in the absence of local organizations.[5] Thus, the complex and often contradictory relationship between these two faces of non-state institutions at the local level – their governance and representational roles – is played out increasingly in a transnational field.

Governance and representation: an example

Non-state organizations typically engage in a delicate mix of practices that simultaneously (1) *represent* a set of identities and interests to authoritative

---

[3] See his chapter in this volume.   [4] See the chapters by Obi and Schmitz in this volume.
[5] Callaghy's chapter documents the activities of Western debt relief organizations that, in some sense, claim to represent the interests of citizens of debt-impoverished nations even when few local non-state organizations are making such appeals (although, of course, the states "representing" those nations are making them).

institutions such as the state, international organizations, and other "local" organizations and (2) *govern* their own members (and possibly others) through an internal politics of legitimation, resource allocation, and social control, which is itself influenced by extra-local connections.

Let me offer an extended example of the representation – governance dialectic inherent in non-state organizations from my research on the Catholic Church in Uganda. Few non-state organizations combine the practices of representing and governing in such a dense and complicated way as the Catholic Church. Historically, its governing role led it into great tension with processes of state-formation, and later democratization, in Western Europe. But it is crucial to remember that, even after the Church's begrudging acceptance of secular states and democratic institutions, it never stopped "governing" its members through canon law, education, socialization, and more informal mechanisms – only now within a more delimited and truncated sphere.[6]

In Uganda, the contemporary Church is involved in a contradictory project of, on the one hand, encouraging its members to take an active role in public affairs, while on the other insisting on its monopoly of who can legitimately and publicly represent Catholics in a religiously plural context and on its governing authority over particular spheres of social life. The Church itself is still formally structured, like states, on a bureaucratic and territorial administrative model, and lines of authority between bishops, priests, and laity are formally unambiguous. This governing dimension of the Church allowed it to contribute to a semblance of local order when the Ugandan state virtually stopped "governing" and made war on its own people in the 1970s and 1980s. It took on some elements of a "state-within-a-state" that has been the historical accusation hurled at the Church by secular rulers and other critics. The Church has entered a much more ambiguous status since the reconstruction of secular political institutions began in 1986 under the National Resistance Movement (NRM) regime of Yoweri Museveni (Kassimir 1998a).

However, there are other dimensions to the institution that are not captured in canon law, organizational charts, or the Church's own narrative

---

[6] The rise of liberation theology movements was initially narrated by its theorists, and by some scholars, as the passage of Latin American churches from a governing role (in alliance with secular rulers) to a representational one. But more recent work in that region has shown that, not only do powerful factions within the Church still take their governing mandate (and the hierarchical division of labor between clergy and laity) very seriously, but that liberation theology movements themselves relied on governing practices (the provision of services, elimination of "superstitious" religious expressions seen as producing a fatalistic world view) as part of their political strategy. On the limited success of this strategy see Burdick (1993).

which claims for itself the mantle of a leading civil society organization. In some ways parallel to William Reno's notion of the "shadow state" (1995), the Church has its non-bureaucratic shadows as well. These include the social networks that link Church leaders to NRM officials, local politicians, and the Curia in Rome. But many other Church members also use Catholic networks, often for different purposes and in ways that constitute "disobedience" to the hierarchy. Members of the lower clergy, as well as some well-placed lay people, are able to draw on resources available from a range of networks outside the formal structure of the Church: state organs, the private sector, NGOs, and, increasingly, international contacts with Catholic aid agencies and local parishes in the USA and Europe. Many of these priests lobby for educational opportunities abroad, in part to create or deepen these networks. Other priests and lay people forge ties with the global network of Catholic charismatics, which is viewed with suspicion by some bishops and clergy for its implication of the leveling of religious charisma between clergy and laity. Every day Catholics participate in "shadow" and sometimes public organizations as they seek remedies for ill health and misfortune in distinctly heterodox ways from the point of view of official Church doctrine (Kassimir 1999). Thus, the Church's governing role, especially in terms of social control, has serious limitations.

The broadest effect of all these extra-formal practices and interactions, in a political sense, is to render the Church's formal capacity to back up its claims to representation surprisingly weak given how visible a presence the Church evinces on the ground. Limited in mobilizing its own structures for the purpose of "governing" its members, it is unable to mobilize in "external" arenas via its representational role.[7]

While the Catholic Church may exemplify an extreme in the degree to which a non-state institution is involved in governing, it allows for comparison with other kinds of organizations and networks with different purposes and different degrees of formality in their organizational structure. While differing in the degree of their governing role, and in the way they exercise authority, one can ask empirically how, how much, and how successfully do NGOs, labor unions, agricultural cooperatives, youth groups, women's organizations, and ethnic associations govern as well as represent their members? The variation in non-state-governing practices

---

[7] At the same time, the formal bureaucratic quality of these structures may impede the possibility of mobilization in the name of Catholics through extra-formal channels. The result has been the reproduction of both the formal and "shadow" dimensions of the organization. While priests do not attempt to destroy their bureaucracies (as Reno shows that some African rulers did), they may have priorities other than developing them. See Kassimir (1998b).

may occur along many dimensions. Non-state organizations may produce formal constitutions or operate under informal tacit understandings that establish membership criteria, the recognition of leaders, and mechanisms for choosing the latter. They will differ in the degree to which they shape social identities (religious, ethnic, class, gender) and control the behavior of members through coercive or other means. Their role in acquisition, accumulation, and distribution of resources will vary, as will the centrality of these resources to the lives of their members.

Non-state governance and representation

While it is unconventional to apply the term "governance" to non-state organizations, there is a growing recognition that such actors are in some sense engaged in "governing."[8] In an era of privatization, where not only economic activity but aspects of health provision, education, and security are shifting to non-state actors, non-state governance demands deeper attention and understanding. Non-state organizations are increasingly cited as a key element in the production of local political processes. Olowu writes:

> The search for alternative non-state structures that can respond to the economic and social needs of African people is one of the most important rationales for the new emphasis on local governance. Local governance implies a focus on the totality of structures within the local community that comprise both state and society organizations. (1999: 288)

Charlick, in arguing for recognition of the governance role of NGOs and civil society, has defined governance as "the way a society organizes *to use power* to manage public resources, involving the making and implementation of collective decisions, enforcement of rules and resolution of conflicts" (Charlick forthcoming, emphasis added). This is a politically astute starting point, from which we can begin asking about what are the

---

[8] David Hecht and Maliqalim Simone coined the term "invisible governance" to characterize "the informal frameworks for justice, morality and social balance" (1994: 13) in urban Africa under conditions of state incapacity and venality. This has some affinity to what political scientists call "local order," although Hecht and Simone are rather elliptical in what they mean by "governance." In a similar vein, James N. Rosenau writes that "governance refers to activities backed by shared goals that may or may not derive from legal and formally prescribed responsibilities" and thus defines governance (as opposed to government) as "a system of rule that is as dependent on inter-subjective meanings as on formally sanctioned constitutions and charters" (1992: 4). In any case, here I am interested in both the visible and non-visible aspects of non-state governance, which I do not assume is necessarily productive of "justice, morality, and social balance," nor is necessarily based upon "shared goals" or "inter-subjective meanings." Both of these definitions give too great a priority to the consensual aspects of governance and underplay the conflicts that are central to non-state governing practices.

sources of the power that produces governance, and what components of "society" are managing and which are being managed.[9] Non-state organizations, I argue, govern through an internal politics of legitimation, resource allocation, and social control (and, on occasion, coercion). Thus, the enactment of "state-like" functions such as service delivery by NGOs is directly linked to the politics within these organizations, the determination of who is recognized to speak for and lead members,[10] and what members must do in order to gain access to resources and services that the organization may provide.

The temptation to cast the governance practices of non-state organizations as the performance of "state-like" functions is a strong one but must be treated with some caution. In the model of the ideal-typical Weberian state, legitimate force or coercion is the only attribute of governance for which the state claims a monopoly. Even in this domain, non-state actors have begun to take on a greater role through the activities of local security and vigilante groups that address both peacetime criminality and wartime protection against the predations of both national armies and rebel forces.[11] Empirically, non-state organizations have always performed a wide range of public governance activities that have local political effects (Charlick forthcoming). Those non-state organizations that undertake some kind of service – humanitarian assistance, credit provision, education, health care, women's empowerment, etc. – may fall into the same kind of political logic that Ferguson describes for states: " 'Government services' are never simply 'services'; instead of conceiving this phrase as a reference simply to a 'government' whose purpose is to serve, it may be at least as appropriate to think of 'services' which serve to govern" (1994: 253).

---

[9] There is a tendency to speak of governance as both a systemic property (of a "society," a "political order") and as a capacity of a specific social organization. In this chapter, I am clearly emphasizing the latter. For a perhaps more conventional use of governance that emphasizes the former, see Hyden (1999). For Hyden, governance "refers to that aspect of politics that aims to formulate and manage the rules of the political arena in which state and civil society actors operate and interact to make authoritative decisions. In more operational terms, governance refers to those measures that involve setting the rules for the exercise of power and settling conflicts over such rules" (p. 185). This builds upon his earlier work on this theme, especially Hyden (1992).

[10] Drawing on the work of Bruce Lincoln, Michael Barnett writes that some definitions of authority are "less about domination *per se* and more about actors who are given a presumptive right to speak and act because of their position or standing." See his chapter in this volume.

[11] For the former, the Sungusungu movement in Tanzania has been the most thoroughly documented. Recent work shows the growing connections of the movement to the state over time. See Fleisher (2000). For the latter, see the work of Casper Fithen, Paul Richards and others on the Kamajo militias in war-torn Sierra Leone.

This may be too cynical, recalling Michels' famous dictum with reference to political parties: "Who says organization, says oligarchy" (1962: 365). One cannot read the purposes to which power is put directly from the way it is organized and distributed, and the particular interest of power-holders and the broader interests of the groups they "serve" can coincide under certain conditions. It is here where the "representativeness" of non-state organizations figures so prominently as it connects the purpose of organizational action to the modes of decision-making and mobilization. Consider how the dialectic of governance and representation is played out through the involvement of non-state actors in development projects, even those working under the precepts of participatory development approaches. In a study of participatory forest management in West Africa, Ribot analyzes the governing aspects and social control mechanisms of local cooperatives that operate as "administrative bodies to control the use of local labour and resources, legitimated by quasi-representative local appointed or 'customary' authorities" (Ribot 1999: 48). In such cases, non-state governance distorts the possibilities for accountable local representation as state officials and international environmental groups engage local actors and organizations that may not represent community interests.

Paralleling colonial concerns, current participatory efforts appeal for their legitimacy to local, non-state authorities, supporting those authorities in the process. Chiefs are used in participatory projects as state administrators, as intermediaries or just as symbols of the "indigenous," thus legitimating the project to local populations while providing it with a local and indigenous flavor for project personnel and advocates supporting participation from afar. Although used as if they were representative, chiefs may not represent or be accountable to local populations. (p. 25)[12]

The representativeness of chiefs is, of course, centrally connected to the most pervasive sources of non-state political authority in Africa: ethnic organizations and communities. Ethnic identities and organizations are critical cases where governance and representation are intertwined. On the one hand, even in places where they have no formal political authority, let alone those instances where they do (e.g. northern Nigeria), ethnically based institutions exercise their own governance role both visibly and in the shadows. Sklar may go too far in calling these institutions a "separate dimension of governmental authority" that constitutes "an auxiliary or second state, behind-the-state," (1993: 86, 96), but the basic point that they are loci of authority and social control is clear.

[12] Also see Guyer (1992).

At the same time, the governing scope and capacities of any ethnic organization are contingent upon who is recognized as representing a specific identity and thus in a position to articulate its interests. The politics of representation is two-sided. On the one hand, governments, international agencies, and other communities serve as audiences, responding to the representative claims of ethnic group leaders and potentially seeking to manipulate who is formally regarded as representing a group. As de Boeck notes: "to a large extent the arguments of identity today centre around the question of who represents whom, and to/for whom" (1996: 94). With regard to the Luunda in the Democratic Republic of the Congo, he suggests that the success of representational strategies is "linked apparently to the capacity to objectify one's own culture by creating an appropriate 'ethnic identity' for outward use, in a form that allows collective action in collaboration with or in opposition to broader political and economic networks" (p. 89). On the other hand, ethnic organizations are themselves frequently riven by internal political struggles over the power to represent the group. They are sites of contestation over wealth, power, and status that often crystallize in struggles over who has the right to legitimately represent an ethnic identity to the state and the world. Mamdani (1996) has recently characterized ethnic mobilization as a "civil war" within groups that can become externalized into inter-group conflict.[13] The internal conflicts can have many bases – class, clan, gender, and generation. The control and possible resolution of these representational conflicts are contingent upon internal governance practices that, as Mamdani argues, are tied to the manipulation of state authorities that empower some claimants at the expense of others. Fearon and Laitin (1996) make the related point that inter-ethnic cooperation or conflict is contingent on the "self-policing" capacities of ethnic groups to control extremists who propose alternative representational claims.

Through social control, resource allocation, modes of establishing and legitimating leaders, and the shaping of identities, governing practices affect both the representational activities of non-state organizations and their capacity to mobilize. Indeed, it is difficult to imagine that, without some mechanism for defining goals, identifying leaders, or controlling members, social organizations can have sustained impact in the broader

[13] "An internal civil war . . . cannot exhaustively explain the phenomenon usually referred to as tribalism, for we all know that media references to tribalism accent more the interethnic than the intraethnic, the conflict between tribes and not that within a tribe. My point is not to deny the existence of the former, but to claim that the nature of conflict between ethnic groups in the larger polity is difficult to grasp unless we relate it to the conflict within a tribe. Without that connection, we will be left with no more than a tautology: different tribes fight because they are different" (Mamdani 1996: 183–184).

political arena. Dunn writes that "what does furnish and sustain political representation" is "the capacity and confident self-organisation of the bearers of social interests" (1986: 162). Thus, non-state governance shapes the effectiveness of representational action and the (particular and collective) interests that it serves. How representational claims are received and acted upon by various audiences depends, in part, on how and how much organizations govern (and are perceived as governing) their members and others.[14] However, there is a recursive quality to this process. For representatives, the status of intermediary implies a set of expectations, both for local constituents and for other audiences (the state and the international arena). A normative framework is created within which representatives must operate or risk a breakdown in their governing authority. Thus, the nature of non-state governing may also depend on representational practices.

Local politics and non-state organizations

Before discussing how this dynamic plays out when global dimensions of non-state organizations enter the picture, it is worth considering how one might begin to conceptualize "local" politics in relation to non-state authority. In the past, the association of "the local" with backwardness invited powerful critique. More recent analysis has called attention to tendencies to romanticize and essentialize "the local" as a site of authenticity or resistance to state predation or global forces.[15] Hannerz has written on the changing views of the local within the discipline of anthropology. The local, he writes, conjures notions of "everyday life" and emphasizes the "continuous importance of place" (1996: 26).[16] He argues that, even in a more intensively globalized world, "the local" maintains its analytical utility, but with two important qualifications. First, the "continuing importance of the local"

could be true as far as experienced reality is concerned even when much of what is in a place is shaped from the outside. We are thus giving up the idea that the local is autonomous, that it has an integrity of its own. It would have its significance, rather as an arena in which a variety of influences come together, acted out perhaps in unique combination, under those special conditions. (p. 26)

---

[14] See Schmitz's chapter, where both the limited reach of Kenyan human rights organizations to the public, and the (perceived) connections of their leaders to ethnic networks, affected their capacity as political mobilizers and the recognition of their claims to represent "civil society."

[15] For an excellent survey of these critiques, see Haugerud (forthcoming). Also see Watts (1999).

[16] He lists the attributes that typically comprise the local: "the everyday, the face-to-face, the early and formative, the sensual and body experience" (Hannerz 1996: 27).

This leads directly to a second qualification – contrary to more common usage, "the local" is tied to, but not fully defined by, territoriality. The local may be a place, but it is also "an arena where various people's habitats of meaning intersect, and where the global, or what has been local somewhere else, also has some chance of making itself at home" (p. 28).

The notion of the local as an "arena in which a variety of influences comes together" is thus an appropriate one, but so broad as to limit its usefulness as an analytical construct, and particularly as a political construct.[17] Parallel to Appadurai's (1996) labeling of the local effects of the cultural dimensions of globalization as the "production of locality,"[18] we can discern the "production of local politics" – the internal dynamics of "the local" as it interacts with broader forces (which include, but go beyond, the institutions of the nation-state).[19] In this sense, "the local" is construed as a political arena where order and disorder are constructed, and spheres of authority are forged and intersect. As John and Jean Comaroff put it, "no social world may be properly understood without reference *both* to its internal historicity and to its unfolding relationship with its wider context" (1994: 96, emphasis in original).

In connecting non-state organizations to the production of local politics, I have concentrated on non-state organizations that express, influence, maintain, and transform local authority and that are thus engaged in interaction with other "locals," translocal networks, the state, and global forces.[20] Of course, not all non-state organizations operating in Africa are "local" in origin, and few are exclusively local in terms of their political connections.[21] National (and international) organizations have local branches, or may be umbrella groups of local associations that vary in

---

[17] The use of the term "arena" was prevalent in political anthropology in the 1960s. See, in particular, Swartz (1968). Indeed, Hannerz's sense of the local as an arena (largely in cultural terms) parallels Swartz's claim (in his volume's introduction) that local-level politics occurs in a space where "politics is incomplete in the sense that actors and groups outside the range of the local, multiplex relationships are vitally and directly involved in the political process of the local group" (1968: 1).

[18] He writes that the "production of locality" is a "structure of feeling" not necessarily tied to place (Appadurai 1996: 181).

[19] For a related point, see Watts (1993).

[20] "Community" is a term often used for "the local" in that it implies a spatial boundedness. Within the discussion offered here, one would need to distinguish between communities as "polities" and the various organizations (state and non-state) that act within communities and may claim to represent not only particular interests, but the interest of "the community" as an (imagined) whole. Since my main point here is that non-state organizations are themselves "polities," provisionally equating the category of local/community with non-state organizations makes some analytical sense.

[21] At the same time, associations of journalists and lawyers tend to be "national," although in reality their "locality" is principally urban areas, and most typically the capital city.

their autonomy. And as mentioned above, non-state organizations are but one element in the production of local political processes.[22]

The notion of transboundary formations used in this volume provides a key lens with which to view local political processes in terms of the internal dynamics of "the local" as it engages with broader forces. The extreme variation we see in local political outcomes in Africa is a "product" of both the myriad ways in which external forces impinge upon the local and the local's own, often contradictory and conflictual fields of power. This is where a focus on representation and governance, as key dimensions of non-state authority, can be helpful in understanding the intersection of forces that comprise transboundary formations.[23]

Representation, governance, and transboundary formations

Thus far I have discussed the dynamics of non-state authority within local and national entities, but without systematic attention to the connections between non-state organizations and transnational forces. It is widely recognized that these organizations, like the communities in which they operate, are not bounded, and that African "civil societies," like others, are not strictly "national" or state-wide phenomena. Indeed, many non-state organizations in the region have close ties and complex interactions with cross-border groups and transnational organizations.[24] However, we are only beginning to understand how these connections are formed and what political effects they generate through transboundary formations.

---

[22] See Olowu (1999). Local governments are the subject of longstanding research in Africa and are receiving renewed attention via the latest cycle of decentralization reforms. However, since in most parts of Africa local government bodies remain extensions of central administrations (rather than semi-autonomous federal units accountable to local populations), they will be treated here as part of the context within which local politics is played out and local orders are made. Located at the margins of political science (with its primary focus on the central state) and of anthropology (with its primary focus on non-state actors), local government as a research domain remains tangential to major debates on politics in Africa.

[23] With regard to political representation, it is striking how rarely this key concept of political theory has been problematized in the post-colonial African context. For an important exception, see Dunn (1986). Writing in the mid-1980s, Dunn argues specifically that "the representation of *place and local community*" is "the aspect of authentic political representation that has been most successfully (and least coercively) institutionalised in African societies since independence" (1986: 167, emphasis added). He continues: "Only within more geographically constricted confines, where localities in themselves can coincide with localities for themselves with rather little ideological fiction, does a real continuity of representative exploration and exertion subsist, as national governments come and go" (p. 169). Also see several of his essays in Dunn (1980).

[24] As evinced by many of the chapters in this volume, and especially those by Obi and Schmitz. Also see Guyer (1994) and Woods (1995).

Examples of such formations, which include non-state organizations, abound in Africa. International agencies have been active in nurturing and even creating local human rights organizations and "civil associations" in the context of political liberalization. Even in conflict situations such as that in Somalia, international NGOs attempted to "find" authentic or legitimate civil leaders (i.e. clan elders) who held, or were perceived as holding, both representational and governing authority. The World Bank and private foundations have assisted in the formation of networks of technocrats (especially economists), part of whose agenda is to constitute domestic lobbies for economic reform measures. Similar practices have been common in the arenas of environmental protection and women's empowerment. International organizations have extended support to "indigenous peoples" – ethnic groups whose ways of life are seen as in need of either change or preservation, especially nomadic peoples such as the Maasai in Kenya and Tanzania. Religious missionary societies, most prominently American Christian evangelical groups and Saudi, Libyan, and Iranian Muslim organizations, have cultivated clients who compete with older, more established religious organizations for followers and claim to represent "true" Christians and Muslims. They often develop public agendas, mobilize followers based on reshaped social identities, and introduce new resources and new mechanisms of non-state governance.[25]

In addition, through transterritorial deployments, international institutions establish a physical presence in African localities. Intentionally or not, these non-state organizations often become bound up in local processes of governance and in the formulation of representational claims. Such organizations include transnational corporations, development and refugee relief organizations, and mercenary forces. Their "deployments," Latham (this volume) argues, vary in terms of their scope and their status as temporary or permanent. To return to the example of the Catholic Church, its permanent presence allows it to be seen both as an international organization with local branches and as a local organization "networked" globally. The Ugandan Church is a local "representative" both *of* and *to* a global institution, its bishops appointed by the Vatican, its administrative structure and its doctrine provided externally by a model that is formally similar everywhere, its funding largely provided by overseas agencies, even some of its personnel provided from outside (although now missionaries constitute a rather small percentage of active clergy). The Vatican even has formal diplomatic standing, with a

---

[25] On the recent influx of mostly American evangelicals to Africa, see Gifford (1994, 1998). On Islam, see Kane (1997) and, for a case study of rural Niger, see Masquelier (1996).

representative – the papal nuncio – engaging in direct relations with the Ugandan state. But the transnational shadow-like practices of local Church members, discussed above, operate alongside these formal structures and relations, but more along a network than a bureaucratic model.

Another transnational religious community combining network and bureaucratic structures, and governing and representative practices, albeit in ways quite distinct from the Catholic Church, are Ismaili Muslims. Ismailis resident in East Africa form strong religious, economic, and social ties to others in South Asia, Europe, and North America, through a "transnational system of governance that is clearly articulated in their constitution" (Kadende-Kaiser and Kaiser 1998: 462). A recent study of Ismailis in Tanzania reports that this system provides the infrastructure through which resources and information flow while representing the Tanzanian community to government and other communities: "Just as the modern state protects and regulates religious expression, administers justice, and collects and redistributes resources that affect the financial solvency and social welfare of the national community, these Ismaili institutions accomplish similar goals at the transnational communal level" (p. 468).

Again, religious organizations are but one example, but one that points to analytic categories open to comparison. We may ask, for example, how local, non-state organizations compare in terms of the extent of their embeddedness in global networks (e.g. dependence on external resource flows) as well as of the nature of that embeddedness (e.g. the balance between formal and informal relations, between bureaucratic and network-type structures). Non-state organizations surely vary in the ways in which authority, resources, ideas, and information flow, formally and informally, through and from transboundary channels.

Many "shadow-like" transboundary formations have shaped the direction and content of the politics of local, non-state organizations. These include trading diasporas of African ethnic or religious groups (e.g. the Hausa and Wolof) (Kane 1997; Perry 1997) or outsider citizens or residents (e.g. East African Asians, West African Lebanese) who cut across state and continental borders in ways that influence the structure of private sector interests. Diaspora or exiled members of ethnic groups have also been active in the flow of resources and representational strategies that affect the internal politics of their groups at home and the latter's relations with states, sometimes supporting political opposition. These are modes of interaction for states whose regimes are neither under violent assault nor facing sub-national regions that are "governed" autonomously from the center. For those states facing armed opposition, the cross-border flows of arms, money, and tradeables and the use of mercenaries are gaining greater documentation. The chapters in this volume by Reno, Nordstrom, and Roitman all demonstrate how a mix of coercion, wealth accumulation, and a shared strategy of abjuring formal institutions for a "networking" ·approach can maintain a contingent and often brutal form of local order which is itself inextricable from the presence of external actors and connections to transnational flows.[26]

The conflict between the Nigerian state, transnational oil companies, and local communities is an example of the representation–governance dialectic in action.[27] On the one side, Shell and other multinational firms exercise "governance" in collaboration with the Nigerian state. Enclaves of ostensibly national territory are not merely exploited but managed by the company, with the Nigerian army acting more as a private security firm than a neutral and national force. Shell has even attempted to ease local pressures by engaging in community development projects, thus developing local clients and enhancing its "state-like" presence. On the other side, factions within the Ogoni community, unable to find redress for their grievances from a state beholden to the oil companies, make representational claims to the international arena on three interconnected but distinct bases: human rights, environmentalism, and the rights of indigenous peoples.[28] The vertical networks which local opposition organizations form with international organizations serve as useful weapons with which to oppose the state and oil companies.[29] However, they also provide resources and legitimation in struggles within the Ogoni community – between collaborators and opposition, and between moderate and hard-line opposition forces. Perhaps unwittingly, the material and moral support those international NGOs provide, and the universalistic discourses they propound, are appropriated in contests not only with Shell, but also within the local community. These are struggles over who has the right to represent the Ogoni externally and to participate in the governance of the community. The entrance of the international NGOs into this scenario did not create these struggles. However, their availability and willingness to provide resources changed the calculus of local politics.

One other effect of transboundary formations is that the external organizations and discourses help to create and reproduce a stratum of professional organizers who develop careerist incentives to maintain their status as intermediaries. In cases such as the Ogoni struggle, this can be a

---

[26] In addition, see Bayart et al. (1999).

[27] This draws on the chapter in this volume by Cyril Obi as well as Watts (1999).

[28] The last mentioned is perhaps the one internationally legitimate way in which ethnic claims can be framed.

[29] On vertical networks, see Schmitz's chapter.

double-edged sword. The international community needs individuals to serve as interlocutors. The support of international activist organizations depends in part on the trust that develops between them and local leaders. But these relationships can deepen hierarchies within local organizations and can foster competition for the resources and the legitimacy that the international arena bestows.[30] This raises a more general issue. Not unlike the way in which Bayart has characterized African states, many local non-state organizations are well versed in the art of "extraversion."[31] Familiarizing themselves with the priorities of international organizations and their discourses, some non-state actors represent their situations and the interests of their members strategically in order to gain access to resources and politically useful networks. Such strategies may, but need not be, part of accumulation and governing strategies for organizational leaders. Indeed, they may be part of very real political projects – improving the status of women, extending the control of resources by "indigenous" groups, even strengthening civil society.

But it does raise questions. Transboundary connections to "the global" may reframe the political purposes and practices of non-state organizations even as they empower them. Material dependence on international support may create or deepen a patrimonial logic within non-state organizations and shift accountability "upward" to donors rather than "downward" toward constituents.[32] In doing so, it may reinforce existing patterns of non-state governance and representational practices that belie the stated objectives of many international organizations.

Conclusion: transboundary formations, "weak states," and "civil society"

In an important and prescient review essay, "Beyond the State: Civil Society and Associational Life in Africa," published more than ten years ago, Michael Bratton argued that state–society interactions "need not always be confrontational but, under certain conditions, may be complementary" (1989: 428), and identified two ways of imagining non-state organizations:

---

[30] For an analysis of the Ogoni case that highlights this dimension, see Watts (1999).

[31] See Bayart (1993) and his discussion of the "social institutions of globalization" in Bayart (2000).

[32] Global support for non-state organizations can indeed be capricious, both as global priorities change and as situations change on the ground. In the case of South Africa, the end of apartheid has meant a major shift in international support from civic associations to the state, and the movement of civic leaders to governmental positions. If the global pendulum ever swings back to betting on states in Africa, we may witness a similar process elsewhere.

One the one hand, a civic organization can represent the interests of a social constituency and influence the formation of public policy, thus improving the coincidence between public policy and the needs of some segment of society. On the other hand, a civic organization can play an auxiliary role in policy implementation, relieving the state of part of the administrative burden of *extending authority* and delivering benefits to a large and scattered population. (p. 429, emphasis added)

Bratton's point was both analytical and normative: that political pluralism (through representation) and administrative pluralism (through a "governance" role for non-state organizations) *could* strengthen state performance and legitimacy in sub-Saharan Africa.[33] The notion of "extending authority" in reference to non-state organizations is critical here. As I have argued, there is a growing need to understand how, and how much, non-state organizations exercise authority within, outside, and across juridical states. In this chapter, I have focused on the juxtaposition of the two dimensions of non-state authority identified by Bratton, which I have coded as the "representational" and "governing" authority of non-state institutions. Many non-state organizations, in varying degrees, take on both a representational role *and* a role in what I have referred to as governance practices.

In addition, the governance–representation dialectic of non-state organizations at the local level is played out increasingly in a transnational field. This is not unique to Africa, but the limitations of the formal state apparatus and the porousness of boundaries, as well as the international community's post-Cold War inclination to disregard some of the norms of state sovereignty (Clapham 1996: ch. 10), make these connections even more consequential in the ways the "local" represents and is represented, the way it governs and is governed.

Imagining local politics and local order in this way forces us to rethink what we mean by "state weakness." What is typically seen as the marker of "weakness" for states in Africa and elsewhere in the contemporary world is the intersection of a limited *capacity* for extraction, mobilization, social control, and policy implementation with a limited *autonomy* from both local and global forces that constrains policy choice.[34] Implicit in this now conventional view of African state–society relations is a question: how is

---

[33] More than ten years later, it would be telling to see if the myriad economic and political reforms that were implemented on the continent in the 1990s moved in this direction. Most indications, I would imagine, would either answer in the negative, or argue that it is too early to tell. For a recent assessment, see Joseph (1998).

[34] The classical general statement remains Migdal (1988). On the variable intersection of capacity and autonomy, both for states and for non-governmental organizations, see Bratton (1994).

order being constructed (to the degree that it is produced) if African states are limited in constructing it? This question, while not ignored, has largely been viewed as secondary to the question of the effect of local politics on the state.

One of the major difficulties with the imputation that African states are weak is that their actions, and sometimes even their discourses are, at least in many parts of the continent, highly consequential in citizens' survival and social mobility strategies, the provision of security and other public goods, the formation and transformation of collective identities, and the inhibiting of social mobilization.[35] One particular dimension stands out along which African states are relevant: their location as interlocutors between the global and the local. And it is here that the connections of transboundary forces to political changes on the ground have shifted the state from its pretensions to a monopolistic gatekeeping position to a looser, more mediating role. Through privatization and other structural adjustment measures, as well as the expansion and pluralization of global networks, more spaces have opened for direct global–local connections to be made, for transboundary flows of commodities, people, ideas, cultural products, and technologies to be transited, uncontrolled by state institutions. To be sure, the ability of African states to serve as gatekeepers has always been limited. But the contemporary intensification of the promotion of international norms, of transnational networks (from human rights activists to arms merchants to diasporas), and of transterritorial deployments (of everything from economic consultants to providers of humanitarian assistance to TNCs to mercenaries)[36] has made state management of "the global" even more contingent and limited.

But if the state as an institution is weak in this managerial process, it is again rarely irrelevant in the way that transboundary connections are formed and institutionalized. International norms of sovereignty are part

---

[35] While arguments have been made that states are not only weak but irrelevant in Africa, debates on this topic are often framed by selecting those cases that most fit the point being made – i.e. "collapsed states" as evidence of and harbingers for African states' irrelevance vs. states' reconfiguration as evidence of a renewed relevance. See Villalón and Huxtable (1998). Forrest, in his contribution to the Villalón and Huxtable volume, comes close to making the irrelevance argument: "a greater proportion of Africans are now experiencing political life with no minimally viable state presence than at any time since the precolonial period." In what Forrest calls "inverted states," "we can analyze intimate business connections between some state leaders and traders, while we bear witness to the demise of the institutional and policy capacity of the state, rendering it increasingly unable to affect the political and economic life of its citizens" (1998: 45, 46).

[36] See Latham's chapter.

of what makes states relevant.[37] But beyond this, state rules help to frame the mode of engagement (e.g. most international NGOs must conform to state regulatory laws or risk being thrown out) and state officials often play important roles in shaping (if not controlling) transboundary formations (how goods are smuggled, where INGOs operate and how they are provisioned, etc.). There is little evidence that such practices are reversing state institutional weakness, but they are evidence of a kind of state relevance. African states may not be monopolistic gatekeepers in the process through which global forces impinge upon local political orders, but they are, for the most part, important mediators of transboundary formations.[38]

The purported weakness of African states led analysts, beginning in the 1980s, to examine the "strengths" of society (Rothchild and Chazan 1988). This focus has tended to oscillate between analyzing the impact of social forces on state forms and state governance on the one hand, and as constituents of local order and local governance on the other. The almost exclusive attention to processes of political liberalization and democratization in the 1990s naturally emphasized the former. Within this, the local and the non-state are subsumed in much of academic and practitioner discourse within the frame of "civil society." Social organizations classified as outside civil society became interesting largely as pathological and negative forces in the democratization process. Thus, the questions of where power is located, how local politics are produced, and the role of global forces in this production became occluded. But given that a change in regime type (i.e. from authoritarian to formally liberal democratic) has no necessary positive effect on state strength (capacity and autonomy), then what produces local politics and local order remains a plausible question to ask, one that is relatively autonomous from questions of regime type and regime change. The subsuming of the local and the non-state into the civil society problematic (as either supportive of or pathological for democracy) leaves us few tools for understanding local politics, as well as for grasping the insertion of transboundary forces into the local.

This chapter has been premised on the notion that, whether we call them civil society associations, non-state organizations, or local communities, these entities are themselves fields of power and authority, not only

[37] See Reno's chapter.

[38] A related point is made by Latham (1999) and Krasner (1995). Hannerz describes political science's core object of study, the state, in ways that parallel his earlier-cited statement about "the local": that the state "should be treated ... as one player among many, with its own interests and logic, rather than as the universe of analysis" (1996: 22).

collective actors arrayed against the state or massed in support of democracy. Given the attention currently given to non-state actors, capturing the balance and the contradictions between their representational and governing practices may provide a deeper understanding of their political possibilities. Two of these possibilities are especially consequential in the production of local politics. The first is the issue of enfranchisement, in the broader sense of effective political participation. Ribot, following the influential recent work of Mamdani, defines enfranchisement as "the shift from subject to citizen" that is "predicated on the existence of a structure for community decision-making that is locally accountable and representative" (1999: 25, 29). Second is the capacity for non-state organizations to achieve collective ends. This is predicated, I would argue, on a structure not only of representation but of governance as well. History provides us with many examples of non-democratic social organizations that accomplished collective as well as particularistic goals, although with many more that achieve the latter at the expense of the former. What worked in the past may not be workable in the present, but we would be sociologically naive to assume the quality of outcomes from the quality of a decision-making process.[39]

Enfranchisement and the capacity to achieve collective ends are critical challenges for non-state organizations in Africa and elsewhere. Whether the enmeshing of these organizations within transboundary formations makes meeting these challenges more or less difficult is an open question, but it is one on which the production of local politics will turn.

---

[39] "While most private governments, unions, professional societies, veterans' organizations, and political parties will remain one-party systems ... it is important to recognize that many internally oligarchic organizations help to sustain political democracy in the larger society and to protect the interests of their members from the encroachments of other groups." (Lipset 1962: 36).

Part III

Transboundary networks, international institutions, states, and civil societies

6   Networks and governance in Africa: innovation in the debt regime

Thomas M. Callaghy

Introduction

One of the most dramatic, systematic, and intrusive forms of external intervention in Africa over the past two decades has been "structural adjustment" – the efforts of the International Monetary Fund (IMF), the World Bank, and the major industrial states to get governments to reform their economies in significant ways.[1] Structural adjustment is seen by powerful external actors as the way to reverse the decline and marginalization of African states as globalization accelerates. Most of these countries, however, have seen structural adjustment, with its high and detailed levels of conditionality, as a major threat to their sovereignty and politically dangerous; they have resisted it through the passive strategies of what I have called the ritual dances of reform (Callaghy and Ravenhill 1993). The result has been increasingly weak, sometimes failing, states.

One of the primary results of structural adjustment has been rising levels of external debt. It is mostly "official" debt owed to major Western countries, the International Monetary Fund, and the World Bank. Since the late 1950s, bilateral debt has been rescheduled by creditor countries organized into a mechanism that came to be known as the Paris Club, while multilateral debt could not be rescheduled. The Paris Club became the core of the international debt regime for official debt – that is the actors, norms, processes, and mechanisms focused around countries unable to service their bilateral debt. As will be shown below, the practices of the international debt regime evolved in important ways during the 1980s and 1990s as it became increasingly clear that poor countries, for whom structural adjustment worked least well, were usually unable to cope with their mounting debt loads.

---

[1] On structural adjustment in Africa, see Callaghy and Ravenhill (1993). In addition to the cited sources, this chapter is based heavily on confidential interviews with officials from the IMF, the World Bank, the USA, Britain, France, and several African governments, as well as representatives of NGOs working on debt, conducted in Washington, New York, London, Paris, and Brussels between September 1997 and July 2000.

The growing debt burden of poor countries, most of which were African, thus became an increasing concern of key actors in the international arena – some creditor countries, agencies of the United Nations system (UNCTAD in particular), a wide-ranging group of non-governmental organization (NGOs), and, of course, debtor countries themselves. During the New International Economic Order (NIEO) negotiations of the late 1970s and early 1980s, debtor countries, especially the poorest, insistently demanded more generous relief of sovereign debt, a simplified debt restructuring process, including generalized norms, and special treatment for the poorest debtor countries. In short, they wanted a reform of the Paris Club debt process, especially its case-by-case procedures. None of this came to pass as a result of the struggle for the NIEO. Yet by the late 1980s, the Paris Club countries began slowly and incrementally to offer more generous (the debtors would say less onerous) terms for its poorest debtors, and occasionally for some of its biggest and most strategically important debtors (Poland, Egypt, Russia, and Indonesia). By the end of the 1990s, however, the debt regime for poor countries had changed dramatically, first with the advent of the Heavily Indebted Poor Country Debt Initiative (HIPC) in 1996 and then a major revision of it in 1999, creating the "Enhanced HIPC Debt Initiative" (HIPC II). How did this happen and why? I believe that the changes in process are as important as, if not more important than, the actual substantive changes that have emerged from them.

The sources of change in the debt regime lay elsewhere than in the state-to-state bargaining of the NIEO. They lay in the complex and uneven relations between some of the actors in the international debt regime (select creditor and debtor governments and the World Bank); in the activities of NGOs focused on debt, constituting what have been called principled-issue networks with their largely normative discourses and evolving capacities; and in fragments of an epistemic community of economists and other scholars who work on development issues, some of whom have played key roles as consultants and advisors to actors on both sides of the battles over debt. These three sets of actors have constituted a triple helix of relationships, of connections, which have led to important but limited innovations in the way that the international debt regime functions, helping in a fragile but important way to recapture some sovereign space for a few African governments.

The three "genetic" strands of the triple helix – the institutions of the international debt regime, the NGO debt networks, and the epistemic community – are wrapped around a central structural dilemma of the international political economy to which actors in the three strands have reacted in varying ways. The driving force for change in the governance of official debt has been the synergy between these various forms of power, knowledge, and discourse as they interacted with the underlying structural dilemma. Each of the strands has used its power, knowledge, and discourses to alter or retain the overall pattern of governance of official debt. The actors of the international debt regime reacted haltingly and unevenly as they came to the realization that something had to be done about the structural dilemma despite its lack of geostrategic importance. This realization was fostered, forced to the fore, by the networks of NGOs working on debt and development that deployed an increasingly coherent moral discourse about social purpose and equity meant to gain representation and accountability for debtors.

This NGO discourse was backed by growing social movement capabilities and progressively more sophisticated knowledge about the technicalities and functioning of the international regime for official debt. The NGOs were assisted by sympathetic fragments of the epistemic community of economists, mostly but not exclusively by those outside the institutions of the international debt regime. Some of those inside the organizations of the international debt regime accepted or were influenced by the content of the moral discourse. These and outsider economists – mostly academic – used their technical knowledge of economic theory, debt, rescheduling, and the operations of the international financial institutions to propose alternative mechanisms, norms, and practices to tackle the underlying structural dilemma of official debt. In the process, both groups of economists contributed to and were influenced by the moral discourses on debt and development of the NGOs. Loose, at first mostly informal, networked connections were established between the three strands of the triple helix. These pushed the evolution of the governance structures as the synergy between various forms of power, knowledge, and discourse interacted with the underlying structural dilemma. The triple helix of governance on official debt helped both to reproduce existing national and international structures and to alter in important ways the way they work.

A key implication of this argument is that governance on debt was shifted slowly beyond the largely state- and international financial institution (IFI)-centric strand of the international debt regime. Over time, despite the absence of major positions of structural power, the NGOs and the sympathetic fragments of the epistemic community have grown in strength and influence, resulting in a much more complex web of international governance – one rooted in the democratic nature of the world's highly industrialized states and strikingly different from the pattern of the early Bretton Woods era. But, given the power structures of the international state system and the growing power of global markets, there continue to be distinct limits to elasticity and change. Given a relatively healthy global economy and the absence of major war, such helix-like structures across a variety of issues may slowly weave a more coherent lattice-like structure of governance.

After discussing the structural dilemma of poor weak states, which is at the core of this evolving governance structure, I will sketch out the three strands of the triple helix: first, the international debt regime, second, the NGO principled-interest networks on debt, and third, the more amorphous epistemic community. I will then illustrate the ongoing evolution of "international" and "national" or "local" governance by recounting three interrelated stories and draw some implications from them. The first story relates how Uganda led the way in creating an innovative Multilateral Debt Fund to cope with its severe debt problems. The second story is the creation of a major new international initiative on poor country debt – the Heavily Indebted Poor Country Debt Initiative – in the mid-1990s. The third story is the transformation of the HIPC debt mechanism into the "Enhanced HIPC Debt Initiative" in 1999.

The structural dilemma

A central structural dilemma of our times is the emergence of a group of weak states and economies that have not been able to benefit as easily or quickly from economic reform and democratization as those elsewhere in the world. This dilemma poses major difficulties for the functioning and evolution of the international political economy and for international peace and conflict.[2]

By the early 1990s it had become increasingly clear that many of the poorest states that came before the international regime for official debt had insolvency rather than liquidity problems. This was a realization that was a long time in coming because it did not pose a major short-run threat to the stability of the world economy. It emerged first in Africa, signaled by Zaire's first rescheduling in 1976, but went largely unnoticed until the mid-1980s. By 1996 the IMF and the World Bank had designated forty-one of their members as "heavily indebted poor countries" (HIPCs) whose debt was not likely ever to be repaid in full (see Figure 6.1). The debt of these countries, mostly public or official rather than private, rose from $55 billion in 1980 to $183 billion only a decade later and to $215 billion by 1995, or more than twice their export earnings. Of the forty-one, thirty-three were from sub-Saharan Africa. Most of the HIPCs have high levels of poverty, limited domestic

---

[2] For data provided in this section, see Boote and Thugge (1997) and World Bank (1997a).

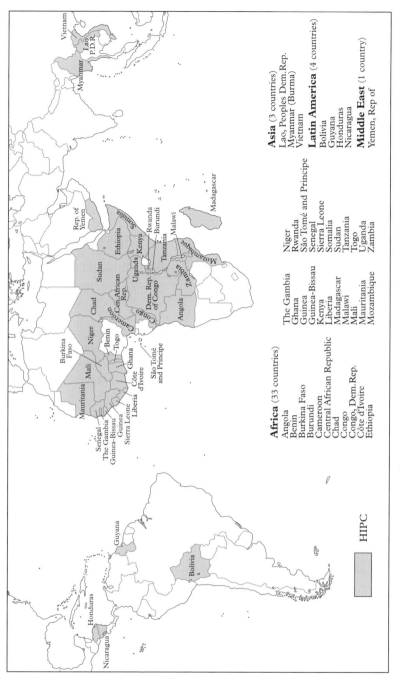

Africa (33 countries)

Angola
Benin
Burkina Faso
Burundi
Cameroon
Central African Republic
Chad
Congo
Congo, Dem.Rep.
Côte d'Ivoire
Ethiopia

The Gambia
Ghana
Guinea
Guinea-Bissau
Kenya
Liberia
Madagascar
Malawi
Mali
Mauritania
Mozambique

Niger
Rwanda
São Tomé and Principe
Senegal
Sierra Leone
Somalia
Sudan
Tanzania
Togo
Uganda
Zambia

Asia (3 countries)

Lao, Peoples Dem.Rep.
Myanmar (Burma)
Vietnam

Latin America (4 countries)

Bolivia
Guyana
Honduras
Nicaragua

Middle East (1 country)

Yemen, Rep of

Figure 6.1 The heavily indebted poor countries (HIPCs).

resources, and weak state capabilities. In effect, they come close to constituting a semi-permanent group of states on the margins of the globalizing world economy. All but six fall into the United Nations Development Program's lowest human development category. According to Oxfam, these countries are in a vicious circle of economic and social decline (Oxfam 1997).

In sharp contrast to other developing countries, the HIPCs have weak economic growth and export performance. Average gross domestic product growth for 1985–1990 was 2.2 percent and fell to only 1.0 percent for 1990–1995. In 1993, thirty-two of them had gross national product per capita figures of $695 or less, debt to exports ratios higher than 220 percent and/or debt to gross national product ratios of more than 80 percent. Over half often had annual debt service due of more than 20 percent of government revenue. The debt payments of Zambia and Nicaragua, for example, used one of every two dollars received in aid, which diverted scarce resources from both economic reform and poverty reduction. Between 1980 and 1996 all but four of the HIPCs had Paris Club reschedulings, with an average of four each and on concessional terms, including some debt forgiveness. Existing procedures clearly were not leading to sustainable debt levels. Since 1982 most middle-income debtors had improved their situations significantly enough to reenter the international capital markets. By December 1996 only four middle- and lower middle-income countries had Paris Club rescheduling agreements. At the same time, many of the HIPCs were being marginalized at a rapid rate. This is not to imply, however, that HIPCs are necessarily consigned permanently to marginalization. As we will see with Uganda, a few of them have made remarkable progress. Examples include Bolivia and Ghana and more recently war-ravaged Mozambique, which progressed despite its debt payments being more than double its combined health and education budgets (Oxfam 1997).

The causes of this structural dilemma are many and complex – external trade and other shocks, heavy reliance on primary commodities, weak formal economies and economic reform efforts, corrupt and oppressive governments with weak state capacities, civil conflict and war, environmental degradation, and disintegrating physical and social infrastructure. All of this is reinforced by limited access to private international capital flows despite the implicit bargain with the IMF and the World Bank that such access would sustain economic reform efforts. A number of these countries are failed or failing states – Somalia, Liberia, Sierra Leone, Chad, Cameroon, Central African Republic, and both Congos (Clapham 1996; Herbst 1996; Reno 1998). Others have ongoing civil strife – Rwanda, Burundi, Sudan, Uganda, and Angola. Even some HIPCs with major resources are in serious trouble – Angola and Sudan, for example. By 1999 Nigeria was no longer a HIPC, although it desperately wanted back in, insisting that this status should be part of its "democracy dividend."

The international debt regime

The international debt regime has largely been a state-centric network of governance, focused on creditor states and the IMF and World Bank, and constitutes a major phenomenon of our era, one that emerged quietly over four decades. Laws and regulations are still enforceable almost exclusively at the national level or through structures, international or otherwise, that are supported primarily by national mechanisms of agreement, constraint, and finance. These processes create flexible networks of coordination that constitute forms of cooperation and regulation based on the interaction of officials with similar concerns and often similar normative frameworks and backgrounds, and they lead to increasingly dense arrangements of largely voluntary cobinding. These official networks are not, however, free from conflict or larger configurations of power; they are largely rooted in the imposing power structures and hierarchy of the liberal capitalist democracies of the Organization for Economic Cooperation and Development (OECD). Their reach is certainly global, if not always bindingly so. From such official networks and processes emerge new ways of coping with complex problems, often without formally legislated outcomes at either the national or international levels.

The memorandum of understanding is the key operational mechanism of this form of governance. In this sense, these ongoing transnational governance networks of cooperation and response can be considered even less accountable than national structures, although legislatures, national civil societies, and NGOs are devising increasingly better forms of oversight, transparency, and accountability and are attempting to infuse them with more of a sense of global social purpose and responsibility. These official networks, with their multigovernmental core, are major arenas for the activities of both international and non-state actors, all of whom operate wherever they believe they will have the most success. They are, in effect, *transgovernance* networks, and they reflect the reach and the limits of supranational, national, and market structures.[3]

The official networks of transgovernance are increasingly populated by hybrid "intersection institutions" or structures such as the Basle Committee on Banking Supervision, the Bank for International Settlements, and the Paris Club of creditor states; the latter is a prime

---

[3] On transgovernmentalism, see Slaughter (1997).

example of the complex richness and ambiguities of transgovernance processes.

The Paris Club is a complex and powerful, yet rarely recognized hybrid international organization, one that reveals a great deal about the evolution of the international political economy and the nature of transgovernance processes.[4] It has been one of the most powerful international organizations operating over the past several decades, directly affecting the lives of millions of people, although technically it does not exist. It is not a formal organization with a charter, legislated set of rules, fixed membership, large bureaucracy, or fancy building; it is usually described as an ad hoc "forum" of creditor countries that reschedules the public and publicly guaranteed debt of "developing" states. It is far more, however, and has evolved significantly since it began operations with Argentina in 1956. A small secretariat is housed in the French Treasury, and numerous officials are assigned to its operations in the creditor countries and the key international institutions linked to it. From its modest beginnings in the late 1950s, the number and variety of reschedulings accelerated dramatically over time – 26 in 1956–1976, 150 more in 1977–1990, well over 200 by the early 1990s, and 308 by the end of 1997.

The discourse of the Paris Club has revolved around the norm that debtor countries have a moral as well as legal and material obligation to repay all debt in a timely fashion. This has been tightly linked to discussions of moral hazard that surround rescheduling and resistance to considering rescheduling as a form of aid. Such a discourse is reflected in the political culture of the Paris Club. Until the late 1980s, most of its officials viewed themselves as hardheaded debt collectors. A culture of secrecy surrounds its operation, so much so that it has been referred to by some creditor officials as "the most exclusive club" and "a Masonic Lodge." For a long time the Paris Club met at the old Majestic Hotel on avenue Kleber in Paris in its Center for International Meetings. The facts that this venerable building served as the headquarters of the Gestapo during World War II and was the site of an unsuccessful 1977 North–South conference failed to escape the notice of the debtor countries.

As a linchpin of international debt management, the Paris Club influences the prospects for social peace and development in many of the world's states – mostly middle- and low-income countries in Africa and Latin America and, more recently, in Eastern Europe and the former

---

[4] This chapter is part of an ongoing book project on the Paris Club as one lens through which to analyze the evolution of international economic governance since the mid-1950s. There is amazingly little written about the Paris Club; as examples, see Rieffel (1985), Sevigny (1990), Bakker (1996: 100–109), and Noyer (1994).

Soviet Union. The Russian Federation assumed the debts of many of its successor states, which were then rescheduled by the Paris Club. Russia received the largest Paris Club rescheduling ever in 1995, and, in October 1997, it was granted membership as a Paris Club creditor country! Two years later it was deeply in arrears and negotiating for yet another Paris Club rescheduling.

Since the late 1970s, the Paris Club has become increasingly embedded in a complex web of interactions with other important actors in the international political economy – the International Monetary Fund, the World Bank, regional development banks, UNCTAD, OECD, the Bank for International Settlements, the "London Club" (private debt rescheduling fora of international banks), the Consultative Groups (country aid consortia), investment bank advisory groups (which sometimes represent debtor countries), and, of course, the debtor governments themselves. These actors take part directly in the operations of the Paris Club or act as observers and advisors.

Debt rescheduling is one of the easiest and quickest ways to provide badly needed foreign exchange to countries in economic, social, and political trouble, but Paris Club relief is at the center of a complicated set of nested games. Rescheduling is possible only if the debtor country has economic reform programs in good standing with the IMF and the World Bank. In addition, London Club rescheduling is supposed to come only after Paris Club rescheduling, and Consultative Group aid coordination is also linked to prior Paris Club rescheduling.

While Paris Club debt relief is contingent on maintaining economic reform programs with the IMF and the World Bank, the debt owed to these "multilateral" institutions was not eligible for rescheduling. This norm was meant to protect the "preferred creditor" status of these institutions. In short, the international debt regime did not cover multilateral debt. Given the high dependence of African countries in particular on loans from the IMF, the World Bank, and to a lesser degree the African Development Bank, multilateral debt became an increasingly severe problem during the 1980s, and a seriously threatening one by the early 1990s.

The structural dilemma has been one important factor driving the evolution of the international debt regime. By the 1970s, while continuing to deal with middle-income countries, the Paris Club focused increasingly on weak states in Latin America and Africa. Such states often fell into debt service trouble quickly and did not come out of it easily because economic reform was not working well. They came back to the Paris Club repeatedly, and, as result, over time forced the Paris Club to bend, stretch, manipulate, "redefine," and even eliminate some of its rescheduling rules – in a sort of ratchet effect. One of the first norms to go, for example, although incrementally, was the one prohibiting rescheduling previously rescheduled debt.

Far from smooth, generalized, or orderly, and with very interesting politics, this evolution of norms shows the complex interplay of the varied and often shifting interests of the major creditor countries as they interact with their respective legal structures, bureaucratic cultures, and domestic politics – electoral, legislative, and special interest. It is fascinating to see how some special deals evolved into more generalized norms while others did not. The impact of these efforts on the underlying structural dilemma was minimal, however. As a result, the Western countries that form the core of the Paris Club started proposing more flexible "menus of terms" that could be applied to "severely indebted" countries – the Toronto Terms of 1988, the London Terms of 1991, the Naples Terms of 1994, and the Lyons Terms of 1996.

This complex bargaining over individual country deals fostered the creation of new understandings about the management of the international financial system and the emergence of new institutional and personal linkages and networks that facilitate everyday cooperation and coping with crises. From my work on Africa's debt problems in the 1970s (an unrecognized harbinger of things to come), I am convinced that the Paris Club's handling of these early problems of poor country debt created much of the "case" or "common law," normative consensus, appreciation of long-term consequences, social networks, and institutional linkages that made possible the swift and largely successful handling of Mexico's crisis of August 1982 which exploded the Third World debt bomb. This is but one example of a more generalized phenomenon shaping the treatment of other important international collective action problems.

State capabilities vary enormously in the international system. The structural disadvantages of the poor country debtors have been seriously aggravated by their poor state capabilities, resulting in poor performance at the Paris Club. As a result, some countries hired merchant banks and even international law and public relations firms to represent them, leading to quite varied outcomes and fascinating politics. These weak state capabilities need to be taken very seriously as level of stateness will be one of the major determinants of reconfigured global hierarchies.

NGO principled-issue networks on debt

Over the past two decades several hundred largely religious, humanitarian, labor, and environmental NGOs have focused on the issue of Third

World debt and its negative impact on the welfare of millions of people.[5] Their activities have revolved largely around a moral discourse that portrays developing country debt as an immoral burden on the backs of the poor. This discourse employs powerful notions of justice, representation, accountability, transparency, and equity. It challenges the notion of who should have authority over such issues in the global community, calls for intervention to rectify injustices and end what is considered to be blatant exploitation, and aims to provide space for debtor representation and agency in the transgovernance processes involving debt. In the process, the NGOs determine to a large degree who is empowered and who is not, who is represented and who is not.

In 1997, a loose coalition of more than fifty NGOs in Britain created the Jubilee 2000 Coalition that called for "a one-off cancellation of poor country debt by the year 2000 of the backlog of unpayable debt owed by the world's poorest countries, under a fair and transparent process" that would involve the establishment of a new international bankruptcy procedure. Characterizing this as a debt-free start to the next millennium, this network of NGOs portrayed itself explicitly as "New Abolitionists" out to abolish the "slavery of debt":

Billions of people in the world's poorest countries are enslaved by debt. Debts run up by governments on their behalf. Debts which started as easy credit pushed by rich lenders. Debts which the poor will never be able to repay. Debts which enrich lenders, but leave children malnourished, while families live in desperate poverty.

The Coalition's success will be an irreversible achievement for humanity like that of the abolition of slavery – and is particularly well suited to a Jubilee that will not occur for another 1000 years. (Jubilee 2000 1987)

The activities, capabilities, and interests of the NGOs that work on debt vary significantly, but most of them believe that IMF and World Bank structural adjustment programs are an evil that needs to be abolished. These principled-issue networks[6] have some of the characteristics of transnational social movements. Most of the network members are Northern NGOs, but increasingly they help to create, link up with, and foster Southern NGOs interested in debt. Several of the strongest Northern NGOs have a network of offices in poor countries through which they can gather information, work with local governments and social organizations, and interact with the local representatives of the IMF, the World Bank, and the major aid-providing "donor" countries, which are, of course, also the major creditors. In this context, the NGOs

---

[5] On NGOs see Simmons (1998), Clark (1991), Florini (2000), and O'Brien (2000).
[6] On principled-issue networks, see Keck and Sikkink (1998) and Finnemore and Sikkink (1998).

are parts of both translocal networks and transterritorial deployments as described by Latham in his chapter. One of the key characteristics of transterritorial deployments is their flexibility of entrance and exit. In this case, they help to create a space for debtor governments and local NGOs to operate and foster linkages to international and regional NGO networks. Because of this gate-keeping function, they have a real say in who becomes empowered and who does not.

Two of the most important NGOs on debt are Oxfam International and Eurodad – the European Network on Debt and Development, a coalition of NGOs from fifteen European countries, funded in part by the European Community. These and other NGOs, such as the Debt Crisis Network in the United States and Britain, have worked assiduously to collect and analyze information on debt and the operation of the international debt regime; educated themselves and other NGOs; demanded that the Paris Club governments and their legislatures provide greater debt relief both in general and for specific countries; lobbied hard with the IMF and the World Bank and at each of the annual G-7 summits for broader debt relief and new mechanisms for it; attended and demonstrated at the joint annual meetings of the Fund and the Bank; organized public education and letter-writing campaigns;[7] and worked closely with the media. Jubilee 2000 was specifically meant to become a social movement that enveloped these NGOs and extended their efforts. It has operated with considerable verve and kept the pressure on the IFIs and the G-7 for much more substantial debt relief. It has been backed by major celebrities, from rock stars such as Bono of U2 to heavy-hitter academics such as Harvard's Jeffrey Sachs[8] and religious leaders such as the Pope.

Coordination increased considerably over time, facilitated by growing fax, email, and Internet capabilities as well as frequent travel and network conferences such as the ones organized by Eurodad. Information and

---

[7] As I was leaving an interview, a senior British financial official said, "Please ask them to tell the nuns to stop writing; we get the point." The nuns had been writing hundreds of letters advocating much greater debt relief, and the government had to hire people to respond to them. Prior to the 1998 Birmingham G-8 meeting, the British NGO Christian Aid, in a particularly creative ploy, had printed 15,000 postcards with the photograph of the signing of the 1953 London Agreement that considerably eased the repayment of Germany's pre-war debt. The idea was to embarrass the German government into greater flexibility on debt relief. The flood of cards became such an issue that Chancellor Helmut Kohl took it up the with Prime Minister Tony Blair. At the Birmingham G-8 summit in May, Jubilee 2000 organized a human chain of thousands of people to encircle the meetings in support of large-scale debt write-offs for poor countries. These examples of debt NGO activity demonstrate the social movement aspect of the NGO networks.

[8] For a nice academic analysis, see Sachs et al. (1999).

documents collected by one organization have been shared quickly with others. Above all, as NGO capabilities and sophistication grew, personal ties based on respect if not always on agreement developed between NGO representatives and officials in creditor governments and the Fund and the Bank; this significantly improved the exchange of views on growing debt problems, especially multilateral debt. In turn, this led to significantly more influential position and briefing papers and special issue alerts from the NGOs about the functioning of the international debt regime and ongoing discussions about what to do about debt.[9]

This process facilitated the growing professionalization of the more important NGOs working on debt, which was also promoted by increasingly close relations between fragments of a large and amorphous epistemic community concerned with development, one rooted to varying degrees in neo-classical economics.

An epistemic community on debt

Mainstream economics, in its academic, business, and official varieties, provides a relatively widely shared set of understandings, language, causal and policy ideas, and technical knowledge about both the functioning of the global economy and the complex issues of development, including debt. Within this epistemic community and its various fragments, however, there exists considerable diversity of views about specific policy issues and how to tackle them.[10] Some members of this loose community dominate the structure of the institutions and processes of the international debt regime, primarily the Paris Club and its member governments, the IMF, and the World Bank. In short, they are the "insiders" of the international debt regime. Other members, who might be labeled "outsiders," those not in major positions of structural power – academic and think tank scholars, officials of "soft" international organizations such as the Commonwealth Secretariat, and private consultants – have played an important role in the ongoing debates about debt by providing

---

[9] For example, on October 17, 1995 seventeen NGO representatives met with the US executive directors of the IMF, the World Bank, and the regional development banks; and on March 17, 1997 NGO representatives met with World Bank staff specifically about Uganda's HIPC Debt Initiative situation. Eurodad even managed to organize two meetings on January 16, 1996 and February 4, 1998 with the usually secretive Paris Club staff, although the discussion remained strained and limited. Over time regular contact, both informal and formal, has increased in density and quality with the IMF and World Bank. Eurodad, Oxfam, and Jubilee 2000 participated in a seminar on "Approaches to Debt Relief" with IMF, World Bank, and Paris Club officials at the October 1998 Joint IMF–World Bank annual meeting in Washington.

[10] On epistemic communities, see Haas (1992).

independent analyses of the existing state of the debt regime and about the status of individual country cases for NGOs, creditor and debtor governments, and the international financial organizations. The individuals, and the networks they create, have often become an important bridge between actors because they are perceived to share at least the basic tenets, technical knowledge, and analytic capabilities of the larger economics epistemic community, and their input has become important as tensions in the debt regime have mounted and policy uncertainty grown. Their influence has been facilitated by the fact that key actors in the international debt regime are far from homogeneous in their views and sympathies.

An important factor in the evolution of the international debt regime has been the role played by some epistemic community members inside the major governments and international institutions that are sympathetic with the NGO discourse on debt. When conjunctural conditions permit, these "insiders" form important network connections with "outsiders" of the epistemic community and with the more sophisticated NGOs that have helped to move things along. In part they help to do this by legitimating new ideas, knowledge, and approaches in their own institutions and delegitimating existing ones (Stern 1997). As we will see, such people played pivotal roles in the triple-helix transgovernance processes in regard to the Uganda, HIPC I, and HIPC II stories.

Uganda and the international debt regime

In the early 1980s Uganda was one of the first African countries to be perceived as a failing state. To the surprise of many, however, Uganda under the remarkable leadership of Yoweri Museveni became one of the major indications of hope for Africa. Uganda engaged in a decade of vigorous economic reform efforts under the auspices of the IMF and the World Bank, with its GDP growing at an annual average of 6.4 percent. This impressive economic reform effort was achieved despite the fact that before coming to power Museveni was an avowed opponent of the IMF and structural adjustment. None the less, despite this progress, Uganda was by the mid-1990s only beginning to approach its 1971 GDP per capita income level; in fact, it was only back to 78 percent of the 1971 figure. The task accomplished is striking, and the job ahead remains enormous, now complicated by Uganda's central involvement in Africa's first major inter-state war of the post-colonial period. Uganda received considerable outside support for its effort (about $500 million a year) and earned the image of a confident, proactive, and increasingly capable player. It has garnered the respect, if not the total confidence, of the key players in the international debt regime.[11]

Between 1980 and 1995 Uganda had six Paris Club reschedulings of its bilateral debt. The last one in February 1995 was under Naples Terms, supposedly making it an "exit" rescheduling. Uganda was the first country to receive a Naples Terms rescheduling. As a result of a vigorous and creative debt-reduction strategy since 1991, its debt service ratio fell from 54 percent in 1993–1994 to 18 percent in 1996–1997. None the less, by mid-1997 its debt burden remained at $3.5 billion, equal to 62 percent of its GDP and 294 percent of its exports of goods and services. Given the high levels of resource flows from the international financial institutions to support its vigorous economic reform efforts, by 1996 roughly three-quarters of Uganda's debt was multilateral debt, which by the norms of the international debt regime was not eligible for rescheduling. By the mid-1990s, multilateral debt was one of Uganda's major problems, one central to its effort to rebuild the country and the capacities of the state.

This story is about the establishment of an innovative Ugandan Multilateral Debt Fund and the creative practices that grew out of it. The Multilateral Debt Fund resulted from network connections that were created between a core group of small European social democratic countries active as both Paris Club members and aid providers whose norms on debt and structural development were more flexible and sympathetic to reforming poor countries than those of most of the G-7 Paris Club creditors. It was a loose-knit and floating group of countries that worked together on various debt-related projects and included Sweden, Norway, Denmark, the Netherlands, Austria, and Switzerland.[12]

Supportive of more generous debt relief, this group of countries quietly provided NGOs and epistemic community consultants with information about Paris Club operations and the handling of individual debtor cases, and discussions on the state of the debt regime by the IMF, the World Bank, and the G-7 creditors. In 1991 they hired a European consultant to do a study of Uganda's debt situation and to work with the Ugandan government as an advisor on developing a coherent and comprehensive debt strategy. They supported creative efforts to strengthen Uganda's debt management capabilities and lobbied the major creditors for more generous debt relief. Given that Uganda had increasingly heavy multilateral debt service burdens (including some arrears), a number of

---

[11] This confidence has been tempered by the involvement of the Museveni government in the civil war in the Congo with the fear that it will endanger the striking economic progress made over the past decade.

[12] This section draws on confidential interviews, unpublished reports, Government of Uganda (1995), and Debt Relief International (1997).

them contributed funds to service this multilateral debt. Out of these activities and interactions with the Ugandan government emerged the idea of creating a special Multilateral Debt Fund just for Uganda to which sympathetic countries could contribute funds to service multilateral debt.

One of the innovative aspects of the proposal was that Uganda would manage the Fund itself in consultation with the donor countries, the IMF, and the World Bank. The general idea was first broached at the Consultative Group meeting on Uganda in July 1994, and after further study and preparation, it was approved at the July 1995 Consultative Group meeting.

The Consultative Group is an especially interesting mechanism of the international debt regime. It is organized under the auspices of the World Bank and brings together the countries that provide assistance to a particular developing country in order to coordinate aid flows. The donor countries are essentially the same as those of the Paris Club, but they are usually represented by officials from their aid agencies, giving the meetings a different tone than the Paris Club ones, which are clearly focused on debt collection. The point is that it is possible for creditor countries to play varying roles in the different fora of the debt regime, especially as not all of them have fully coordinated policies. More importantly, given that the Paris Club operates under a norm of consensus, which means less generous positions tend to become the norm, countries that would like to provide more bilateral debt relief in the Paris Club but are unable to do so can play a more generous role in the context of the Consultative Group.

Not all members of the Consultative Group were supportive of the proposal for the Uganda Multilateral Debt Fund (UMDF), but it was approved none the less. Neither was there substantial support from the IMF or the Paris Club secretariat. It proved to be a major success, however, and eventually all actors came to support it. The idea subsequently spread to other debtor countries, including Bolivia, Guinea-Bissau, Mozambique, and Tanzania. UMDF succeeded because it increased the ownership and management of Uganda's debt strategy by the Museveni government.

The bedrock of the success was that UMDF entailed quarterly meetings in Kampala between the Ugandans and the local representatives of the creditor/donor countries, the World Bank, and the IMF. Over time these discussions broadened to include most of the major economic reform issues. The meetings were often contentious, as the views of the parties did not always coincide, but in the process mutual respect was generated and the capacities of the Ugandan government increased substantially. At the same time, the Ugandan government maintained ties with its consultant and key NGOs both at home and overseas, and their influence on the evolution of events is clear.

The consultant, as part of the epistemic community, played an important role in establishing and maintaining connections within and between networks. He had close ties to the Commonwealth Advisory Group on Multilateral Debt, OECD policy makers, senior staff of the IMF and the World Bank, and Ugandan officials at all levels. In addition, he maintained close relations with key NGOs, especially Oxfam (both in Uganda and overseas) and Eurodad for whom he had written an influential report on what NGO debt strategy should be. Other scholars and consultants played similar if less significant roles.

Several other innovations emerged from these ongoing connections between the various networks, especially with the creation of the HIPC Debt Initiative in 1996. From the operations of UMDF came the idea of creating a social fund to act as the operational arm for using the resources saved from HIPC, laying the groundwork for important changes discussed later in this chapter. Of particular importance was a move to institutionalize the role played by the consultant and extend it to other countries. The governments of Austria, Denmark, Sweden, and Switzerland helped to create and fund an organization called Debt Relief International that helps to prepare countries for the HIPC Debt Initiative, develop debt-management strategies, and coordinate capacity-building efforts. By early 1998, Debt Relief International had started projects in eighteen countries, including non-African ones such as Bolivia and Guyana. At the same time, significantly larger innovation was underway in the international debt regime with the emergence of the HIPC Debt Initiative. This is our second story.

The rise of the HIPC Debt Initiative

The innovation of the Paris Club debt menus in the late 1980s and early 1990s was a sign that major actors of the international debt regime were beginning to recognize the existence of the underlying structural dilemma but only in relation to bilateral debt. The emergence of the menus resulted from the quiet lobbying of small European countries on their G-7 colleagues; the important leadership of Britain, Canada, and to a lesser but important degree, the United States; the persistent work of the debt-oriented NGOs in encouraging both sets of countries; and suggestions that emerged from the epistemic community on debt, both from outsiders and quietly from those inside some Paris Club governments, the World Bank, and, to a much lesser degree, the IMF. With each new menu, however, it quickly became clear that it was not adequate, and pressure would build for additional measures, but again only within the context of the Paris Club.[13]

After the onslaught of Mexico's debt crisis in 1982, many far-reaching and innovative debt proposals were made, all to no avail because they did not resonate with the major actors of the international debt regime at the time. Despite increasing recognition of a multilateral debt problem, however, most of the Paris Club countries, the IMF, and the World Bank continued to defend the preferred creditor status of the Bretton Woods institutions, in large part because they were worried about the cost of tackling the problem for a group of countries that was not as a whole perceived to have major strategic or economic importance. At the same time, the realization was growing inside the NGO networks and parts of the epistemic community that the problem of multilateral debt needed to be confronted, irrespective of cost or the absence of strategic importance, largely for developmental and normative reasons.

By 1992 the NGOs geared up their activities in regard to multilateral debt, especially with the G-7, while some of the like-minded smaller creditor countries also quietly lobbied the G-7. At the joint IMF and World Bank annual meetings in Madrid in 1994, the United States and Britain proposed that the two institutions conduct a study of multilateral debt. The issue reemerged at the spring 1995 meetings of the IMF's Interim Committee and the Bank's Development Committee, and then again at the G-7 summit in Halifax in June of that year.

While the influence of the NGOs was certainly important, larger factors had come into play, resulting in part from the nature of the structural dilemma and in part from the quiet restructuring of the major powers themselves. For Britain in particular, but also to a lesser degree for the United States and Canada, very real budget constraints were cutting into aid budgets with the prospect of not being able to support client states among the HIPC countries as the multilateral debt problem grew in importance. This was the case because structural adjustment was having only a marginal effect in many of these countries. As a result, both the Fund and the Bank were extending part of their loans to facilitate the repayment of earlier ones that were used to launch economic reform efforts. As already noted above for Uganda, some of the Paris Club countries helped as well by repaying multilateral debt. In fact, those advocating multilateral debt relief used Uganda as the primary case to illustrate the need for it.

---

[13] This section draws on confidential interviews, Boote and Thugge (1997), World Bank (1997b), (1997c), and (1998), and Oxfam (1995), (1996), and (1997).

A crucial point was reached when American banker James Wolfenshon became the ninth president of the World Bank on June 1, 1995. He was more open to the views of debtor governments and the NGOs, especially after a trip to Africa, was less worried about the financial market consequences of altering the Bank's preferred creditor status, and needed a major policy initiative to demarcate his arrival at the head of this powerful international organization. He chose debt and empowered sympathetic elements of the Bank staff to accelerate its ongoing work on a new debt initiative. Just before the joint Fund/Bank annual meeting in the fall of 1995, a Bank staff report that proposed the creation of an international Multilateral Debt Facility was leaked to the *Financial Times*. Many in the NGO community believed that the report was leaked by Bank and Fund staff opposed to the proposal. The leak had the effect of galvanizing opposition to the plan among more hard-line G-7 governments and some of their legislatures. The primary worries were cost and modality, although not always expressed in those terms. Despite earlier support for multilateral debt relief, the USA also expressed some reservations about both concerns. The Paris Club secretariat was highly suspicious of the plan, as was much of the IMF staff.[14]

The more technically capable NGOs such as Oxfam International and Eurodad made important contributions to the design of the HIPC apparatus, not always getting what they wanted but certainly making a difference as advocates of the debtor countries. In fact, it was one of the NGO consultants from the epistemic community who came up with the key compromise formula that the IMF and World Bank were to be "preferred but not exempt." Oxfam in particular had excellent access to key executive directors on the boards of both the IMF and the World Bank, to staff in each institution, and to finance ministry officials of key creditors. The same holds true for some of the academic fragments of the epistemic community interested in debt.

Planning shifted to a proposal that eventually became the complicated Rube Goldberg mechanism of the HIPC Initiative, with the Paris Club continuing to have a central role while allowing the IMF, the World Bank, and the other multilateral creditors to tackle their debt problem with the HIPC countries. The IMF was brought on board as its managing director, Michel Camdessus, eventually saw the wisdom of trying to steer the design of the mechanism rather than resist it. In addition to seeing the writing on the wall, some evidence exists that he was influenced by the arguments of the Catholic Church and its debt-focused NGOs, as well as by other religious figures. Over the previous years Pope John Paul

---

[14] On the relationship between the IMF and the World Bank, see Polak (1997).

had sent senior aides to the IMF and the World Bank to argue for debt relief. The HIPC Initiative was formally approved and announced at the September 1996 Fund/Bank joint annual meeting.

The intent of HIPC was to provide an exit from the rescheduling process by reducing debt to "sustainable" levels so that it is not an impediment to growth and poverty reduction. It was billed as a "new paradigm" for international action, despite the fact that it built on existing mechanisms in a very complicated way. It was meant only for those countries that demonstrated a strong commitment to major IMF and World Bank economic reform for at least six years and was conditioned on continued compliance with their dictates. In a complex, multistage process, the Paris Club countries would provide concessional debt relief and reduction on a case-by-case basis to eligible countries, with the IMF and the World Bank providing important formal debt relief for the first time. In fact, the HIPC apparatus shifted the center of gravity from the Paris Club toward the IMF and the World Bank because they are tasked with conducting the debt sustainability analyses central to the process. All non-Paris Club creditor countries and commercial creditors were supposed to provide comparable treatment, although how this would be achieved was not clear. With Russia now a member of the Paris Club, about $170 billion dollars of Soviet-era debt was to be brought under the HIPC umbrella. Initial estimates put the cost to the creditor countries, the IMF, and the World Bank at about $5.5 billion, with the hope that it would catalyze private financial flows and help reintegrate these countries into the global economy in productive ways. The cost would prove to be much higher, however, and the catalytic effect much lower.

Although the initiative was likely to help only about twenty countries and not quickly, it was resisted strongly from the beginning by Japan, Germany, and Italy because of concerns about cost, burden-sharing, moral hazard, and issues related to the proposed sale of IMF gold reserves; it was likewise seen to undermine the credibility of the IMF and the World Bank as enforcers of major economic reform. The United States and the IMF continued to have doubts along the way.

Uganda became the first country to enter the complicated multistaged HIPC process, but not without considerable controversy. Some actors did not want to start with Uganda precisely because its case for relief was so strong that they feared making precedent-setting changes in the delicately negotiated framework. Major battles were fought over funding and technical design with respect to Uganda. The Ugandan government lobbied effectively, in part by using its own and international NGOs to push the country's case over a wide range of issues. It freely shared data with the best of the NGOs, Oxfam International in particular, and used its epistemic contacts to great effect. It also sent a high-level delegation to Eurodad's annual conference in January 1997 and, working with the NGOs, especially Jubilee 2000, it actively used major international media to make its case. Oxfam, for example, weighed in with a hard-hitting press release:

> This decision [to delay] will hurt the poor people in Uganda. This year many children, especially girls, will not be going to school, many health clinics will go without basic medicines. The decision also sends the wrong signals to those other countries undertaking painful economic reforms. If Uganda, which is seen as the jewel in the economic reform crown, is so shoddily treated what incentive is there for other countries? (Forsyth 1997)

A Ugandan debt NGO, the Uganda Debt Network, also lobbied both in Uganda and at the global level for quick application of HIPC to Uganda.

In April 1997 Uganda became the first country approved for HIPC treatment after important battles were fought on several fronts. Uganda did not achieve everything it wanted but far more than it would have without the efforts of the NGOs and their epistemic community allies. Similar processes played out with Bolivia, Côte d'Ivoire, and, more contentiously, Mozambique. Hence, the NGOs and their epistemic community allies played a major role in affecting the design of HIPC and altering the structure and process of its implementation, and they continued to be influential with each country case as it came up, helping to defend the debtor's interests in the face of powerful larger forces. Finally, in April 1998, Uganda actually received its first HIPC debt relief. One Western diplomat praised Uganda's proactive approach in "adopting the reforms as their own and not using the IMF and World Bank as scapegoats when the going gets tough" (Reuters 1998).

Many of the rules were bent or stretched right away in order to provide more relief, some as a result of debtor and NGO pressure on specific cases, some from the creditor side as they wanted special deals for their clients (France for Côte d'Ivoire, for example). A new indicator had to be created so that Côte d'Ivoire could become one of the HIPCs eligible for relief – a debt to revenue ratio of more that 280 percent.[15] At the same time Ghana was ineligible because it had been adequately and responsibly servicing its debt, which was thus not considered unsustainable.

Serious doubts remained, however. Major NGOs, led by Oxfam and Eurodad, maintained that the Paris Club and the IMF, in particular,

---

[15] This addition of a new indicator is an example of how HIPC subtly shifted some of the debt regime's long sacrosanct norms. Within the HIPC process, countries are still treated individually, or "case-by-case," but the indicators used for debt sustainability analyses apply to all countries of the group. The new debt/revenue indicator created for Côte d'Ivoire then had to be applied to all other HIPC countries.

lacked the will to achieve serious debt relief. They claimed that IMF conditionality was much too stringent, challenged the way sustainability, vulnerability, and threshold indicators were assessed, and pointed to weak comparability mechanisms and commitments to poverty reduction. Oxfam charged the IMF and some of the major countries with systematic attempts to delay and restrict implementation, partly through data manipulation, while asserting that industrialized countries could easily afford the cost. Not all of the forty-one HIPC countries were to be eligible for HIPC relief. In fact, only about half of the original forty-one were likely to even be considered, and only seven countries had even entered the process after three years – five of them African.[16] On both the technical knowledge and moral discourse fronts, the battle for greater representation, accountability and, hence, better transgovernance would continue.

HIPC II, poverty reduction, and NGOs

The shock of the Asia crisis temporarily slowed the momentum of the debt relief movement, a fact about which African leaders were particularly bitter. Kwesi Botchwey, the architect of Ghana's mini-economic miracle, noted that the projected cost of HIPC was only "about a fifth of the resources that were mobilized in the space of a few months for bailout operations for a handful of countries as a result of the Asia crisis" (Botchwey 2000). But as a result of renewed pressure from the NGOs, spearheaded by Jubilee 2000, the World Bank in late 1998 and 1999 undertook a quite wide-ranging and intensive process of consultation and review of HIPC. Informal consultation and exchange had now become formal and institutionalized. This review involved regional meetings, including one in Africa,[17] with NGOs and debtor governments, as well as consultation via specially created web pages administered by the World Bank. At the same time, close consultations and negotiations took place among the creditor players in the debt regime.

---

[16] The seven were Bolivia, Burkina Faso, Côte d'Ivoire, Guyana, Mali, Mozambique, and Uganda: packages for Ethiopia and Guinea-Bissau were discussed but put on hold due to armed conflict (a criterion never applied to Uganda, however). Benin and Senegal were evaluated and declared to have sustainable debt.

[17] HIPC Review Seminar, July 29–30, 1999, Addis Ababa, hosted by UNECA. It was attended by twenty-one African countries, including Nigeria, Ghana, and Sierra Leone; donor countries such as Canada, the Netherlands, Switzerland, the United Kingdom, and the USA; international organizations such as the African Development Bank (ADB), IMF, World Bank, IDB, OECD, UNICEF, UNDP, and WHO; research organizations such as the Institute for Development Studies and the Overseas Development Institute; and NGOs such as Afrodad, Uganda Debt Network, Eurodad, Oxfam, Christian Aid, World Vision, Debt Relief International, and Jubilee 2000. Honduras, Russia, and the European Commission also attended the meeting.

First stage

Country establishes three-year track record of good performance and develops together with civil society a Poverty Reduction Strategy Paper (PRSP); in early cases, an interim PRSP may be sufficient to reach the decision point.

- Paris Club provides flow rescheduling as per current Naples terms, i.e. rescheduling of debt service on eligible debt falling due during the three-year consolidation period (up to 67 percent reduction on eligible maturities on a net present value basis).
- Other bilateral and commercial creditors provide at least comparable treatment.
- Multilateral Institutions continue to provide support within the framework of a comprehensive poverty reduction strategy designed by governments, with broad participation of civil society and donor community.

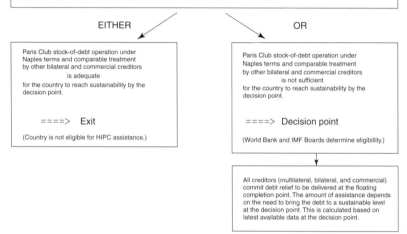

EITHER   OR

Paris Club stock-of-debt operation under Naples terms and comparable treatment by other bilateral and commercial creditors
is adequate
for the country to reach sustainability by the decision point.

====> Exit

(Country is not eligible for HIPC assistance.)

Paris Club stock-of-debt operation under Naples terms and comparable treatment by other bilateral and commercial creditors
is not sufficient
for the country to reach sustainability by the decision point.

====> Decision point

(World Bank and IMF Boards determine eligibillity.)

All creditors (multilateral, bilateral, and commercial) commit debt relief to be delivered at the floating completion point. The amount of assistance depends on the need to bring the debt to a sustainable level at the decision point. This is calculated based on latest available data at the decision point.

Second stage

Country establishes a second track record by implementing the policies determined at the decision point (which are triggers to reaching the floating completion point) and linked to the (interim) PRSP.

- World Bank and IMF provide interim assistance.
- Other multilateral and bilateral creditors and donors provide interim debt relief at their discretion.
- All creditors continue to provide support within the framework of a comprehensive poverty reduction strategy designed by governments, with broad participation of civil society and donor community.

"Floating" completion point

- Timing of completion point is tied to the implemention of policies determined at the decision point.
- All creditors provide the assistance determined at the decision point; interim debt relief provided between decision and completion points counts towards this assistance:
  - Paris Club goes beyond Naples terms to provide more concessional debt reduction of up to 90 percent in NPV terms (and if needed even higher) on eligible debt so as to achieve an exit from unsustainable debt.
  - Other bilateral and commercial creditors provide at least comparable treatment on stock of debt.
  - Multilateral institutions take additional measures, as may be needed, for the country's debt to be reduced to a sustainable level, each choosing from a menu of options, and ensuring broad and equitable participation by all creditors involved.

Source: World Bank

Figure 6.2 HIPC Debt Initiative: flow chart.

Out of this process came HIPC II in September 1999 (see Figure 6.2).[18] Almost everybody took credit for it, of course, including the major creditor countries. US Treasury officials asserted that the United States led the effort to redesign HIPC, claiming that the USA got everything it wanted. That may be so, but it got things that it had not wanted even two years earlier.

HIPC II was meant to be "enhanced" – bigger, better, and faster. Four key debt sustainability ratios were altered, the timeframe became more flexible, additional types and levels of relief were instituted, and the process streamlined to make it work faster. The World Bank claimed that it would cost about $30 billion, possibly more, and that it would cut in half the approximately $90 billion in public debt of the thirty-three HIPC counties it considered likely to qualify for relief. Many actors had doubts, however. Funding was not ensured even for the first couple of years,[19] the amount of increased debt relief remained questionable, and the NGOs and debtors worried about the issue of "additionality" – that is, whether debt relief would be in addition to all other assistance and not just another version of it at the same level. While loosened somewhat, major conditionality remained. In fact, despite their longstanding opposition to it, the NGOs ended up creating new forms of conditionality, but this time it was their type of conditionality.

One significant change incorporated in HIPC II is that all HIPC debt relief is now to be tied directly to poverty reduction. This is to be ensured by the creation of Poverty Reduction Strategy Papers (PRSPs) put together by debtor countries *in consultation with civil society groups*. IMF and World Bank adjustment lending programs are to be formulated only after these efforts have been taken into account. The PRSP process will be very demanding. The IMF notes that "these strategies must be genuinely country-owned and reflect the outcome of an open participatory process involving governments, civil society, and relevant international institutions and donors" (IMF 1999). An elaborate process of consultation is being developed for the PRSPs.

If seriously implemented, this new process could be an important change in international governance on debt, aid, and development more generally and may have major implications for the unfolding of democratization processes in Africa and elsewhere. In addition, it has the potential to be a major avenue for enhancing state capacity and legitimacy. A report by

---

[18] For the most current information on the status of HIPC II, see http://www.worldbank.org/hipc/.

[19] The cost was to be split about half and half between bilateral and multilateral sources, although there was much fighting and finger pointing about this. Burden sharing had been a very contentious issue right from the beginning of HIPC.

a leading NGO was, uncharacteristically, almost giddy about the possibilities:

The IMF and World Bank have now agreed to provide assistance to countries within a framework whereby countries will, through a process of consultation with civil society, the private sector and external donors, develop their own poverty reduction strategies. This could become a *turning point* in the way these institutions and the wider aid community support development. Poverty reduction is intended to be "front and center" of all IMF/World Bank operations, including macroeconomic policies.

These changes could mean that civil society becomes truly engaged in the design of national policy. It could mean that the existing economic paradigm would be debated openly in poor countries, with the potential impacts on the poor, both positive and negative, discussed and addressed. Clearly there are difficulties with this new approach. Some governments may not want to open up and may want to continue a closed system with the Bank and the Fund.

For the first time, it could be that policy design will not be done in Washington or by a few Ministry of Finance officials, but openly in the country concerned. ... The changes therefore offer major opportunities to civil society in developing countries, and their partners in the North, to address this agenda and to hold both institutions, and governments, to account. (Oxfam 1999)

The NGOs quite properly see the changes incorporated into HIPC II as major victories with implications far beyond debt relief for poor countries. These victories are part of a larger ongoing process of making the IFIs more transparent and accountable, resulting from a combination of discourse, networks, expertise, bargaining, and pressure. The NGO networks have thus become an important new part of international economic governance. They are, however, aware that this process could go astray. As a result, the NGOs have made it very clear they will be vigilant and protective of their newly won gains: "Finally, powerful governments and the Boards of the Bank and the Fund are aware that Jubilee 2000 and civil society organizations around the world are watching these developments and will raise havoc if these changes are not implemented seriously" (Oxfam 1999). And after Seattle, they believed this threat to be much more credible, especially since the social movement capabilities of the NGOs have grown significantly. The NGOs sought to prove this with their A16 or "Mobilization for Global Justice" mass direct action campaign at the IMF/World Bank spring meetings in Washington, DC, April 8–17, 2000, using the slogan "De-Fund the Fund! Break the Bank! Dump the Debt" and then again at the annual meetings in Prague in October.

In fact, the NGOs may be correct. "The battle for Seattle" may have been both a substantive and symbolic turning point. The social and political weight and influence, via both public and private channels, of the NGOs and their related social movements have reached a maturation point that has been building for about twenty years such that they can hold the feet of the major players to the fire. This is achieved not by the state-to-state bargaining of the NIEO era, but rather by taking the politics of this and other issues inside the political arena of the major industrial democracies. Does this mean, as some have grandiosely claimed, that a "global civil society" has emerged? No, far from it, if for no other reason than that it is still mostly a "Northern" phenomenon, although "Southern" NGOs are growing rapidly in number and capabilities. None the less, something basic has changed.

Major actors on the creditor side have, often with gritted teeth, praised the role of the NGOs while trying to co-opt them via consultation or deflect them. It is not at all clear who is being co-opted, however. US Treasury Secretary Larry Summers commented on how "grateful we are to the many committed NGOs and others in the development community who have kept debt relief high on the international agenda this year and helped to generate the political will for action ... Thanks in large part to the efforts of the Jubilee 2000 coalition, the advent of the millennium has given us an historic opportunity to accelerate these efforts, and help these countries finally build an attractive environment for private investment and market-led growth" (Summers 1999). Referring to the fragile nature of HIPC II, especially given inadequate funding, the IMF's Michel Camdessus noted that "it shows us above all, how fragile our collective commitments are, and how small the chances that they will be fulfilled without a universal mobilization of public opinion, as has been the case with Jubilee 2000" (Camdessus 1999).

One World Bank official put it more directly. After acknowledging that the NGOs in Jubilee 2000 have provoked a necessary and healthy debate and played a critical role in forcing a discussion in industrialized countries on debt, he noted that "we are continuously being monitored and told what needs to be improved. Groups have proposed different ways to ensure that countries channel the savings from debt relief into social programs. And other groups have asked that projects financed with debt relief, as well as new lending, be closely monitored to avoid mistakes of the past" (Van Trottenberg 1999). The NGOs, of course, give themselves much of the credit. Oxfam, for example, has claimed that "without such visible public pressure, politicians in the G7 and other countries would not have given HIPC reform the impetus required; and without strong advocacy from a wide range of NGOs and other actors, policy makers would not have been pushed into improving mechanisms with such strong linkages to poverty reduction" (Oxfam 1999). This assertion is largely correct.

The NGOs sense that they are caught in a dilemma of their own creation – the tension between the need for swift debt relief and the newly won imperative of consultation with civil society. Their main response is that extensive civil society capacity-building efforts are needed, and they want the IFIs and the donors to pay for it, while they help provide it. Despite their longstanding opposition to structural adjustment and conditionality, they are now very much part of the process. For their part, many African countries see an even longer structural adjustment laundry list and a much more complicated, and politically sensitive, process. African leaders wondered what they were to do if the PRSP consultation process led to demands for the return of subsidized food, health, transportation, and educational programs as part of a poverty reduction strategy! President Chiluba of Zambia said, "Then we were told, no, no, no, Africa needs to embrace the spirit of partnership with NGOs but the NGOs where I come from, ZCTU [Zambian Confederation of Trade Unions] also wants increased wages. And then the IMF says do not give them, we do not know which way to go" (Saluseki 2000). In fact, in October 2000, a complex Jubilee 2000-led bipartisan coalition, which included major business support, convinced the US Congress to fully fund the US contribution to HIPC, grant approval to use IMF gold proceeds to fund it, *and* declare its opposition to the imposition of user fees for basic healthcare and education in structural adjustment programs for poor countries. The latter is to be enforced by the Treasury and US representatives to the IMF and World Bank.

For savvy governments that already have experience and have developed state capacities in this area, such as Ghana and Uganda, the new HIPC process offers real opportunities; for others, this is far less clear. Many hope that the PRSP process will strengthen democratization and state capacity-building efforts, but actors of all types are skeptical. For the IFIs and the creditor countries, this process also quietly shifts important responsibility to the international and African NGO community, which should generate some of the local representation–governance tensions discussed by Kassimir in his chapter.

On the donor side the hope is that this process will build legitimacy and "ownership" of structural adjustment programs without cutting the heart out of them. This will be difficult to accomplish. Expectations have been raised very high by HIPC II, and there is plenty of room for failed expectations. The PRSP process in its grandest form could be viewed as a somewhat meager attempt by creditor countries to extend their own "compromise of embedded liberalism" to the poorest countries of the world, based on a relatively small "pot of gold."[20] The longer-run question is how the partial extension of embedded liberalism might be financed. The major creditors are having trouble financing HIPC II. The political fact is, however, that the NGOs have won the battle over HIPC debt savings; they are to go exclusively to "poverty reduction." The primary focus of key NGOs and some debtor governments has been on health and education, with a secondary emphasis on rural and other infrastructure. In addition to HIPC, a number of creditor countries, including the USA, Britain, France, Germany, and Italy, have taken steps to write off significant amounts of bilateral concessional debt.

HIPC is not a magic bullet; it is important for a number of countries but very far from turning African and other poor countries around.[21] For some countries, such as Uganda, the benefits will be real and supportive. As with HIPC I, Uganda was the first country to benefit from HIPC II. It will receive debt relief of about $55 million annually over the next thirty years under HIPC II in addition to the $45 million annual relief agreed under HIPC I. At a Consultative Group meeting in March 2001, donors pledged about $2.5 billion over the following three years for poverty reduction under Uganda's new Poverty Eradication Action Plan (PEAP). At the same time, they criticized official corruption as well as Uganda's involvement in the war in the Congo.

The Uganda Debt Network continued to grow and increase its capabilities. By 2000 it had more than sixty members as well as strong ties to the Uganda Joint Christian Council and business, student, and labor organizations. The Catholic Church gave it particularly strong support. The Network held several campaigns in Uganda to raise the level of awareness about debt relief, as well as participating in Jubilee 2000's international activities, especially lobbying about the HIPC II treatment of Uganda. It launched a major anticorruption drive to make sure debt savings are used properly and lobbied parliament about future debt levels. Above all, however, it was becoming very active in coordinating civil society participation in the PRSP process, which it was doing with the help of Northern NGOs. Lastly, it had improved its own organizational capabilities and was running it own independent website.[22]

---

[20] Embedded liberalism is the notion that industrial democracies have long handled the processes of economic adjustment, especially to external change, by buffering the social and political costs of adjustment in ways not congruent with neo-liberal economic doctrine and that they have preached the latter to developing countries while doing the former. See Ruggie (1982).

[21] For a good analysis of the limits of HIPC II, see General Accounting Office (2000). To see the current status of HIPC, see the IMF and World Bank HIPC websites at http://www.imf.org/external/np/hipc/hipc/htm and http://www.worldbank.org/hipc/.

[22] For a good look at the activities of the Uganda Debt Network, see its fine website at http://www.udn.or.ug.

In April 1998 Jubilee 2000 helped to form Jubilee 2000 Afrika in Accra, Ghana, as a regional coordinating body for debt campaign work in Africa. By late 2000, Jubilee 2000 had campaigns in more than twenty African countries, with active organizations in at least fourteen of them. Many of these were based on existing local NGOs, such as the Jesuit Centre for Theological Reflection in Zambia, which in 1998 joined with the Zambian Catholic Commission for Justice and Peace to launch a debt campaign: the Jubilee 2000–Zambia campaign. By early 2000 the main focus of this campaign was on making the PRSP process operate in an open, accountable, and effective manner. It worked to build the capacity of civil society groups to take part in the process and helped to coordinate it. As with the Uganda Debt Network, Jubilee 2000–Zambia ran its own website and had its own international and regional ties. In February 2000 it held a national conference on debt and proposed a Zambian Debt Mechanism to ensure that all debt relief goes to poverty reduction. The group's coordinator summed it up succinctly: "Jubilee 2000–Zambia has come a long way in a short time. A silly idea, a crazy dream. But now the reality! Please keep giving us your hard work and dedication – we have a long ways to go yet. But we are moving and the goal – poverty reduction in a society of greater justice – is too great to be slow about" (Jubilee 2000–Zambia 2000).

Similar strong efforts exist in Mozambique, Tanzania, and elsewhere. In short, African NGO work on debt was sinking real roots and moving beyond the confines of campaigning for debt relief, facilitated by the victory of the international NGOs on the issue of debt relief and poverty reduction. They were beginning to take on viable social movement characteristics. In addition, it was already possible to find situations where African and international NGOs did not completely agree on how debt savings should be applied to poverty reduction in particular countries and where African NGOs were influencing the views of the international NGOs on other matters.

Unforeseen events can get in the way, however. Although excluded from HIPC I because it was servicing its debt, Ghana was included in HIPC II and should have been next in line after Uganda. It was not to be, despite Ghana's expectation of obtaining much-deserved early relief. Japan announced that any country that took advantage of HIPC II debt relief would forgo any further concessional aid from it. Japan is Ghana's biggest donor country. As a result, one of Africa's two star economic reformers "voluntarily" withdrew from HIPC II. As Kwesi Botchwey, the architect and contractor of Ghana's impressive economic reform effort, laments with understatement, "It is worth noting that Japan's decision to make countries, notably Ghana, choose between HIPC relief and continued Japanese assistance is an unfortunate development." He adds that "Ghana has in fact opted out of the HIPC Initiative for this reason, although it is by no means clear that this is in its best long-term interest" (Botchwey 2000).[23]

Uganda is a case in which a proactive African response to decline created halfway houses of representation and capacity building via better transgovernance. Unlike other types of networks discussed in this volume, there is nothing very shadowy about the networks and connections that helped to achieve this result. They have helped to make Museveni's Uganda stronger while increasing creditor country and international financial institution accountability by intensifying global–local interactions. Uganda succeeded because it was perceived by the major actors in the debt regime to be doing what was expected of it. Without Uganda's decade of impressive economic reform, it would not have been able both to make changes in the debt regime and to benefit from them. In many ways, it is still a self-help world as international relations theorists have so long asserted. With its proactive behavior and the help of other actors, Uganda has been able to grab back some sovereignty and capacity, while increasing its legitimacy. In the current African context, this is no mean feat.

In sum, Africa has been central to the evolution of the international regime on public debt, although not its primary driving force. New actors and processes have been unleashed in response to Africa's plight that might significantly alter the way the larger development regime functions. In the long run, the most significant changes may well not be HIPC itself, but rather the new processes and transboundary formations that it has helped to unleash.

Conclusion

In discussing networks, moral discourse, and history, Fred Cooper (1998) shows "both the possibility of mobilization across borders, across conceptual frameworks, across interests, and the possibility that discourses can be changed." Within the domain of international debt, I have tried to show that this is possible. By using the notion of a triple helix of transgovernance regarding debt, I have also attempted to show what Cooper notes is harder to think about:

[23] Ghana made the decision hastily and without running net resource flow calculations because it was dealing with a major crisis with Ashanti Goldfields. Mozambique, on the other hand, made the decision to stay with HIPC and do without Japanese assistance. Other major donors did not place much pressure on Japan to change its position, hesitating to rock the boat, given what they considered to be more important cross-cutting issues. Personal communication from Kwesi Botchwey, March 25, 2000.

how one connects the different elements of the picture: structures (such as states), networks (such as the antislavery movement), and discourses (free labor ideology, anticolonialism, panAfricanism)... What structures? Within what limits? By the power of whose voices, via the workings of what mechanisms? And how do new networks, new discourses, new structures channel possibilities for action in particular ways, while excluding other possibilities? (Cooper 1998: 10)

As characterized in this volume,[24] there are three dimensions within which transboundary formations take form – international arenas, translocal networks, and transterritorial deployments. The interwoven strands of the debt triple helix are part of a very complicated transboundary formation in which three fields of action and meaning become intertwined in intricate ways creating a new "genetic" form of transnational governance. These fields have not just bumped up against each other, but rather they have become tightly linked in a variety of ways.

Similar helix-like structures exist for other issues and are likely to become a more common and influential form in the global realm. NGO translocal networks, for example, have expanded their reach from human rights to the environment to security issues such as landmines and now to more technical issues of development and economics revolving around structural adjustment. The debt triple helix and others like it are making the global realm more robust without necessarily making the major states or international organizations of the international system less consequential. The international debt regime strand of the triple helix is by far the "thickest" – has the widest amplitude of practices and discourses – of the three. The other two strands are "thinner," with the epistemic one much more so, but both of them are growing and central to this transboundary formation.

The argument here is that in conjunction with elements of an epistemic community, the NGO translocal networks have shaped the amplitude and sway of the international debt regime in important ways. The triple helix has powerfully affected the way a number of African and other states function; it has intervened in the day-to-day operation of these states in very detailed ways. In their interaction with the international debt regime, the epistemic and NGO strands of the triple helix have helped to create new forms of governance at both the national and international levels.

The international debt regime strand of the triple helix can be characterized as an international arena. With its widely amplified norms and discourses, it constitutes an international public sphere made up primarily of states and international financial institutions. The epistemic community

[24] See Robert Latham's chapter in this volume.

and the NGO principled-issue network strands are most akin to translocal networks. Yet both the international debt regime and the NGO networks have transterritorial deployment aspects as well. The IMF, the World Bank, and Western aid agencies often have transterritorial deployments in African countries. So do some of the bigger development NGOs that are part of the debt translocal networks, for example, Oxfam, Bread for the World, and Catholic Relief Services. As Jubilee 2000 has made an effort to extend its campaign into Africa and other parts of the developing world, it has linked up with local NGOs and societal groups or created its own transterritorial deployments from scratch. The degree of externality, scope, and sway of these deployments is constantly being negotiated in complex ways.[25] The hope of the international NGOs is that these territorial deployments will become central to African national governance both on debt and increasingly on wider development issues such as reducing poverty via the PRSP process, attacking corruption, and making governments more transparent and accountable. At the same time, it is hoped that they will become more autonomous nodes in the international NGO debt networks, making direct contributions of their own to the evolution of the debt transboundary formation.

These transterritorial deployments have become hinges that join international and local forces and discourses. NGO transterritorial deployments have much less scope and sway than those of the IMF, the World Bank, and the aid missions of the major powers, but they are attempting, with some success, to increase their influence while turning their local presence into a more permanent one. In addition, connections grow between the transterritorial deployments of all of these institutions and between them and the African states and societies in which they operate. International NGOs try to create transterritorial deployments and strengthen existing local NGOs while retaining the flexibility to operate differently or withdraw if they so choose. With their particular combination of vulnerability and power, they also, of course, always run the risk of being forced out if they tread too heavily with national governments on issues related to debt such as corruption, transparency, and accountability. The international NGOs that work on debt have deployed themselves as translocal networks and transterritorial deployments, but they have also deployed themselves as an increasingly effective and global social movement. In the process, they have changed the rules and discourse of the debt regime, increased resource flows, brought about new forms of international and local governance via HIPC and the PRSP process, and

---

[25] See Ron Kassimir's chapter in this volume.

created or strengthened local NGOs. In short, they have reshaped the forms and process of intervention.

Given the complexities and power structures of the current international system, reform usually comes slowly. Very little came of all the heat and rhetoric of the efforts of developing states in the 1970s and 1980s to set binding, generalizable rules for a New International Economic Order and very little may come from all of the recent discussion of a grand "New Financial Architecture." Resulting from the complex interactions of the debt triple helix, the Uganda Multilateral Debt Fund, HIPC I, and HIPC II are innovative extensions of the transgovernmental Paris Club mechanism. The Paris Club evolved slowly in the 1960s and 1970s without the influence of NGO principled-issue networks or an epistemic community. Beginning with the explosion of the Third World debt bomb in 1982, these other two strands of the triple helix came increasingly into play. In their more highly organized forms, both of these strands are relatively recent additions to the way the international system operates. Yet while the functioning of the triple helix reminds us that states are not the only consequential units, they remain powerful actors. In this sense, the triple helix of interactions helped both to reproduce existing national and international structures and to alter the way they work.

A key lesson of this chapter's stories is that it is important to disaggregate actors and actor types. Not all creditor countries resisted more debt relief, and some of those that did, did not do it all the time; sometimes they changed their minds. Over time the two major Bretton Woods institutions had quite varied views and played quite different roles in regard to debt issues. Not all NGOs supported HIPC I and HIPC II; many have refused to support them because of the very tight link to the often harsh and intrusive conditionalities of structural adjustment. Another lesson is that the NGOs with the best understanding of the international debt regime and the economics epistemic community were able to bring about the most change.

What are the prospects for more dramatic change? Discourses have the most impact when they resonate with important parts of an existing context, and in a compatible language, even though they challenge other parts of it in major ways. Like institutions, discourses have varying capabilities, varying resonance at any given time. This is not to say, as Cooper nicely reminds us, that major perceptual change brought about by discourse struggle is impossible. As with the nineteenth-century anti-slavery movement, it is possible that industrial democracy leadership and public opinion could change to such a degree that the type of broad debt cancellation advocated by the Jubilee 2000 campaign might come about at some point. In the meantime, efforts like it continue to increase pressure on key actors to accelerate the evolution of HIPC.

An illustrative effort to shift the discourse on debt came in 1998 when Pope John Paul issued a major Papal Bull entitled "Incarnationis Mysterium" ("The Mystery of the Incarnation") which argued that wealthy countries should relieve the debts of poor ones as acts of charity as the world enters Christianity's third millennium. The Pope noted that "Some nations, especially the poor ones, are oppressed by a debt so huge that repayment is practically impossible. It is clear, therefore, that there can be no real progress without effective cooperation between the peoples of every language, race, nationality, and religion." He called for a new culture of international solidarity and cooperation "where all – particularly the wealthy nations and the private sector – accept responsibility for an economic model which serves everyone," noting that it is no longer tolerable that a poor man should be forced to feed on the scraps that had fallen off the banquet table of a rich man (Pullella 1998). At the time of the Prague IMF/World Bank meetings in October 2000, the Pope was very critical of the slow progress in implementing HIPC II. It is interesting that in August, Michel Camdessus, who had stepped down as managing director of the IMF in February after being elected for an unprecedented third term, joined the Vatican's Pontifical Council for Justice and Peace, which has taken a central role in the debt relief campaign. An Oxfam spokesperson noted that "until recently, one would not have mentioned Mr. Camdessus and the Pope in the same sentence. But during his last few months at the fund, Mr. Camdessus began to speak the same language as the Pope about debt relief." The spokesperson went on to comment that "no one asks why Paul did not have his conversion earlier than on the road to Damascus – they are just pleased that he had it" (Beattie 2000).

7 When networks blind: human rights and politics in Kenya

Hans Peter Schmitz

The tremendous growth of the non-governmental sector both in the Western and Southern world has lately also led to an increasing academic interest in the subject matter.[1] In the human rights area, a sizable literature has emerged which identified international and domestic human rights groups and their networking activities as an increasingly influential factor for regime change (see Brysk 1993; Risse et al. 1999; Schmitz and Sikkink 2001; Smith et al. 1997).[2] In particular, this literature highlights strategies on the part of those actors that aim at building direct connections between the local and the international level (see Keck and Sikkink 1998). These actions tell previously untold stories and represent attempts to connect what is traditionally separated by "Westphalian sovereignty" (Krasner 1999: 20–25) and the norm of non-intervention in internal affairs. Challenges to the status quo presuppose the emergence of alternative networks and discourses. The emergence of such transboundary formations in the non-governmental realm makes "extraversion" (Bayart 1993) a viable strategy not only for state leaders but also for their challengers. During the 1980s, international human rights organizations, but also Western states and international organizations, have increasingly taken up such requests for support and supplemented pressure from below with pressure from above. In the Kenyan case this has forced the regime under attack to adopt an introverted strategy of mobilizing its own domestic support.

---

[1] For insightful comments I would like to thank the participants of two workshops at the European University Institute in Florence, Italy (March 28–29, 1998) and at the University of Pennsylvania in Philadelphia, USA (December 5–6, 1998) as well as the three editors and two anonymous reviewers. This chapter represents my continued research on the role of human rights organizations in East Africa. While I explore in greater detail in an earlier work (Schmitz 1999) the transforming potential of such activism, I emphasize here some of its ambivalent long-term effects as well as the counter-strategies developed by repressive regimes.

[2] Others have highlighted the influence of such transnational networks with regard to global environmental and security issues. See Price (1998); Wapner (1995); Zürn (1998).

149

While the named literature has been successful in putting such transnational human rights networks on the research agenda of scholars in international relations and comparative politics, there is still little reliable knowledge on the long-term effects of their activities. In this contribution, I will suggest ways of understanding such effects by comparing the role of transnational human rights networks prior to and after the reintroduction of multipartyism in Kenya in late 1991. First, I argue that during the 1980s the domestic opposition to authoritarian rule successfully relied on international contacts for its very survival and the creation of alternative forms of authority. These contacts not only protected a number of individual human rights activists from serious harm but transformed the entire composition of the domestic opposition movement. The transnational mobilization in the late 1980s and early 1990s crucially contributed to the "remapping" (Brysk 1993: 268) of Kenya's image abroad and the donor decision in November 1991 to temporarily cut aid. However, the subsequent (re-)introduction of multipartyism offered new opportunities for the Moi regime to control the political playing field.

Second, I argue that during the subsequent period of protracted (and still ongoing) regime transition transnational human rights actors and their domestic allies have fallen significantly short with regard to translating their authority into the creation of a new, more democratic order. While the main reason for this development is a recalcitrant authoritarian regime, I argue that transboundary formations such as transnational human rights networks can have ambiguous long-term effects on domestic regime change. Not only do they offer protection and support; under certain conditions they create "blind spots" for dialog and compromise. While the international contacts remained in the 1990s an important safeguard for human rights actors, *long-term* and sometimes even *exclusive* reliance on such networks with the outside world constrained actors in the domestic political struggle for political reforms. International contacts in the form of "vertical networking" cannot substitute for the development of a solid domestic political following and successful "horizontal networking" simply because international actors are not a reliable constituency in Kenyan national affairs.

The main reason for the ambiguity of human rights mobilization in the Kenyan case is an ethnically divided civil society.[3] Although the expansion of the civil society sector after 1991 also led to intensified horizontal networking, these networks tended to be ethnically biased. Hence, they often simply added international voices to their political demands without broadening beyond their narrow ethnic boundaries. At the same

---

[3] For a similar concern for ethnicity see Ndegwa (1997).

time, this led to continued hostility from the regime and its supporters. The challenge to authoritarian rule in the 1980s was successful when a marginalized ethnic coalition began to seek the outside support of juridical institutions such as internationally recognized human rights norms. In the 1990s, the authoritarian regime answered this challenge by going in the opposite direction and resorting mainly to non-state and non-juridical means in mobilizing its own ethnic base. After losing donor confidence and battling the label of a "pariah state," the regime's preferred strategy of the 1990s became introversion. Both sides' efforts, combined with declining aid levels, have contributed to a weakening of the state as a repressive tool, and also as a potential guarantor of human rights.

Vertical and horizontal networking as forms of social action

Emirbayer and Goodwin commended the network literature for offering a "new mode of structuralist inquiry" that goes beyond traditional structural accounts with their sole emphasis on categorical attributes of individual and collective actors (1994: 1413). Network analysis moves structuralism beyond a concern for the position of actors toward the recognition of dynamic modes of interaction between participants: "From the network point of view, analytical approaches that direct attention to the 'intrinsic characteristics,' 'essences,' attributes, or goals of individuals, as opposed to their patterned and structured interrelationships, are all inherently suspect" (p. 1416). In the Kenyan example, I show for the 1980s how a transnational human rights network constituted and strengthened domestic actors whose authority increased not merely because of their essential attributes (e.g. lawyer or church representative), but because they chose to be part of a particular transboundary formation. In the 1990s the authoritarian regime countered this attack not only by exploiting the formal (but dwindling) state resources it controlled, but also by mobilizing its own informal network of ethnic support.

In order to establish a network perspective as a viable alternative to other forms of social inquiry, earlier scholarship overemphasized the role of "empty" formal network relations at the expense of the "causal role of ideals, beliefs, and values, and of actors that strive to realize them" (Emirbayer and Goodwin 1994: 1446). There is no necessary trade-off between a sophisticated analysis of the social structure in a network perspective and an equally refined recognition of agency and (non-)material conditions. Emirbayer and Goodwin are correct in maintaining that any explanation of an actor's behavior in a network perspective has to analytically separate the social structure (network) from the equally important "cultural structure" (e.g. norms and symbols) (p. 1439). Cooper in this volume refers to this "as the crucial intersection of structures, networks, and discourses."

A basic distinction between vertical and horizontal networking as forms of social action represents a valuable addition to recent scholarship on regime change in Africa (comparative politics) and the role of norm-promoting transnational advocacy networks (international relations theory). While the scholarship on regime transitions still tends to under-estimate the role of transboundary links (see the introduction to this volume), the research on transnational advocacy networks focused mainly on the role of vertical connections in supplementing or substituting domestic horizontal networks. This contribution takes emerging transboundary interactions seriously without neglecting the continued importance of domestic politics in processes of regime change. I argue here that the interaction between different modes of social action expressed in horizontal and vertical networking activities on the part of regime opponents but also supporters can help to explain the direction of political transitions. While vertical networking through transnational human rights networks was successful in establishing alternative forms of authority on the domestic level, it inhibited the emergence of more inclusive horizontal networks expressed in a non-violent civil society as a basis for a new and more democratic political order.

Establishing alternative sources of authority, 1984 to 1991

At the time of Kenyan political independence, two parties, the Kenya African National Union (KANU) and the Kenya African Democratic Union (KADU), competed for national power. While KANU represented the interests of the larger ethnic groups (mainly Kikuyu and Luo), KADU was formed as a coalition of smaller, pastoral groups (mainly Kalenjin and Maasai) to counterbalance the threat of an imminent dominance by larger tribes. Supported by British settlers, KADU strongly advocated federalist ideas (*majimbo*) in order to protect the independence of the smaller ethnicities. Shortly after the electoral victory of KANU in the first post-independence elections in 1964, KADU dissolved and its leadership crossed over to KANU. The result was the emergence of a *de facto* one-party system led by the first independence president, Jomo Kenyatta. Subsequently, one of the former KADU leaders, Daniel arap Moi, was named vice-president. Until Kenyatta's death in 1978, the country's political system was stable compared with those of most of its neighbors and the executive tolerated a "semi-competitive" (Barkan 1992: 168) process within the KANU ruling party. None the less, fundamental political opposition was repressed and human rights abuses for political reasons had been on record since the early 1970s. The situation worsened when the vice-president, Daniel arap Moi, succeeded Kenyatta and began to consolidate his domestic power position against the still powerful Kenyatta cronies (see Karimi and Ochieng 1980; Schatzberg 1987). The significance of this power shift became apparent when Moi began to expand the security apparatus and slowly replaced Kikuyu and Luo within the ruling elite with his own loyal (and former KADU) followers.

After an unsuccessful coup by air force officers on August 1, 1982, Moi took increasingly repressive measures to suppress the political opposition (see Howard 1991).[4] He used KANU as an instrument to sharply increase the executive control over parliament, the judiciary, and society at large (see African Rights 1996; Kibwana 1992; Widner 1992). The government justified its repressive measures by claiming that radical opponents of the regime had gone underground and formed the clandestine organization *MwaKenya*. In particular, members of the country's universities became targets of the state security forces. University lecturers, students, and other alleged opposition members were regularly arrested and tortured in the infamous Nyayo House in downtown Nairobi (see "Arrest and Detention in Kenya" 1987).[5]

As a result of the domestic repression, the Kenyan opposition sought protection and assistance from the outside world and began to engage in vertical networking. Amnesty International and other transnational human rights organizations began to expose the pattern of abuses in Kenya (see Amnesty International 1987). A number of Kenyan dissidents were subsequently granted political asylum in Western countries, most prominently the former member of parliament Koigi wa Wamwere in September 1986 in Norway. While Amnesty International relied on domestic sources for its reports, the presence of political exiles such as the charismatic Koigi wa Wamwere intensified vertical networking and mobilization: "Arguably, he was the most important opinion leader in Kenyan affairs in Norway in the late 1980s" (Baehr et al. 1995: 68). Koigi not only linked intellectual circles in Kenya to the Norwegian public, but also maintained contacts to similar groups in the United States where he had studied for one year at Cornell University in the early 1980s. While Koigi's identity as a Kikuyu and his political activism made him a prime target for the government in Kenya, Western perceptions of his identity concentrated exclusively on his fate as a political refugee.

---

[4] For a recent review of academic freedom issues in Kenya see Adar (1999).
[5] Moi frequently used the Swahili term "Nyayo" to claim that his presidency "follows the steps of Mzee Kenyatta." Ironically, whoever the Moi government identified as not following those steps ended up for days or weeks in the basement of Nyayo House.

Domestically, almost all societal organizations had in the meantime succumbed to the interventions by KANU and the executive. Only the churches and a group of lawyers organized around the Law Society of Kenya (LSK) were able to resist usurpation because they already had established ties to the outside world and controlled financial resources of their own. Apart from individual lawyers, the churches and in particular the National Council of Churches in Kenya (NCCK) put up the first coherent challenge against authoritarian rule. While the NCCK had been working closely with the state bureaucracy of the newly independent Kenya during the 1960s and 1970s, the relationship became now increasingly strained. The NCCK's theology was liberal and its "gospel as much social as individual." The staff "had no organic or historical connection with the local environment," a situation which enabled the NCCK "to be 'alongside' the new African politics ... in a way in which the local churches would have found difficult even if their leaders had thought it desirable" (Lonsdale et al. 1978: 269–270).

The strong outside ties of the NCCK became now important channels for enlisting additional international support. Similarly, many university teachers and lawyers had been trained abroad and now used these contacts to inform the outside world about mounting repression in Kenya. In a situation where the domestic opposition was trying to survive and was too weak to exert significant pressure from below, the international arena served as an alternative avenue for networking and mobilization. While the Kenyan government was in complete control of the domestic arena, vertical networking enabled the opposition to threaten the international image of Kenya as a stable and reliable partner of the Western world. To this end, the weak domestic and growing international part of the transnational human rights network in 1987 took advantage of Moi's planned state visits to the United States and Europe. When Daniel arap Moi met US President Reagan on March 12, the *Washington Post* ran the headline 'Police Torture is Charged in Kenya.'[6] Immediately, the US State Department spokesman, Charles Redman, declared his agency's grave concern for human rights violations in Kenya: "The allegations of torture, apparently supported by signed affidavits from those in Kenya who claim to have been tortured, raise serious questions of human rights abuses." (African Contemporary Record 1987). Later that year, a defiant Moi canceled a visit to Norway and Sweden and complained about

---

[6] In order to protect himself, a defense lawyer in the MwaKenya trials, Gibson Kamau Kuria, had provided the detailed information to *Washington Post* correspondent Blaine Harden. After submitting his allegations of torture to the court, Kuria was arrested and disappeared for two weeks. In 1989, Kuria received the Robert F. Kennedy Memorial Award for Human Rights.

continued human rights attacks in the media. The networking activities of non-governmental human rights organizations now also began to affect state actors and representatives of international organizations and Western governments.

While the international image of Kenya had markedly deteriorated by 1989/1990, the situation of the domestic opposition and human rights conditions remained highly precarious. The more outspoken domestic critics were met by an even more repressive reaction by the government. In February 1990 the Kenyan Foreign Minister Robert Ouko was found murdered not far from his farm.[7] On May 3, 1990, the former cabinet ministers Charles Rubia and Kenneth Matiba announced for the first time since 1981 the creation of a new party and demanded multiparty elections. Their arrests and extended detention without trial fueled massive street demonstrations all over the country, culminating in many deaths during the *Saba Saba* demonstrations on July 7.[8] In August, Anglican bishop and high-profile government critic Alexander Muge died under still unresolved circumstances in a car accident. The first major confrontation between the regime and a more independent civil society occurred when a National Council of NGOs resisted legislation by the government intended to increase its control over this increasingly vocal part of society (Ndegwa 1996: 31–54). Although the NGO community could not prevent the establishment of registration and reporting requirements, it was able to water down the legislation and retain some of the *de facto* independence gained during the 1989/1990 period. The struggle between NGOs and the executive over the legislation was a turning point that indicated slowly changing power relations between the government and its critics.

In September 1990, the International Bar Association moved its biannual meeting with more than 3,000 participants from Nairobi to New York. The Kenyan government remained largely unmoved by the growing international isolation and even contributed directly to it. On October 22, the Moi regime severed diplomatic relations with Norway,

---

[7] Ouko had accompanied Moi on a visit to the United States only two weeks prior to his murder. There were rumors that the United States government favored him as a possible successor to Moi, after he had announced he would address the issue of high-level corruption. Based on her interviews, Widner wrote that "upon his return [from the United States] Moi was so furious with Ouko that he ordered his assassination" (Widner 1992: 193). Hempstone even discussed accounts of events involving the direct participation of the president in the torture and subsequent death of Ouko (Hempstone 1997: 66–70).

[8] For a comparative analysis of the dynamics of street demonstrations in Kenya see Lafargue (1996). *Saba Saba* is Kiswahili for the seventh day in July, a date chosen by the political opposition for annual nationwide protests for democracy.

indicating its dismay with Norwegian Ambassador Niels Dahl's regular attendance at court proceedings against Koigi wa Wamwere (Baehr et al. 1995: 69). The following year, Human Rights Watch published *Kenya: Taking Liberties*, the first comprehensive human rights report on the country (Africa Watch/Human Rights Watch 1991). On August 2, the opposition created a broad coalition called the Forum for the Restoration of Democracy (FORD) that was "inspired by Civil Forum in East Germany and Czechoslovakia" (Throup 1993: 390). The creation of FORD was a breakthrough in establishing a political alternative to KANU and the Moi presidency. At the November donor meeting, the transnational mobilization finally had tangible material effects when financial aid amounting to $850 million was suspended for six months: "Kenya, the long-time favorite of the West, was being treated as one of Africa's pariah regimes"(Throup and Hornsby 1998: 84). Within a few days of this decision, President Moi ordered parliament to repeal section 2a of the constitution that declared Kenya a one-party state.[9] Multiparty elections were set for late 1992.

The period between 1984 and 1991 highlights the role of transboundary formations in withstanding and challenging the expansion of authoritarian rule. This challenge was successful because it enlisted the support of principled human rights actors advocating universally shared norms embedded in juridical institutions. Mainly urban and middle-class elites were able to form the nucleus of a reviving domestic opposition because of their traditional ties to the outside world and some retained financial independence. As Cooper writes in this volume, the "possibility of internationalist action ... made it possible for opponents within any given territory to imagine their opposition in wider – and more optimistic – terms than would otherwise be the case." The international non-governmental mobilization originated in the narrow human rights sector and later affected Western media, and other non-governmental and governmental actors as well as international organizations. However, the increasing number of actors drawn into the domestic arena also led to a much greater diversity of interests. In particular donor countries such as the United States not only pushed for multipartyism in 1991; they were relying during the same time period on the Kenyan government as a strategic ally for the military operations during the Gulf War, and against Libyan forces in Chad in 1991, and in Somalia in 1992 (Hempstone 1997: 136–141, 214–231). While the outside voices for change increased in quantity, this process brought in competing interests with material and strategic, rather than principled interests.

---

[9] For details on the decision see Hempstone (1997: 252–257).

Domestically, the struggle for political power pitted against each other two ethnic coalitions that, by and large, had already been present at the time of independence. While Kikuyu and Luo had dominated Kenyan politics for almost twenty years under Kenyatta, under President Moi they lost this control to representatives of smaller ethnicities. Hence, the emerging civil society actors concerned with regime change were recruited mainly from the disenfranchised Kikuyu elite. Their call for human rights was principled inasmuch as it reflected a means to the end of regaining their influence in national affairs. International actors interested in furthering the cause of human rights and democracy in Kenya did not simply work with principled domestic groups; they also began to affect this ongoing struggle between different ethnic coalitions. These more ambivalent effects of local–international connections are the subject of the following section.

The struggle for a new political order, 1991–2000

The decision to return to multipartyism had three major consequences. First, opportunities for the sustainable institutionalization of domestic political dissent increased. Within months, the executive lost much of its control over the (mainly) urban-centered societal realm where dozens of opposition groups now reclaimed the previously lost terrain. Individual members of the opposition took advantage of the window of opportunity and now created NGOs with more solid transnational connections. Donor organizations with their new funding strategies were now able to choose between dozens of domestic groups claiming to promote human rights and democratic change. At the same time, those new actors also found more avenues for expressing their opinions because the domestic press was also able to regain some of the freedom it lost during the 1980s.

Second, the advent of multipartyism shifted attention away from immediate political reforms and toward the struggle over the control of national power as well as efforts to replace Moi as president. Several ministers of Moi's cabinet and other leaders used the opportunity to quit KANU and form their own (often ethnically narrow) opposition parties. To the mainstream the opposition politicians' issues of constitutional reform were only of interest in so far as they contributed to a level playing field for the upcoming presidential and parliamentary elections. Multipartyism not only created an opportunity to contest Moi and KANU in elections; it also increased incentives for competition within the opposition. Hence, the previously united political opposition split along two lines. The first divided those who demanded sustainable political reforms before an election and others who struggled for an advantageous position assuming that domestic and donor pressure would remove Moi from power in any case. The second dividing line was ethnic and split the opposition over the next ten years into a growing number of smaller parties.

Third, the ruling elite reacted to this new situation by developing new strategies designed to defend its threatened power position. Emphasis was now given to narrower, shorter-term objectives such as the control of the 1992 election process, rather than the continued stifling of the civil society sector. An important part of this strategy was the deliberate instigation of ethnic violence directed against Kenyans expected to be in favor of the political opposition. As the opposition had successfully used "extraversion" strategies to challenge the regime, the latter now turned inside, rhetorically revived the earlier *majimbo*-debate, and mobilized its own ethnic base. As a result, more than two thousand Kenyans were killed in 1991/1992 and several hundred thousand displaced (Africa Watch/Human Rights Watch 1993; Amisi 1997).[10]

The return of multipartyism did not mean that the Kenyan government now ended its repression of the mainly urban-based civil and political opposition. Domestic critics were still regular targets of security organs and many attempts to institutionalize dissent were met with open threats and harassment. However, compared with the situation in the 1980s the regime could no longer sustain complete control of the political system, the press, or society at large.

The process of political liberalization opened up opportunities for the establishment of domestic human rights groups and other political NGOs. For the first time, Kenyan non-governmental organizations specializing in human rights advocacy emerged as significant actors in the domestic arena. One of these organizations, the Kenya Human Rights Commission (KHRC), constituted itself in September 1992 as a transnational group when it opened offices simultaneously in Nairobi and Boston, USA. KHRC became the major donor-funded local organization providing human rights information to local and international observers. KHRC essentially copied the working methods of Amnesty International and regularly issued *Quarterly Repression Reports* (e.g. Kenya Human Rights Commission 1993, 1995). Amnesty International became the main international partner of KHRC, while its work and publications were financed by various donor agencies, including the Ford Foundation, the National Endowment for Democracy, and the Swedish NGO Foundation for Human Rights.

---

[10] A parliamentary investigation not only reaffirmed the political character of the attacks, but also found evidence for the leading role played by high-level KANU representatives (Republic of Kenya 1992). As usual, this report was shelved without further action against the perpetrators.

Other organizations such as Release Political Prisoners (RPP), the Center for Law and Research International (CLARION), or the Citizens' Coalition for Constitutional Change (the 4Cs) followed suit. These organizations now supplemented the voices of protest previously sustained only by church organizations and the lawyers' community. Moreover, the whole NGO sector was increasingly politicized: "A majority tended not only to address community development and institution building, but also human rights issues with civic education constituting the core of their activities" (Tostensen et al. 1998). Thus, the number and stability of domestic "nodes" of a transnational network on human rights increased significantly. However, the sharp increase of NGOs and subsequent horizontal networking was mainly due to the fact that many of the former government critics now set up their own organizations and could attract donor funding for them. The institutionalization of domestic dissent tended to stabilize already existing informal networks rather than creating new ones.[11] Hence, ethnic bias also pervaded the emerging sector of organizations pressing for constitutional reforms. Politically active members of the Kikuyu ethnicity had created many of those "nodes" in pursuit of a distinct political agenda.

The December 1992 elections

Shortly after the introduction of multipartyism, the opposition coalition FORD disintegrated and in December a total of eight parties and presidential candidates competed in the elections. Although the opposition accounted for more than two-thirds of the vote, the gerrymandering of constituencies (Ndegwa 1998: 207) and the splits within the opposition enabled Moi and KANU to retain power. The electoral defeat and the continued harassment by state security forces ended any hopes for a fast "Eastern-European"-style transition to more democratic rule. Moreover, the parliamentary opposition was further weakened when fourteen members of parliament crossed over (or back) to KANU within the next few months. Hence, the NGO sector became in the mid-1990s the main source for continued reform pressure on the Kenyan government from below. International material and ideational support remained crucial for the sustainability of that challenge, in particular after the donor community resumed some aid programs in late 1993.

---

[11] One Nairobi representative of a foreign donor organization during interviews in 1996 called Kenyan NGOs "very territorial and elitist." Kenyan NGO representatives usually also acknowledged the problem of urban bias.

Although the period between 1993 and early 1997 brought seemingly little progress with regard to the political reform process, a number of significant developments indicated that the transnational mobilization had more sustainable effects than either donor intervention or domestic resistance would have had on its own. The efforts of the domestic political opposition and the donor community in 1991/1992 to solve the issue by rushing to multiparty polls were successfully countered by the regime's strategy to mobilize its own ethnic power base. However, gains such as press freedom and a more autonomous civil society survived this period and opened opportunities for further mobilization. In 1993, the government lifted the ban on members of Amnesty International who had previously been barred from visiting the country. The same year, the Attorney General, Amos Wako, announced the creation of several commissions charged with a complete overhaul of the constitution and remaining repressive laws from the colonial period. Although the government delayed the actual appointment of the commission members, the announcement put the government under additional pressure to live up to the promised steps.

In 1996, two days prior to a donor meeting, Moi appointed a Standing Committee on Human Rights charged with monitoring the domestic human rights situation and reporting directly to the president. Again, the committee remained completely dependent on Moi and none of its reports have been published so far, but it represents a potential step toward the creation of a more independent domestic human rights body.[12] Other significant concessions of the period included the final release of Koigi wa Wamwere on December 13, 1996 and the accession to the United Nations Convention against Torture and other Cruel, Inhuman or Degrading Treatment or Punishment in February 1997.

The re-formation of the political opposition

Fearing a repeat of the 1992 electoral disaster, the extra-parliamentary reform groups within civil society decided in 1996/1997 to step up their domestic and international mobilization for constitutional reforms. Intensive efforts in horizontal and vertical networking became a crucial instrument in further cornering the Moi regime. Meanwhile, the government

---

[12] Amos Wako has already asked the Kenya Human Rights Commission (KHRC) to give up its name for this government institution. Following the publication of a damning report by the United Nations Special Rapporteur on Torture, Nigel Rodley, in March 2000, Wako pledged the implementation of all eighteen recommendations made by Rodley (UN Commission on Human Rights 2000). On June 22, the cabinet agreed to the creation of a more independent human rights body.

continued to delay serious reform steps and tried to repeat the successful 1992 tactics by offering only minor concessions. This time, the opposition reacted with greater unity to the regime's tactics. In April 1996, a coalition of parliamentary opposition members called the Inter-Parties Group (IPG) invited civil society groups to participate in their deliberations. One year later, from April 3 to 6, 1997, a coalition of thirteen opposition parties, church organizations, and NGOs held a follow-up meeting to press for constitutional reforms prior to the upcoming general elections. The first National Convention for Constitutional Reform in Limuru formed an executive committee (NCEC) charged with representing the coalition in national affairs. The meeting repeated the opposition's longstanding demands and threatened to resort to mass action such as street demonstrations or general strikes if the government refused to sit down for negotiations.

The plan to mobilize on the streets was well attuned to other plans that sought to bring renewed pressure from above. The NCEC called for the first street demonstration on May 31, one day before the first visit of an official Amnesty International delegation led by the organization's General Secretary, Pierre Sané. On the day of their arrival Moi announced the abolition of the Public Order Act, a law frequently used to curtail the opposition's freedom of association. However, he maintained his refusal to talk about constitutional reforms prior to the elections. The coordination of international and domestic forces marked an important step toward intensified vertical and horizontal networking as Amnesty International launched a "Human Rights Manifesto for Kenya" together with seventeen Kenyan human rights organizations.[13] In the following months, the NCEC became the main force behind the intensified campaign for constitutional reforms. In turn, the NCEC represented many of the already internationally well-connected human rights activists, including Gibson Kamau Kuria, Kivuta Kibwana, and Paul Muite. Moreover, popular leaders, such as Kenneth Matiba, initially lent their support and local mobilization capabilities to the cause of the NCEC.

Thousands of Kenyans responded to the call for nationwide protests on May 31. Subsequently, Moi blamed "foreign-funded NGOs" for the street chaos and threatened them with deregistration: "There are some NGOs such as the ones that have been engaged in feeding famine victims, but there are others which have gone against their mandate and are seeking to influence political developments in this country ... They

---

[13] Although President Daniel arap Moi himself refused to meet the Amnesty representatives, many other government officials agreed to meetings, including Vice-President Saitoti and the Attorney General, Amos Wako (Amnesty International 1997).

are not allowed to play politics, because that is how Africa has become the experimental playing ground for everything" (Moi, quoted in *Daily Nation*, June 21, 1997). More fundamentally, Moi held that the NCEC was nothing but a "congregation of self-styled leaders" not elected by the Kenyan people. Moi's strategy was to frame the conflict as an issue of "us" (the Kenyan people) against "them" (foreigners). This argument was intended to resonate not only with basic democratic norms, but also with the powerful discourse of political independence and sovereignty. The fact that forces with exceptionally high international contacts and a comparatively smaller domestic base dominated the NCEC gave Moi's arguments some domestic leverage.

The NCEC reacted to Moi's rhetorical attacks with another call for street demonstrations on July 7, the anniversary of the original *Saba Saba* demonstrations in 1990. The antiriot measures taken by the Kenyan police left twelve demonstrators dead and many more injured. Several dozen parishioners were severely beaten when the police stormed Nairobi's All Saints Cathedral during a service. At the same time, ethnic violence flared up again, this time in the coastal region of Mombasa, where more than one hundred Kenyans were killed and thousands displaced. Once again, the news made it to the headlines of international media and the Kenyan government had maneuvered itself into international isolation. Moreover, due to the government's failure to address rampant corruption, the renewed isolation began to spill over into the aid sector again. Two weeks after *Saba Saba*, the World Bank and the International Monetary Fund (IMF) gave Kenya one week to "show tangible signs of transparency and accountability" with respect to the agreed economic reforms. When Moi withdrew a letter by Finance Minister Mudavadi that indicated compliance with the demands, the IMF suspended the disbursement of a $220 million low-interest loan.

In late July Moi finally agreed to reform talks with selected religious leaders, but he still rejected the inclusion of other civil society actors. The announcement immediately split the opposition. While the leaders of the opposition parties in parliament saw this as an opportunity to reenter the reform process, members of the extra-parliamentary civil society groups rejected the proposals and called for all-inclusive talks. Consequently, the NCEC called for a general strike on August 8 to press for the inclusion of civil society actors. However, without the support of many popular opposition leaders, the call for a general strike found little resonance in the population. By the end of August, the government and the NCEC exchanged increasingly hostile accusations. Moi and his ministers claimed that the NCEC was "backed by foreigners to start a revolution in Kenya" (quoted in *Daily Nation*, August 31, 1997). The president claimed that the NCEC was about to stage a "civilian coup" and intended to subvert the elected government. This statement followed the Limuru II meeting held from August 25 to 28 where the NGO representatives had decided to constitute the NCEC as a parallel government if KANU did not finally enter dialog. The meeting also resolved to call for two other major rallies on September 9 (*Tisa Tisa*) and October 10 (*Kumi Kumi*). Faced with the threat of continued mass action, Vice-President Saitoti and other moderate KANU politicians tried to break the deadlock and called on the closing day of Limuru II for a meeting of KANU and opposition MPs. Saitoti invited the opposition MPs to form the Inter-Parties Parliamentary Group (IPPG) which would be charged with kicking off the constitutional reform process.

Minimal constitutional reforms

On September 2 negotiators agreed on minimum legal reforms, including a reform of the Electoral Commission and the deletion of the ban on forming a coalition government. The IPPG created three committees: on legal and administrative issues, on electoral reform, and on problems of domestic security. The NCEC reacted to its exclusion from the reform talks by reaffirming its call for demonstration on September 9. However, similar to the failed general strike in August, the demonstration did not attract many Kenyans on to the streets. While the extremely popular opposition politician Kenneth Matiba had earlier supported the NCEC's calls for mass action, he now distanced himself from the organization's policies. At the same time, the moderate opposition accepted KANU's refusal to admit non-elected NCEC representatives at the negotiating table. The leading representatives of the NCEC themselves had no significant domestic constituency as they had mainly used vertical networking strategies and outside support to establish their authority on the domestic level.

On the day of the first IPPG talks, Amnesty International launched its six-month campaign "Kenya – The Quest for Justice" which continued its cooperation with several domestic human rights groups. During the entire period, joint Amnesty – RPP groups visited all major European countries and briefed government representatives, parliamentarians, and the general public on the human rights situation in Kenya. Africa Watch published two extensive human rights reports as reminders of the upcoming general elections (Human Rights Watch/Africa 1997a, 1997b). However, domestic affairs were now completely dominated by the surprising pace of the reform process. This represented a major departure from the previous intransigence of the government, although the prominence of

KANU moderates in the negotiations and Moi's aloofness were certainly important enabling factors.

Within only two months, the committees completed their work and Attorney General Amos Wako tabled the reforms in parliament. Amnesty International cautiously welcomed the progress made on constitutional reforms, but maintained that many issues were still unresolved. On October 30, parliament voted with more than the required two-thirds majority in favor of the IPPG package (156 in favor, 26 against, 1 abstention). One week later, Daniel arap Moi signed the IPPG proposals into law.[14] Even though the NCEC had contributed to these results by its continued mobilization of domestic and international voices, it rejected the compromise as insufficient. On September 11, the NCEC stated that "the recommendations of the IPPG Sub-Committee change NOTHING whatsoever of real substance concerning reforms towards free and fair election in Kenya" (quoted in Tostensen et al. 1998: 37, emphasis in original). Similar statements followed from critical church representatives. However, an initial resolution by the NCEC to boycott and disrupt the elections was shelved on November 11 "pending public feedback."

The fast and successful completion of the IPPG talks would not have been possible without the presence of an opposition divided into moderate and radical sections. The latter presented a constant threat of mass action to the government, which strengthened the moderates at the negotiating table. On the side of the opposition the NCEC was excluded as a result of the government's insistence on the participation of elected representatives only. Hence, the beginning of constitutional reforms in Kenya highlighted the classical emergence of hard- and softliners on both sides of the political divide. The civil society component within the NCEC had become a significant force in the domestic arena mainly because it maintained relations with international human rights groups and partially reproduced their activities on the domestic level. However, these outside connections were also one of the NCEC's main constraints in the political struggle for reforms. The Moi regime, with an almost paranoid attitude toward outside interventions, resisted such civil society participation, claiming that only elected officials should decide on the future of the country. While this position revealed the perceived strength of those

---

[14] The reforms included the explicit proclamation that Kenya was a "multi-party democratic state," the appointment of opposition members to the Electoral Commission, the deletion of "detention without trial" and "sedition" from the Penal Code and the Preservation of Public Security Act, major curbs on the powers of local authorities in the Chief's Authority Act, and measures to ensure equal presentation of political standpoints in the media. Finally, the Constitution of Kenya Review Commission Bill set up a commission that would undertake a comprehensive review of the constitution immediately after the elections (*Daily Nation*, September 12, 1997).

actors as much as the government's intransigence, the possible long-term ramifications could not be easily ignored. What had started in the 1980s as a survival strategy against governmental repression now turned into a potential burden for political activists who had to play by democratic rules. Those rules favored actors and groups with strong domestic bases no matter how these had been obtained. Moreover, the independence struggle as a leitmotif of Kenyan identity could always be turned into an argument against any form of foreign intrusion, no matter what goals such interventions pursued.

The December 1997 elections

The December 1997 elections were again dominated by President Moi and KANU, although the playing field was more level and the opposition was able to capture almost half of the parliamentary seats (Ajulu 1998; Tostensen et al. 1998). Moi was returned to his (supposedly) last term of presidency and KANU was able to retain 113 seats in parliament against 109 won by opposition parties. The domestic situation remained highly volatile. The NCEC and the government continued to clash on the constitutional reform process, while ethnic violence returned to the Rift Valley. When the Catholic and Protestant church leaderships claimed that the Moi government had "no moral legitimacy to lead" and called upon Western governments to press for all-inclusive reform talks, Moi accused the church leaders of joining "the many shady and illegal groupings" and further held that "a Philippine-like revolution would not succeed in Kenya." Moi repeated his threats that he would outlaw NGOs supporting the "illegal" NCEC and advised domestic political activists to "join the legally constituted parties if they wished to engage in politics" (quoted in *Daily Nation*, February 21, 1998).

Despite prior negative experience, the NCEC returned to its 1997 tactics and called upon the population to strike on March 3, April 4, and May 5, for a full week in June, and indefinitely starting from July 1. In early April the NCEC was again forced to call off all plans for strikes and demonstrations as the expectations for a high turnout of demonstrators were not met. While the urban-based elites dominating the NCEC had acquired some leverage because of their international contacts, they obviously overestimated their capabilities to mobilize domestic support. The impressive international resonance of their campaigns and the subsequent emphasis on vertical networking had discouraged them from building strong domestic networks beyond the groups they belonged to in the first place. The new social relationship across national boundaries that originally created an enabling environment for

challenging a repressive government now increasingly blinded its participants to its uncompromising attitude and narrowed its choices. While
such a position may have been the only possible one when faced with the
regime's repressive tactics, it was not backed up by a significant domestic
base.

Reflecting the preferences of the Moi government, Attorney General
Amos Wako on April 1, 1998 announced the creation of a twenty-five-
member Inter-Party Parliamentary Committee (IPPC) to supervise the
constitutional reform process. Although the electoral victory gave the Moi
government some new leverage to resist the pressure for political reform,
the ongoing mobilization and the 1997 negotiations with the opposition
had considerably weakened the hardliners within KANU. This resulted
in two major defeats of the hardline faction around President Moi. First,
in the area of economic reforms a majority of parliamentarians called
upon the government to implement the anticorruption measures agreed
in negotiations with the IMF and the World Bank. During a seminar
organized by the World Bank and the German Friedrich-Ebert Foundation, Finance Minister Nyachae admitted that "Kenya was broke and
corruption was rampant" (*Daily Nation*, April 30, 1998).[15] The participants resolved that economic reforms were a necessary condition for
the resumption of the aid withheld since August 1997. A subsequent
meeting of the KANU parliamentary group rejected Moi's proposal to
officially distance themselves from the recommendations of the seminar.
After this defeat, Moi agreed to the reform package, but insisted that all
measures must be taken under the leadership of KANU (*East African*,
May 7, 1998). Second, KANU hardliners failed to prevent in parliament the creation of a commission charged with the investigation of all
instances of ethnic violence in Kenya since the early 1990s.[16] Although
KANU members were in the majority, the motion for the commission
won a 54 to 49 majority. The growing dissent within KANU forced Moi
to accept Raila Odinga's National Democratic Party (NDP) as a *de facto*
coalition partner in the National Assembly.

Moi's negative attitude toward the participation of civil society groups
in the process of constitutional review was now also challenged from
within KANU. The KANU members of the IPPC agreed to organize
a day-long seminar of 400 political, religious, and NGO leaders on the

---

[15] Nyachae was dismissed by Moi in February 1999. After the 1997 elections, Vice-
President Saitoti was not reappointed to his position until April 1999, in another in-
dication of Moi's disapproval of prominent roles played by cabinet ministers in leading
political or economic reforms.

[16] The government refuses to give a date for the release of the report by the so-called
Akiwumi Commission. However, most of the evidence is available, since the press was
free to cover the hearings of the commission.

constitutional reform process. Attorney General Amos Wako chaired the meeting at the national cultural center Bomas of Kenya on May 11. NCEC representatives Gibson Kamau Kuria and Kivutha Kibwana repeatedly walked out of the meetings in protest, because KANU representatives maintained a negative attitude to civil society participation. Before the second round of the Bomas talks planned for June 8–9, thirty-six participating groups led by the Catholic Church, the NCEC, and the NGO Council threatened to boycott the meeting if their demands for greater inclusiveness were not met. They were supported by forty-two MPs including five from the ruling party. The following day, Moi gave in to the continued pressure and announced an expansion of the review committee (*Daily Nation*, June 2, 1998).

On June 22, thirty-three civil organizations and all political parties met to decide on the future of the constitutional reform process. The NCEC was now officially included in the talks. During the meeting, hardline KANU representatives remained opposed to the inclusion of civil society representatives in the constitutional reform process and suggested the enlargement of the IPPC on the basis of district representation. The NCEC rejected the plan as "tribalist" and demanded representation based on existing civil society organizations. After intensive debates, both sides agreed to set up a three-tiered structure under the leadership of the Constitutional Review Commission. One of the two other bodies would consist of representatives from the sixty-five districts (District Consultative Forum, DCF), while the other would bring in a broad range of politically active domestic organizations (National Constitutional Consultative Forum, NCCF). Shortly thereafter, KANU hawks rejected the compromise and Moi returned to his original position, declaring that he was only willing to accept a number of church organizations as partners in the constitutional debates.

On August 7, three days before the next round of talks and another possible stand-off between regime and civil society actors, bomb explosions ripped through Nairobi and Dar-es-Salaam. The explosions targeted the US embassies in both East African capitals and killed an estimated 250 people, the large majority in Nairobi. In the wake of the tragedy, the meeting on the constitutional reform issue was rescheduled for August 24. In the course of the meeting, President Moi changed his position again and agreed to NGO participation: "The fact that 'radicals' such as Prof. [Kivutha] Kibwana were sitting on the same committee with Mr. Sunkuli, an ultra-right wing KANU politicians, shows just how much transformation Kenyan politics has undergone over the past few months" (Githongo 1998). However, most of the envisioned substantial step toward democratization were still not yet agreed upon, let alone implemented. So far, the compromise was only about the formal conditions under which reforms would take place. While the DCF secured representation according to the majimboist ideas advanced by the incumbent minority groups supporting the government, the NCCF represented the liberal ideas of the civil society sector. The former preferred constitutional reform based on ethnic communities and their representation in parliament, which would secure an overrepresentation not only of KANU, but also of the smaller ethnic groups. In contrast, the NCEC, as a group representing not only liberal values but also the narrower personal and ethnic interests of the larger tribes, advocated a process based on national citizenship and majority rules.

One day before the drafting committee was supposed to spell out the details of the compromise (October 5), the NCEC and one of the opposition parties withdrew their support and declared that the whole process was still controlled by Moi and KANU. NCEC officials again threatened mass action and called for the formation of a coalition government. The other participants went ahead and agreed on the composition of the Constitutional Review Commission. Of the twenty-five members, thirteen were now to be chosen from the parties in parliament and twelve from religious, women's, and other civil society organizations. Of these from parliament, five were supposed to be nominated by KANU, the other eight by the opposition parties. Within the civil society sector, the churches were supposed to nominate three members, the women's organizations five commissioners, and all other civil society organizations the remaining four members through the National Council of NGOs (*Daily Nation*, October 31, 1998).

Continued resistance to meaningful political reforms

In February 1999, twenty-two cabinet ministers stormed into a meeting on the creation of the Constitutional Reform Commission. They announced that KANU would no longer participate in the process unless it was given more seats. In June, Moi reneged again on his promise to give civil society actors a voice in the reform process and announced that only elected officials chosen from the National Assembly would carry out the review of the constitution. On June 10, riot police injured dozens of protestors, including many opposition parliamentarians and representatives of the once again excluded civil society groups.

However, on the economic front, the regime finally agreed to demands by the IMF to curb corruption. In an attempt to end the 1997 suspension of a \$200 million loan,[17] Moi appointed in July a long-time critic of his government, the paleontologist Richard Leakey, as head of the Civil Service.[18] While economic reforms began slowly to take root, the political reform process retreated, at least in the eyes of the political opposition. In December 1999, the National Assembly formalized Moi's decision and appointed Raila Odinga, the NDP leader and *de facto* coalition partner of KANU, to start a new initiative for the constitutional reform process. Immediately thereafter, church leaders and NGO representatives started a parallel reform initiative (the Ufungamano Initiative) in order to press for their inclusion. Over the next few months Raila's committee settled for a small review commission consisting of fifteen commissioners who will be selected by parliament and appointed by the president. On July 25, 2000 parliament passed this proposal as the Constitution of Kenya Review Bill. All opposition members and many KANU parliamentarians walked out before the vote. Meanwhile, Moi's succession and the upcoming 2002 elections begin to overshadow the reform process (again). The opposition has again been discussing an election boycott, while prominent members of KANU seek to occupy a leading position in the race for the succession.

Conclusion

Comparing the effects of transnational human rights activism during two distinct periods of regime change in Kenya offers important insights into the possibilities and limits of transboundary networking between non-state actors. While in the 1980s this strategy was successful in creating and strengthening alternative sources of authority to challenge the repressive government, the 1990s expose the problems of translating this authority into a new, more democratic order. International human rights norms can serve as a platform to successfully challenge authoritarian rule. However, subsequent efforts to ensure regular and fair

[17] The approval by the IMF is crucial, because all other multi- and bilateral donors only join once the IMF has given clearance.

[18] More than one year later, the IMF announced that it would resume aid under clearly defined conditionalities (http://www.imf.org/external/np/sec/pr/2000/pr0045.htm). The conditions included the enactment of anticorruption laws, weekly inspections of the Kenyan Central Bank by IMF officials, and a shift of powers away from the president's office to the Treasury. Moi denounced the measures as "too severe" and declared that "without political stability, there can never be economic development and the IMF should know that" (*Daily Nation*, August 22, 2000). In the annual corruption perceptions index published by Transparency International (TI), Kenya was in 2000 rated as one of the ten most corrupt nations, ranking 82nd out of 90 states. It scored 2.1 on a scale of 0 (highly corrupt) to 10 (highly clean) http://www.transparency.de/documents/cp:/2000.html.

competition as well as democratic participation require both a shift of attention away from transboundary to domestic relations and an effort to resurrect the state as the main vehicle to enforce such a transition. In the Kenyan case, the vertical networks have become solidified during the 1990s, while their purpose remained largely the same as in the 1980s and only slowly adapted to the new circumstances. The success of the challenge in 1991/1992 and the subsequent increasing aid flows to civil society actors contributed to the failures on the part of the network members to create horizontal networks for democratic change across ethnic lines.

This case study contributes to a literature on regime transitions that replaces a structuralist focus on economic or cultural preconditions with an interest in an analysis of more contingent, strategic interactions between different domestic elites (see Karl 1990; O'Donnell and Schmitter 1986). Although modernization scholars were able to show that the stability of democracies increases with their economic wealth, this finding does not support the conclusion that economic growth is a necessary condition for democratization (for this argument, see Przeworski and Limongi 1997). Moreover, the evidence from the "third wave of democratization" (Huntington 1991) did not support the conclusion that economic development always precedes (and causes) the establishment of sustainable democratic institutions. The subsequent shift of scholarly attention away from preconditions has opened additional avenues for analyses of regime change even under the extremely depressed economic conditions in most African nations. However, despite this fundamental challenge to the modernization paradigm, many of the agency-centered approaches continued to share a general skepticism toward the role and influence of international factors.[19] This contribution argues for a systematic recognition of such international influences and traces some of their effects on regime change. In doing so, it has mainly focused on the activities of transnational advocacy networks mobilizing around issues of human rights.

The research on the role of norms and transnational advocacy networks in affecting domestic change has mainly focused on the strategies developed to challenge authoritarian rule and the likely paths of subsequent regime change (Keck and Sikkink 1998; Risse et al. 1999). However, many of the more prominent cases show that change caused by such mobilization occurs over a long period of time, often in the range of several decades.[20] This contribution adds to this literature by paying particular

---

[19] For an example of such skepticism with regard to the recent "democratic experiments in Africa" see Bratton and van de Walle (1997).

[20] For Eastern Europe, see Thomas (2001); for South Africa, see Klotz (1995).

attention to the long-term effects of interactions between international and domestic actors seeking either to maintain or to change the existing political order. I use vertical and horizontal networking as two different forms of social action to show both the potential and limits of principled transboundary mobilization. While vertical networking activities were a necessary survival strategy for Kenyan human rights advocates and government critics during the 1980s, the growing success had increasingly ambivalent effects in the 1991–2000 period. Donor involvement and their narrow push for multipartyism ironically helped the Moi regime to hold on to power for another decade.

I further argue that networking not only is a strategy for non-governmental actors, but can also be successfully used by the groups defending the status quo. This led in Kenya to the emergence of new forms of gross human rights violations after 1991. The ethnic violence of the 1990s killed many more Kenyans than the now partly dismantled security apparatus in the 1980s. The shift of repressive strategies away from using traditional state institutions, such as the police, to mobilizing non-juridical ethnic networks or groups of "youths" represents a major new challenge for the international human rights community. Among the main reasons why this challenge has not been adequately met are the quality and long-term effects of the vertical network relations. Inside Kenya vertical networks have made parts of the opposition overconfident about their domestic power capabilities and, thus, contributed to the disunity within the opposition camp. Multipartyism split the principled opposition to the regime and put sustainable democratic reforms on the backburner. For some opposition members the call for human rights was little more than a thinly disguised anti-Moi slogan, or worse, represented a convenient way of promoting an ethnic agenda.

Outside Kenya such relations of vertical networking temporarily turned the attention of a wide range of actors with very different interests toward that country. Most of these outside observers had their own agendas, which had little to do with the issue of democratic regime change in Kenya. Donor governments in the early 1990s felt pressured to support democracy around the globe, but had little clue on the means that were appropriate for each individual country moving away from authoritarian rule. Principled human rights groups in the Northern hemisphere had a much clearer agenda, but tended also to ignore the urban and ethnic bias of the most vocal part of the opposition movement in Kenya. Their narrow human rights mandate inhibited a more comprehensive perspective on the unfolding transition process in Kenya. Outside support for the democratization process requires the development of a broadened perspective beyond the narrower realm of support for a few urban-based human rights activists. A more-inclusive approach would have to go beyond both the opposition's majoritarian and KANU's federalist proposals and develop alternative ideas about the equal participation of different ethnic groups in Kenyan national politics.

8 Global, state, and local intersections: power, authority, and conflict in the Niger Delta oil communities

Cyril I. Obi

Introduction

This chapter analyzes how transboundary formations are reflected in the conflicts ravaging the highly volatile and militarized Niger Delta oil communities. It inquires into the effects and forms of international intervention, of local co-opting of discourses in international arenas, and state mediation of global and local forces. This is an important step towards explaining how the dialectics of international interventionism and local governance fuel conflict in the Delta.

The conflict in the Niger Delta provides a concrete case of transboundary formations as they emerge in points of conflict and alliance. This complex terrain of conflict and social coalitions needs to be systematically "unpacked." Such unpacking will help us interrogate some zero-sum assumptions about the impact of globalization on the state as well as on local conflict in Africa.

In relation to the ongoing struggles in the Niger Delta, it is possible to discern the role of four major actors/forces: the multinational oil corporations (MNOCs); the Nigerian state; local leaders, organizations, and movements; and international non-governmental organizations (INGOs). With the exception of the MNOCs and, to a lesser extent, the INGOs, these actors, particularly the state and local leaders and movements are fractionated, and form alliances that are as complex as they are contradictory. The reasons for this lie in a host of historical, cultural, economic, and political factors. In the first place, the Nigerian state is a site of constant struggles for access to power and resources, in which those in power defend themselves at all cost, and those outside seek entry at any cost and through any means (Ake 1996). Second, this state is dependent on the MNOCs which produce oil (and provide oil rents). Thus, the state's internal dynamics dictate that it defends global oil capital by forcefully asserting its authority and power locally. This is in order to provide a shield behind which the state–MNOC–local partners alliance will continue to share the "spoils of oil" while degrading the fragile ecosystem of the Niger Delta, directly threatening the livelihoods and futures of millions of impoverished villagers. These villagers, since the late 1980s, have thrown up resistance movements that have hit hard at the MNOCs operating in their areas. To cite a report on the depth of resistance, "Between January and August this year, Shell recorded 55 attacks on its installations and equipment loss of close to N51 billion. Total work days lost as a result of work stoppage is estimated at 103 days" (Onanuga 1998).

On the part of the local leaders and groups, issues of power and authority are central to the struggle over access to resources (oil rents). This places local resistance forces on a collision course with the state–MNOC alliance. But the local forces are not without their transboundary allies, the INGOs. There is a bifurcation in the politics of oil multinationals and those of INGOs. The MNOCs forge alliances with collaborating "local" authorities to extract more oil from the Niger Delta, and to contain reprisals from the forces of local resistance. The INGOs, on the other hand, largely support the local forces of resistance in the latter's efforts to strengthen their claims/grievances, and earn legitimacy within the international community. The INGO–local movements alliance is mutually empowering, even if it contains complexities and contradictions that may weaken the capacities of local forces, in ways that will be discussed later.

Some conceptual issues

The conceptual framework of this chapter hinges on a radical and eclectic interpretation of global environmental change. It recognizes the centrality of a range of actors whose activities are "transterritorial" and tied to their objective position in the "processes of accumulation, production and reproduction central to capitalism" (Williams 1996: 41).

As the most viable source of energy, oil in globalized capitalism enriches the transterritorial producers (and to a lesser extent their local allies). But the inhabitants of the Niger Delta are largely alienated from the oil produced from their lands and waters, while facing the deprivations linked to the degradation of their ecosystem and the lack of local autonomy. The forces of local resistance construct a collective metaphor of the victim and mobilize their complaints along the lines of victimized ethnic minorities to make demands on the international community. Thus, the capacity of transnational movements to mobilize the opposing local forces along the lines of rights or profit depends on the position of such forces in the global political economy.

How then are the globalized relations of power relevant to the situation in the Niger Delta? In the first place, they imply that the Delta is transformed via capitalist (oil) relations into a local site for global accumulation in Nigeria. MNOCs are deeply immersed in the control of resources and the environment with implications for political, economic, and social life. In the second place, they enable us to raise the critical question as to whether globalized relations take power and authority away from the state and local forces. As far as the struggles in the Niger Delta show, at the level of extraction and repression, transterritorial producers reinforce the power and authority of the state and those of local leaders and groups aligned to it. In some cases, however, the MNOCs have carried out state-like roles in the locale, including local patronage and payoffs (Onishi 1999) and the provision of limited services and facilities in the areas of education, agriculture, health, and water supply. On the other hand, the INGOs have broadly empowered local forces in the struggle against the forces of transterritorial extraction.

Like any locale, the Niger Delta is a site of the "meeting of levels" in the contest for resources, power and authority. The minority ethnic nationalities which inhabit the oil-bearing lands of the Delta seek to reassert their autonomy, and claim the land and the oil under it *vis-à-vis* the contending claims of oil multinationals and the state. The ethnic minority nationalities of the oil-rich Delta are equally critical of the majority ethnic nationalities (Hausa-Fulani, Yoruba, and Igbo) that control power and resources at the federal level and exercise *de facto* control of oil revenues to the exclusion of the oil minorities. The oil minorities see this as an inequitable and unjust situation and seek an end to such "internal colonialism" by the hegemonic ethnic groups backed up with state power. Thus, the struggle for ethnic minority rights is deployed in the quest for liberation from exploitation and pollution. For instance, the success of the campaign of the Ogoni people, one of the smallest ethnic nationalities in the Niger Delta, partly lay in the capacity of the Movement for the Survival of Ogoni People (MOSOP) leadership in welding local discourses of the survival of the Ogoni nation on to the global discourse on the rights of indigenous peoples. The image of the Ogoni as a victimized indigenous people, excluded from the benefits of the oil industry while facing imminent genocide from oil pollution and repression by the militarized Nigerian state, empowered MOSOP's appeals and complaints to the international community. In order to reinforce its presence in international arenas, MOSOP (and some of its affiliates) opened offices in Europe and North America. From this global "refuge" it coordinated the local struggle on a global scale.

It is apposite to attempt to "theorize" further the concept of "local resistance." Indeed, the forces are not an undifferentiated whole. They are made up of various factions, classes, interests, and ideologies, broadly united against a common enemy – the oil multinationals and (to a lesser extent) the federal government. They are, however, divided along the lines of the strategies to adopt in wresting concessions from these "enemies." Up to a point, the local forces are divided between those who play the role of a "loyal opposition" to the MNOCs and the Nigerian state in return for patronage, others who demand compensation and direct rents from MNOCs, and those who challenge the legitimacy of the state and the MNOCs and seek to exercise direct control (through ethnic autonomy) over oil, and their oil-bearing lands.

The last, in the Ogoni case, connect the people and, the INGOs, and appropriate global rights discourse and the "technology" of global networking. INGOs, in effect, empower local resistance as allies. This, in turn, legitimizes and concretizes the relevance of the INGOs as actors in the transnational human rights movement.

From the foregoing, the struggles involving "global-local" alliances/net works tend to be complex, reflecting varied interests, overlaps, and contradictions. Yet the forces of local resistance are clear about the need to capture power (and exercise authority) at their locality as a basis for seeking equitable distribution of oil revenues to their communities, pushing an agenda for social justice within the Nigerian federation, and forcing oil multinationals to conform to internationally recognized environmental standards and respect the rights of the local people.

From the global to the local: the deconstruction of local resistance

The partnership of the Nigerian state and the MNOCs lies at the heart of the deconstruction of local resistance. The role of the state as facilitator for the reproduction of oil-based accumulation in Nigeria carves for it a mediatory role in global – local relations. The multinational oil corporations in the course of oil production become immersed in the local politics of the oil-producing communities. Acting in partnership with the state, but operating directly in the oil community, the oil company becomes "domesticated." It is a powerful and rich "tenant" of the impoverished communities, which despite being the "hosts" remain largely excluded from the operations of the companies and the distribution of benefits accruing from oil. The Niger Delta, while hosting the sophisticated MNOCs, is paradoxically one of the poorest regions of Nigeria. Most of the oil communities lack electricity, piped water, and basic infrastructure. There is virtually no development, with the people torn between a life of subsistence and the stark reality of unemployment. Worse still, these pauperized villagers bear the full costs of pollution and degradation arising from oil production. In some instances, the MNOCs directly "govern," in the sense of exercising power and allocating resources in the oil-producing communities, patronizing local chiefs and opinion leaders, and influencing some of the decisions of local authorities.

The history of the extractive and polluting activities of multinational oil corporations (particularly Shell) in Nigeria is well known and will not be repeated here (see Obi 1997; also Niboro 1997). Suffice it to say that this has been facilitated by a legal framework which vests the ownership of all land (and oil) in the federal government. It also provides that the federal government is a joint-venture partner to the oil multinationals operating Nigeria's most lucrative oil wells in a context where state regulation of environmental standards and safety is inadequate. Due to the headstart Shell had over other MNOCs operating in Nigeria (Soremekun and Obi 1993), with the most widespread operations in the Niger Delta, pumping out close to half of Nigeria's total daily oil production and exports, it has faced the brunt of, and suffered immense losses arising from, the growing protests in the region. In the same way, local resistance in the Niger Delta has targeted Shell as the biggest and most visible operator, and a major symbol of wealth and power, backed by the state. This has opened up a global front (when Shell and the state ignored local demands for restitution and compensation), while Shell deploys its huge resources toward neutralizing the forces of local resistance.

The strategic issues for Shell include ensuring the local order necessary to continue its extractive (and polluting) activities and protecting its corporate reputation, particularly in Europe and North America (thus protecting the company from international protests and hostility). Shell has worked hard to protect its image from damaging reports exposing the details of its exploitative and ecologically devastating activities in the Niger Delta. A great deal of energy has been directed against such reports by denying outright that they are true and publicizing huge sums spent by Shell on community development in the Delta. Shell's spokespersons have addressed press conferences in which Shell's corporate image is properly packaged and articulated. Other strategies include publicizing Shell's losses arising from violent protests and acts of sabotage.

Shell, Chevron, and other oil companies are also involved in the patronage of some state-appointed traditional rulers, local elite, and elders in the local communities,[1] and sponsoring of Western journalists on specially

---

[1] Local information in this chapter is drawn from interviews conducted by the author between December 1997 and August 2000 under conditions of anonymity with two groups of actors in the Niger Delta: activists and MNOC community relations officials in Nigeria and the United Kingdom.

packaged tours of the Niger Delta to "see things for themselves." They have also resorted to the hiring of high-flyer public relations consultants and environmental advisors to polish their image and strengthen their Nigerian community relations component. In relation to the human rights situation in the Delta, the MNOCs continue to insist that they cannot be held liable for the actions and non-actions of the Nigerian state and the military. However, since the execution of nine Ogoni activists in 1995 and the damage to Shell's image locally and globally, the company has begun to restructure its community development program to allow for a measure of community participation, working directly or with development agencies, INGOs, NGOs, and some local community-based cooperatives. But it must be noted that this new direction is still at its infancy and is still subsumed in the logic of "community relations."

In relation to the dialectics of local governance, oil multinationals have continued to back state repression of local protests and resistance (Rowell, 1996a: 282–451; see also Rowell 1996b; Boele 1995). Shell's links with the dreaded Rivers State Internal Security Task Force, which has since 1994 been violently "pacifying" Ogoniland, have been revealed (Robinson 1996). Its connections with some local leaders act as a lever for the classic "divide and rule" tactics of truncating the forces of local resistance. The local allies of MNOCs are rewarded with gifts, lucrative contracts, positions in the oil companies or government, and logistical support for special projects and assignments designed to bolster their relevance and authority within the arena of local politics.

From the foregoing, it is clear that, rather than change, the oil multinationals largely prefer to keep their transaction costs down, and ride roughshod over the human and environmental rights of the people of the Delta. They try to ensure that the true dimensions of the ecological damage are kept away from observers so that the reputation of MNOCs in Africa is not damaged.

With the Nigerian state being largely excluded from the actual production of oil, and reduced to a collector of oil rents, its dependence on MNOCs means that mediation is broadly a function of two phenomena: state weakness *vis-à-vis* the MNOCs and divisions within the ruling class, which mean the hegemonic faction is fragile, while paradoxically appearing strong. Both combine to define local resistance as subversion, to be crushed by the state.

But, as mentioned, there has also been direct MNOC involvement in local governance, unmediated by the state. This occurs especially in the area of community development. However, the impact of this on the Delta is unfortunately comparable to little drops of water in an ocean of poverty.

The entire Niger Delta has been militarized to provide the oil multinationals the law and order (security) necessary to produce oil, while complaints (demands) have been ignored, protests violently crushed, villages sacked, and thousands killed, exiled, or displaced by armed troops. Indeed, matters came to a head in the Ogoni tragedy of November 10, 1995, when Ken Saro-Wiwa and eight other MOSOP leaders were hanged, after being found guilty by a tribunal of inciting a mob to murder four (allegedly pro-state) prominent Ogoni leaders.

These executions – which were condemned around the world as illegal as the verdicts resulted from a tribunal that fell short of internationally recognized standards of a fair trial (Birnbaum 1995) – failed, however, to ensure victory for militarized state mediation as events in the Delta since 1995 clearly show (Human Rights Watch 1999).

It is necessary to dwell, albeit briefly, on how some government institutions were deployed against local resistance. At all levels, the resistance groups were denied access and representation. Even when delegations of federal government toured the Delta in 1993 and 1994, and the MOSOP leadership was invited to Abuja, the federal capital, in 1994, it was essentially to explore federal possibilities of co-opting the leadership of local resistance. When this failed, that leadership was marked for elimination. Two past decrees were significant in charting the historical course of this action: the Treason and Treasonable Offences Decree of 1993, which branded ethnic minority agitation for self-determination an offence punishable by death, and the Rivers State 1994 Special Tribunal (Offences Relating to Civil Disturbances) Edict, under the Civil Disturbances (Special Tribunal) Decree of 1987, which ousted the jurisdiction of normal courts and granted the power of appeal to the Provisional Ruling Council (PRC) of the federal military government. It was under this decree that the "Ogoni nine" were tried, found guilty, and executed.

Militarized mediation dialectically strengthened the radical arm of local leadership. With formal structures of power and authority closed to them, they established parallel structures of "loyalty, governance, and representation," became militant, with youth factions in the vanguard, branding the colluding elite and leaders as traitors to be scorned, or in extreme cases attacked.

Even within the state–MNOC alliance, there are contradictions, for in some ways the oil multinationals are no match for the Nigerian state.

At certain conjunctures, the state is treated with contempt, passed off as inefficient for failing to provide basic infrastructure and services in the Niger Delta,[2] and blamed for the problems the oil multinationals are facing in the oil communities. Yet the fact that the Nigerian state provides access to high-quality, cheap petroleum with little regulation provides the oil multinationals with immense profits. Whatever reservations the officials in the field may have, these pale into insignificance in the face of successive impressive annual revenues.

The oil multinationals actively engage local structures of power and nurture a client class of contractors, informants, and local leaders to smooth over their operations. However, such clients are increasingly having their authority challenged and undermined in the face of the radicalization of local movements. It has become more expensive to protect these clients, especially as their legitimacy in certain local communities wears thin in the face of their inability to persuade the state and MNOCs to address adequately the grievances of the people. These clients are seen either as self-serving leaders or, in extreme cases, as traitors, to be either defied or punished. In some of these communities, traditional chiefs are "tried" and "exiled" by militant youth movements, who increasingly exercise (alternative) power and authority in the community, and even confront MNOCs and state security forces in their locality.

In order to reverse the trend, in which legitimacy, power, and authority were slipping out of the hands of these client-chiefs, the Nigerian state has poured more troops into the Delta. Some elders/chiefs are now struggling hard to retain their legitimacy and relevance, even to the extent of opposing the militarization of the Delta and offering to act as mediators between the protest forces and the state–MNOC alliance. The reaction of the protest forces across the Delta to such offers ranges from cautious cooperation, to suspicion and outright rejection.

Thus, the forces of transterritorial extraction that forge links with client structures of power, as well as some local NGOs and individuals, clash with the forces of local protest (which in turn have support from their international allies). It is this violent engagement that defines the ongoing conflicts in the Delta. As the tensions escalate, the possibilities of local order continue to erode, resulting in more violence and the episodic disruptions of the global extraction of oil from the Niger Delta.

---

[2] Interviews, 1997, 1998 (Nigeria).

International arenas, transnational discourses, and local protest

It is necessary to note the relevance of the openings offered by the end of the Cold War in the late 1980s. These openings, such as the prominence given to the need to uphold minority rights or the rights of indigenous peoples by organizations such as the European Union, the United Nations, and some INGOs in Europe and North America, provided a platform for the internationalization and legitimization of the struggle of the Niger Delta ethnic minorities. It would seem that the activities of INGOs in supporting democratic/opposition groups in the Third World are perhaps shaped by a neo-liberal multiparty/democratic framework which seeks to universalize the values of democracy through an emphasis on human, environmental, and group rights. Other INGOs showed more specialization, with some focusing on humanitarian, conservation, and environmental issues. Altogether, these INGOs have constituted "associational allies," and facilitators of resistance in the Niger Delta. They rarely do so uniformly, and in a few cases they actually weaken local protest efforts by imposing agendas on groups seeking their support. In such cases, donor funds or projects have provoked internal struggles over distribution, goals, and priorities.

The INGOs offered a nice handle with which groups such as MOSOP, the Chikoko Movement (CM), and the Ijaw Youth Council (IYC) have strengthened local struggles. Operating across borders, and without obvious state control, INGOs have supported the campaigns of oppressed groups, providing them with platforms and resources to lobby, protest, and bring their plight to the attention of the people and parliaments of the industrially advanced states. It is expected that these will in turn pressure their home governments and the citizens to call the Nigerian state and the MNOCs to account.

With regards to networking with INGOs, MOSOP was perhaps the earliest local group in the Delta to connect with these transnational organizations (Obi 1999; see also Saro-Wiwa 1995). What is, however, fundamental to this study is how the forces of local resistance have represented their grievances, the strategies of networking, and how they mobilize forces in the quest for power over the oil-rich locality.

The foregoing can be located in some of the strategies of MOSOP, and more recently, Chikoko and the IYC. Right from its beginning in 1991, MOSOP claimed to represent the liberation of Ogoni people from decades of exploitation, pollution, and voicelessness. The Ogoni Bill of Rights (OBR), which was presented to the federal government of Nigeria by Ken Saro-Wiwa in his capacity as president of the Ogoni Central

Union in 1990, involved the widest consultations with all sections of Ogoni society. MOSOP established grassroots support for the belief that the struggle for self-determination, compensation, and control of the oil-rich Ogoni territory was morally correct and just. The OBR received local legitimacy when it was endorsed with the signatures of most Ogoni traditional rulers and leaders. It was translated into the Ogoni dialects and understood by the villagers. MOSOP became the umbrella organization of the various Ogoni interest groups: Federation of Ogoni Women Associations (FOWA), National Youth Council of Ogoni People (NY-COP), Council of Ogoni Churches (COC), Council of Ogoni Professionals (COP), Council of Ogoni Traditional Rulers (COTRA), National Union of Ogoni Students (NUOS), Ogoni Students Union (OSU), Ogoni Teachers Union (OTU), and Ogoni Central Union (OCU) (Barikor-Wiwa 1996).

In 1991, MOSOP mobilized the local populace not only to expand the demands made in the OBR, but also to receive popular authorization to internationalize the Ogoni struggle. It took the Ogoni case to the Unrepresented Nations and Peoples Organization (UNPO) at The Hague in 1992, and helped produce documentaries on Shell's environmental activities in Ogoniland. A great deal was done to promote the Ogoni cause. This involved protests against Shell and the Nigerian state, and other activities coordinated by the highest decision-making organs of MOSOP: the executive and the steering committee. In terms of its relations to other movements in the Delta, MOSOP efforts to provide leadership for a pan-Delta effort of local resistance petered out as a result of a host of historical reasons, ethnic, ideological, and personality differences.

As a "minority within minorities," the Ogoni were discriminated against by the larger ethnic minorities in the Delta in the intra-elite squabbles for power and resources. Such large groups (such as the Ijaw) were unwilling to accept Ogoni "leadership." The 1993–1994 clashes between the Ogoni and their neighbors – Andoni, Okrika, and Ndoki – were covertly instigated by the Nigerian military, which had infiltrated these communities with the intention of subverting the MOSOP struggle.

Offering the Ogoni masses the opportunity to participate directly in decision-making and providing them with a platform to voice their grievances, MOSOP became an alternative source of power and authority for local forces. This partly explains the determination of the state and Shell (and their local allies) to crush the MOSOP "revolution" and set it as an example to other restive groups in the Niger Delta. Yet MOSOP has continued to enjoy broad support among the Ogoni, representing their interests at local and global levels, while the MOSOP example has spread to the Ijaw ethnic group, with the IYC fiercely engaging the state and the oil companies operating across the Delta.

MOSOP has not been without its own internal contradictions, being divided into three broad factions: the conservatives/elite/moderates, the radicalized youth/peasantry/women, and the vigilantes. It is important to note that these are more "analytic categories" designed to address the Ogoni struggle and illustrate how the widening of the cleavages within the struggle has had severe consequences for the movement since 1994. It is equally important to note the rather fluid nature of these factions and the ways is which actors move from one to the other, based on disagreements over goals, tactics, and leadership styles.

Within the conservatives, there were those who were clearly pro-state and pro-Shell as they were direct beneficiaries of patronage, contracts, and protection, and thus were labeled as sell-outs, traitors, or "vultures." There were those who believed that MOSOP was "spinning out of control," and its politics undermining long-valued norms of respect for tradition, moderation, seniority, and age, with younger radical leaders excluding or demonizing all those who disagreed with MOSOP's tactics. The radicalized groups on the other hand (NYCOP and FOWA played prominent roles) believed that a social revolution based on self-determination and social justice was possible with total commitment, courage, and sacrifice. They allowed little room for doubt, disagreement, or indeed compromise once the "majority" had reached a decision. It was the cleavages between the conservatives and the radicals that were exploited by the state – Shell alliance to undermine MOSOP. This took different forms: repression of the activists, ample support of the conservatives, disinformation on both sides, fanning of the embers of hatred, distrust, and anger, and the infiltration of the ranks of the radicals by paid agents programmed to inform on and subvert them from within.

The vigilantes on the other hand were made up of extremist elements or *agents provocateurs* who took the law into their own hands, holding summary trials (and allegedly in some cases executions), effecting the banishment of "vultures," and setting up illegal road blocks or manhunts for traitors. Their style was largely violent, illegal, and often condemned by MOSOP (Obi 1997). Yet the activities of the vigilantes, among other factors, provided a pretext for the military occupation of Ogoniland from 1994, in order to restore "law and order".

As the cleavages within MOSOP widened, and the basis for compromise wore thin, the movement became increasingly vulnerable. Since MOSOP lacked strong ties to neighboring oil communities or social movements in the Niger Delta region, it was relatively easy for Shell and the Nigerian state to work against the Ogoni revolution.

In terms of representation in local formal structures, the state ensured that radical MOSOP members or sympathizers were excluded from participating in state governance. Denied access, MOSOP operated largely outside these structures. As such, in the heat of the struggle a zero-sum relationship developed between those who accepted the power and authority of MOSOP and those who recognized the power and authority of state structures. This zero-sum context provided fertile ground for the hegemony of the radical faction of MOSOP, driving the most conservative elements to seek the "protection" of the state–Shell coalition. The latter exploited these cleavages to undo the "MOSOP revolution."

The chain of events starting with the disagreements arising over the decision to boycott the June 1993 presidential elections resulted in the resignation of the president and vice-president of MOSOP and the assumption of those positions by the radicals, led by Ken Saro-Wiwa. This culminated in the murder of four "conservatives" by a mob on May 24, 1994 and set the stage for the military siege of the Ogoni and the hanging on November 10, 1995 of nine MOSOP leaders, which thus eliminated an entire generation of the leadership of the Ogoni movement.

MOSOP's strategies for entering international arenas

The insertion of the Ogoni cause into the global rights agenda from 1991 underscored the Ogoni people's success in waging one of the most sophisticated struggles against the excesses of the oil companies. MOSOP strengthened their case, and won the support of significant sections of the INGO community to the cause of local resistance.

In the face of the non-response of the Nigerian government and Shell to Ogoni demands, MOSOP took the struggle to the global level, with its strategy of putting international pressure on the Nigerian state and turning the heat on Shell in its own home, Europe, exposing it as a violator of the rights of an indigenous people, the Ogoni, who had been excluded from the benefits of the oil industry and whose lands and waters were being poisoned by oil pollution. Shell was chosen because of its vulnerability as the largest onshore operator in the Niger Delta, the fact that it had enormous wealth in the midst of abject poverty in the oil communities, and its symbiotic relationship with the Nigerian state, among other reasons. It was hoped that once Shell capitulated, a domino effect would occur within the ranks of other oil multinationals and force the state to respond to the demands of the oil minorities.

MOSOP's first port of call was the Unrepresented Nations and Peoples Organization in The Hague in 1992. Here the Ogoni case was presented to the world, as that of an indigenous people facing imminent ecocide/genocide at the hands of Shell and the Nigerian state. It provided Ken Saro-Wiwa with the opportunity to network with INGOs involved in the area of rights – human and environmental – and helped MOSOP establish the necessary contacts, strategies, and alliances, for "globalizing" its struggle (Obi 1999). UNPO thus became the early global platform for legitimizing Ogoni local resistance and immersing it in the global rights "community." In the same year, the MOSOP presented its case to the United Nations Working Group on Indigenous Peoples. On January 4, 1993 MOSOP organized a peaceful rally against Shell and the state. This demonstration involved over 250,000 Ogoni people as part of the celebration of the United Nations Year of Indigenous People. Since then, every January 4 has been marked as Ogoni day, thus transforming a global statement into a local idiom for the cause of Ogoni freedom. The United Nations Human Rights Commission later became interested in the Ogoni struggle, and was to set up a fact finding mission, which toured Ogoniland after the 1995 hangings.

MOSOP's "complaints" were well packaged for the global audience, through networking with human and environmental rights INGOs such as Amnesty International, FIAN International, Human Rights Watch Africa, Article 19, Inter-rights, the Body Shop, Greenpeace, Friends of the Earth, and others (Skogley 1997) (see Table 1 below). The image of the Ogoni, as a victimized minority ethnic nationality, an indigenous people denied its rights, discriminated against by the big ethnic groups, faced with extinction, and confronted by the combined might of Shell (a global oil giant) and the authoritarian Nigerian state, strengthened MOSOPs appeals to the international community. It also formed the basis for networking with the INGOs and activists based in the West, who "adopted" the Ogoni struggle, completing the circuit of the connection of the local to the global.

The use of modern communications technology in the globalizing of Ogoni resistance was critical. Computers, the Internet, telephones, and fax machines were essential elements in informing the world about the excesses of the state–Shell alliance and in representing it in visual form. Contacts were speedily arranged and the shortening of distances also enhanced the capacity of INGO missions to visit, experience firsthand, and report on the situation in Ogoniland. At the same time, MOSOP activists were able to give lectures all over the world, attend workshops, and address politicians, parliaments, and pressure groups in order to win them over to the side of the forces of local protest.

The role of the media, Nigerian as well as foreign, in popularizing the Ogoni struggle cannot be overemphasized. The Ogoni campaign was promoted through widely circulated reports in the leading newspapers and news magazines in Europe and North America. Television stations and networks beamed the "ecological violations" against the Ogoni to shocked audiences across the world. Examples include documentaries such as "The Heat of the Moment," "Delta Force," and "Drilling Fields." In one program, Bop Van Dessel, Shell's former head of environmental studies in Nigeria, confirmed Shell's complicity in damaging the Niger Delta's fragile ecosystem: "they were not meeting their own standards, they were not meeting international standards. Any Shell site I saw was polluted. It is clear to me that Shell was devastating the area" (quoted in Clothier and O'Conner 1996).

From the foregoing, the "globalizing" of the MOSOP campaign turned the heat on Shell and the Nigerian state, while popularizing the cause of the Ogoni. MOSOP, empowered by the support abroad for its local claims, confronted the state, and especially Shell, head on, forcing Shell to abandon operations in Ogoniland after 1993. Even after the militarization of the Delta by the state, the execution of some MOSOP leaders in 1995, and the displacement or forcing into exile of thousands more, the state is still far from enforcing law and order in the Niger Delta. The "MOSOP revolution" has been counting its gains and losses, amid efforts to heal the deep cleavages in the movement. Developments since the death of Nigerian military strongman General Sanni Abacha in June 1998 have contributed to a slight loosening of the military siege on Ogoniland.

On September 4, 1998, the "Ogoni nineteen" were freed on the orders of a Port Harcourt High Court, four years after they were arrested and detained, and after a sustained local and international campaign for their release from the harrowing conditions under which they were held. Since then some MOSOP leaders have returned from exile to coordinate the struggle, which is rather unfortunately immersed in factional politics – this time involving a group led by Ledum Mittee, MOSOP's president (the sole survivor of the Justice Auta Tribunal which sentenced the nine Ogoni activists to death in 1995), and a rival faction led by Dr. Owens Wiwa, the late Ken Saro-Wiwa's younger brother. Chikoko, the IYC, both factions of MOSOP, and other rights movements in the Delta have sites on the Internet, through which they promote their international campaigns against the Nigerian state and the MNOCs.[3]

While there is a reduced tempo in the Ogoni campaign, as a result of continued repression and factional struggles within MOSOP which have led to the confusion of both local and global supporters of Ogoni resistance, the struggles in the Delta have spread and have continued to reach

[3] For example, http://www.oneworld.org/mosop, http://www.mosopcanada.org, and http://www.oneworld.org/delta.

Table 8.1 *A selection of INGOs networking with rights groups in the Niger Delta*

Africa Policy Information Centre	Netherlands Committee of the International Union for the Conservation of Nature
BookAid International	Project Underground
Both Ends	Rainforest Action Network
Delta	Sierra Club
Friends of the Earth International	Trocaire
Human Rights Watch	World Council of Churches

Sources: Fieldwork, interviews, and NGO reports/newsletters.

out into international arenas. Other resistance movements have come to the fore. For the purpose of this study, we shall mention four. These are Environmental Rights Action (ERA); the Niger Delta Human and Environmental Rescue Organization (ND-HERO); the Chikoko Movement (CM); and the IYC, which in December 1998 launched the Kaiama Declaration. This contained a list of demands to MNOCs and the federal government, which, if they did not meet them, would face forceful expulsion from the Ijaw-controlled parts of the Niger Delta. These resistance movements are working with some of the INGOs listed in Table 8.1.

Drawing lessons from the MOSOP experience, the other protest movements have concentrated on raising the level of awareness of the local population. They have also worked with people in the areas of community empowerment, resource management, and compensation to strengthen organizational capacities in relation to the demands made in the course of their struggle. Apart from documentation and collection of information, these groups inform the world of occurrences in the Delta and organize campaigns against the violation of such rights. Through vertical networking (see Schmitz this volume) they have kept the campaigns against Shell alive, resulting in pressures on the company and the boycott of its products in some countries in the West.

Within the Delta itself, the Environment Rights Action (ERA), established in 1993, which also networks with Chikoko and the IYC, is involved in several projects with INGO support. These include community resource development projects in Anyama, Sangana, and Okoroba, and a proposed one in Olugbobiri (information from author interviews in Nigeria in 1997). A few INGOs working with participatory development models are a new trend in the Delta. This is a departure from the technical, wasteful, top-down community development programs of the MNOCs. It is interesting to note that some MNOCs are linking up with these INGOs, NGOs/community-based organizations (CBOs), and protest movements to co-partner community-owned and designed development projects (there have been a few of these scattered across the Delta since 1996).

The ERA is also involved in the collation and dissemination of information about the state of human and environmental rights in the Niger Delta, the activities of Shell and other petroleum companies, and the human and environmental rights implications of the actions or inactions of the central and state governments in the Niger Delta. These activities are carried out in the field, and also through the Delta Information Service (DIS) and its monthly publication, *Niger Delta Alert*. While ERA is an arm of the Civil Liberties Organization (a national human rights NGO), its Delta-specific focus hinges upon "the defense of human ecosystems within the context of human rights" (ERA/Friends of the Earth Nigeria 1998a, 1998b, 1998c, 1999a, 1999b). The ERA is a member of the African Forest Action Network (AFAN) and an associate of Friends of the Earth International (FOEI) and serves as the coordinating NGO of the OilWatch Network in Africa. As noted earlier, ERA also has close ties with and support from some of the INGOs identified in Table 1.

Despite limits to horizontal networking (see Schmitz this volume) in the past, the beginnings of a pan-Delta network of local protest can be seen in the Chikoko Movement (CM), which was launched on August 17, 1997 at Aleibiri, in Bayelsa state. Chikoko is a mass organization of the ethnic minorities of the Niger Delta seeking to defend their rights, as well as confronting their oppressors. Its launch was reportedly attended by over 10,000 people including representatives of rights groups such as the Democratic Alternative (DA), ERA, OilWatch, MOSOP, and the Movement for Reparations to Ogbia (MORETO), as well as women's, youth, and community representatives from other parts of the Delta.

What the CM seeks to forge is a unifying platform for an emancipatory pan-Delta project on the basis of social justice, equity, ethnic identity, and democracy. In a sense, it seeks to elevate the struggle in the Delta to include all the ethnic nationalities, and to put the issues of self-determination and control of resources on the front burner of national and global discourse (author interviews in Nigeria, 1997 and 1998).

Chikoko also seeks the political restructuring of Nigeria into a federation of ethnic nationalities based on the people's right to self-determination, equity, and access to resources. This implies ethnic groups should control natural resources and be free to negotiate the terms of their membership of the Nigerian federation. The same logic of local (grassroots) autonomy is extended to the realm of the traditional authorities, who are scared of the militant youth movements of the Niger Delta and who often rely on the state and the oil companies for their personal security and comfort (author interviews).

While a note of caution must be sounded to the effect that the drive toward a pan-Delta network of local resistance is not altogether smooth, beset by its own internal contradictions and complexities, Chikoko has none the less begun to be successful in connecting its local struggles with global discourses on rights and democratization in the ways described above for individual organizations.

As an intrinsic part of their struggles, the social movements of the Niger Delta challenging the state have linked up with the national-democratic movement within Nigeria. The Ijaw Youth Council, Isoko National Youth Movement, Oron National Forum, Egi Youth Organization, Ogoni Solidarity Movement (an affiliate of MOSOP), Chikoko, O'odua Peoples Congress, and the Pan Igbo Youth Council among others have formed the Coalition for Self-Determination (COSED), which is pushing for self-determination for the ethnic nationalities of the Niger Delta, and the institution of a national government based on a Sovereign National Conference involving the elected representatives of all ethnic and interest groups with the aim of restructuring the Nigerian federation (COSED 1999).

There is no doubt that since 1995 there has been a radicalization of local resistance in the Niger Delta. While the discourse of resistance is not anticapitalist, the politics of the leadership of the social movements is basically radical, challenging the inequities spawned by the oil capital in the region. The use of rights discourses – environmental and human – supports both immediate goals and long-term political ones. For the movements are as concerned about the safety of their fragile ecosystem as they are about the defense of their rights as a people. To cite a part of the Chikoko statement, "now is the time to reclaim our destiny and humanity. We must defend our ecosystem and means of subsistence from further devastation and looting" (Chikoko 1997; see also Chikoko 1999). Unless the state–MNOC alliance responds to demands for the employment of indigenes of oil communities, compensation for pollution and damage of economic crops, provision of basic services, and a fairer distribution of oil incomes, these local movements are ready to block oil production in the Niger Delta. At certain junctures, however, the conservation and compensation considerations contradict each other (even if this is not immediately obvious).

There is also the realization across the grassroots in the Niger Delta that an emancipatory project, while including "material and social justice objectives," must involve a radical restructuring of the Nigerian federation with emphasis on the respect of rights of ethnic minority nationalities, democracy, and local autonomy for the nationalities of the Niger Delta. While not being directly involved in the provision of basic or social services in the Delta, the forces of local resistance acting with INGOs and local NGOs have carried out some community development projects in the Delta: micro-credit finance and savings schemes, natural resource management, conservation, and income-generating activities. Considering the swampy and difficult terrain of the Delta, provision of infrastructure and services is a very costly venture beyond the present resources of these local groups, hence the premium placed on an increased share of oil revenues, and payment of reparations and compensation for the exploitation and degradation of their lands by the MNOCs.

There is no doubt that the organizational capacities of the forces of local resistance in the Niger Delta have grown since 1995. Rather than following the Ogoni example which led to the heavy local costs of a state-led pacification via military occupation and repression, with the aim of frightening other communities into submission, this resistance has fed into covert, militant action by other groups in the Delta, especially among the Ijaw, Urhobo, Oron, Egi, and Isoko. While "globalizing" their struggles, they have been representing their claims and grievances through the use, among other things, of protest and "guerrilla" tactics in blocking MNOC oil installations or waging local wars such as the Ijaw – Itsekiri fracas in which youth "forces" have fought a bloody "oil war" in 1997, 1998, and 1999. Protesting Ijaw villagers have been fired upon by troops, as in the case of the Parabe incident in May 1999, the invasion of Ijaw communities in January 1999, and the destruction of Odi in November 1999. The joint operations of Nigerian police, army, navy, and security forces remain directed at forcefully lifting the siege on the MNOCs and oil installations in the Niger Delta.

In August 1998, "armed villagers forced Shell to suspend exports at both the Bonny and Forcados oil terminals . . . in all both Shell and Agip could not export close to one million barrels of oil, out of Nigeria's quota of two million daily" (Onanuga 1998). The virtual shutdown of about half of Nigeria's oil export capacity for weeks (bringing it down to its lowest level since 1995) by the forces of local protest and the renewed military operations by government (even while giving notice of intentions to introduce "reforms") offer little hope of a respite in the short to medium term (Economist Intelligence Unit 1999: 29). It is quite clear that MNOCs' old tactics and those of the state are becoming more costly, amid the rising incidence of acts of violent protest against them. Yet it is still unclear how effective the Chikoko Movement is in its pan-Delta drive. An unresolved point is the suspicion that Chikoko may yet be a ploy for Ijaw ethnic hegemony over other minorities in the Delta.

Some also believe that the MOSOP leadership is more "battle-tested" and experienced. There is also the problem of Chikoko's being eclipsed by the militancy of the Ijaw Youth Congress and other militant groups currently engaging the oil companies and federal forces in an "oil war" in the Niger Delta. Beyond this, Chikoko is faced with the complexity and ethno-cultural diversity of the Delta, the problem of the logistics of mobilizing people across the difficult terrain of the region and the presence of the formidable forces of the state–MNOC alliance. However, through its networking with other resistance youth movements in the Niger Delta and beyond, the Chikoko is overcoming some of the initial limitations.

In addition, some cracks have been noticed in the INGO movement *vis-à-vis* local protest in the Niger Delta. Some INGOs have "dropped" the Ogoni campaign, moving on to other "hot" global concerns, or losing interest following the execution of the charismatic, well-known writer and Ogoni rights campaigner, Ken Saro-Wiwa. Others have diversified their support by adopting other resistance movements in the Delta. However, other INGOs are reportedly penetrating the local by engaging in community development projects covertly funded by MNOCs (and overtly by donors).

The contradictions within local movements (and even the INGOs) without doubt reduce the capabilities of the forces of local resistance. Local movements to some extent are dogged by leadership crises, institutional weaknesses, disagreements over principles and tactics, and the activities of "professional activists" who seem to be keener on making a career of seeking compensation from MNOCs, attracting resources from donors, and reaping the material benefits of "global" activism, than the defense of the rights of the people. This to some extent has caused confusion and divisions in the ranks of local protest movements.

At the same time the militants are growing increasingly numerous and confident of their ability to outwit state forces either through guerrilla-like operations in the maze of creeks and swamps of the Niger Delta or by bringing global pressures to bear on the state–MNOC alliance. This is not in any way to downplay the major strides recorded in the advancement of local movements in the Niger Delta, but to note that, rather than being a straightforward or linear process, it is largely driven by its own dialectic, in a zigzag, backward–forward motion. But on the whole, the forces of local protest have developed the capacity to block extraction and draw global attention and resources to their cause.

Before going further, it is apposite to capture the difference that Nigeria's return to democracy since May 1999 has made to local – global junctures and the volatile relations between major actors in the Niger

Delta. The democratic opening has reduced the level of the militarization of the region, even if extra-judicial killings and rights violations are yet to stop (author interviews; see also Esparza and Wilson 1999). Local movements and INGOs now operate freely and continue to engage the state–MNOC alliance which has not changed in any fundamental manner. Local resistance forces still deploy "the collective metaphor of the victim" in attracting global support to their claims. This, together with an alarming wave of sabotages of petroleum product pipelines, abduction of company staff, shut-down of oil installations, and tragic pipeline explosions leading to many villagers in the poverty-stricken Delta either being burnt to death or gravely injured (*New York Times* 2000), continues to draw global attention.

Exploiting the window of opportunity opened up by democracy, the Nigerian state has started to engage the Niger Delta through other (non-violent) means. A development board – the Niger Delta Development Commission (NDDC) – has been established, after some bickering between the federal executive and legislature, to address the growth issues in the troubled region. Apart from this, the derivation principle of revenue allocation has been increased from one to 13 percent to the advantage of the state governments of the Niger Delta, providing increased oil funds for developmental purposes. Yet both initiatives remain controversial and their effectiveness limited. The federal executive and the legislature are yet to settle the gray areas in the NDDC Act, after it was passed into law (without the president's assent). Thus, the commission is yet to fully take off, even though a measure of progress has been recorded in getting the senate to approve most of the president's nominees to the board and management of the NNDC. Additionally, the oil-producing states of the Niger Delta protest what they allege is the non-implementation of the 13 percent derivation formula by the federal government which continues to hold on to half of the derivation funds. On the part of the social movements of the Niger Delta, nothing short of local autonomy and total resource (oil) control would satisfy their demands; hence they remain unimpressed by the reforms being introduced by the democratic regime (author interview 2000).

Conclusion

The Nigerian case is illustrative of the issue of how the state still matters even when transboundary networks, arenas, and deployments become intensified. If anything, the Nigerian state has found new mediation roles by enforcing order and extraction at the local level. The centrality of the state under the conditions described above in the Niger Delta clearly shows the danger in some of the zero-sum assumptions about how globalization renders the state an irrelevant actor.

It must be pointed out, however, that the task of freeing the Delta from the contradictions spawned by global oil capital is a very difficult one, but the chances can be enhanced if the oil multinationals and the Nigerian state agree to be fair and transparent in their dealings with the people of the oil-bearing communities. Yet the capacity of the hegemonic forces of globalized oil capital to resist change must not be underestimated. In the same vein, the strategic and vital interests of the G-7 countries in cheap and steady supplies of oil (and gas) cannot be simply wished away.

There is no doubt that the intersections of the global, national, and local are significant for the struggles over power and authority in the Niger Delta. It would seem that the emancipation of the Delta would be enhanced by a unified global campaign connected to a local democratic one, defined by the rights of the people, on the basis of a co-equal partnership.

Ultimately, the possibilities of conflict resolution and the protection of the oil-rich Delta environment lie in the organizational capacity of the social movements of local protest to protect their rights and represent interests in ways that constructively engage international actors in the project of building a people-centered democratic project in Nigeria. But both local and global actors must learn, through struggle, to deal with the Nigerian state and the networks of globalized capital, which remain resolute to crush any opposition to the extraction of petroleum and gas – the vital propellants of capitalism in the era of globalization.

Part IV

Political economies of violence and authority

9   How sovereignty matters: international markets and the political economy of local politics in weak states

William Reno

Where do local power and authority lie in Africa when formal bureaucratic state institutions are either very weak or non-existent? At first glance, it seems that in Africa's worst-off states, places such as Nigeria, Congo, Liberia, and Sierra Leone, rulers cannot control associates, much less shape societies and economies within their borders. "Some states," writes Christopher Clapham (1996: 273), "have been so thoroughly privatized as to differ little from territories controlled by warlords." In Nigeria, for example, private groups even collect taxes, generating complaints that state officials ally with armed brigands to extort money from citizens for purely private gain (Olarewaju 1998: 16). Misrule and politicians' failure to satisfy even minimal popular expectations can lead to the collapse of order. Internal sovereignty in parts of Africa, argues Robert Jackson (1993), in the sense of a capacity even to preside over regime associates, much less control a specific territory, is increasingly either very weak or non-existent.

Jackson explains this weakening of internal control as being related to the growing unwillingness among officials in non-African states to give material assistance to help rulers compensate for weak bureaucracies. Proliferating insurgencies and the outright collapse of state order in Liberia, Somalia, Congo, and intermittently in Sierra Leone and Congo-Brazzaville appear to indicate a significant decline in external resources and internal capabilities available to rulers of weak states. This internal weakness calls into question the capacity of rulers to benefit from juridical, or external, recognition of nominal sovereignty. Holsti (1996: 40) expects that "weak states – not in the military sense, but in terms of legitimacy and efficacy – are and will be the locales of war." Clapham (1996: 9) even questions "whether international relations can exist without states, and if so, what form such relations might take."

Private economic transactions, John Ruggie (1993) claims, overwhelm the bureaucratic capacities of even strong states outside Africa (see also Ruggie 1983; Strange 1996). Africa's rulers in fact distinguish themselves in terms of meddling in clandestine markets, use of private violence to deal with rivals, and appropriation of state assets for personal gain, all at the expense of formal state institutions.[1] This suggests that local power has shifted away from norms and conventions of states. This affects its concrete, bureaucratic manifestations – and in terms of what the editors of this volume in their introduction call intangible social forms and practices, challenges the international expectation that all Africans live within political units that at least resemble states.

This chapter explains how Africa's rulers really exercise power amidst the apparent collapse of external support for weak state bureaucracies and vulnerable regimes. To address this question, I examine private commercial transactions in Africa that supposedly undermine the form and purpose of Africa's weakest states. I explain how these transactions bolster a new internal configuration of power in place of formal state bureaucracies. Related to this is an important extension of international practices regarding transnational aspects of commerce in Africa. Rulers' participation in commerce in Africa unintentionally favors non-bureaucratic means of exercising local power. Specifically, some rulers of weak states recognize that they can manipulate transnational commercial connections and outsiders' willingness to recognize them as mediators between local and world economies to accumulate wealth and control associates. External support for this interaction also plays a key role in bolstering the attractions to foreign firms of weak states and dealing with their rulers.

For weak state rulers, these relationships constitute a new form of extra-territorial political power. They manipulate commercial connections and recruit foreign firms as allies in battles with local challengers, exhibiting features akin to conventional diplomacy, which Jackson (1990) recognized as the (diminished) bedrock of weak state rulers' internal capacity. This action is now more informal and varied, using a wider range of outsiders to control commerce and people. Unlike in state-to-state diplomacy, rulers of weak states who exercise power through these relationships abjure efforts to control territory within internationally recognized frontiers, or even control territorially contiguous areas. At the same time, they may exercise a *de facto* control of people and areas outside state frontiers, seemingly at odds with the decrepitude of their state administrations.

Outside norms regarding the relation of internationally recognized sovereignty and transnational commerce play key roles in underpinning this new arrangement of power. Firms operating in Africa still require guarantees of protection of fixed assets, enforcement of contracts, access to credit, the capacity to indemnify operations, and certifications

---

[1] African critics of weak conventional norms of state rule include Ansah (1991), Koroma (1996), Takaya and Tyoden (1987), and Wonkeryor (1985).

of credibility sufficient to satisfy regulators in headquarter countries, rating services, and investors.[2] Rulers of very weak states and agents of foreign firms team up to use these conventions and norms to minimize inefficiencies associated with doing business in unpredictable, violent environments in places that lack state bureaucracies. Foreign firms benefit from the ruler's manipulation of the prerogatives of his sovereign status in the international realm. Other interested outsiders accept this arrangement because it reestablishes or preserves an outward semblance of internal hierarchy, appears to settle disputes, and metes out punishments. Some rulers of weak states thus prove adept at manipulating global commercial "issue networks" (akin to Frederick Cooper's use of the term in this volume to mean the intersection of interests that frame an issue in a particular way) to garner resources. This creates a widely accepted alternative order, alongside the (collapsing) state and its decrepit bureaucratic institutions, and helps mitigate the negative effects of this collapse, both for rulers and those outsiders who do business with them.

Broad, tacit acceptance of new arrangements even bolsters the power of rulers who already enjoy international recognition as sovereign. This creates two paradoxes. First, the willingness of outsiders to relax notions that sovereignty should include control over territory and an internal hierarchy changes the role of Africa's weak states. More particularly, this enhances the role of the internationally recognized sovereign status that accompanies even minimally capable states, as interlocutors between local and global economies. This gives weak state rulers privileged access to resources associated with this role, prerogatives insurgents lack. Second, weak state–foreign firm partnerships benefit from *international order* that international norms create. Thus armed, these partners exploit *internal disorder* to manipulate sovereign prerogatives to exclude commercial and political rivals, violently appropriate resources, and shield transactions from the eyes of outsiders. Together, they reshape internal arrangements in ways compatible with international economic competitiveness and internal control. Their actual exercise of power strays from conventional norms of internal state sovereignty, but conforms outwardly to outsiders' expectations that a state system exists everywhere in the world.

The shift from bureaucratic to commercial tools

Observers of politics in many sub-Saharan African states have long noted that rulers have exercised political power through family connections,

---

[2] My discussion of international commercial norms benefited from Dezalay and Garth (1996).

informal agreements with local intermediaries, or deals with trading communities, as much as through the authority of formal state institutions
(see, for example, Bayart 1989b). Direct state-to-state diplomatic ties,
however, helped rulers weather the major drawbacks of neglecting bureaucratic efficiency. For example, France's deployment of troops in six
states and thirty separate military interventions between 1963 and 1994
protected many regimes from their inability to effectively coerce rivals or
build popular legitimacy among populations (Martin 1995).

Declining international aid and more stringent conditions attached to
loans have weakened the centralization of patronage networks, posing
security threats to rulers. In former Zaire, for example, the decline of
bilateral aid from $823 million in 1990 to $178 million in 1993 reduced
President Mobutu's abilities as a patron (World Bank 1997a: 309). This
occurred not only as a consequence of Mobutu's inability to provide payouts to associates. Bereft of military aid or assistance from the USA and
its African allies, Mobutu could no longer enforce discipline among his
associates. Nor could he rebuild state bureaucracies to generate revenue
inside Zaire. The delegation of power to effective bureaucrats would pose
the risk to Mobutu that they would use increased revenues and popular
support for services to build their own power bases from which to challenge the president.

None the less, like some rulers of other weak states, Mobutu did not
face as drastic a decline in resources as first appeared. Overall, US state-
to-state aid to Africa fell from a peak of $2.4 billion in 1985 to $1.2 billion
in 1990 (both figures in constant 1997 dollars), and remained below that
figure for the rest of the 1990s (Copson 1994: 4). Some of this loss, however, shifted over to state support for private commercial activity in Africa,
or as aid to local societal organizations. In doing so, it increased the incentives to rulers of weak states to seek accommodations with foreigners
and local entrepreneurs who would have access to this aid. US aid, for
example, increasingly takes the form of credit and loan guarantees via the
quasi-official Overseas Private Investment Corporation (OPIC) to firms
willing to risk investment in impoverished African states (Rice 1997).
Likewise, legislative initiatives such as the Africa Growth and Opportunity Act (enacted in May 2000) designate $150 million for a private
investment equity fund and $500 million to back private investment in
African infrastructure. The official US Export-Import Bank helps ar-
range financing for overseas projects and exports. Similar shifts in priorities characterize financial flows to Africa from other states (Schraeder
et al. 1998). French officials increasingly back "aid" through agencies
such as Coface and Agence Française de Developpement, Koreans
through the Korean Export Insurance Corporation, Italians through

SACE (Istituto per i servizi assicurativi del commercio estero), and so forth.

The importance of controlling these and other commercial transactions lies in the tendency for regime opponents in weak states to strike out on their own when a ruler's attractions as a patron diminish. Liberia and Somalia demonstrate this danger. Liberia's President Doe (1980–1989) and his successors faced a growing array of strongmen competing to dominate the country once military and fiscal aid from the USA declined sharply in the late 1980s. Doe's total overseas aid fell from $105 million in 1986 to $55 million in 1989 (World Bank 1997a: 309). By 1994, all six of the major insurgent groups were headed by former Doe regime officials, each of whom built a private army on the resources and commercial connections that he had enjoyed while working for Doe. Likewise, Somalia's "warlords" arose from President Siad Barré's internal security and military hierarchies to challenge him, once he lost US patronage in the late 1980s. Thus political conflict in failing states tends to shift toward control over markets at the same time as officials in foreign states shift resources from aid to African states to aid investors in Africa.

The declining resources of state bureaucracies relative to the resources of markets appear to influence the behavior of insurgents as well. Most post-Cold War insurgencies exhibit an anti-bureaucratic bias as a consequence of their need to avoid delegating authority to potentially threatening associates while still desperately seeking resources, much like the weak state regimes that they challenge. During the Cold War, however, insurgencies such as South Africa's African National Congress, the Zimbabwean African People's Union, and the Eritrean People's Liberation Front, pursued external relations with confidence that a non-African state patron would help finance and provide diplomatic support to a centralized organization that presented itself as a reformist alternative to the incumbent regime (Clapham 1996: 222–226). Lacking a dominant external patron, contemporary insurgencies are forced to gather resources locally. Consequently, organizations such as Uganda's West Nile Bank Front, Lord's Resistance Army, Uganda National Rescue Front, the Allied Forces for the Liberation of Congo-Zaire (before assuming power in 1997), the Revolutionary United Front (RUF) in Sierra Leone, a plethora of Liberian groups, and others, appear more preoccupied with tapping into trade networks and less with presenting a reformist version of the state.[3]

---

[3] The demarcation is not absolute. US indirect assistance plays a role in strategies of the Sudanese People's Liberation Army. Conversely, the Union for the Total Independence of Angola received external aid while conducting diamond trade in the early 1990s. None the less, widespread state support of insurgents who style themselves as reformers is not likely to reemerge under current conditions.

Even a close look at the structure and capabilities of weak states and insurgencies that challenge them appears to indicate that insurgencies and weak states occupy a more level playing field. Jeffrey Herbst (1996), for example, proposes that insurgencies that do a better job of marshaling resources should be permitted to dismantle and replace some of Africa's weak states, borders and all (see also Herbst 2000). Herbst's suggestion appears to respond to African reality. For example, Charles Taylor's National Patriotic Liberation Front (NPFL) from 1990 to 1996 controlled the bulk of Liberia and parts of neighboring states, popularly known as "Taylorland" in distinction to Liberia. Taylor controlled far more resources than did the recognized government of Liberia, which was confined to a tiny coastal enclave centered on the country's capital, Monrovia. Taylor's income from 1990 to 1992 was roughly $200–$230 million.[4] The coastal enclave reportedly benefited from an income of only $250,000 in 1993 (Clapham 1996: 230) and state employees worked as unpaid "volunteers" in the words of a finance minister (Tarr 1993: 75). Likewise, the Congo's one-time insurgent and late president, Laurent Kabila, might have fared better as head of a new state, situated astride cohesive cultural and trade networks that cross currently recognized state frontiers.

And yet the Republic of Liberia remains in existence not only in international eyes but also in Charles Taylor's own publicly stated objectives (National Patriotic Reconstruction Assembly Government 1991). Taylor repeatedly asserted throughout Liberia's 1989 to 1996 civil war that his goal was to become the internationally recognized president of the Republic of Liberia, which he accomplished in an internationally mediated election in 1997. Nor did Kabila's 1996–1997 offensive in Zaire portend the disintegration of the country, as some predicted (see French 1996).[5] Kabila hastened to Kinshasa to assume the mantle of international recognition, rather than exploiting his standing in a trading area that had its own currency and far more cultural ties to eastern neighbors than to the distant capital. The same is true of Sierra Leone's RUF rebels, who contested control of Freetown, the capital, instead of basing their rule on their control of diamonds, the country's main source of wealth, 200 miles to the east. In Guinea-Bissau, army mutineers abjured a formal link-up with the transnational clandestine trade networks controlled by ethnic kinsmen which overshadow the formal income of the impoverished

[4] Taylor's wartime income is calculated from William Twaddell, US Assistant Secretary of State for African Affairs (1996), *Marchés Tropicaux* (1995): 1603–1606, Reeves and Moulard (1993), and documents from Taylor's National Patriotic Reconstruction Assembly Government, Forestry Development Authority & Economic Affairs Committee and liner bills of lading collected by the author.

[5] Instead, observers had to settle for Kabila's decision to change the name of the country from Zaire to Congo.

Guinea-Bissau state. Instead, they sought control of the capital, a small, decrepit town in hostile territory (*Africa Confidential* 1998b).

Apparently international recognition of sovereignty offers material and political advantages to insurgents that exceed the resources that come with *de facto* control over a specific territory. It is not surprising in this light that no major post-Cold War insurgency group, even in Africa's weakest states, has articulated an irredentist or separatist agenda that challenges Africa's boundaries inherited from colonial rule.[6]

Commercial advantages of sovereignty

A closer look at potential state-building insurgencies reveals how their lack of international recognition hobbles their efforts to build even *de facto* administrations. Some firms did do business with Charles Taylor when much of Liberia, but not its capital, was under his control. Firestone Tire & Rubber's subsidiary, for example, produced and exported rubber from "Taylorland." This activity gave Taylor access to several million dollars in the form of "tax" payments (National Patriotic Reconstruction Assembly Government 1992).[7] In addition, the firm allegedly permitted (or was forced to allow) Taylor to base his "Operation Octopus" offensive against the Monrovia enclave on Firestone's plantation. At the same time, Firestone faced legal action in US courts when the internationally recognized Monrovia enclave sued for violation of commercial agreements when the firm paid a "tax" to Taylor (Republic of Liberia 1993). In this and several other cases involving claims on behalf of and against the internationally recognized Liberian government, US courts affirmed the rights of recognized governments to seek standing in US court.[8] District courts also affirmed that the US president retains the prerogative of determining whether US authority (including courts) would recognize a particular insurgency as a public authority.

[6] The Eritrean People's Liberation Front (EPLF) secured independence in a 1993 referendum after prolonged warfare. Yet all combatants recognize the legitimacy of colonial boundaries (though dispute their location). The EPLF couched independence claims in terms of recognizing Eritrea's history as a colony separate from Ethiopia. Likewise, the Somali Democratic Movement's claim for Somaliland independence is based upon that territory's separate identity as a British colony before Somalia's independence in 1960.

[7] Also "Firestone Restart Table," January 16, 1992 – photocopy of original in author's possession.

[8] See Marian Nash, Office of the Legal Advisor, Department of State (1996). This view links standing to recognition of sovereignty. It underlines the rejection of standing in US state and federal courts of National Patriotic Reconstruction Assembly Government of Liberia vs Liberian Services, Inc. (92 Civ 145, E.D.Va 1992). In contrast, Taylor's US agents stressed Taylor's claims to control the territory and institutions of the Republic of Liberia during Liberia's civil war: Lester Hyman and H.P. Goldfield, "Notes on Liberian Fact-Finding Visit," September. 1991 [typescript].

Not only could a firm doing business with insurgents face enforceable legal claims from a recognized government. Non-recognition of insurgents denies firms that do business with rebels recourse to foreign courts for claims against their business partners.[9] Thus commercial jurisprudence, at least in its American form, provides a predictable framework external to weak states themselves to insure assets of firms that do business with internationally recognized weak states. In contrast, those who do business with insurgents do so without these legal protections, and thus, with higher risk. In practical terms, this legal exclusion makes it nearly impossible to indemnify operations with insurgents. Lacking insurance, such firms have a difficult time convincing investment rating services and institutional investors of the viability of their operations.

Yet as noted above, insurgents have attracted foreign firm backers. These firms likely calculate, however, that their insurgent partners will quickly assume the mantle of sovereignty. This is where Firestone miscalculated; after the failure of Taylor's "Operation Octopus," Firestone withdrew and many of Taylor's smaller foreign firm partners abandoned him. In Zaire (Congo), American Mineral Fields (AMF), a Canadian firm with headquarters in Hope, Arkansas (former president Clinton's hometown), reportedly provided Kabila with logistical services and "taxes" prior to his assumption of the office of president (*Africa Confidential* 1997; Brümmer 1997). AMF later faced confiscation by Kabila's government. But AMF's calculated risk paid off in the sense that the firm has recourse to US courts to sue a rival firm accused of poaching on AMF's concession agreement and to force underwriters to compensate for the seizure of their assets by Congo's government (*Africa Energy & Mining* 1998b). So tied were firms to the formal aspects of Congo's sovereign existence, yet so frustrated with Kabila's tendency to sell concessions several times over, some reportedly offered the president $200 million if he would leave the country (Strandberg 1999). But none appears to encourage insurgent partners to seek international recognition as head of a completely separate state.

---

[9] Queen's Bench Division Commercial Court, Case No. 1991, 2567, Yona International vs La Reunion Français Société Anonyme d'Assurances et de Reassurances, et al. did not resolve in British commercial courts whether a logging firm's claims of expropriation by NPFL fighters constituted an act of appropriation by a "public authority." In contrast, a plaintiff's right to press claims of expropriation against the Monrovia enclave were upheld in US courts in Meridien Bank Ltd vs Government of the Republic of Liberia (92 Civ 7039, S.D.NY 16 Jan 1996). Taylor's NPFL asserted they should receive recognition in foreign courts on the basis of their participation in inter-state agreements: National Patriotic Reconstruction Assembly Government, "ARE: Consultations on Pending S.C. Resolutions on Liberia,"Gbarnga, March 25, 1993.

Likewise, it appears that the decision of the French oil producer, Elf Aquitaine, to bolster the position of Denis Sassou-Nguesso, the former president of Congo-Brazzaville, and his "Cobra" militia in 1997 against the elected incumbent president was based on the company's (correct) assumption that Sassou-Nguesso would quickly become the republic's internationally recognized president. Sassou-Nguesso defeated his rival, securing for his foreign business partners the assurance that they could gain access to the predictable benefits and reduction of risk that international commercial jurisprudence offers. At the same time, Sassou-Nguesso's official status shielded the oil firm from the consequences of its earlier actions on his behalf when he was an insurgent leader.

Private firms on the weak state's battle front

As long as there is preferential access to foreign courts, political instability and weak state capacity need not inhibit certain kinds of foreign investment and trade in Africa. For example, the five countries that the World Bank (1994: 260–261) rated among its worst of four tiers of commitment to economic reform in a 1994 report (Cameroon [from 2000, site of a multi-billion-dollar oil pipeline project], Congo-Brazzaville, Côte d'Ivoire, Mozambique, and Sierra Leone) registered a 149 percent increase in private foreign investment, averaged over the years 1994–1996, compared with the period 1985–1989. This compares with a 139 percent gain for the fourteen countries in the World Bank's next higher tier. More revealing was the 215 percent increase in investment in Angola, Equatorial Guinea, Zambia, and Zaire during the same period (World Bank 1997a: 82). World Bank officials judged these four countries ineligible for loans due to very poor fiscal performance and the absence of a significant commitment to economic reform. Of course the common element of all of these "good performers" (from the point of view of attracting investment, not reform) lies in the fact that investors are attracted to compact, valuable and easily transportable natural resources to which the sovereign prerogatives of heads of states can allow them privileged access.

In contrast, I argue that political instability can be beneficial to some kinds of foreign investors. Once provided with legal capabilities abroad and the credibility to investors that comes from this standing, firms that can manage risks associated with the weak state's internal instability through special deals with local authorities can gain access to resources that will give them an improved market position *vis-à-vis* more established competitors. This is especially true of enclave mining operations. Neither the miners nor their host governments need to bear the social costs of fostering, regulating, and protecting local markets to generate a profit. They need only directly control a fairly limited piece of ground and secure access to the relevant external market.

The prevalence of smaller Canadian, Australian, and South African mining companies in places such as the Congo, Angola, and most recently Chad underscores this point. Desperate local authorities are not likely to impose stringent and costly regulations (such as environmental ones), nor insist that business be practiced in a particular way. Firms that are willing to invest in this setting are usually adept at managing their own economic environments. As a European businessman observed in Congo: "The absence of a banking system is far more of an opportunity than a hindrance. You set up your own network and make your own rules ... I find it quite inspirational (in Wrong 1995)."

Internal anarchy gives opportunities to some firms that are more adept than their competition at managing risk for commercial advantage. For example, AMF's reported association with International Defense and Security (IDAS), a Dutch Antilles registered security company, helped AMF secure relative local stability (McGreal and Brümmer 1997). While AMF's dealings with Kabila gave AMF access to the externally constructed benefits of Congo's sovereignty and the promise of preferred internal access to natural resources, Kabila's administration could not provide internal protection of AMF's property rights. The mining firm hired the security firm to provide this service. This arrangement denied Kabila's rivals access to natural resources, while controlling a politically reliable source of revenues. Reported partnerships between mining firms such as Branch Energy and the South African military service firm Executive Outcomes in Sierra Leone, Angola, and Uganda have also appeared able to manage their economic environments through private military means, a task now performed with lower profile "industrial security" firms (Goulet 1997; *Indian Ocean Newsletter* 1997; for a counter-claim see *Jane's Intelligence Review* 1997).

Stability can be sought more peacefully too. Further afield, companies promoting a multi-billion-dollar oil and gas pipeline through Afghanistan proposed a "pipeline council" to which companies would make contributions. A spokesperson also indicated that companies planned to seek matching funds from aid donors. "We want to really leverage this thing," said the spokesperson (Corzine 1996: 1). Such arrangements respond to the increasingly diverse channels for foreign aid. The Afghan case also illustrates the earlier point about the advantages of international recognition of sovereignty. The Taliban's general failure to date to gain widespread recognition inhibits any large-scale pipeline deal, and investors have turned their attentions to other locales. On the other hand, the internationally recognized sovereignty of Equatorial Guinea is critical enough to oil and gas firms to prompt them to help organize a conference, which also included international jurists and government officials, to discuss frontier disputes between Equatorial Guinea and its neighbors (*Africa Energy & Mining* 2000). This is a clear case of the growing importance of activities of multinational firms in a process of "internationalization," yet these activities strengthen the outward appearance of sovereignty's norms.

Vulnerable rulers of weak states therefore possess a powerful advantage as commercial partners over their insurgent rivals. Even if power is contested on the ground, firms will prefer to side with the individual who will (or is most likely to) enjoy international recognition of sovereignty. Paradoxically, once ensconced in a privileged deal with a weak state ruler, internal anarchy may deter competitors who are less willing to provide their own security. In this sense, foreign firms that do business in weak states can commercialize the externally constituted benefits of their partner's sovereign recognition for themselves.

Smaller firms can quietly hire mercenaries to protect investments, a course of action less attractive to larger, more established firms that worry that assertive action would alarm officials in states where reliable bureaucracies and indigenous militaries protect assets, and who define these tasks as an exclusive prerogative of the state. In addition, those who challenge existing power structures may discover that high-profile firms make easy targets for criticism, which in turn mobilizes other issue networks. As Cyril Obi's chapter in this volume illustrates, ethnic Ogoni activists in Nigeria have enjoyed some success in mobilizing international advocates for indigenous rights and environmental protection in their campaign against tight security ties between the Nigerian regime and oil companies (Civil Liberties Organisation 1996). Smaller firms that ally with mercenaries and weak state rulers can thus gain market shares of resources that are unavailable to the larger firms that face scrutiny in managing their own economic environments. This offers investors a chance to use small firms to grab rights to resources, then to sell them to a larger firm. The small firm becomes a contractor to insulate the larger firm from political risk and enable it to reclaim market control in exchange for a handsome return for investors.[10]

Conversely, firms seek to limit risk through international certification of their political partners' sovereignty so that agreements can be enforced in foreign courts, operations can be indemnified, credit on attractive

---

[10] Several small mining firm operations in Sierra Leone, Angola, and the Congo were sold to larger firms at prices that indicate local access and control over market share, rather than elusive production figures, determine the values of these firms. See reports in *Africa Energy & Mining* and *La Lettre du Continent*.

terms can be procured from multilateral and bilateral agencies (such as OPIC), and capital markets can be tapped. Those who profit, either politically or materially, benefit from this capacity of firms and rulers to manipulate this dichotomy between internal anarchy and external stability. The intersection of interests extends beyond internal security and profit, however, and includes officials in strong states who are worried about broader issues of stability in peripheral areas.

The role of violence in expanded coalitions

Firms that choose to do business with rulers of very weak states have to take on tasks of ensuring regular trade and break barriers that freelancing local strongmen may set up. In this regard, the task of the firm is similar to the concern of traders in Africa's hinterland in the nineteenth century to "keep the roads open."[11] Thus Branch Energy in Sierra Leone benefited from Executive Outcomes' successful anti-insurgency campaign in 1995–1996. Likewise, some firms in Angola are reported to require private militaries to secure their mine sites (Venter 1997: 10).

This commercial arrangement offers to local state authorities a more extensive security relationship with outsiders too. Alliances with foreign investors who bring their own armies permit the ruler to rid his political alliance of subordinate officials or directly oppose armed rivals. In Sierra Leone, for example, Executive Outcomes trained "kamajor" irregulars, which then served the dual function of guarding small-scale mining joint-venture operations between individual foreigners and Sierra Leone's state officials, while defending the regime that paid Executive Outcomes and granted a concession to Branch Energy. This enabled the regime to reduce its reliance on the underpaid rank-and-file military, which had a tendency to spawn "sobels," or soldier-rebels who looted and engaged in clandestine mining like their erstwhile rebel enemies. Likewise, privately defended mine sites in Angola, Central African Republic, and Uganda are found in areas plagued by insurgencies. Some firms involved in these operations seek protection from companies that train local irregulars who defend contracting regimes while protecting mine sites.

The private provision of security addresses the concerns of other outsiders. In Sierra Leone, for example, the country's creditors could hardly expect the regime to pay arrears on debts when, as in 1995, the regime spent 75 percent of its revenues on an ineffective effort to fight insurgents, for a total cost of about $250 million from 1991 (Karimu 1995/1996). In contrast, the 1995–1996 Executive Outcomes operation cleared rebels

---

[11] This is the theme of Hopkins (1974).

from major highways and cities in six months at a cost of about $40 million (*New York Times* 1997). One report even alleges that newcomers advanced money to Sierra Leone's government to make a token payment on arrears at a critical point in discussions with creditors in 1995.[12] In any case, Sierra Leone received relatively good treatment at Paris Club debt negotiations in early 1996, which reduced Sierra Leone's debt by 20.1 percent to $969 million (Bank of Sierra Leone 1996; Swaray 1996). Improved relations with creditors also cleared the way for bilateral aid projects and budget support, totaling $204 million in 1995, compared with $62 million in 1992.[13]

This "private solution" for the Sierra Leone government's security problems provides a sharp contrast to conventional diplomatic solutions to internal wars. Sierra Leone's diplomatic backers, particularly the USA, in 1998–1999 shifted to a preference for a formal, negotiated settlement. The Lomé agreement, signed in July 1999, incorporated Revolutionary United Front insurgent leaders in a coalition government, overseen by a UN peacekeeping force. Though not its intention, this arrangement allowed insurgents to continue to occupy diamond-mining areas and manage their own trade in diamonds to the detriment of official government capacity to collect revenues. Widespread violence again returned to Sierra Leone in mid-2000 when UN forces attempted to challenge insurgent control over mining operations. The UN was not capable of nor were its member states willing to pursue armed enforcement of the agreement once it became apparent that insurgents would not give up their domination of the country's resources. This failure encouraged the Sierra Leone regime's British diplomatic backers to investigate possibilities for assisting the Sierra Leone government's efforts to find private military trainers and suppliers. This strategy mirrored earlier British government efforts to back the intervention of the private firm Sandline International in 1997–1998 on behalf of the besieged regime, an effort that encountered considerable criticism in parliament.

Farming out security operations to private firms also simplifies the task of cutting civil service rolls. Creditors recommend this measure to reduce expenditures and remove corrupt state officials. Rulers who preside over very minimal bureaucratic capacity generally accept the measure, since the prospect of eliminating teachers, healthcare workers, and agricultural extension services removes people who, if they were actually efficient, might become popular enough to become a pole of criticism of the

---

[12] *Lettre du Continent*, December 21, 1995. Most mining and security firms involved deny such claims.
[13] Compare these figures with Sierra Leone's visible gross product of about $700 million. Economist Intelligence Unit (1996).

regime. This also conserves scarce resources that can be distributed to remaining loyal clients or be used to pay security forces. This order of priorities explains how Sierra Leone's government could lay off 60,000 civil servants, or a quarter of the country's salaried workforce, while fighting a civil war (Hudock 1996: 337).

Officials in non-African states also find positive fiscal and political interests in supporting private security. The US-led intervention in Somalia from December 1992 through 1993 cost the US military $3 billion, a deployment of 18,000, 26 dead, and political damage done in Washington to the notion of official intervention in troubled states (Johnson and Dagne 1996: 202). In Angola, a United Nations brokered peace agreement between insurgents and the regime broke down in early 1993, leading to a resumption of fighting in an eighteen-year civil war. The failed UN mission cost $132 million, while Angola's military spent $500 million on weapons in 1993 (Anstee 1996: 14). The military stalemate in Angola threatened not only efforts to rebuild this potentially rich country, but also unstable neighboring states such as the Congo (former Zaire) and Zambia where UNITA rebels maintained rear bases and received supplies.

Finding its own solution, in 1994 Angola's government hired a South African firm to train Angolan soldiers at a cost of $60 million. The firm and their trainees helped tip the balance of power decisively in favor of the regime, leading to a more lasting peace agreement (Gordon 1997). Furthermore, the recipient of this "aid" paid for this service through a convoluted process of awarding mining concessions to firms associated with the mercenary force. This opened the way for privileged access for other South Africans willing to serve the material and security interests of Angola's government officials. For example, the director of Sonangol, Angola's state-run oil company, later had a hand in establishing Teleservices International, a security firm that employs South Africans in partnership with South Africa's Gray Security Services to protect private and government installations in Angola (*Africa Confidential* 1998a). Other operators joined the fray. An American mining company teamed up with a European security firm while a Brazilian mining firm used a Russian security firm to gain access to diamond mine sites near rebel-held areas (*Africa Energy & Mining* 1998a).

This arrangement helps concerned officials in other states recruit proxies to influence events in very weak states. Executive Outcomes' agents, for example, met in Washington with US Defense Intelligence Agency officials in a "Privatization of National Security in Sub-Saharan Africa" workshop in 1997 to discuss the positive role of private militaries in stabilizing vulnerable regimes at a low cost. Another firm, Sandline

International (mentioned above), later helped funnel arms to the ousted Sierra Leone civilian regime of Ahmed Tejan Kabbah, which continued to enjoy international recognition (but not official aid) while in exile after a coup in May 1997. Sandline spokespersons claimed that support for its contacts with the Kabbah regime came from Britain's Ministry of Defence and Commonwealth Office. They also claimed that the US State Department and Department of Defense supported their role in Kabbah's restoration.[14]

The academic community also lends support to the notion that internal conflicts are resolved when one side wins militarily. Roy Licklider, for example, finds that 76 percent of ninety-one conflicts that he classifies as "civil" between 1945 and 1993 ended when one side won a decisive victory. Of negotiated settlements (24 percent), half collapsed and fighting recommenced (Licklider 1995: 68–690). A US State Department official expressed a frustration with Sierra Leone's conflict. "We find it difficult to envision talks with RUF," he said, because of these groups' unwillingness to renounce violence.[15] David Shearer of Oxford University's prestigious International Institute for Strategic Studies notes in this context: "Private companies can help in peacekeeping. They are willing to go where governments do not want to send troops" (Shearer 1998: 20). The work of Shearer (1998) and others indicates that even more "liberal" groups accept arguments in support of private intervention on behalf of threatened rulers of weak states.

Part of the justification for this support lies in the assertion that security firms are more likely to protect states – and are thus compatible with maintaining internal order (and by extension, security for vulnerable populations) – while remaining consistent with the strictures of a state-based international system (Zarate 1998). This argument is used to promote the licensing of private security firms. Licensed firms will presumably desire to remain in the good graces of home states, and will try to acquire a professional reputation for respecting human rights. Likewise, they will be reluctant to do business with clients whose legitimacy in international society is unclear (Republic of South Africa 1998).

The use of proxies in the foreign policy of strong states is not new. Unlike Cold War practice, however, private firms that act as proxies in Africa's weak states do so to make a profit in the weak state itself. More autonomous than most Cold War era front companies, these firms work at greater arms length from their strong state clients, serving both the

---

[14] Letter from S.J. Berwin & Co., counsel for Sandline International to British Foreign Secretary, April 24, 1998. Reports in the London *Sunday Times* backed Sandline's claims.
[15] Testimony of Ambassador Johnnie Carson, Principal Deputy Assistant Secretary for African Affairs before the House Subcommittee on Africa, June 11, 1998.

political and commercial interests of themselves and their weak state ruler partners. Indeed, their engagement with strong state officials occurs around the precondition of profitable operations. Different from Cold War practice, this arrangement more closely resembles nineteenth-century conventions in which officials in non-African states preferred to protect commercial advantages and their citizens with "strong native powers" bolstered against disruptive strongmen with help from European trading houses (Robinson and Gallagher 1961: 33–41). The overall dilemma of development and order was – and is – understood as a problem of "uncivilized parts of the world where the early stages of development do not admit of heavy revenues or of indolent administration (due to native uprisings)," and where "progress and security can only be attained by administration and commercial work being in the same hands" (Sir George Goldie, head of the Royal Niger Company, quoted in Doyle 1986: 190).

The interests of some private charities and development organizations also intersect with this international coalition concerned with stability in weak states. Said a worker for Save the Children in Sierra Leone: "They [mercenaries] bang heads very efficiently, the fighting stops – and that's when babies get fed" (Brian 1997). Security is also a concern for multilateral creditors. World Bank officials in Sierra Leone recognized in 1997 (before a coup in May) that "security is likely to remain an issue for some time ... To counter this threat project preparation will be coupled with discussions with other donors with a view to developing parallel security measures" (World Bank 1997e). The interests of non-African states also intersect with non-state relief and conflict management operations. For example, the US government hired a private de-mining company to serve in Rwanda in 1995. This provided a way to privatize state-to-state diplomacy, sidestepping a UN weapons embargo to supply the Rwandan military with hardware and training (Isenberg 1997). The American firm Pacific Architect Engineers played a similar role in the Liberian conflict of 1990–1996, enabling US officials to indirectly coordinate security interests with Nigerian intervention forces in that country (Jeter 1997).

"Privatized" foreign policy favors factions that possess internationally recognized sovereignty, since this coalition of outsiders also relies upon the international legal prerogatives of sovereignty to legitimate and indemnify their operations. Ironically, the end of the Cold War reduced prospects for insurgents, since it has become more difficult for these organizations to present themselves to foreign backers as a proxy in a strategic battle for diplomatic allies in Africa. This change is reflected both in the shift of resources toward factions possessing sovereignty and in the declining tendency for insurgents challenging weak states to present themselves to external patrons as a reformist alternative to an incumbent regime.

Insurgents adapt to this situation with strategies that resemble those of groups resisting imperial incursions in the nineteenth century. As noted above, they are forced to seek resources through alliances with regional trade diasporas. The head of the rebel group United Liberation Movement of Liberia for Democracy, for example, tapped into a trade network of Malinké-speaking ethnic kinsmen. He took advantage of these ties to a faction of the Guinea army, giving him access to weapons and some benefits from army participation in commercial ventures in Guinea. These connections also enabled this leader to recruit Casamance Malinkè rebels from Senegal to fight in Liberia.[16] This and other insurgent groups are also forced to organize their own accumulation of resources. Angolan rebels, for example, relied extensively on small-scale mining operations to finance weapons purchases and (with limited success after 1993), to attract private entrepreneurs, mostly from the southern and central African region (de Boeck 1996: 76–80).

Groups that battle sovereign opponents resort to tactics such as targeting foreigners associated with the incursion. The RUF in Sierra Leone, for example, has kidnapped employees of mining companies and relief agency workers (Saccoh 1995a, 1995b),[17] and repeatedly has taken UN peacekeepers hostage. Ugandan insurgents have killed tourists. This tactic may reflect the insurgents' relative lack of external contacts, compared with their opponents, as well as an effort to pressure the regime's backers to flee. To outsiders, this interfactional warfare appears as a collapse into anarchy, as insurgents launch "unjustified" attacks on the regime and foreigners who (in their own view of how business and power are related) go about peaceful, legitimate activities.[18]

This creates further pressure on officials outside weak states to assist with the provision of weak state security. Just as missionaries contributed to the destabilization of politics in the Niger Delta in the 1880s, and then called for military rescue (Platt 1968), Leslie Gelb of *The Washington Post* advocated a "shoot to feed" intervention in Somalia in 1992 (cited in de Waal 1997: 183). The 1880s saw the more assertive policy of using the imperial power's own soldiers and bureaucrats. The contemporary response is more thoroughly private, relying on contractors and a wide variety of private groups as proxies. In this regard, the

---

[16] "L'unité nationale doit être plus forte," *Horoya* [Conakry], 16 April 1996; "Lécheveau, casamançais," *La Lettre du Continent*, 14 December 1995. This connection traces a precolonial trade and kinship network.

[17] A similar connection between commerce and warfare appears in Smith (1989).

[18] This analysis appears in Kaplan (1994).

power in Sarawak in the 1840s of Sir James Brooke's family ("The White Rajahs") as commercial-political agents of a reluctant imperial power more closely resembles the current politics of interfactional fighting in very weak states in Africa and the role of outsiders in it (Baring-Gould and Bampfylde 1989). Brooke was an entrepreneur who found that possessing a state was good for business. His commercial interests also served the interests of the British Empire in assuring some degree of predictability and stability on the imperial periphery. None the less, the Brooke family had to pose as heads of a state to became incorporated into a European vision of the world that grew increasingly intolerant of political units that were not states, or colonies of states.

The unexpected capabilities of "weak" states

But international conventions and norms regarding sovereignty for the White Rajahs have undergone considerable change. Imperial officials switched sides more readily in African wars, since usually no "native" combatants enjoyed a clear claim to the mantle of sovereignty in European eyes. Contemporary rulers of weak states exercise the comparative advantage of secure recognition (provided they can hold the capital city, or in the case of Sierra Leone's temporarily deposed president, enjoy accreditation as an elected civilian ruler), making it far more likely that they will find help against more cohesive and internally capable rivals.

Greater heterogeneity in the capabilities of individual states in the international system of states also gives possessors of sovereignty freer diplomatic rein than their nineteenth-century counterparts. Middle powers such as Israel, Libya, South Africa, and France have long been more sensitive to the benefits of using private firms to address the internal vulnerabilities of weak state rulers, even during the Cold War, since these governments have had fewer resources to distribute directly. This practice at times has placed firms in these states in an advantageous position to exploit contacts through which to profit from the new vulnerabilities of weak state rulers.

Africa's weak states also appear to exercise more leverage than did their nineteenth-century counterparts to negotiate the terms of their sovereignty. This is due as much to the continued strong external support for the notion of juridical sovereignty as it is to the superior wisdom of contemporary weak state rulers. Weak states exist within the state system because they and their private firm partners continue to benefit from and manipulate their juridical equality with other states, even though these states lack centralized systems of government and do not provide much in the way of collective goods to citizens. Thus the dichotomy between internal and external sovereignty in Africa is likely to continue, especially as it offers commercial and political advantages to a wide range of outsiders. Furthermore, the marginality of very weak states constitutes the primary tool that rulers can use to extend non-bureaucratic control within commercially viable parts of their realms through a lucrative private diplomacy.

10 Out of the shadows

Carolyn Nordstrom

This is an ethnography of the shadows.[1] The term shadows as I use it here refers to large-scale systems of affiliation and exchange that occur apart from formal state structures. Ethnography underscores the fact that much of the data presented here comes from fieldwork conducted in epicenters of political violence.

In the frontier realities that mark political upheaval, the people, goods, and services that move along shadow lines are often closely and visibly linked to the most fundamental politics of power and survival. Significant amounts of arms, actors, and supplies flow into a country at war while extensive amounts of valuable resources flow out of a country to pay for these inflows. A good deal of this takes place outside formal state institutions and international law. In fact, shadow transactions can equal a third to a half of a country's entire GNP in many locations in the world. Globally – the shadow networks along which goods and personnel flow are by definition transnational – shadow economies can involve trillions of dollars annually, and this brokers significant political power.

This is also an ethnography of power and socio-political transformation. Shadows represent a juncture of global politico-economic trends and local dynamics, a juncture that can represent sites of power capable of reshaping the character of states in the world today. Power is essentially transformative (Bhabha 1994; Comaroff and Comaroff 1991; de Certeau 1986; Nordstrom 1995). This is best understood by recognizing that "the global" can only be produced in action, and action is by definition localized (Strathern 1995). A transnational organization ultimately rests on the actions of the individuals comprising it. Their

---

[1] An ethnography, in anthropology, is a long-term, in-site field study, usually where the anthropologist learns the language, customs, and cultures of the people among whom they are working. The research here is based on a number of years of research conducted in Mozambique in 1988, 1989, 1990–1991, 1994, 1995, 1996, 1997, and 1998, in Angola in 1996 and 1998, in Namibia in 1997, and in South Africa in 1994, 1995, 1996, 1997, and 1998. I have also conducted shorter length fieldwork on several visits to Kenya, Tanzania, Zimbabwe, and Somalia.

actions are located – in time, space, locale, structure, and culture. At another level, the transnational networks of affiliations themselves, in a phenomenological sense, come to comprise structures, processes, and cultures located in time and space, however vast. These junctures are simultaneously transnational and located: inseparable on one level from the local actors that make the networks and on another level from the affiliations that bind them. So where exactly is the global?

Following Saskia Sassen (1998a), it is everywhere and anywhere; but having said that, there is a real place to start investigations. The global is strategically located in key people and institutional configurations. As Sassen reminds us, economics, like politics, is a system of power, and it is grounded in institutions and the relations that define them – not many key actors are necessary to affect global processes.

Themes of state and power have long been the domain of political science, and a formidable literature has developed. Anthropologists, with their focus on cultural systems and social networks, have focused less on the state than have political scientists, but in its stead, have followed different kinds of power formations. This is one such study. My interest here is in vast, international networks – those residing in the shadows – whose economic and political power can match, even exceed, that of some states.

Introduction: defining the shadows

A person can stand at the epicenter of practically any war in the world and watch an extensive assortment of international actors pass through. If a person works in different war zones, even ones located on different continents, she or he will begin to recognize the same actors moving from one zone of political violence to another. Arms vendors, military "advisors," merchants of survival, diplomats, profiteers, non-governmental organizations, and a host of others ultimately make war and peace possible. This international cast of characters moves substantial amounts of goods, influence, and services across the countries of the world. A significant portion of these exchanges take place outside formally recognized state channels: some moving along brown and gray market routes, some along incontestably illicit and blackmarket pathways. Given all wars' reliance on the vast array of technologies and alliances produced throughout the world, war today, by definition, is constructed internationally. We may speak of internal wars, but they are set in vast global arenas. We may speak of contests within or between states, but a considerable part of war and post-conflict development takes place along extra-state lines. War and peace unfold as much according to these extra-state realities as they do according to state-based ones.

The work presented here is grounded in the political violence that marked Mozambique and Angola in the post-independence era, and in the struggles for peace and development each sought to fashion in the post-accord periods. I have set this piece in several states rather than a single one, not to stand as test cases, but to show the way in which local, regional, and international trends intersect to shape the social, economic, and political possibilities across countries. It is the ethnography of the shadows that provides the framework for these investigations.

I will follow the "shadows" across Mozambique and Angola.[2] Some might say that following sets of interconnecting questions across countries is the equivalent of comparing apples and oranges. I suggest just the opposite: this method of presentation reflects the larger practical and theoretical orientations of this work. Thinking only in discrete and bounded states cannot come close to approximating the reality of states today. Nations are defined within a broad sweep of history and through extensive international associations; they are shaped by the hand-to-hand interpersonal exchanges of non-formal economies and the complex sets of power that attend to these. Each country, and each citizen, struggles to pull away from war years and forge viable solutions within vast interrelated sets of relationships across the region, the continent, and the globe. Power, authority, change, and identity are forged within these complex sets of interrelations.

The phenomena I am dealing with here are not simply (shadow) markets or economies (Ayers 1996): they are a compilation of political, economic, and socio-cultural forces. Shadow associations are characterized by several core features. First, in configuration, these are networks, not formal state structures. Second, they are international. Third, they are transactional; they are networks that function not only by exchange and alliance, but by internalized norms and cultures of exchange and alliance. While benefiting from studies like those of William Reno's (1995, 1998.) "shadow states" – nation-based systems of power and patronage paralleling state power – my work focuses on a different, and more distinctly *international*, set of criteria that constitute a set of "institutional frameworks"[3] in their own right. These networks are more integrated and bound by rules

---

[2] As this work is ethnographic in base, it is based on primary data collection – on firsthand field research. Publishing data on shadow phenomena entails a responsibility to one's informants, to those who will be affected by data disclosures, and to one's own professional obligations. Thus, much of my direct fieldwork disclosures protect these sets of responsibilities and the identities of those affected by these discussions.

[3] I use institution here in the dynamic sense: in anthropology, institution has a flexible definition, so that the specific and formally constituted "institutions" of government and the fluid and non-formally constituted "institutions" of family are equally recognized by the same word. Institution is a social phenomenon.

of conduct than the studies of gray and blackmarkets that focus on high-risk items such as armaments and drugs, or studies that focus on basic informal markets such as foodstuffs, imply. They represent *cultural*, as well as political and market systems (Appadurai 1996; Granovetter and Swedberg 1992).

While shadow networks work both through and around states, they are distinct from them. This point is an important one. They form a different kind of power formation than the state does. For this reason, I refer to these powers as "extra-state," *denoting that while they may partake of state structures, they are not modeled on state systems*. Extra-state does not mean that shadow networks function outside all state boundaries, but that they are phenomenologically distinct from state-order organization. States and shadow networks exist simultaneously, each representing distinct kinds of authority and politico-economic arrangements.

Extra-state denotes non-formal economies and political transactions. The distinction I use in this analysis for non-formal is precise: formal, as applied to the state, refers to *formally* recognized state-based institutions and the activities they support. Non-formal applies to institutions and activities that exist apart from formal state structures and processes. This is *not* to say that formal and non-formal are physically separate locales of power and action. A businessperson or government official who uses legally recognized oil sales to purchase armaments in Angola is acting in the formal market, but when that same person sells oil or diamonds for military supplies or personal gain outside the state's public channels, they are adding to the non-formal economy. Non-formal, as distinct from conventional definitions of informal, refers to more than small-scale economies, for these markets can rival and exceed state markets in strength and profit. This is a critical point. The traditional use of the word "informal" has confounded an understanding of the relationships among (small-scale) survival economics, (large-scale) corruption, and (international) non-formal empires. Chingono (1996: 101), writing on Mozambique, observes:

The International Labour Organization (ILO), the agency that has formalized the term "informal economy," characterized the informal economy as "a sector of the poor" in which "the motive for entry into the sector is essentially survival rather than profit making" (ILO/JASPA 1988) . . . On the contrary, not all of those who participated in the grass-roots economy were poor nor were their motives for entry merely to survive. Corrupt bureaucrats and professionals used their office, influence or contacts to acquire via the grass-roots war economy, through for instance, smuggling, fraudulent export, barter, speculation, bribery, and embezzlement, and invest in building houses, hotels/restaurants, or in transport. Similarly corrupt commercial elites, religious leaders, international agency personnel, as well as international racketeers and their middle-men, smugglers, money-dealers, pirates, and slavers and abductors, not to mention soldiers in the warring armies and foreign troops, were among those who yielded substantial benefits, and in many cases, became obscenely rich, by participating in the grass-roots war economy.

It is anyone's guess how many dollars are actually generated each year through all extra-state activities worldwide, though, taken as a whole, this represents one of the larger monetary and power blocs in the contemporary world. Nor does anyone know how many people are involved in these exchanges in total, though the number will run into millions. But indications of the extent of these sprawling networks are visible in studies which have revealed details such as the following. As much as 20 percent of the world's financial deposits are located in unregulated banks and off-shore locations (Lopez and Cortwright 1998). UN estimates of illicit drugs earnings run at $500 billion a year (United Nations Research Institute on Social Development 1995). Illicit weapons sales produce another half trillion US dollars a year (Alves and Cipollone 1998). It is not surprising to note that roughly one-half of Mozambique's economy is generated non-formally, along with 58 percent of Kenya's and 90 percent of Angola's. But it is interesting to note that over half of Russia's economy, 50 percent of Italy's, and up to 30 percent of the USA's economy are extra-state (Ayers 1996; Greif 1996). Even single non-formal industries in the world's smaller states can add up to significant sums: estimates of Sierra Leone's extra-state diamond earnings on the world market have been placed as high as $500 million a year (Clement Jackson, economist, UNDP, personal communication; Richards 1996).

Shadow networks, then, are not marginal to the world's economies and politics, but central to them. If we do not yet know the exact financial and personnel strength of the non-formal sectors of the world, perhaps more dangerously, we do not know how these vast sums affect global (stock) markets, economic (non-)health, and political power configurations. What we can surmise is that these extensive transnational transactions comprise a significant section of the world's economy, and thus of the world's power grids.

To summarize: extra-state political economies, licit or otherwise, are more than sprawling value-neutral international market networks (Appadurai 1996). They fashion economic possibilities, they execute political power, and, importantly, they constitute cultures, for these networks of power and exchange are governed by rules of exchange, codes of conduct, hierarchies of deference and power – in short, as this chapter will demonstrate, they are governed by social principles, not merely the jungle law of tooth and claw.

The development of war – Mozambique

In 1990, at the height of the war in Mozambique, I traveled to a remote town in the middle of the country. It was remote, but it was of strategic importance: it was the site of gem mines. This remote location, largely forgotten in the sweep of nationwide war atrocities and power-war development history, captures the deep linkages between shadows and war. As I conducted interviews, I came across scores of stories from local civilians and soldiers about the foreign white men and troops who passed through to collect large quantities of precious gems. I also collected photographs of soldier-drawn graffiti on the barren walls poking up from the bombed-out buildings. The graffiti chronicled the war from the young bush soldier's perspective. There were pictures of battle plans; of helicopters strafing villages and villagers; of soldiers proudly holding the latest in automatic weapons. There were pictures of the human tragedies of war: soldiers raping women, and old grandmothers carrying the wounded on their backs.[4] The drawings held a deeper truth: these soldiers were not merely villagers fighting a local bush war – these were people trained in the latest international technologies. Soldiers in tattered uniforms wield the latest superpower arms. The pilots flying the helicopters have been trained in cosmopolitan military centers. The methods of the rapes are enactments of the latest pornographic magazines that are yet one more military currency in battle zones. The political slogans inscribed in the drawings are battlecries forged in distant nations and other wars and carried across time and continents by military allies, mercenaries, gem and arms runners, military texts, and the latest fads in the Rambo genre.[5] In these graffiti and in these gem mines I saw perhaps as clearly as anywhere the powerful intersections of local and transnational, and of the curious ways power insinuates itself into the fabric of living and dying.

War requires enormous capital. This capital (and the resources it purchases) is not rooted in a single country, nor a power bloc. It is international in the most fundamental sense. Consider the typical cycle: war requires supplies, yet no government or rebel group can fully supply themselves solely by internal means. Nor can most governments support all their political and military (financial) needs solely through government-generated revenues and tax bases. Vendors of every necessity from fuel through weapons systems to antibiotics span the globe, and vendors work

---

[4] I took photos of these pictures, and a few have been published: see Nordstrom (1995, 1997, 1998).
[5] See Richards (1996) for a discussion of the role of Rambo movies in directing paramilitary ideology in Sierra Leone.

for profit. They want political alliances, or they want hard currency. A country at war rarely has the power to deny allies, or a currency that is tendered internationally. A nation's resources become hard currency: oil, gems, gold, timber, seafood, ivory, and precious metals become the tender of war-purchases. But these purchases may break a number of laws, sanctions, and political alliances, both in the country doing the purchasing and internationally. These proscriptions do not stop inter-state trafficking in goods-for-arms; they just ensure the exchanges move into non-formal or illegal channels. Thus, as a host of international diplomats and allied advisors enter the country legally, mercenaries and rebels from around the world cross unmarked borders. As goods from the many cosmopolitan production centers of the world are brought into the country along formal channels, a plethora of mafias, informal trading, and sheer blackmarketing slide through the interstices of the world's states.

Consider the case of Mozambique during its fifteen-year post-independence war (see Geffray 1990; Hanlon 1984, 1991; Isaacman and Isaacman 1983; Minter 1994; Nordstrom 1997; Vines 1991; also see War-Torn Societies Project unpublished documents). Mozambique at that time was listed by the United Nations as being the poorest country on earth. How, then, did Mozambique foot the bills for a war that raged nationwide? There are those who argue that bush wars – guerrilla tactics and low-scale conventional warfare – are inexpensive. Those people have not walked the frontlines of wars. Ironies abound in war, and a classic image of such an irony in Mozambique was that of soldiers in remote outposts sitting in tattered remnants of uniforms working state-of-the-art cosmopolitan laptop sat-linked computer communications equipment. What vast networks of exchange, corruption, and political power moved computers, trainers, and communication links from urban centers in peacetime countries to the remote outback of Mozambique? I had the good fortune to meet some of the people in the chain of relationships that moved this equipment into the bush in Mozambique.

The story is relatively straightforward: computers were circuitously routed through various international ports to avoid sanctions, fees, and in some cases laws. But the details marking such deliveries are not as straightforward. It is common knowledge that cargo planes violate airspace to deliver anything from illicit goods to weapons. But how this is done without detection is less often considered. Discretion is paramount, and an unknown or foreign plane is likely to call attention. In Mozambique, the familiar workhorses of the air were the national airlines, limited to a handful of planes, a few small freight lines, and several humanitarian cargo services. The airplanes used in humanitarian aid were provided by international businesses, and paid for by large INGO service groups and governmental agencies such as USAID. In these cases, the humanitarian aid was shipped to war-torn civilian centers under Frelimo government authority. Unbeknownst to the aid donors, planes were sometimes hired out in secret to another customer. Under cover of night, the planes crossed international borders, picked up illicit cargo, including computers, and delivered the cargo to military base camps deep in the interior of Mozambique. Payments were flown out in everything from cash to the hard currencies of gems, precious goods, and human workers. The next morning the planes were again flying humanitarian service routes.

A substantial network of people is necessary to move supplies from a computer company to a base camp in Mozambique. Shipment requires not only airplanes, but pilots, mechanics, technicians, loaders, "border-experts" (who figure out how to navigate every restriction from air traffic control to border guards and military checkpoints), and a host of others who make such transfers possible. Many of these people are not from the country receiving the goods, but represent a truly international cast: trained pilots, military advisors, and technicians for sophisticated computers and weaponry. They are cosmopolitan professionals, working out of the world's urban centers. They thus bring with them not only their areas of expertise, but the cultural underpinnings of their own political, economic, and social agendas. War in the outback of Mozambique is infused with the politics and personal foibles of every advisor, trainer, profiteer, and mercenary who passes through Mozambique, or any other war zone.

This network along which computers and armaments flowed is not an isolated, single series of economic links. Broaching borders, bypassing laws and regulations, transferring illicit goods and personnel, and securing the service of specialists is time-consuming, difficult, and dangerous. People thus use existing networks. Computers flow along similar routes to those traveled by the weapons, mercenaries, and other goods coming into a war zone; as do the gems, human cargo, and precious materials coming out of a war zone to pay for military necessities. This is not to say that there is one large transnational network that all war supplies and illicit goods move along, for that is clearly ridiculous. Instead, I am pointing out that networks are constituted by complex economic and political alliances that can involve, as Reno's chapter in this volume shows, multinational corporations and political rulers. As Castells (1998: 169) writes:

This internationalization of criminal activities induces organized crime from different countries to establish strategic alliances to cooperate, rather than fight, on each other's turf, through subcontracting arrangements, and joint ventures, whose business practice closely follows the organizational logic of what I identified as "the network enterprise," characteristic of the Information Age. Furthermore, the bulk of the proceeds of these activities are by definition globalized, through their laundering via global financial arrangements.

Though Castells is writing specifically of criminal networks, I want to underscore that the international transfers I speak of here often blur the boundaries of legal and illegal. Gems, ivory, oil, and other goods and resources brought out of rebel areas to pay for military supplies cannot be said to fit the description of legal or illegal: international law applies to formal states, not to rebel-held regions. The computers and weapons coming in from cosmopolitan centers may be purchased legally by middlepeople, sent along formal legal channels for a part of their journey, and then enter quasi-legal and illicit channels. The financial gains from these exchanges are reinfused into the global economy either directly or through laundering, and impact global economic in/stability in ways that are as yet poorly understood.

It is perhaps useful here to add an example that involves the more lethal aspects of war. One day, flying in the cockpit with humanitarian pilots ferrying food and emergency supplies to a bombed-out region, I saw a sheet of flame eating its way across the countryside such as I have never seen before or since. Viewed from the cockpit of an old DC3, it appeared hundreds of meters high, yet – and the image struck me then – as thin as a giant shower curtain drawn across the landscape. It snaked its way, unbroken, across a good kilometer, perhaps more. It was hundreds of kilometers from any provincial capital: only those directly involved or passing by in an emergency supply plane would ever see it. Every formal war statement by the various militaries denied the use of napalm-category inflammables in the Mozambican war. But I questioned this being napalm. I have wondered whether it represented some new "product" of some country in the world looking for some place, some war far from prying political and journalist eyes, to test it. It becomes an interesting project to track all the paths necessary for that sheet of flame to wind its way across the interior of central Mozambique. Who authorized this, selected the product from overseas vendors, negotiated with providers, transported it along "blind" channels outside formal public accounting? Who taught troops in its use, flew the mission, and got killed? Who paid for it and how? All told, what does it cost – both in financial and in political terms – to dump a load of flammable explosives over a town in a military exercise?

The economic answer is in part supplied by returning to the planes that flew humanitarian supplies and aid. A wartime economy can yield considerable riches for the canny and the powerful, and these riches move far beyond war supplies. They also move beyond the military. At times these aircraft were taken, under cover of secrecy and unbeknownst to international donors and local officials, from their aid service to fly industrial components, luxury goods, electronic equipment, vehicles, and a plethora of other goods to various places in Mozambique. Businesspeople, profiteers, industrial wildcatters, and politicians engaged in war economies, both legal and illegal, and reaped untold profits. The paths of their trade often followed the same routes as war supplies and employed similar border-crossing and law-evading strategies.

This is not merely the movement of goods around a country. Consider the fact that the parallel economy sets the black, or street, exchange rate for currency, and that this street rate is considered by many, including the banks, the IMF, and governmental agencies, as the accurate one. The official bank rate is often more a political than a factual rendering. The businesspeople with the power to commandeer humanitarian aircraft for private use, to set up wartime economic enterprises, and to dictate economic policy on the ground are also the people who set the daily street currency exchange rates. Not the government, not formal international governmental economic alliances. *The true value of currency, in these instances, is set in the shadows.* It is set according to transactions that partake of formal and shadow economic and political realities. And it is this that undergirds the foundations of economy.

The links between the shadows and the formal sector should be evident by now: profiteers assist the transfer of military goods and payments in precious resources; these profits fuel formal businesses as well, and the profits – both material and political – that can be gained in business can be converted into political power when successful businesspeople run for office or back others of their choice. Military, business, and politics intersect in these transactions that blur il/legal distinctions, and public policies are often in actuality crafted in the shadows.

The gains are as international as the goods that produce them. A ground-eye view demonstrates the "war payments:" coastlines fished out by foreign trawlers for millions of dollars' worth of seafood shipped internationally; gem mines hosting a brisk, lucrative, and illegal international trade; war orphans sold into international prostitution and labor rings; looted goods being carried across borders to purchase everything from luxury items to war supplies; future resource (oil, timber, land-lease, industrial) rights sold off to (super)power and multinational corporation interests. While "armies," as Chingono (1996: 106) calls them, of local profiteers risked their lives smuggling, poaching, slaving, money changing, etc. in Mozambique, the true benefits went outside Mozambique:

On the contrary, it was the "big fish," the professional racketeers in their fancy suits and posh cars, not only from Mozambique but from other countries as far north as Zaire, Nigeria and Sierra Leone and Germany. Indeed, by 1992 Maputo had become a "camp haven" for foreign dealers, who resided in the city's hotels, and who were busily creaming off the wealth of the country and setting up big "legal" enterprises in their own home countries . . . In short, trafficking involved a number of actors, interwoven in an extensive worldwide network linking local dealers to international barons, and with respect to Renamo, to arms peddlers in the informal international arms market.[6]

I have written elsewhere that a vast international cast of characters moves across war zones offering every possible commodity, including the intangible ones of ideological commitments, alliances, soft aid, and propaganda (Nordstom 1995, 1997). Each of these actors moves within a cultural system that imparts meaning, values, and emotional orientations to the commodities they move. This is core to understanding "networks" as I use the term here: they are systems imbued with and inseparable from the currents of culture, power, ideology, and social significances of the people and politics that comprise them. They are not free of such considerations as ethnicity, affiliation, nationalism, inequality, and thus of identity (Appadurai 1996; Pasha 1997; Wilmsen and McAllister 1996; Zulaika and Douglas 1996). For example, foreign advisors not only train soldiers in the use of weapons; they also impart ideas and ideals about who should use that weapon, who it can and cannot be used against, and how to rationalize these usages. Diplomats and non-governmental aid organizations variously seek to retool ideas of who may and may not be targeted, and to impart emotive ideologies to violations of what are defined as basic human rights. International black-marketeers can support an honorable trade in hard-to-obtain medicines, or an immoral one in child prostitution – both supporting certain war and economic practices, however moral or immoral they may be.

The cultures each player brings to a war zone help shape the very notions of what war is, what future political systems are possible, what peace is tolerable. The compendium of state and extra-state transactions configures the shape and character of the country, and the ways in which people, as a society, meet their basic needs. An "internal war" is a very "interstate" fact and international construction. It is a cultural hybrid. It is here we can most clearly see the intersections of local actors and transnational

---

[6] Chingono goes on to say that "Local rumours abound that some of the NGOs and international agency personnel were also involved in this racketeering" (1996: 106). It is important to realize that corruption and extra-state activities do not pass solely through local governments and suspect characters. Those who may be on the forefront of aid may as well be in the backyard of profiteering.

actualities, and cultural orientations are the product – created in the interactions of actors in the larger world of meaning and action. As Campbell (1996: 23) notes: "Likewise, neither is 'everyday life' a synonym for the local level, for in it global interconnections, local resistances, transterritorial flows, state politics, regional dilemmas, identity formations, and so on are always already present. Everyday life is thus a *transversal* site of contestations rather than a fixed level of analysis."

As with all human social endeavor, people must share a number of cultural presuppositions in order to interact. Thus, people follow codes of conduct and rules of behavior when engaging in illicit transactions as developed as those followed by people interacting in legally recognized society. People must know with whom they can and cannot engage, how these patterns of association must evolve, and where they can take place (Ross 1997a, 1997b). "Corruption," writes Gambetta, "requires trust" (Gambetta 1997b: 59). Quite simply, people must *trust* that the people they are acting in concert with are acting in good faith, that these people will not denounce, betray, shoot, or otherwise harm them (Gellner 1989).

Return, by way of example, to the appropriated humanitarian flights commandeered by businesspeople in Mozambique. Let us say on a particular run they are transporting (German-made) cars and lorries stolen in Johannesburg and Maputo, (French- and Japanese-made) industrial equipment for their factories and (Russian-made) weapons for the militias guarding their interests, some (United States-made) computers and (Chinese-made) electronic equipment both for their own use and to sell or barter, and luxury items such as (European) alcohol, (American) cigarettes, (Western and Indian) videos, and (open market) foodstuffs for profiteering. For a businessperson to pick up cargo at point X and fly it to point Y an extended chain of associations, and of trust, must be in place. The cargo itself is transnational, and businesspeople must trust that the middlepeople in the chain of shipments do not release their names to authorities or steal their cargo; they must trust that the border guards and customs officials do not arrest their minions, implicate them, or steal their cargo. As these are international alliances, people cannot rely exclusively on family, ethnic, and national loyalties, but must forge associations across distinct language and identity groupings. To fly the cargo, the businesspeople require aircraft, pilots, mechanics, loaders, and a host of workers from air traffic controllers to aviation fuel attendants. The levels of trust extend exponentially from here: the officials who oversee flights must be bribed, kept in the dark, or otherwise compensated; the pilots, mechanics, and other professionals must be trusted to do their work without breaking loyalties or stealing the cargo. As these professionals are themselves cosmopolitan and come from numerous language and

ethnic groups, the chances for betrayal are extensive, and thus trust is a
finely honed business survival strategy. These businesspeople transport
everything from personal items to industrial components, and a percentage of these will by necessity pass through some form of governmental
(or military) regulatory agency. To open an industry in a war zone, to
have the only all-terrain vehicle in a town, and to have the means to set
the currency exchange rates in a region all invite regulatory inspection.
Gains associated with these exchanges can be of such proportions that
they can result in confiscation, imprisonment, or a death sentence. The
businesspeople must also trust that their alliances with regulatory and
security officials are strong, hidden, or important enough to avoid any of
these disadvantageous outcomes. They must also trust that other businesspeople at any point in this chain of transfers will not simply shoot
them and take their goods. This whole process of transfer and trust is
then reversed as the payments for these goods and services are conveyed
back along the networks.

At each step of the way illicit, gray, and legal institutions intersect:
middlepeople transfer legal purchases across unmarked borders; pilots
paid in Eurodollars with pension funds taken out by their employers fly
uncharted runs with unrecorded merchandise and personnel; businesspeople evade taxes bringing unlicensed goods into legal industries; government officials set regulatory law and simultaneously grease the flow of
illicit goods into development industries. Without trust, such vast enterprises are impossible, and networks could not function. The fact that a
significant proportion of paramilitary and military goods and personnel –
and of a nation's development infrastructure – passes through the shadows shows that the trust, however difficult it is to negotiate, does work.
The fact that large-scale massacres, wars, and trails of dead bodies mark
shadow networks to no greater extent than they do states attests to the
fact that the systems function efficiently (Gambetta 1988b). This is no
mean feat when we consider that we are talking of millions of people exchanging billions of dollars' worth of goods and services.[7] Gellner (1989:
150) highlights the irony in this: "The Hobbesian problem arises from
the assumption that anarchy, absence of enforcement, leads to distrust
and social disintegration ... but there is a certain amount of interesting

---

[7] Gambetta (1988a: 230, emphasis in original) stresses a key consideration here in writing
that "*economizing on trust* is not as generalizable a strategy as might at first appear, and
that, if it is risky to bank on trust, it is just as risky to fail to understand how it works,
what forces other than successful cooperation bring it about, and how it relates to the
conditions of cooperation. Considering the extremely limited literature on this crucial
subject it seems that economizing on trust and economizing on understanding it have
been unjustifiably conflated."

empirical evidence which points the other way. The paradox is: it is precisely anarchy which engenders trust or, if you want to use another name, which engenders social cohesion." And in a final irony, Gambetta (1997a: 59) observes a democratizing element in mafias' corruption: "the mafia democratizes access to rents for colluding firms in a cartel. By increasing the number of firms able to participate in a cartel and protecting their access to rents, the mafia ensures widespread participation. Firms are no longer afraid to join cartels because they no longer fear that other firms will jump the queue, submit competing bids, and so on."

As I have pointed out, shadow networks do not always involve corruption. Nor, in response to the quotes above, are they always restricted to powerful interests pursuing profits. As Chingono (1996: 114) shows, they represent concerns that range from the rational to the religious:

Although operating within these constraints, the grass-roots war economy was more predictable and rational in many respects than the official one. Illegal and unrecorded trade was not haphazard but institutionalized, operating according to a system of rules known to all participants. Examples included the standardized equivalences observed for barter transactions, the set rate for paying border guides, the arrangements set up for the terms of clientage, and the reciprocal obligations of other personal ties. The organization of a grass-roots war economy depended to a great extent on these reciprocal obligations of personal ties. The trust and confidence inspired by personal relations or common cultural background provided the reliability and predictability that were conspicuously lacking in the official economy. To some extent, therefore, the grass-roots war economy generated alternative economic opportunities for people as well as an alternative society, with parallel religio-economic institutions alongside official ones.

Extra-state exchanges are not a minor chapter in the book of political relations. Vast amounts of wealth and goods change hands along extra-state networks during wars, and sophisticated national and international machinery must be in place for these exchanges to occur. It is here we can most visibly see the intersections of formal state institutions and extra-state networks in one and the same place: the *simultaneous existence of different configurations of power* shaping extant political realities.

Consider an example from the *non-formal* realm. A military that seeks to acquire goods and arms in ways that violate international laws and sanctions, or that it cannot cover through state taxes, must raise money through alternative "hard currencies" (whether through bargaining the state's resources or downright illicit actions); it must negotiate gray and black international markets.

While at the same time in the *formal* realm a military must rely on internal security systems for backing and on internal judicial systems for support.

Essentially, a country's political institutions – and the ideologies shaping them – must be in line to support the cause of political control by removing distinctions between in/formal policies and il/legal actions when it is politically and militarily expedient to do so. Non(-formal) state-based and criminal activities become embedded in the everyday functioning of the country's governing institutions. This is not to say everyone is implicated, for they are not. Nor is it to say that the institutions are fundamentally criminal, for they are not.

I have already pointed out that criminal and extra-state should not be considered synonymous. In the same way, network alliances and state practices cannot be conflated. They represent two distinct modes of power and exchange, and they are capable of operating in the same sphere of influence – that is to say, *networks and state structures intersect, but they do not give up their own identity in this intersection.* For example, if a military needs to engage in extra-state activities to raise money, procure necessities, and conduct operations, it will encounter formal state barriers. To survive, these barriers must be bridged, and the bridges consist of professionals who operate both formally and non-formally: law enforcement personnel who assist the military in illicit operations, customs officials who turn a blind eye to cross-border trade, and judges whose courts do not ferret out or prosecute military excesses or extra-state activities. I return to my point above: this does not mean a country's core institutions are fundamentally corrupted. A view that posits such corruption is based in an "either/or" position that posits a state – as the paramount political entity – as healthy or failing. Instead, I underscore here the ways in which power adheres to states and to extra-state networks and each arena variously configures political and economic realities in any given context.

Political violence reconfigures a society's most fundamental political and social institutions. Reconfiguring a society's core institutions essentially amounts to redefining both the nation and the state. And redefining a state can reconfigure international relations. It is here that we can begin to investigate my observation that the self-same extra-state networks that leave a country dangerously militarized may also be the primary mechanism whereby development can begin to restructure war-devastated economies. In these conditions the complexities of power become apparent as new forms of authority emerge to challenge established governing structures, or to fill vacuums left in the wake of failing state institutions and crippled regimes – for good or for bad.

War and development – Angola

Angola continues to face ongoing cycles of war in the conflict between the MPLA government and Savimbi's rebel UNITA forces. The impact of this political violence on the citizens of the country has been devastating: a million people have lost their lives to the post-independence war, and in 2000 there were 1.7 million internally displaced people. Conditions, for many, seem impossible. Since the resurgence of the war after Savimbi lost the 1992 elections to the MPLA government, Savimbi's UNITA troops have controlled some two-thirds of the country, primarily the rural areas and the regions of food production. The MPLA controls the major cities and infrastructure, and the flow of hard goods. Areas of no-man's-land divide the two powers and their resources. UNITA has food, but not commodities. Those in MPLA-controlled towns have goods, but little food. When I was in southern Africa in 1997, a representative of the government of Angola estimated that 60 percent of the population was malnourished or starving. Civil and military crime and violence are rampant. Military repression and forced settlements are common. People in many locations in the country live amidst the rubble of war ruins and pick their way across landmine-strewn roads and fields,[8] largely bereft of social services, of a viable economy, of freedom of movement, and of access to the resources necessary to rectify these conditions. A key question in my research was that of how people in such conditions survived at all. It is not a question classical theories of economics or development easily address.

An irony in this analysis is that the very extra-state activities I have been discussing are also those by which a significant amount of development and more stable transitional peacetime economies are created. Traditional economic textbooks and much INGO wisdom posit conflict transformation and development as taking place through the strengthening of societies' formal infrastructures (Hancock 1989; Lawson 1997). Thus aid and development monies go to existing state institutions and officials to instigate formal programs. My fieldwork suggests this model little matches the actual dynamics of reconstruction.

Consider the conditions that characterize wartime and greet most post-war societies. In addition to militarized and decimated infrastructure, agricultural lands lie fallow, and water sources may be polluted. Old currencies may have collapsed, and with them, banking systems. New

---

[8] I went out with the de-mining group Halo Trust in Huambo and Kuito provinces. The locations that average civilians most need to survive are heavily mined: roadways, water sources, fields, and buildings. Illustrating the international character of war, in one spot they found landmines from thirty-three different countries.

currencies may be only as valuable as the paper they are printed on in international markets. Even the most legal of companies – those that haven't been bombed, looted, raided, or taken over – find they have to exchange monies, and possibly goods, on the blackmarket. Currency exchange rates often fluctuate to extreme levels, making formal business transactions virtually impossible: who can buy goods one day not knowing if they will sell them for a profit or a loss the next day depending on the vicissitudes of a powerful, but formally uncontrolled, financial market? In 1996 in Angola, I exchanged US dollars variously for 120,000, 200,000, and 270,000 kwanza in the space of a week: a rollercoaster of currency valuations. If I bought kwanza at 270,000 per US dollar, I worked not to spend money necessitating more currency exchanges when the price dropped below 200,000. When I bought at 120,000 and the prices soared to 270,000, I paid over twice the amount for goods as those who had changed at more auspicious times. By 1998, I received nearly half a million kwanza for a US dollar. What industry can function in such financial uncertainty? But of course, who takes kwanza anyway? Most goods must be networked across numerous international borders: war-devastated countries often are unable to produce many of the basics they need, much less the luxury items. To buy internationally requires "hard currency" from dollars and marks to gold and guns. To raise these resources frequently entails having to gray or blackmarket local resources. The bread and butter industries – and by that I mean the basic industries of everyday life from bakeries through clothing manufacturers to equipment plants – do not survive easily in these conditions (driven out as well by landmines, roving militias, severe corruption, and destroyed trade routes), and pack up to leave for greener pastures.

In countries like Angola, it is difficult to distinguish what is wartime and what is peace. When I was in Angola in the summer of 1998, technically the UN was implementing peace accords, and demobilization was progressing. Technically a government integrating the MPLA government and the UNITA rebel forces was voted in during 1997. Technically there was peace in Angola. But it was a very violent peace. All professional and aid workers were restricted to capital cities because of the intensity of fighting countrywide. Tens of thousands of refugees flooded more secure areas. People from outlying provinces were evacuated, as several told me, "dodging heavy fire and jumping over piles of dead bodies." For people in Angola, the country was suffering war. But in formal diplomatic terms peace prevailed. The contradictions were profound: while the head of Catholic Relief Services was scrambling to make sure her fieldworkers were alive and safe, she received notice from international headquarters that workers' hazard pay had been stopped as Angola was now classified as "at peace." For locals the contradictions could be lethal: conscription sweeps became so intense that young men were taken from the major streets of the capital heedless of watching journalists, UN officials, or family members. Each military's need for supplies and the money to purchase these increased, while social services often slowed to paralysis and wildcatting of goods and services escalated substantially.

Who then thrives in such economies? From urban centers to remote rural communities there are those who do well in such conditions, who profit from the political instability or social chaos that reduces legal restraints. Informal markets surface to provide the daily requirements to the broad spectrum of citizens. Non-formal banking systems emerge to transfer funds and provide loans. Gray market economies function on the borders between government regulations and practical survival, between formal international systems and the realities of daily life. Black-markets can function on a massive scale. For example, at the time of the collapse of Mobutu's reign in Zaire in mid-1997, highly organized traffickers were smuggling out 80 percent of Zaire's diamond wealth. Figures were not mentioned for Zaire's cobalt and copper trafficking, except to mention it has amounted to a "king's ransom"(Bearzi 1977). In the mid-1990s, fully half of Mozambique's GNP was smuggled out of the country illegally, primarily in gems and mineral wealth, and seafood from the coastlines. Mafias and international cartels function smoothly in these circumstances, as do multinational industries and consortia with wildcatting enterprises. In many ways, these non-formal markets parallel, and even make use of, colonial-style market systems: simple extractions of labor and resources channeled along equally simple routes to cosmopolitan centers around the world.

These are the conditions of a frontier: the perilous transport of daily necessities to the millions who need them; the wildcatting of vast fortunes; and the systems of protection, usury, and domination that see these various ventures to fruition. From kindly women trading tomatoes for medicines, through mafias trading in gems, drugs, and high-tech computers, to violent gun runners selling post-war weapons to urban criminals, the non-formal sector steps into the limelight in these transitional times.

One can start anywhere in mapping these networks: from the "nocturnal" military flights from Namibia into Angola carrying in medicines, food, and clothing and carrying out gems, to the massive trade in everything from food grains to weapons along the border of the Democratic Republic of Congo. I would like to start an example of the mapping of these shadow networks with a small boy I met in a town in the center of Angola that had been completely bombed out during the 1993–1994 battles. The fighting took place in the center of town: a dividing line down the main street marked the division between the government forces and Savimbi's UNITA forces. The loss of civilian life was extensive, numbering in the tens of thousands. War orphans are one of war's more tragic legacies. I befriended some of the orphaned street children, and struck up a conversation with a boy below the age of ten. He was selling foreign brand cigarettes, and I asked him about it. "One of the businessmen sells them to me and I sell them on the streets for a little profit." "How do you start out if you have no money to buy?" I asked. "He gives them to you to start with, and you must come back to share the profits." "And if you cannot make a profit, or if some larger street kid takes your cigarettes?" I inquired. "Then your life can be short, like in the war." We began walking down the street, and he showed me the shop of the man who "sponsored" him. In a bombed-out building (all the town's buildings were in ruins), new gleaming television sets, VCRs, and other luxury items peeked out from darkened backrooms – darkened as much by a lack of electricity and repair as for protection. In a town bereft of basic foods and electricity, much less a table to put a television set on, cosmopolitan dreams from the world's urban centers called out to passersby without shirts or shoes. But someone had to have the means to buy these luxury items, and to use them. People who did not deal in the local currency, kwanza. People who dealt in resources that translated to hard "international currency:" gems, medicines, weapons, precious resources, prostitution, and illegal substances.

A vast network stretched from this town in central Angola through its gem mines and along its valuable resources, through troops and civilians, profiteers and thieves, and then across international borders to link into large exchange systems that operate both legally and illegally, running all the way to far-flung mafias and superpower urban commodity centers. The irony made me stop and sit on the crumbled curb with the boy. "You mean," I asked, "that if you didn't sell cigarettes for this shyster that you would not be able to eat?" "What is a shyster?" the child replied. A question that cuts to the heart of the matter in war-torn societies: this child selling foreign cigarettes on bomb-cratered roads far from the world's economic centers links into global extra-state economies that reap trillions annually.

The man who fronts cigarettes to street children is a prime example of a lynch pin in the intersection of shadow transactions, business development, and political power. Like the businesspeople in Mozambique, he is linked into international networks capable of bringing valuable goods across international borders; he is linked with networks inside Angola that produce the resources that can convert to the hard currency to buy these goods; and he is linked with formal state systems in running his business and developing his industries. With financial and business success – that is to say, with power, and with all the alliances that attend to these – this man also has political power. He can back politicians, he can formulate policy through major state institutions, or he can stand for office directly. He can also work in INGOs, become a UN representative, sit on multilateral trade boards, or attend forums on international law. He will be unlikely to give up his network alliances, or his reliance on the shadows, when he enters a formal state role. As I wrote above, with wildly fluctuating currencies, war-locked economies, and a country where 90 percent of the economy is non-formal, he probably could not conduct business solely along formal lines even if he wanted to. But as the young street child cigarette vendor reminded me, why would he want to? It is where he acquired money and power in the first place. As Castells (1998: 178) notes, there is a "thin line between criminal traffic and government-inspired trade."

The development of Angola is largely jump-started along non-formal economic lines – far from the laws and taxes of failed government institutions. Here we can see the traditional divisions of "informal" economy and "high-tech gray/blackmarket networks" are both theoretically and practically misleading. Gems are traded for armaments and VCRs, which are brokered for cigarettes which are bartered for basic food. As with the war orphan selling cigarettes, the old woman carrying tomatoes into food-impoverished communities is linked into the same system as the man who is carrying out gems worth $20 million. Seeds and electronic equipment are smuggled in along similar routes to armaments. It is in this way that people gain the means to plant crops, start up industries, develop trade routes, and further development. As Chingono (1996: 109) observes, "In other words, the grass-roots war economy – a by-product of violence – has offered the participants involved *relative* freedom from the suffocating grip of the state and from (direct) exploitation by big capital, as well as freedom of movement across national-boundaries in spite of the celebrated sanctity of the nation-state."

The final irony in this is that virtually all aid and loan dollars go through government channels. The government that controls only 10 percent of the economy in Angola;[9] the government whose banks are largely closed because military spending, failed institutions, and corruption have taken their lasting toll.

[9] This figure comes from the UN Development Program, Humanitarian Assistance Coordination Unit (UCAH), World Bank, and many INGOs (personal communication in interviews). See also Human Rights Watch Arms Project (1994); Maier (1996); Minter (1994).

A question evolved from this research, a question that I incorporated into my ethnography of the shadows:

If the formal sector is largely inoperational; if what is operational largely assists the fortunes of very few and for the most part barely affects the daily life of the population as a whole; and if the massive informal market (including gray, brown, and black) largely sustains the population as a whole – *where does actual political and economic (post-war) rebuilding power come from?*

It was a question I put to numerous INGO development workers and economists.[10] From Angola to Mozambique, most responded that non-formal economies are central to development processes. But answers were vague as to exactly what comprises non-formal economic and political powers: who is involved, how they work, and what relationships hold between non-formal and formal economies both nationally and internationally. In the discussions of non-formal and extra-state activities, there is a general tendency to postulate that non-formal markets, whether of Africa or of Eastern Europe and Asia, are the result of a combination of changing political regimes, social transitions, and economic opportunism. The belief is that as these countries settle down in the course of normal state development, their economies will become increasingly defined by state-regulated institutions. In this view, while illegal goods (e.g. drugs and weapons) and service rings (e.g. mercenaries and prostitution) will always exist in the countries of the world, they comprise a marginal part of the world's real economy.

My research to date suggests we need to rethink these assumptions. As Chingono (1996: 115) writes, "the informal economy seems here to stay,

---

[10] As part of my ethnography of the shadows, I interviewed a number of representatives and economists from major INGOs on their views on the relationships of non-formal economies to the formal sector, and to development policy. These included UNDP, World Bank, UNHCR, UNICEF, WFP, UN-UCAH, Save the Children, Africare, CRS, Christian Children's Fund, IMC, Halo Trust, USAID/US embassy and other embassy officials, WHO, UNESCO, ICRC, Italian Aid, Concern, MSF, Oxfam, Care, World Vision, Red Barne, and journalists, among others.

The senior economists of the World Bank and UNDP provide two (fairly common) points on the spectrum of answers I received. The head of the World Bank responded: "We simply don't deal with those things, they are not issues we are concerned with." Dr. Aboagye, the senior economist of the UNDP office, gave a completely different answer: "We have a serious interest in figuring out how people actually survive in these (seemingly impossible) conditions; how the informal and illegal markets work in affecting the dynamics of economic realities of the country; and where the true bases of economic power are located in the economy – but like most formal agencies, we are bound, by mandate, to dealing with formal economic arenas *only*. To compound matters, classical and contemporary economic theory simply does not have the capacity to deal with these questions."

For research on related issues, see Callaghy and Ravenhill (1993); Fox and Starn (1997); Hanlon (1996); Hansen (1997); MacGaffey (1991); Richards (1996).

and may even become the mainstay of the economy." On a larger scale, local non-formal economies link with worldwide economic and political concerns: I can stand in the most remote war zones of the world and watch a veritable supermarket of goods move into and out of the country. Tracing the supply routes of these goods takes one through both major and minor economic centers of the world. The sanctions-regulated satellite-linked laptop computers I saw on the battlefields of Africa were made in major cosmopolitan centers of the world, and the gold, diamonds, ivory, and seafood that pay for these commodities move along the same channels back to those cosmopolitan centers. These international transactions are not comprised such luxury goods alone. Clothing, watches, industrial components, VCRs, books, and medical supplies travel these same routes. At the bottom line, it would appear that non-formal economies play a formidable role in countries such as Japan, Germany, and the USA as well as in areas of more rapid economic and political change and development – when the gems and oil of Angola buy computers and armaments (or clothing, medicines, and VCRs) from cosmopolitan centers, the money helps define the financial realities of these centers, regardless of whether it arrives through formal or shadow means. All these factor into corporate sales, bank (laundered) revenues, stock market prices, cost of living indices, and so on, whether these facts are recognized in formal analyses or not. "The flexible connection of these criminal networks in international networks," writes Castells (1998: 167) "constitutes an essential feature of the new global economy."

These realities are belied in development programs. Virtually every aid, development, and economic enhancement organization deals directly, and generally exclusively, through the formal sector, which, in turn, deals little with the vast majority of people in countries such as Angola. So most of the development monies coming into the country are going into the formal sector that, to a large extent, is taking money out of the country, either in agreements such as large weapon and foreign goods purchases, or in corruption. The last issue is critical: the corruption that is currently a prime topic of concern in development circles has its main font in the formal sector – the formal sector through which intergovernmental loans and aid monies are channeled. In addition, aid may well be channeled into the very structures that are most likely to foment continuing conflicts.

Few economic indices and political theories have been constructed to show – with the degree of complexity and detail accorded to studies of formal political and market institutions – the interpenetrations between state, formal, and non-formal economic realities shaping political violence and peace in the world today. If this seems overstated, consider finding a World Bank, International Monetary Fund, or United Nations single country or international fact sheet publication that charts non-formal economic and political indicators alongside, and in relation to, formal indices; or economic indices that chart how the wealth created by extra-state gem and weapon sales affects, for example, European and Asian stock markets or international currency valuations. When I ask WB, IMF, and UN economic specialists why there is a dearth of such data, they typically reply: "Such work is dangerous." The implied assumption is that it is dangerous because it can be aligned to criminal networks and they are, by definition, dangerous. If you study gem smugglers and gun runners – or the underside of security – you might end up little more than the statistics you are collecting. But perhaps the better question is: "dangerous to whom?" If these networks of power, services, and goods rival formal state structures in important ways, non-formal economies do not merely represent monetary concerns; they can comprise socio-political powerhouses. Considerable fortunes are made and lost outside the traditional formal sector, and these fortunes intersect with formal states and economies in myriad complex ways. In truth, the divisions between non-formal and formal states and economies are far less distinct than classical theory and popular discourse would have. The danger might thus be to our very conceptions of power and economy, to our theories about the nature of the relationships between state, individual, and authority.

Postscript

Anthropologists have long worked with multiple nodes and trajectories of power defining any given site (Bhabha 1994, Comaroff and Comaroff 1991, Fabian 1990, Tambiah 1996, Taussig 1987). Heuristically, the state represents one such model: a form of organizing power that coalesced after the Middle Ages along territorially bounded, legally codified, and representationally hierarchical lines. Concurrent systems, such as the shadow powers I discuss here, operate coexistentially across time and space. Understanding the complexities and relationships between different configurations of power is crucial to grappling with the dilemmas of war, development, and peace, whether in Mozambique and Angola or in Europe and Asia.

The relationships holding between different formulations of power do not stay constant. As the modern (Enlightenment) state is reconfigured by the realities of twenty-first-century globalization, the nodes of socio-political and economic power shift as well. In the same way that the international networks of traders during the time of *king*doms helped preconfigure the modern state, and their market tribunals presaged contemporary international law – the shadow sovereigns of today may foreshadow new power formulations barely emergent on the horizons of political and economic possibility. It may be convenient to think that globalism most powerfully affects the cosmopolitan centers of the world. But perhaps, as Ngugi (1993) implies in *Moving the Centre*, Mozambique and Angola, Africa and Asia, are the sites where new configurations of power shaping the world are most visible. For it is here that flexibility, the breakdown of entrenched institutionalization, the politics of survival, and the creativity of development meet in the most direct of ways.

11   New sovereigns? Regulatory authority in the Chad Basin

Janet Roitman

The frontiers of power are changing. Or at least this is what we are compelled to conclude when we see how transformations in local, inter- and transnational politico-economic relations have caused unprecedented relationships in the contemporary world. This is evident in instances of mass mediation, which have allowed community and place to become largely unhinged, and in the transnational realms created by new financial instruments and technologies, where time and place are uncoupled and hence jurisdiction unsettled. Under the somewhat vague rubric of "globalization," these complicated phenomena are apprehended in terms of certain tropes: territory, place, and space are perhaps foremost among them.[1] Their predominance has significant consequences for how we confront the problem of transformations in the nature of power and authority in the world today.

This emphasis on space and place – on the changing geography of power – is, of course, warranted. A great part of what we are witnessing – the increasing mobility of capital and labor, the intensification of disciplinary mechanisms and regulatory authority associated with world financial institutions, the rupture of boundaries brought on by new technologies and media forms, and the extension of diasporas as distinct geopolitical entities – results from, and contributes to, the destabilization of the territorializing project of the nation-state (most clearly demonstrated by Appadurai 1990, 1996). Thus while inter- and transnational phenomena are by no means new aspects of nation-based geo-politics, the idea, for example, that "the national economy" is a naturally occurring part of the nation-state – that "economy" is naturalized as "national" – is only now being interrogated or rethought.[2]

---

[1] See, of course, David Harvey's writing (1989) on "space–time compression" and the annihilation of space.

[2] Benedict Anderson (1996: 7) claims that the concept of the "national economy" dates from "[a]s late at least as the founding of the League of Nations," being intrinsically linked to the very doctrine of self-determination.

240

My own concerns follow this line of thought. In a very general sense, I approach the problem of circumscribing the economy – or "the economic" – in terms of modalities of power. In the following remarks, I will consider the exercise of power in trans- and sub-national regions (e.g. regional economies dependent upon transnational markets in capital, goods, services, or labor) and ambiguous territories (e.g. borders). In doing so, I will be particularly concerned with the exercise of power. While one cannot avoid the subject of space/place when reflecting on contemporary geographies of power, emphasis placed on "locating" power – in its new forms and expansive networks, for example – tends to obstruct our understanding of historical practices of power. In other words, there is a tendency to seek out the supposed locations of power while slighting the matter of its modes of exercise. Although perhaps warranted as a first step in delineating unprecedented relationships and connections across national space, one wonders how power can be perceived outside its mode of practice. How do we know that it is there unless its effects have been noted, its exigencies performed by its very subjects (Foucault 1990 [1978])?

This is the question I take up in this chapter. I will do so by referring to the Chad Basin, where emergent sub- and transnational regimes of accumulation and authority have come to dominate the Nigerian, Nigerien, Cameroonian, Chadian, and Central African Republic's borders. Their effective authority over certain economic activities, regional or international resources, and local populations puts them in competition with the nation-state. I will argue that, while this situation seems "oppositional," it does not necessarily imply the demise of the nation-state in the face of non-national forms of accumulation and power. In fact, one can argue that the relationships between the two realms are highly ambiguous: they are often reciprocal and complicitous as much as they are competitive and antagonistic. That is, while antagonisms exist with regards to the state's official regulatory authority over these regional economies, complicity is also evident insofar as the state is dependent upon these regional economies for rents and the means of redistribution. Likewise, while these networks can be described as trans- or sub-national, they make important, or even essential, contributions to the national political economy. Moreover, while these regimes of power and wealth may be described as novel realms of thought and action, they are none the less inscribed in the same logical – or epistemological – order as that of the nation-state.

The Chad Basin can be described as a region of competing sources of wealth, regulatory authority, and welfare (redistribution). In order to clarify this situation, I will first briefly review the ways in which networks of wealth creation arise from strategies for accumulation that are defined by, and take advantage of, opportunities and constraints produced by the imperatives of the global political economy (e.g. deregulation, privatization). In the Chad Basin, this latter process has resulted in a military–commercial nexus, which has become the legitimate basis of livelihood for many people of the region. This means that the very production and continuity of these networks, as a complex of relationships, is partly ensured by the exercise of newly articulated claims to rights in wealth, which, while often working to undermine the integrity of the national political economy at the point of regulation, are none the less often deemed licit by participants.

What we see, then, is the institutionalization not only of relationships that define networks, but of particular definitions of licit wealth and manners of appropriating wealth. I suggest that this process is dependent on the frontier, both literally and conceptually. The transgression of national economies and political regimes is a border and bush phenomenon in the Chad Basin. And as I explain below, the political frontier and the economy of the bush are defined by new concepts of wealth (e.g. spoils) and manners of appropriating such wealth (e.g. rights-in-seizure). But these are not marginal: these concepts and practices are assumed by those who work the bush and border, as well as those tending to the state bureaucracy and the national economy. While defined by their subversive relationship to official regulatory authority, these trans- and sub-regional activities are on the frontiers of wealth creation. They represent one of the few means of accessing hard currency, scarce luxury goods, and state-of-the-art technology, as well as markets in small arms, minerals, gems, and drugs. More generally, they produce wealth in times of austerity and serve as essential mediations between the state and the global economy. As such, they are an important resource for representatives of the national economy, providing new rents for the management of internal conflict and the redistributive logics of national politics, and a means of insertion in the world economy. Therefore, although some practices associated with emergent regimes of accumulation and wealth may undermine forms of authority defined by the nation-state, they also contribute to its capacity to exercise power over wealth and people.

This conclusion runs contrary to certain observations about the relationship between transnational networks and the state. For instance, since regimes of wealth and power such as those described herein demonstrate effective authority over certain resources, activities, and persons, they are often described as antagonistic to the nation-state.[3] That is, beyond

---

[3] For various interpretations and commentary, see Brown 1995; Camilleri and Falk 1992; Ong 1999; Rosenau 1990; Strange 1996; Walker and Mendlovitz 1990. For general critique, see Sassen 1998a; Smith et al. 1999.

undermining a particular regime, they are said to be new sites of potential sovereignty and hence possible threats to the absolute and unique status of the nation-state. Without necessarily ushering in the demise of the nation-state form, networks of power which seem to parallel or compete with the nation-state (e.g. financial markets, agglomerations of non-governmental organizations, international legal regimes, transnational mafias) are said to constitute domains of sovereign power.

Regimes of wealth and power do compete with the nation-state in the Chad Basin, but only insofar as they undermine official regulatory authority. New manners of creating wealth, and articulating and exercising legitimate rights-in-wealth have been normalized through the military–commercial alliance described herein. This has given rise to new figures of regulatory authority in the region. However, these arrangements are part and parcel of the political logics of the state. They contribute to the viability of state power through the production of rents and possibilities for redistribution but, more importantly, the precepts underlying apparently novel relationships, activities, and modalities issue from, or are consistent with, those practiced in the existing political economy or historical socio-juridical order. As a final rumination on this point, I close by indicating how conclusions as to the emergence of novel forms of sovereignty in the contemporary global political economy are driven by the mutually constituting problematics of locating power and conceptualizing the state as sovereign.

The global context of the regional political economy

In many ways, the scenario I refer to in the Chad Basin illustrates the local effects of global processes. While commercial networks that span the borders of Cameroon, Nigeria, and Chad have historical precedents in the trans-Saharan and east–west Sahelian economies, their resurgence in recent years is in part due to the effective incorporation and novel use of resources derived from international markets. As elsewhere on the continent, marginalization from certain world markets (e.g. export crop commodities) and the proliferation of certain resources for accumulation (e.g. drugs, small arms) have resulted in a drive for new forms of economic integration (Bayart et al. 1997). These include sometimes risky and hence often lucrative ventures such as the trade in small arms flowing through the Sudan, Libya, Chad, Cameroon, Nigeria, Niger, and Algeria; provisioning of ongoing conflict in Niger, Chad, the Central African Republic, and the Sudan which involves transiting petrol, hardware, electronics, grain, cement, detergent, and (most often stolen) cars and four-wheel-drive trucks; the ivory trade centered around Lake Chad and the Central African Republic; the transfer of drugs between the Pakistani crescent, Nigeria, and Western Europe; and large-scale, highly organized highway banditry.[4]

These types of commerce and the trading regimes they forge are influenced by the global political economy in several ways. First, the deregulation of both world and local markets has exacerbated dependencies on certain international markets in the regional political economy. This is the case for the international markets in small arms, mercenaries, securocrats, and militias, which recently have gained prominence in the region. Today, one notes a proliferation on the continent of arms from Eastern Europe, the independent republics of the former Soviet Union, China, South Africa, and Angola, and the increased circulation of mercenaries from France, Belgium, South Africa, the former Yugoslavia, and Pakistan.[5] The formalization of these once secretive flows is summarized by the comments of Capitaine Hoffman: "I am a mercenary. I 'rent' my services to foreign countries for money. Many of us prefer the term, technical consultant ..." (Friedman 1993). This increasingly explicit and normalized presence has led both private concerns and public power increasingly to employ private security forces (e.g. Wackenhut, Executive Outcomes) to defend oil fields, mines, airports, company headquarters, government buildings, and residential neighborhoods. High-placed government officials and military personnel are often implicated in the operations and revenues of this economic sector such that the security business is now an important vocation in the regional political economy, helping to sustain the international traffic in arms and men.[6] This has been abetted by the fact that programs for economic and political liberalization put forth by the World Bank and the International Monetary Fund have resulted in the privatization of state-run industries as well as internal security.

Indeed, the conditionalities of international financing are another factor contributing to transformations of the regional economy. This can be seen through the impact of structural adjustment programs, which privatized industries and downsized armies, leading to swollen ranks of the unemployed, who seek opportunities for accumulation in the emergent

---

[4] On kalashnikovs and the Chadian economy, see *Jeune Afrique* (1992). On the continental drug economy, see "Observatoire géopolitique des drogues" (1995). On highway banditry, see Soudan (1996) and Dorce 1996. More generally, see Bayart et al. (1997) and Bennafla (1996, 1997).

[5] These points are briefly underscored in various parts of Bayart et al. (1997) as well as in numerous recent issues of *L'Autre Afrique*. See also Friedman (1993), Harding (1996), and Banégas (1998).

[6] See Banégas (1998), as well as Hibou (1997) and Ellis (1996).

markets of the region. No social category of the population has been spared. In Chad, for example, the military demobilization program started in 1992 has generally been eclipsed by soldiers' ability to recycle themselves through various regional rebel groups (e.g. the Mouvement pour le développement around Lake Chad or the Forces armées pour la République fédérale in southern Chad); to enter into the small arms traffic, for which they have contacts and expertise; or to "enter the bush," often working as road bandits with organized groups of Cameroonians, Nigerians, Nigeriens, Centrafricans, and Sudanese.[7] Likewise, the local urban-based merchant class, which produced its rents through debt-financing up until the late 1980s (Bayart 1989b), was forced to reconfigure its economic activities with the contraction in bilateral and multilateral aid. These merchants' past engagements as transporters and suppliers for public works projects have been reformulated in terms of the remaining or evolving possibilities for enrichment: their convoys have taken up the paths running through Nigeria, Cameroon, the Central African Republic, Chad, Libya, and the Sudan (e.g. smuggling petrol).

Since privatization and the downsizing of public enterprises accompanying structural adjustment programs have inflated the ranks of unemployed youth, growing hordes of young men have followed the paths of the merchants' convoys. Those who once found employment in local agro-industry, the health and education sectors, and development and public works projects now work as transporters, guards, guides, and carriers along the Nigerian, Cameroonian, and Chadian borders. One might argue, in fact, that the urban networks that have predominated over the countryside for several decades are becoming increasingly dependent upon economic strategies pursued by the unemployed and recently dispossessed. In many ways, the urban economy is now subservient to the "economy of the bush." As a recent report on the monetary situation in the franc zone notes, the "urban exodus" of bank bills and coinage (notably smaller denominations, which are virtually impossible to procure in large towns and cities) is largely attributable to the vitality of the

---

[7] Between 1992 and 1997, 27,000 Chadian military personnel were to be demobilized and disarmed. Since kalashnikovs had become a veritable currency as well as a means of accumulation in the region (circulating especially between Chad, Niger, and Libya), upon collection of the 30,000 CFA promised in exchange for their military uniforms and arms, most Chadian soldiers reinvested in the arms market. See *Jeune Afrique* (1992); *Le Progrès* (1997); *N'Djamena Hebdo* (1997a); Teiga, (1997); and Bennafla (1996: 65), who notes that "Many 'deflated' soldiers rush to buy back a khaki uniform and an arm as soon as they are pensioned off" (my translation). This was confirmed in interviews with military and civil administrators, as well as human rights activists in N'djamena.

rural sector, and especially the "informal," or border and bush, economy (*L'Autre Afrique* 1997a).[8]

Producing wealth on the frontier: the economy of the bush

In sum, the stimulation of economic activity in the bush is partly a result of the combined efforts of the economic refugees of structural adjustment programs and decreased foreign aid, on the one hand, and the military refugees of downsized and under-financed armies, on the other. In the Chad Basin, those recently discharged during the demobilization campaign in Chad have joined up with unpaid soldiers from Cameroon, Nigeria, Niger, and the Sudan, as well as the young guards and guides who have worked the bush trails trafficking contraband goods (especially petrol) for almost a decade now. Together, they raid border markets and highways (Dorce 1996; *N'Djamena Hebdo* 1997a; Pideu 1995; Soudan 1996). Their activities have transformed border areas, which are speckled with settlements that serve as depots, hide-outs, and bulking and rediffusion points. Some "are quietly flourishing ... as local entrepôts specialized in precision goods such as radios, cassette-recorders, watches, etc. as well as petrol retailing and currency exchanges" (Achu Gwan 1992: 23).

What is especially novel about this situation, and what makes it worth noting with respect to the dynamics of transregional political economies and the nation-state, is that the dismissed, dispossessed, and unemployed who have taken to the bush, highways, and borders are making claims to rights to wealth. Many unemployed young men have some form of education (sometimes having finished high school) and yet they find themselves obliged to scavenge and traffic for money. They often talk about their situation as a state of "war," where forced appropriation and seizure are the norm, being practiced by customs officials, police, gangs, armed bandits, and themselves.[9] And those who normally benefit from rights-in-seizure also complain about lack of compensation: regular soldiers protest (often

---

[8] F. de Boeck (1999) describes how young Zairean urbanites have migrated to rural areas along the Angolan border in order to partake in the diamond economy. This has led to their inclusion in a "dollarized" economy – the bush economy, as opposed to the city, becoming the very source of tokens of wealth and consumption. This does not mean, as de Boeck (1999) and Bennafla (1998) note, that investment practice has also been reoriented from the urban centers to the bush. Revenues procured through commercial and financial activities transpiring in the latter are often invested or consumed in cities and major towns.

[9] Commentary on visions of wealth, freedom, and violence by young illegal petrol sellers in northern Cameroon can be had in Roitman (1996, 1998).

through mutinies, as in the Central African Republic and Niger) against insufficient and irregular salaries, lack of basic infrastructure (e.g. sleeping quarters, food), and even essential equipment to carry out their duties (petrol, ammunition).[10] Likewise, demobilized soldiers maintain that their indemnities are inadequate. For many, this, combined with lack of training for occupations in the civil or private sectors, is what compels them to "enter the bush" (the implication being that, for those who join rebel groups, their rationale is "alimentaire" – or about food more than politics).[11] In that sense, entering the bush is not just about "shadow" economic and political activities. The economy of the bush may have its covert or even insurgent aspects, but it is equally a realm of well-known strategies of accumulation, legitimated patterns of establishing rights over wealth, and definitive organizational and financial connections to state power.

As is the case for the urban merchant class, the economic wellbeing of the political class is in many ways dependent upon this pool of supposed surplus labor. While seemingly expendable (as the "downsized"), the latter's position on the frontiers of wealth creation has rendered them indispensable to the political logics of productivity and especially extraction.[12] This apparent contradiction arises from the logics of displacement and combinatory strategies pursued by those who have "entered the bush": they are productive, thus being targeted as sources of wealth, and yet unstable, so confounding to manners of extraction based on traditional methods (such as taxation based on a census). Those working the bush and border roam from city to hinterland; make simultaneous use of the franc CFA, French franc, Nigerian naira, and American dollar; procure several national identity cards; exercise the vote in various national elections; and refer to heteroclite renderings of various Islams, Christian movements, Western ideals of democracy and human rights, and local practices of power and agency relating to self-realization and community.

[10] This has been reported in many places. See footnote 5 above as well as the descriptions of various national armies in *L'Autre Afrique* (1997b), including the section on Chad (pp. 14–15).

[11] This does not mean that the "Politics of the belly" (Bayart 1989b) is irrelevant. No doubt, state resources for public spending have diminished as a consequence of structural adjustment programs and embezzlement. None the less, presidential guards and private militias associated with executive power are well paid and in a timely manner, these outlays being mostly off-budget. Evidently, the right to redistribution is gauged according to certain representations of utility (be they well judged or not: witness Mobutu's Special Presidential Division).

[12] This ambivalence is a direct consequence of their being targets of regulatory authority, see Roitman (1998). For a more extensive study of the unstable terms of regulatory authority in northern Cameroon, see Roitman (1996), which reviews how "the slave," tax, price, and the population flottante all form an intrinsically related, and significantly unstable, ensemble of regulatory targets.

To be sure, as nomads, migrants, refugees, the unemployed, the home-less, fugitives, brigands, and even separatists, those who work the bor-ders are often pegged as that which has erupted or been expelled from the non-correspondence between nationalized space and deterritorialized practice.[13] While their precarious situations are often correctly attributed to the rise of novel transnational forms of accumulation and their asso-ciated markets, the peripatetic and those living states of dispersion have always been problematic to territorialization.[14] In the Chad Basin today, the domestication of nomads, street hawkers, the ambulatory, the clan-destine, smugglers, and the "informal economy" more generally depends fundamentally on whether or not these categories are represented as "for-eign" with respect to the nation, "subversive" with respect to society, or "irrational" with respect to the economy. Their claims to rights in wealth are judged accordingly; the state consistently refuses to address the ques-tion of the conditions of wealth creation for these populations. And yet their insistent exercise of those claims through seizure, contraband, ban-ditry, highway robbery, and smuggling are intrinsic to the perpetuation of certain aspects of state power.

Legitimating wealth creation: the contest of regulatory authority

Recourse to the bush, the intensification of economic activities along borders, strategies to evade official regulatory authority, and rebel move-ments seeking compensation through violence or retribution all seem to point to the demise of the nation-state in the Chad Basin. It is fair to say that those who control unregulated activity and armed factions are in competition with the nation-state for financial power derived from re-gional and international markets, as well as the authority to extract from local populations. But to speak of competition is not to say that the demise of the nation-state is impending or that the form of power defined by the nation-state is no longer assured. While the failings of state power on the African continent are noted daily in journalistic and academic writing, life on the continent is rife with occasions to experience the efficiencies of state power: mobilization of the opposition in Cameroon met with a crushing militarized response, as did the Ogoni movement in Nigeria.

[13] By "deterritorialized practice" I am limiting myself to situations where the ultimate refer-ent is the nation-state. In that sense, I am refraining from conclusions as to its significance as "nomadology," an alternative mode of representation (or even non-representation) and power. On the latter, see Deleuze and Guattari (1987).

[14] This has been underscored in recent writing about diasporas, although much of that commentary celebrates the novelty of diasporic states.

Nevertheless, and this is perhaps the only point I wish to make, while certain strengths of African states are all too evident for their citizens, it is true that state regulatory authority is no longer assured in most countries of the continent. While this situation varies across states, the financial crises that are now the hallmarks of most African states are largely indicative of the failings of fiscal regulation and the autonomization of certain economic activities with respect to state controls. In the Chad Basin, this is the case for commerce across national borders involving general merchandise as well as drugs and small arms. It is also the case for certain large-scale businesses, such as transport, which generally escape customs controls and other forms of taxation through collusion and creative accounting techniques. Beyond Chad, the failings of state regulatory authority are evident in the autonomization of certain economic sectors, such as mining, which has become essential to the financing of militias, rebel movements, and secessionists in many countries (e.g. Sierra Leone, Angola, Democratic Republic of the Congo) over the past ten years.

This does not mean, however, that the failings of state regulatory authority – which are by no means unique to the African continent – are indicative of a loss of sovereignty. State power and sovereignty are not equivalent, and lapses in the former do not indicate the displacement of the latter. Likewise, manifestations of competing sources of wealth and authority, such as described herein, are not sovereign simply because they exercise authoritative power over specific domains. This is an important point, which I will address below.

To gain a sense of the extent to which state regulatory authority is being displaced by other agents means ascertaining how regimes of accumulation associated with the latter are institutionalized and, more importantly, legitimated. Of course, in the field of state power, alternative forms of power – and regulatory authority – always exist because no form of power is totalizing. But the question remains: are appropriations which found viable regimes of accumulation legitimated in everyday practice, giving rise to new figures of regulatory authority in the Chad Basin? And this, in spite of their being associated with often extreme violence?

As noted above, the commercial and financial activities that constitute regional networks of accumulation are among the few remaining opportunities for employment and enrichment in the Chad Basin. One of the main ways in which regional elites (prominent merchants, ex-military personnel) exercise regulatory authority is by controlling access to such possibilities for accumulation, thus determining the right to employment and enrichment. This takes place at the highest levels of business through commissions on deals, right-of-entry taxes, tribute and royalty payments to maintain political and commercial relationships, protection fees, and even payment for safe delivery of goods procured through customs fraud or for their "legal" passage through customs. It transpires at the everyday level of business through levies on local merchants, protection and entitlement fees paid by young men engaged as guards, guides, runners, and wardens, entry taxes paid at unregulated border markets, and tolls on roads near these economically sensitive outposts.

No doubt, many of these payments are made under coercion.[15] Yet many people are often quite willing to make payments for access to privileged commercial relationships, international markets, and the more lucrative local sites of accumulation since these provide the means for socioeconomic mobility in times of scarcity. Furthermore, payments made to ensure access to markets, essential commercial and financial relationships, and protection serve to formalize the various kinds of traffic involved, be that of small arms across long distances or smuggled petrol through a mountain pass. This makes such activities less unpredictable both in terms of logistics and revenues. Moreover, contributions to those who regulate access to, and participation in, these commercial and financial activities are not without services rendered. These include protection and a formal cadre, but they also involve the redistribution that takes place through the financing of schools, mosques, churches, and medical clinics. In Chad and northern Cameroon, prominent merchants are famous for building mosques and Muslim schools in home villages; today, these have begun to pepper the no-man's-lands and new frontier towns along national borders. And in Mbaiboum, a mushroom "town-market" on the Chad–Cameroon–Central African Republic border, Ibo merchants from Nigeria built a church in 1996 (Bennafla 1998: 69).

Those who find themselves outside the bounds of national welfare and security come to judge prestations associated with unofficial regulators as legitimate since they grant access to possibilities for accumulation, protection, and services which are not secured through the state or public infrastructures. In this sense, the relationships that local populations establish with those controlling regional networks of

---

[15] See Bennafla's description (1998: 68) of payments made at barricades along the route to Mbaiboum, a flourishing, unregulated (until recently) market at the confluence of the Cameroon–Chad–Central African Republics' borders. Even though the state administration recently attempted to regulate this intense center of border traffic by implementing official "tickets de marché" and licensing fees paid by merchants, unofficial "rights to entry and exit" are still also paid to regional henchmen at the market itself.

accumulation respond to the former's claims to rights to wealth. As the foot soldiers of the economy of the bush insist, the expanding trade in unregulated goods is quite often a source of economic empowerment and freedom. They assert rights to engage in commerce regardless of means.[16] Since state appropriations frequently take the form of seizure (especially in marketplaces, on roads, and on border crossings, where impoverished state officials chain merchants' stores shut and haul them in pick-up trucks to prison, and renegade customs officials and gendarmes skim off of trucks and travelers, usurping contraband), similar (and often violent) modalities of expropriation are perceived as "fair game," or are taken up as an operative rationality.[17] For the local populace, the extractive power of non-state regulators is consistent with certain paradigms of social order, equitable distribution, and retribution; the latter's power is legitimated, then, insofar as they allow local people to aspire to and act upon their understandings of what rights-in-wealth "should be."

While recourse to these networks of accumulation and acquiescence to their associated figures of authority may be inspired by a contraction in material wealth and access to such wealth (the "marginalization of African economies"), it also transpires from the extension of the discursive field in which wealth and value are figured. "Spoils," for instance, is now an ambivalent sign in the regional lexicon of wealth: once associated with war and asocial forms of wealth creation, it now signifies the disavowal of particular social obligations (e.g. tax, debt). As with fraudulent commerce, what is seized cannot be taxed. And for those living in a web of international and local debt relations, seizure is a means of reversing the social order implied by such obligations. Furthermore, spoils now signifies a new sociability of exchange insofar as it is a new means of redistribution.[18]

This is part of the process of legitimation of practices of wealth creation through seizure in the Chad Basin today. Regional entrepôts and border settlements – which are safe havens for refugees, smugglers, guards, and guides – generate distinct, and often validated, regimes of violence. They

---

[16] Those who smuggle Nigerian petrol into Cameroon described their activities to me as part of "democratization" since "anyone can participate" and their supply keeps gas prices low, thus aiding the impoverished consumer. On the relationship between their status as a fiscal subject and their perceptions of the free citizen, see Roitman (1998).

[17] On this last point, refer to Mbembe and Roitman (1995).

[18] This is reminiscent of practice during the nineteenth-century *jihad*, when "spoils" was articulated from within the discourse on legitimate property and wealth. Today, *jihad* is an important reference, but its import stems from its association with a world movement for political affirmation and redistribution. For further commentary, see Roitman (1998).

are not always seen as lawless outposts; depending on one's vision of wealth, authority, and freedom, they can also be sites of protective, sustaining power.[19] Most importantly for the local population, the forms of violence associated with their particular modes of appropriation are inherent to certain strategies for socio-economic mobility.[20] Since they are hubs for the redistribution of wealth, economic competition, and welfare, social hierarchies generated in their midst endure to the extent that they are deemed to rectify or subvert either longstanding or recently created conditions of exclusion.

Those who have managed to direct the financing, labor recruitment, and material organization required by such networks include leaders of factions or rebel groups (e.g. the Mouvement pour le développement around Lake Chad), the local merchant elite (e.g. the Arab Choa elite in Kousseri, Cameroon and N'Djamena, Chad), and military officers who find rents on fraudulent commerce more attractive than their official salaries (leading to their denomination in Chad as "les douaniers-combattants" – literally, "customs officials-soldiers" or, more prosaically, "fighting customs officials").[21] These commercio-military alliances and their counterparts in the bush are emergent figures of regulatory authority in the Chad Basin. Their exactions and levies are often tolerated and even sanctioned by local populations – who achieve socio-economic mobility and gain needed security – as much as those exercised by the state. As regulators, they certainly compete with the nation-state in its capacities to extract.

Yet this scenario cannot be reduced to a matter of national (e.g. Cameroonian or Chadian) involvement in these sub- and transnational networks of trade and accumulation. Commercio-military alliances involve renegade militias, demobilized soldiers, gendarmes, customs officials, well-placed military officers, local political figures, members of the

---

[19] On this notion of power with respect to the *jihad* movement, see Last (1992).

[20] This is not particularly African: refer to Weber, Braudel, Tilly. With respect to the African context, see Bayart (1994) (especially on war as a historical mode of insertion into the world economy).

[21] This was noted during my stay in northern Cameroon and Chad, and from interviews. Scant references include: on the guerrilla movement around Lake Chad, Faes (1997); on demobilized soldiers see footnote 7; and on the military's rent-seeking activities, see Abba Kaka (1997) and Ngarngoune (1997). Although not specifically referred to, the region comprising southern Chad, the north province of Cameroon, and the Central African Republic presents an analogous situation, the main differences being the identity of the rebels (e.g. les Forces armées pour la République fédérale led by Laoukein Bardé) and the nature of wealth (diamonds from the Central African Republic or gold dust in southern Chad).

opposition, and government ministers.[22] To say that this amalgam results merely from the involvement of national figures in corrupt practices perpetrated by regional traffickers would be an oversimplification since sub- and transnational regimes of accumulation, redistribution, and security are legitimated alongside the nation-state. I have argued that these regimes compete with the nation-state for financial power and the authority to extract from local populations, taking advantage of and aggravating the state's failure to assert regulatory authority. However, such competition does not imply that state power, more generally, is being usurped by transnational phenomena.

While it is true that transnational phenomena present notorious problems for state regulation, the scenario of the Chad Basin, like that of other places, demonstrates how such networks become part and parcel of the political logics of the state itself, contributing to its ability to fulfil essential political imperatives such as extraction and redistribution (see Sassen 1995 on the creation of new legal regimes and, more generally, Hibou 1998, 1999).[23] This takes place, for one, through various manners of appropriation. For example, the Cameroonian administration has increasingly implicated itself in the recently established market-town of Mbaiboum. In 1987, Mbaiboum appeared on the Chad–Cameroon–Central African Republic borders as a hub of unregulated commerce in local industrial goods (salt, sugar, textiles) and consumer items (clothing, cassette players, hardware, cement), as well as gold, drugs, arms, and diamonds. In the early 1990s, commercial activities in Mbaiboum intensified dramatically. In 1992, a Cameroonian customs station was established at Mbaiboum. Although the state has provided neither water nor electricity to this booming "town," it now manages to take in

[22] In Cameroon, goods stolen during a road hold-up were discovered later in a sub-prefect's office. In Chad, an administrator with the postal service refused to comment on the identity of road bandits who attacked her convoy because, as she said, "they know me very well," implying that they were, like herself, members of the state bureaucracy. And when people from a Cameroonian village pursued a gang of brigands across the frontier into Chad, they were stopped by the Chadian village chief who handed them over to the very same gang. One report noted that, "These men proved to be dissident members of the Chadian military who obey a certain Commandant Kah." Arms seized on the Cameroonian side of the border included a bazooka, something not in large supply in the local village markets . . .

[23] Some might argue that this is true for a regime or government, but not the state. That is, they understand the idea that the continuity of a regime may stem from appropriating the logics of wealth creation manifest in transnational networks, but insist that state sovereignty is at peril due to the lack of authority exercised over such networks themselves. But if these networks contribute to the very viability of state functions (extraction, enabling productive economic sectors, redistribution), they perpetuate the viability of the state as a political institution as much as a particular regime.

20 million francs CFA each year through the sale of "droits de marché" (market duties) and licenses.[24]

This formalization of once unregulated activity does not imply the usurpation of power. Unofficial regulators of this commerce still exercise their "rights" over local populations: they collect "entry and exit" duties in the market (5,000–10,000 CFA per vehicle) and tolls on incoming roads (10,000–50,000 CFA for trucks), not to mention commissions and protection fees on the more lucrative trade in gold, arms, and diamonds.[25] No measures are taken to quell these unofficial taxes and Cameroonian customs policy has been described as "accommodating" or even "encouraging," with very low levels of taxation on goods, and a minimum amount of surveillance of the national identities of population flows through borders (Bennafla 1998: 66; 1999: 42–49). Furthermore, military escorts have been established between Mbaiboum and certain outlying cities so as to protect merchants from the insistent pillaging and brutalities of road bandits. In Chad, some claim that those who conduct such military escorts (the Garde nationale et nomade) are less concerned with protecting imperiled citizens than with securing fraud:

Unfortunately, in Chad, most of the laws governing the customs service are put to ridicule. The simple resolution stating that "a customs officer must not operate beyond the border" has not been respected. On the pretext of thwarting smugglers, the military and elements of the Garde nationale et nomade du Tchad – or alleged customs officials – ride at breakneck speed through the city crammed into their Toyota [pick-ups], causing numerous accidents. The victims are most often peaceful citizens who have nothing to do with fraud. In reality, this chase between customs officers and smugglers is a pretense. It is, to some extent, a strategy that involves escorting the vehicle containing the smuggled goods all the way to the marketplace, for fear of being intercepted by other customs officials who amble along the roads. Without this tacit complicity, merchandise would not be imported from abroad. (Abba Kaka 1997: 8)

Indeed, the Chadian and Cameroonian states have every reason to facilitate border traffic, which provides remuneration for under- and unpaid military officials, who convert to customs officials, and fills state coffers through licensing.

But this does not necessarily mean rendering "legal" unregulated traffic. The state can offer a legal structure for these activities without altering the fact that they are either formally illegal or based on fraud. This means

---

[24] See K. Bennafla's detailed descriptions of Mbaiboum (1998: 54, 68).

[25] On market and road taxes, see Bennafla (1998: 68). Information on the trade in gold, arms, and diamonds (and perhaps rhinoceros horns) is based on confidential interviews in Cameroon.

producing administrative paperwork for transactions without taking into account certain quantitative or qualitative aspects of the commerce involved, thus producing a false legal status for merchants. This is typical practice along the borders of all states in the Chad Basin, and represents one way in which the state is sometimes at the heart of the proliferation of sub- and transnational networks of accumulation and power. Evidently, this false legalization contributes to the economic wellbeing of under- and unpaid state administrators, who are reimbursed for such services. But it also contributes to the state's financial liquidity. Traffic between the Chad Basin and North Africa has proved one means of accessing hard currency in a context of the non-convertibility of local monies. In Niger, for instance, the state is central to the organization of the illegal trade in American cigarettes. As Emmanuel Grégoire notes,

The Nigerien state has, in effect, set up a legislative framework which organizes this traffic and obtains significant customs receipts, estimated at about 6 billion francs CFA in 1994 and 1995, or the equivalent of a month and a half of functionaries' salaries, which are six months past due (January 1998). Operators act in perfect legality in Niger, with fraud transpiring only at the cost of neighboring states which prohibit imports of foreign cigarettes to protect their own industry (Nigeria) or tax them strongly for the same reason (Algeria and Libya). (Grégoire 1998: 100, my translation)

In this instance, state agents collude with, and are dependent upon, intermediaries (e.g. Tuaregs)[26] who control certain trade routes and are notorious for providing security in dangerous zones (such as the south of Algeria and the Niger–Chad border) not only for personal profit, but also to respond to the insolvency of the state and its associated political risks (e.g. the demands of unpaid state bureaucrats, including police and "gens d'armes"). This scenario partially explains how insolvent states are somehow able to expand their administrative corpus: in Cameroon, for example, 20,000 new functionaries have been added to the rolls since 1987 despite the fact that there has been no new official recruitment since that time (Hibou 1997: 150). It also confirms the point that commercial policy in Africa (and elsewhere, such as in Russia) is defined in terms of lucrative opportunities:

International commercial policy . . . is designed not primarily by the relevant (competent) administration (with its ensemble of rules on customs duties, quantitative restrictions, the standardization of regional commercial agreements, etc.), but by a certain number of influential actors, both public and private, who define

---

[26] Emmanuel Grégoire notes the special talents of the Tuareg of Hoggar as "passeurs" between Algeria and Niger (1998: 95). He also indicates that the Nigerien army often offers protection for convoys running illegal deliveries between Niger and Libya (p. 101).

such policy in function of possibilities for fraud and contraband, so as to insure mastery of access to parallel markets and fraudulent practices. (Hibou 1998: 156, my translation)

The state thus benefits from profitable situations produced by competing regimes of power. It is sometimes also the instigator of proliferating unregulated, underregulated, or falsely regulated activities, and even becomes dependent upon those wielding power (e.g. regulation of access) and expertise (e.g. security) in sub- and transnational networks. While these endeavors potentially undermine state regulatory authority and national security, as noted above, they also contribute to the viability of the state through the production of new rents and possibilities for redistribution among strategic military, political, and commercial personalities.[27] This is, of course, a question of financing both political clients and strategies to prevent the emergence of a counter-elite or counter-power.[28] It is a matter, then, of the very formation and maintenance of a dominant political class – or the stability of a regime. However, beyond political payouts and underwriting political stability, rents (or wealth) thus produced are essential to "an extremely complex system of revenue transfers from formal and official circuits to parallel ones, from urban households to rural ones, from the richest to the most dispossessed (via allocations to families, social expenditures, and diverse benefits such as school fees, health, funerals, participation in customary ceremonies...)" (Mbembe 1993: 367–368). These forms of redistribution are a primary mode of the exercise of state power.

Indeed, appropriating rents associated with sub- and transnational networks of accumulation – and thus collaborating with and managing their associated figures of financial power and regulatory authority – means creating wealth for off-budget activities (e.g. hiring private security companies as presidential guards or financing political parties) and state functions (paying administrative salaries or financing external conflicts). In

---

[27] This is similar to the situation in Algeria, as described by L. Martinez, who demonstrates how the civil war in Algeria has not led to the disintegration of the state. The Algerian state found economic and political advantages through a specific manner of regulating conflict and control of resources. Recourse to the army and private militias as a means of ensuring exclusive control of certain resources (e.g. oil) is legitimated due to the state of war, thus permitting the state to finance the reconstruction and consolidation of essential alliances. Also, surveillance of the general population has been given over to militias, who benefit from accumulation via violence and increase their power. See Martinez (1995, 1998). I thank Béatrice Hibou for referring me to his work.

[28] In Cameroon, the Biya regime's tolerance – if not sanction – of high military officials' involvement in the arms, drugs, and counterfeiting sectors is well-known and generally interpreted as a means of redistribution.

this sense, regional networks are a resource that contributes to the political logics of predation that define the historical exercise of state power in Africa.[29] And yet this is not to reduce this situation to a historical-cultural necessity: similar situations can be found in Colombia, Peru, Algeria, and Russia, where tributary relations between the state and sub- and transnational networks of wealth and power prevail. Moreover, while this form of intermediation between state power and emergent figures of power may be interpreted as in keeping with certain historical continuities (e.g. the role of intermediaries in the Atlantic slave trade or in the enactment of colonial power), today its specificity arises from certain ruptures in the global political economy.

Many observers note, correctly, that state consolidation on the continent is now taking place via indirect (i.e. non-bureaucratic) means (Reno in this volume; Hibou 1999). This is in large part due to the emergence and deregulation of particular markets (e.g. in small arms, mercenaries, private security companies). But is this manner of exercising power via indirect mediations a novel aspect of state power in Africa? Recourse to private, foreign agents, for example, is a longstanding manner of ensuring the effective exercise of state power; in Africa, this has involved the use of external alliances (such as the Cold War powers) or external resources (such as foreign aid) to manage internal conflicts and the demands of factions constituting the basis of state power (Bayart 1989b; Hibou 1997, 1999; Reno 1995). Thus, the reconfiguration of power on the continent today is less a matter of new practices of the exercise of state power than of novel ways of negotiating the changing world economy, or managing extraversion. It is, as Achille Mbembe has argued in another context, an attempt to "redeploy networks of reciprocity, allocations, and compensations that were once amalgamated in the heart of the single party [state]" (Mbembe 1993). In the Chad Basin, sub- and transnational regimes of accumulation are critical connections to today's external rents; they are another means of insertion in the world economy. Figures of regulation associated with these regimes are critical to the consolidation of state power even though they work to undermine state regulatory authority. And they represent, through the production of wealth on the frontier, one place where the tentacular effects of state power are redeployed in its quest for the means to redistribute.

---

[29] This is a longstanding thesis of J.-F. Bayart, articulated in many places. On the multiple manifestations of the predatory logics of state power, see Bayart (1989b), and on the "dédoublement de l'état" in the form, for example, of "conseils administrative," see Bayart (1997: esp. pp. 64–67). On *dédoublement* as a mode of power, see Mbembe (1992).

Conclusion: power is not sovereign

One question remains: are emergent figures of regulation in the Chad Basin alternative sites of political power? If the sub- and transnational networks described above can be defined as both national and non-national, they are "new spaces" insofar as they belie the assumption that the pre-eminent locus of power is the nation-state form. But are they new forms of power arising from the disjunctures between the local and global or the national and non-national? Or are we beginning to approach them from novel points of view, which tend to destabilize the national referent? This brings us to the conceptual question raised at the beginning of the essay: is power located at all?

It is tempting to argue that the situation in the Chad Basin warrants reference to "new spaces" since novel manners of conceptualizing and arrogating wealth are being institutionalized in practice, giving rise to unprecedented power relationships. While these practices arise from the historical templates of wealth, appropriation, and violence in the region (e.g. seizure and spoils in *jihad*), they are none the less driven by novel, transnational phenomena (e.g. emerging markets).[30] For example, the *razzia* has been given new élan with the diffusion of kalashnikovs in the Chad Basin. None the less, to say that power relations have been – or are being – transformed by transnational phenomena is to speak of a *qualitative* change involving not just new spaces *per se*, but new forms, new techniques, new rationalities, etc. In other words, emphasis on new locations of power must not occlude the question of transformations (or not) in the *exercise* of power.

To my mind, this is intrinsically related to the problematization of state power as sovereignty. As I have argued herein, the demise of certain metaphors and historical institutions that once regulated communities (e.g. economic development, national progress, social welfare) has rendered certain modes of appropriation (*razzia*, seizure, debt) and their associated figures of authority (militias, *douaniers-combattants*, foreigners) potential alternative sources of regulatory authority.[31] But are these new sovereigns? More specifically, if the constitution of state power is

---

[30] It is worth noting, however, that, beyond the specifics of the nature of contemporary geo-political relationships, forms of technology, and types of commodities, this situation resembles that existing during the time of concessionary companies on the continent, as well as the Atlantic slave trade. Reflection on the present refiguring of relationships between wealth, appropriations, and violence should take that into account.

[31] See also Paul Richards' writing on the Sierra Leone–Liberia region (1996). Beyond Africa, it is evident that breaches in the association between national progress and the teleology of economic development have given rise to various forms of social movements (e.g. nativist, environmental) and categories of people (e.g. indigenous people, refugees, diasporas) that now make and exercise novel claims to wealth.

dependent upon the power of non-state regulators, do these latter instances represent new forms of sovereignty? Clearly, how sovereignty is
conceptualized matters greatly in addressing such questions.

Since sovereignty, as regards the definition practiced in classical political theory and jurisprudence, is seen as the summation of the founding
properties of "statehood," it is thought to be constitutive of the state
itself and *is thus vested with powers of its own*. As a foundational politico-
legal concept, sovereignty itself is assumed to be self-evident.[32] This is
why most present-day commentary on transnational phenomena often
confounds sovereignty and power. The state, as an abstract, unitary object of knowledge and a political subject in international political theory,
is such because of sovereignty. And yet sovereignty is simply the unre-
stricted and determining power of the state as a political subject in the
system of states.[33] Sovereignty is thus a given as the foundational concept and defining property of "stateness" and the very presence of the
state. The quest to define and, moreover, locate sovereignty stems from
the presumption that sovereignty constitutes the indivisible units of the
international political system (Bartelson 1993: 10–22, 25).[34]

From this conceptual point of departure, it is almost natural to appre-
hend the impact of transnational events and instances in terms of the potential displacement of the sovereign status of the state by emergent forms
of power. These include financial markets or global capital markets and
their associated legal regimes, agglomerations of non-governmental organizations or institutions of transnational civil society, and, more generally,
extra-state politico-economic networks.[35] In spite of its foundational relationship to the politico-legal concept of the state, many observers raise the

[32] "[T]he more sovereignty is thought to explain, the more it itself is withdrawn from explanation. The theoretical sovereignty of sovereignty leaves sovereignty itself essentially
unquestioned; the more constitutive sovereignty appears to be, the less unconstituted
it becomes" (Bartelson 1993: 15). See especially ch. 2 in Bartelson, which has greatly
informed my own thoughts. Very different critiques of the notion of sovereignty as constitutive of the modern state system can be found in both Wallerstein (1999) and Krasner
(1999).

[33] On the circularity of sovereignty, see M. Foucault's writing on *gouvernementalité*, in which
he establishes distinct understandings of the finality of sovereignty as opposed to government. While "to govern . . . means to govern things," and hence has a finality of its
own, "the end of sovereignty is the exercise of sovereignty." He says, "whereas the end of
sovereignty is internal to itself and possesses its own intrinsic instruments in the shape
of its laws, the finality of government resides in the things it manages and in the pursuit of
the perfection and intensification of the processes which it directs; and the instruments
of government, instead of being laws, now come to be a range of multiform tactics"
(Foucault 1991: 94–97). On this point, see also Foucault (1991: 10–22).

[34] See also Bartelson (1993: 23–31) on the problematic of sovereignty and space, or how
space becomes an object of political knowledge, with sovereignty being the metaphysical
condition establishing the unity of the modern state.

[35] Refer to the various interpretations found in the references cited in footnote 3.

question of whether sovereignty inheres in non-state forms, and whether or not there are now sovereigns other than the state.

To answer in the affirmative is to assume that sovereignty *is* some thing. It is a form of power that we can define and locate in human socio-political and economic relationships. While sovereignty is less frequently taken to be a timeless essence of the state,[36] its ontological presence is assumed as constitutive of the modern political system. In keeping with its presumed constitutive conceptual and empirical power, sovereignty is treated as a timeless feature of political reality. Often this form of power is defined as constituted by domains "that are the locus of pre-eminent power in a social field" (Ong, unpublished ms: 4; subsequently published 1999), or zones defined by various modes of governance, which give rise to differential regimes of civil and political rights. These structures, networks, domains, or zones are fields of social authority which produce codes, rules, norms, and significations that structure the practices and relations of those under its dominion. But are they generative of sovereignty?

Emergent figures of regulatory authority in the Chad Basin may be described in such terms. Here, relationships defining the military–commercial complex have been institutionalized over time, and this field of social authority structures practices and induces certain rationalities for those in its midst. But to say that such an emergent domain is a predominant referent for action, understanding, and authority is to speak of the exercise of power and not necessarily sovereignty. Even if these domains are equal to or more powerful than the state in the government of people and things, this does not contradict the extent to which they may be part of the same logical space as the nation-state. If their codes, rules, and norms are structuring in a determining way, or in a way that usurps or parallels state power, how has this become logically possible? That is, how have the claims to authoritative status and unqualified jurisdiction become normalized such that they are not contested as illegitimate (read illogical)? We might answer that question, as I have attempted to do herein, but this does not provide the means to conclude that such power is sovereign.

The idea that sovereignty exists in circumscribed domains where one is compelled to act or even think in a specific way, or where subjects are constituted in terms of particular (non-state based) political and economic rights, is consistent with a particular conception of power. This takes power as productive; it is a situation which gives rise to subjects who are "caught up in a power situation of which they themselves are the

---

[36] See, for example, Giddens (1981: esp. pp. 263–264); some of the contributions to Czempiel and Rosenau (1989); Evans (1997).

bearers" (Foucault 1977: 201). Attempts to grasp the exercise of power understood in this sense have inspired acute attention to the structuring power of relationships and institutions, as well as to the disciplinary effects of codes, techniques, and rationalities. However, much caution is required in incorporating these insights into debates about globalization and its purported effects on state sovereignty. Indeed, this analytics of power was inspired by the very critique of the ever-present subject of the juridical sovereign in analysis and representations of power.[37]

As Foucault maintained, the abiding juridical representation of power is constructed from the prohibitive thematics of repression and law; yet this manner of representation is "utterly incongruous with the new methods of power whose operation is ensured not by right but by technique, not by law but by normalization, not by punishment but by control, methods that are employed on all levels and in forms that go beyond the state and its apparatus" (Foucault 1990 [1978]: 89). Foucault's critique is not, of course, based on the notion that the juridical mode of representing power is "outdated" or fails to account for new forms of power. His move toward an analytics, as opposed to a theory, of power involves the formulation of a "definition of the specific domain formed by relations of power" so as to comprehend historical practices of power.[38] For this agenda, an ultimate source of power and the possibility of its possession are irrelevant since power is productive of relationships and subjectivities and not primarily repressive or a simple matter of interdiction (p. 94).[39] Thus sovereignty (if it *is* anything) is not a condition of unqualified power or absolute authority since the omnipresence of power *is not its totalizing capacity or unqualified unity*: "power is not an institution, and not a structure; neither is it a certain strength we are endowed with; it is the name that one attributes to a complex strategical situation in a particular society" (p. 93). Thus, the networks and domains often described as new spaces of sovereignty or emergent sovereigns – which

---

[37] So much emphasis has been placed on Foucault's thoughts on power and knowledge and disciplinary techniques that his explicit preoccupation with the effects of the language of political philosophy on conceptualizations of power, the relational nature of power, and the seemingly insurmountable problems of origins and history devoid of subjectivity have been slighted. Foucault spoke of "the system of Law-and-Sovereign which has captivated political thought for such a long time. And if it is true that Machiavelli was among the few – and this no doubt was the scandal of his 'cynicism' – who conceived the power of the Prince in terms of force relationships, perhaps we need to go one step further, do without the persona of the Prince, and decipher power relationships on a basis of a strategy that is imminent in force relationships" (Foucault, 1990 [1978]: 97; see also Foucault 1981: 102).

[38] This is possible only if the "juridical and negative representation of power" is finally disarmed ("cutting off the king's head"). See Foucault (1981) 82, 86–91).

[39] For commentary, see the chapter entitled "Thematics of State and Power" in Dean (1994: esp. 152–173). See also Foucault (1977: 167–169).

include emergent figures of regulation in the Chad Basin – are new configurations of power, the question of their sovereign status being irrelevant. In other words, if we accept – again, following Foucault – that states of power are constantly engendered at the multiple points of its exercise, the question of sovereign status, understood as totalizing in any particular domain or an instance of unqualified unity, is nonsensical since such situations simply do not obtain.[40] The infrastructures of the state, or the points of the exercise of state power, extend beyond the specific institutions of the state itself, or even the state as a unified and coherent entity. This is manifest in homes, schools, hospitals, factories, armies, and, I would add, world financial markets, international mafias, and non-governmental organizations. While the latter may be defined as non-state based, they are surely points of the exercise of state power.

In that sense, the precepts underlying apparently novel relationships, activities, and modalities issue from, or are consistent with, those practiced in the existing political economy or socio-juridical order.[41] The endurance of sub- and transnational regimes of accumulation and power depends upon the normalization and legitimation of new registers of value and the articulation of rights to wealth that were heretofore deemed asocial or irrational (e.g. spoils, rights in wealth through seizure). However, these may be perfectly consistent with those exercised by the nation-state; that is, new ways of valuing and governing may emerge in the peripheries of the infrastructures of state power, all the while confirming the right and logic of extant modes of thinking and enacting power.

To repeat, new figures of power may emerge on the horizons (e.g. agents of regulatory authority in the Chad Basin) which do not destabilize our manner of thinking and exercising power. Likewise, instead of wondering about whether or not new types of sovereignty are in our midst, we should pay attention to the precursory matter of whether or not the intelligibility of the very idea of sovereignty has been destabilized with recent changes in the global political economy. Debates about globalization have spurred the problem of the intelligibility of sovereignty insofar as they raise the issue of the status of the nation-state in the

---

[40] "Power's condition of possibility, or in any case the viewpoint which permits one to understand its exercise, even in its more 'peripheral' effects, and which also makes it possible to use its mechanisms as a grid of intelligibility of the social order, must not be sought in the primary existence of a central point, in a unique source of sovereignty from which secondary and descendent forms would emanate…" (Foucault 1990 [1978]: 93).

[41] This point is inspired by Giorgio Agamben's reflections (1997) on how the state of the exception is the very product of the extant regime of truth. He shows how the state of exception is normalized, and how such arrangements endure even though – or perhaps because – they are devoid of "distinctions between outside and inside, exception and rule, licit and illicit (p. 110)" I thank Luca D'Isanto for this reference.

international and transnational contexts. But this is not a new problem; it is, in fact, one of the founding debates of classical political science. The real question is whether we can discern changes in the organization of knowledge, or the production of valid statements about what the state *is*, or is not. Of course, this partly arises from interpretive struggles. But do new claims to sovereignty (e.g. those of indigenous peoples) come from, or contribute to, the reorganization of knowledge? Or are they simply part of the history of "self-determination," and thus part of the extant template of knowledge?

In other words, to say that something has changed in a particular way (e.g. new figures of regulatory authority have emerged in the Chad Basin) does not address the question of *how* such change has become logically possible. For instance, certain figures of regulatory authority may be qualified as emergent in the Chad Basin simply because they were not there previously. But, as I have attempted to demonstrate, this in itself is dependent on qualitative changes in various domains (e.g. the international economy) leading to the definition of new realms of logical thought and action (e.g. the military – commercial nexus described herein). This gives rise to unprecedented possibilities for the organization of economic and political life (e.g. the "bush economy" described herein). The ultimate question is whether such changes across domains are the result of transformations in the organization of knowledge, or in the prevailing manner of producing valid statements: e.g. "this is (legitimate) regulatory authority" or "this is a (legitimate) sovereign."

In the Chad Basin, regulatory authority is clearly in crisis. While not necessarily undermining state power, regulators, acting on the basis of the military–commercial complex, and the regulated, who often assume their tactics of wealth creation and rights to extraction, are political subjectivities that arise from novel configurations of power and wealth while remaining consistent with the epistemological foundations of state power and modalities of exercising power, more generally. In other words, dominion over persons and things may be surfacing out of ambiguous interdependencies (state/non-state) while remaining consistent with the exigencies of the exercise of state power.

Part V

Conclusion

12   Toward a new research agenda

Ronald Kassimir and Robert Latham

The end of the Cold War ushered in a new optimism about the capacities of the international community to contend with a multitude of economic, political, and environmental problems in Africa and other regions around the world. In part, the new era held out the promise that this community would be able to devise intervention strategies and pursue international security free from geo-political calculations and ideological debates and thus be more open to dealing directly with conflict, poverty, and environmental degradation on their own terms (Boutros-Ghali 1992).

Peacekeeping, conflict prevention and post-conflict reconstruction, emergency humanitarian relief, liberalization-driven development programs, environmental cooperation and oversight, democratization, and the building of civil societies still might offer some viable courses of international action. But a considerable degree of pessimism and a growing discourse of failure have emerged recently among policy makers, scholars, journalists, and activists in the West (Rieff 1996).

Nowhere has the tendency toward pessimism been more striking than in Africa. The ongoing crisis in the Great Lakes, which we chronicled in the introduction to this volume, is perhaps the most visceral recent exemplar for the pessimistic position. In the most extreme of these views, the continent's security problems are largely internally driven, and portrayed as hopelessly intractable and impervious to improvement from outside or from within. Africa has become a symbol of the limits of intervention, international security, and of global governance more generally.[1] In a related way, forms of intervention coded as unambiguous "failures," such as Somalia, influence subsequent decisions on future peacekeeping efforts elsewhere, e.g. Rwanda, the Congo, and Sierra Leone.

Thus, the discourse on Africa is bounded by, on the one hand, the immediate post-Cold War optimism (reinvigorated, in the aftermath of

---

[1] Kaplan's (in)famous piece in the *Atlantic Monthly* (1994), of course, comes to mind. But even more scholarly and practitioner-oriented accounts connect with this pessimism, if not for Africa, then for the possibility of international institutions, including humanitarian NGOs, to do more good than harm. For examples, see de Waal (1997) and Tvedt (1998).

267

President Clinton's 1998 visit to the continent, through talk of an "African renaissance") and, on the other, by more pessimistic visions. Either side of this discourse tends to assume that the only relationship worth contemplating in terms of intervention is the one between Western interveners and Africans. However, as each chapter in this volume has shown, there are webs of transboundary relations that have historically extended beyond the norms and operational codes of the juridical international institutions and key states that make up the active "international community." In effect, global managers of intervention do not monopolize the interventions or interactions occurring across boundaries.

As the pessimists (but not only them) point out, the agents of global governance (be they Western states, international institutions, or NGOs) have not found a *tabula rasa* in the countries that have been the recipients or targets of intervention. The international community's very modest success in addressing Africa's problems and possibilities, while surely connected to the way that powerful states and international institutions sometimes pursue narrow interests, is also a result of a lack of understanding of power relations on the ground in African countries. This lack of understanding both stems from and encourages a reliance on universalistic and sometimes overly technocratic formulas insufficiently informed by African realities. It can also lead to a deficit of imagination in the design of intervention strategies, and in the very criteria used in deciding when they are necessary and feasible.

One problem with the pessimistic vision is that it moves from this lack of understanding to the position that if the international community really understood conditions on the ground, it would not bother about getting involved. This willfully ignores those relative "success stories" such as Ghana, Uganda, Mozambique, and South Africa where international involvement can be plausibly claimed to have made a difference (even if this difference is sometimes exaggerated by the optimists). But the more important point is that the pessimistic emphasis on intractable "internal" problems elides the fact that, in almost all cases, "external" forces are already involved, already part of the constitution of order and authority. Thus, the question of whether such forces can influence local processes is a non-starter. They already do. The real question is how this happens, and why, in the cases of conflict resolution, economic development, environmental degradation, and many others, we witness so many unintended consequences. For example, in conflict situations the United Nations has begun to acknowledge both the complexity of local and national alignments and the role of transboundary forces. The recent debate on whether the "international community" needs to focus as much on stopping the illegal trade in precious minerals that fuels African wars (and involves a wide range of licit and illicit, Western and African actors) as it does on peacemaking demonstrates both that some modicum of learning is possible and that international action can at least address other kinds of international processes that clearly are part of the causes of conflicts.

At the analytical level, we need a more rigorous theorizing of globalization and at the same time a more sophisticated analysis of what constitutes local order and authority. New research and new conceptual categories are required. We are suggesting that transboundary formations may be one of the categories to help us get beyond the present impasse. For example, perhaps most central to a deficit of imagination is that African conditions are too often read as the conditions of African states, with states seen as the sole and/or inevitable cause of or solution to poverty and conflict. This discourse includes an "anti-statist" impulse, which can be found in the pro-market designs of the IFIs, and among some academics and international activists. For the latter, oppressive states are typically contrasted with seemingly progressive forces of civil society struggling to resist state predations. Across all these perspectives the state retains its centrality as a reference point, and in the process a very basic question is obscured: when the state's legitimacy is contested or its effective capacity and even presence are severely limited, what forms of authority and governance operate in specific areas of social existence (such as the economy) or in particular locales?

This question is particularly relevant to practitioners faced with the tasks bundled together today under the label post-conflict reconstruction. The term is a thin veil for what is in reality an incredibly ambitious task: state-and-society building. Whether or not official interveners can self-consciously realize these ambitions (especially with the limited resources on tap), the lesson of the chapters in this volume is that transboundary formations (which may include, but also extend beyond the category of official intervener) are constitutive of political possibilities, in Africa and elsewhere.

The future study of transboundary formations

Whether they recognize it or not, international interveners of all sorts, by their very presence, are caught up in dynamic intersections involving international, national, and local forces. We have labeled these intersections "transboundary formations" because they often have lasting and deep impact on the political and social terrain within which they operate. The problem is that we do not yet have a language to describe and analyze these formations.

One reason we lack such a language is that our standard conceptual framework – the "levels-of-analysis" – serves to separate local, national, and international forces so that analysis can be concentrated at each appropriate level, rather than on the ways intersections occur and form hybrid social spaces. This volume suggests that considerable amounts of social power and political outcomes are being generated where international, local, and national forces operate coterminously. Indeed, in these situations it becomes impossible at times even to identify a set of dynamics as squarely part of one level or another.

Even so, the three spatial identities (international, national, and local) still can be part of our conceptual starting point for thinking about transboundary formations. On the one hand, we gain a sense of what transboundary formations are by their violation of the clean analytical breakpoints of the levels-of-analysis framework. On the other, it would be reductive not to recognize that there are different types of social spaces. Indeed, what interests us are the intersections of these spaces.

With this in mind, we believe that lying at the core of the transboundary formations considered in this volume is the interaction of forces associated with localities, states, or international realms. These forces can vary in form and type: sometimes they are institutions or actors (such as the local NGOs discussed by Schmitz); sometimes networks or structures of relations (such as the triple helix discussed by Callaghy); other times norms and codes (such as those associated with sovereignty as discussed by Reno or with regulatory authority as discussed by Roitman). Despite the fact that any given force likely operates in all three spaces, we can still apply the label local, state, or international to these forces because their basic constitution as empirical entities is associated with one space or another – varying based upon who is directly involved in the entity and the nature of its collective social purpose. The militias and rebel armies described by Reno, Nordstrom, and Roitman may be enmeshed in an array of translocal forces such as diamond trading networks and foreign armies, and may see the "international community" as an audience for their claims. But we still apply the "local" label because, as an entity, their range of membership and collective social purpose are lodged in one locality or another. In the case of international norms, they are distinguishable from local norms based on the range of authorities that articulate them as well as on the range of collective (often universalistic) social purposes to which they are purported to apply.

Moving on from this starting point for thinking about transboundary formations is what is actually difficult, since we do not have any recognizable conceptual moorings like the levels-of-analysis to help us. While the chapters by Cooper, Latham, and Kassimir, as well as Barnett, tell us why transboundary formations matter and what some of the important elements in their operation are, we believe we are only at the beginning of the articulation of a new research area that joins a number of fields in the social sciences and humanities (thus the self-conscious addition of "toward" in the title of this conclusion).

For this reason, the editors of this volume ensured that they incorporated a range of case studies that empirically explore various dimensions of transboundary formations. Each empirical chapter offers a different glimpse into the workings of these phenomena. Each speaks to a distinct set of concerns and raises unique questions that should be important to future research.

What links the chapters is a focus on how the intersections of forces associated with localities, states, and international realms produce forms of authority and order in a social space. Perhaps the most easily recognized forms considered in the volume are the process of institution-building and network formation discussed by Callaghy. Through his case study of Uganda, he shows how a mechanism involving the Ugandan state was constructed called the Multilateral Debt Fund. This construction was based on the relationship between Uganda and what Callaghy labels a triple helix of forces in the international realm (comprising an international debt regime, an international NGO advocacy network, and a transnational epistemic community of experts). The relationship between the triple helix and the Ugandan state is a transboundary formation whose effects take a tangible form in the production of a recognizable institution operating in the domestic realm.

What is interesting about this process is that it may be an instance of nascent state-formation that is not directly attributable to war, security competition (Skocpol 1979; Tilly 1975), military occupation, or the repertoires of international organizations applying formulas for state-making (Boli and Thomas 1999; Meyer 1987). Rather, the crucial external force is a structure of transnational governance (the helix). On the one hand, this suggests that we might want to think about how to expand the range of factors taken into consideration in the study of the international dimensions of state-formation. On the other, we ought to reconsider how we study international governance. Typically the study of international governance starts by identifying the web of institutions involved in governance (Rosenau 1997; O. Young 1994) and then tries to show how that web produces governance of one form or another. In contrast, Callaghy underscores how important it might be to turn this formula on its head. Processes of governance can shape or, in the case of Uganda, produce the institutions that are involved in those processes. (Barnett points out that processes of governance can also shape the international institutions involved in those processes in decisive ways).

One other notable dimension of Callaghy's case is sequencing. Initially, the principal "local" actor in the triple helix was the Ugandan government. At the beginning of the debt regime's subtle transformation, debt was not an issue that prompted popular mobilization in Uganda or most other debt-ridden countries. Over time, African NGOs devoted to a resolution of the debt problem emerged, especially when international advocacy groups and African governments created a linkage between debt forgiveness and poverty reduction. This linkage created new stakes in how resources previously allocated to debt service would now be used. Local NGOs arose to make claims on this process. The broader research question is: why do some issues linked to the international realm lend themselves to civic mobilization and others do not? As Cooper reminds us to consider, how does the presence or absence of such mobilization change the international politics associated with an issue?

Schmitz's chapter is directly concerned with such questions. Human rights has become the most noted issue around which connections form between popular contestations and the international realm. The literature that is developing in the field of international relations focusing on these connections is, for Schmitz, a departure point (Risse et al. 1999). While this literature is concerned with how advocates, local and international, form transnational networks that can effect changes in state policies and international norms, Schmitz asks that we consider in the Kenyan case how these networks shape the structure of civil society and the very nature of domestic politics. The transboundary formation he considers is composed of the triad of, first, a horizontal network of local and national NGOs, second a vertical network linking these organizations to international NGOs and intergovernmental organizations, and third, the Kenyan state. He advises us to consider the long-term effects of vertical networks as they empower some kinds of mobilizations (and not others), strengthen certain types of professionals and religious leaders, and (unwittingly) contribute to reshaping the bases for organizing political contestation (especially linked to ethnicity). These effects are clearly consequential for, and indeed constitutive of, formations of authority and order. Here, civil society itself is the political terrain wherein these formations unfold rather than the state (although the state is an essential factor in the changes Schmitz describes).

Schmitz thus suggests that we will have to move beyond the current thinking on transnational networks to directly address the broader political context within which networks operate. One key dimension which he emphasizes, similar to Callaghy, is timing and sequencing – in other words, taking the long view of how transboundary connections shape contexts, whether national, local, or regional, and how these connections are themselves transformed over time.

Another route is to consider the issue of representation. On what grounds, and by what means, do some NGOs claim to represent civil society within local, national, and international realms? How do different audiences receive those claims? Not only is the legitimacy (i.e. representativeness) of many local NGOs often taken for granted by international institutions, but also we know little about the processes that make these assumptions viable and their ultimate impact on the politics of a country such as Kenya.[2] If it is now recognized that domestic mobilization that enters transnational networks can have a "boomerang" effect as it comes back to influence state policy (Sikkink 1993), we need also to study how the boomerang comes back to shape the civil society within which such mobilization emerges and is sustained.

Obi's chapter also documents for us the operation of a transboundary formation involving, first, horizontal networks (of NGOs and protest movements in the Niger Delta), second, the state (Nigeria), and third, vertical networks (of INGOs and IOs). He addresses problems of authority and order formation in a highly charged context within which various organizations, sometimes in alliance and sometimes in competition, seek support from Delta residents as well as the international realm.

But Obi's case introduces a further complication that suggests an original approach to transboundary formations. In the Delta there is a second formation in operation, namely, that between, first, multinational oil companies, second, the Nigerian state, and third, local notables who are clients of the oil firms. The tangle of interests, identities, and contestations that mark the Delta reflects the presence of two formations in the same social space. The juxtaposition of multiple transboundary formations operating in the very same locale is one for which our analytic tools are not well developed. The Delta case suggests that we need to pay careful attention to the relations within and between these different forms of connection.

Obi's chapter calls attention to how this kind of analysis is both critical and complex. Political pressures from Delta networking (vertical and horizontal) shape interactions between oil firms, the Nigerian state, and local collaborators. This ends up taking somewhat bizarre, even perverse form in corporate-sponsored development projects in the very communities that see themselves under siege by the company–state alliance. At the same time, this alliance involves the firms' engagement of state

---

[2] For an exemplary discussion of these issues for Kenya, and one with comparative implications, see Ndegwa (1996).

security forces for protection, which further provokes forms of Delta protest.

The example of the oil companies points to a need to understand how transnational economic actors deployed into localities change the relationship between those places and states. The study of MNCs has been limited mostly to their impact on national economies and wider international economic structures.[3] But foreign firms are political actors in local contexts on many levels – performing "state-like" welfare functions, engaging security forces (public in the case of the Delta, private in the examples that Reno discusses in his work), and raising serious questions about their accountability to populations over which their actions hold sway.[4]

The presence of the state in both transboundary formations in the Niger Delta also points to a crucial issue for future research: what sort of roles does the state take up as a mediator between international, national, and local forces? How does this mediation unfold? What are its political dynamics and impact on various relevant contexts (domestic order, regional politics)? And what are the limits to this role?[5]

While this volume makes clear that states, or at least state officials, are key players in transboundary formations, the configuration of the states involved can diverge quite widely from the classic territorial model. For instance, there are what Reno (1998) has called "archipelago states," where rulers control only certain regions in order to retain access to economic resources such as mineral wealth, often in alliance with MNCs and private security companies. The rest of "the state" may be in the hands of opposition forces, or simply ignored.

In working through this terrain, Reno focuses on a transboundary formation involving, first, multinational firms investing in resource extraction, second, formal holders of state power (and their rebel opponents), and third, the body of international norms associated with state sovereignty upheld by global political and legal institutions. The subtle irony at the core of Reno's argument is that the (public) norm of sovereignty is a means for the expansion of private authority. This authority takes shape in the control of foreign companies over economic assets, based on the assistance of private security firms, and in the "privatization" of resources and power by state rulers whose sovereign claims are recognized internationally.

---

[3] Two superb exceptions that stand out are Biersteker (1987) and Evans (1979).

[4] For a discussion of this kind of accountability in regard to the IFIs, the UN system, and NGOs, see Chege (1998).

[5] A recent monograph based on extensive case studies by African economists asserts a potential positive role for states in managing Africa's insertion in global economic structures. See Mkandawire and Soludo (1998).

In Reno's formulation, the control of territory is a means to control commerce and people, rather than the other way around. While this process may be interpreted by some as an instance of "neo-medievalism," it is complicated by the central role that international sovereignty norms play in its very construction. A contradiction is built into the core of this dynamic, which provides incentives both to establish non-bureaucratic forms of state power and for cycles of violent opposition to capture the prize of sovereignty. Such a dynamic suggests short-term calculations that may have severe limits even for the risk-taking firms that do business with the rulers that Reno discusses. In political and moral terms, this phenomenon may indeed represent the darkest side of the globalization of capital and the ideologies that justify it. But it also opens up a whole range of research issues: for multinational firms, what are the conditions under which they will undertake such risky investments? For states, to what degree does this configuration present a kind of equilibrium and under what conditions might rulers be forced to adopt more traditional state-formation strategies in order to maintain power and retain international legitimacy?

Reno's chapter also suggests that in such situations we need to pay attention not only to disorder, but to the variety of orders in operation that do not fit our standard models and for which there is a clear lack of accountability of powerful state and non-state actors to local populations.

It is on this issue that the chapters by Roitman and Nordstrom are particularly relevant. They both call attention to military–commercial networks or "regulatory authorities," operating within and across national borders, which together with the state constitute two sides of a transboundary formation. Notably, local communities constitute the remaining part. Within this formation, the authors call attention to the relations of trust that develop between state and non-state participants in these networks (Nordstrom) and to the emergent norms of "rights-in-seizure" that legitimate coercive practices (Roitman).

The chapters by Roitman and Nordstrom open up a range of questions about the ways in which authority and local order are constructed in the communities drawn into these kinds of networks. To what degree do rebel armies, mercenary bands, and private security firms employed by local and transnational economic interests maintain order by means other than violence? In the classic language of political sociology, do they translate power into authority, and how is this accomplished?

This in turn raises the question of how transboundary formations are understood and valued by various social groups. In her chapter, Roitman argues that military–commercial "regulatory authorities" are "normalized" in the border regions of the Chad Basin. By this, we take her to mean that they have become taken for granted, that there is a generalized sense of "this is how things are" or "this is how things work." Nordstrom also argues that these networks, and the power relationships that they have engendered, have become "institutionalized" in the war-ravaged countries of Mozambique and Angola. To what degree is this normalization and institutionalization evident elsewhere? Has this taken-for-granted quality reshaped the identities of local populations, their sense of citizenship, and their expectations of their governments?[6]

Conclusion

Transboundary formations are a widespread phenomenon in the developing world. And while the range of forces associated with them is very broad, not all relationships across international, state, and local realms constitute transboundary formations. As we have defined them, transboundary relationships become formations when they produce and/or sustain forms of authority and order. Development aid, for example, can in one context be part of an effort to refashion socio-economic relations in a country (which otherwise would not occur without the aid program). In this case not only are international development experts likely to be deployed directly into one locale or another, but models and norms of development as well (see Cooper and Packard 1997; Ferguson 1994). In other contexts, aid may simply flow to state coffers without directly changing the nature of authority and order in the "targeted" country (however much it might be a resource exploited by existing elites to maintain power or a means to increase donor influence in the receiving country). In the former instance we have a transboundary formation, while in the latter we do not.

Also, transboundary formations are hardly new, as Cooper underscores in his chapter and we discuss in the introduction. They are not just artifacts of the post-Cold War or even a post-World War world. Colonial empires involved transboundary formations of considerable depth and magnitude. Cooper demonstrates how one can view the slave trade system as a transboundary formation involving plantations, colonial governments,

---

[6] To the degree that this sense of normalization is incomplete, we need to know how local populations imagine other possible forms of authority. We owe this point to conversations with Paul Richards who has prompted us to ask: who seeks autonomy from existing transboundary formations? What projects do they undertake in pursuit of this autonomy? Of course, much past analysis has emphasized social groups seeking autonomy from the state. A much-cited exemplar is Rothchild and Chazan (1988), who develop the distinction of social orientations of incorporation with or disengagement from the state. But this distinction has proved problematic, as many empirical studies have shown that both individuals and social groups often display complex mixes of both orientations.

traders, slavers in Africa, and some manufacturers in Britain. He shows us how a formation of this sort can evoke reactions such as the antislavery movement wherein a web of networks was able to make slavery an international issue (the parallels to the kind of protest around indigenous rights and environmental degradation discussed by Obi, human rights discussed by Schmitz, and debt forgiveness discussed by Callaghy are difficult to miss). Cooper makes it clear how complex the contexts and cross-currents have always been (involving imperialism, ideologies such as humanitarianism, and socio-economic structures).

Although we have focused on sub-Saharan Africa, transboundary formations have widespread historical and contemporary resonance. We know of dramatic cases where it has applied to places such as Europe (e.g. the Marshall Plan) and Japan. Yet we are only at the beginning in our understanding of how formations of order and authority within the developed world emerge from transboundary economic regulatory institutions (e.g. credit rating organizations [Sinclair 1999]), global financial structures (networks of currency trading), or new modes of transnational legal arbitration (Dezalay and Garth 1996).

Like these dimensions of contemporary globalization, several of the transboundary formations discussed in this volume may be seen as "innovations": the strategic use of sovereignty to benefit from a changing global economy, the use of networks to compensate for institutional limitations, the extraversion of non-state organizations to gain resources and support from the international community, and the emergence of new governance mechanisms.

It is tempting to view these innovations, such as they are, through the lens of "hybridity" as actors combine "local" and "national" ideas, institutions, and practices with those available through transboundary connections. However, we want to call attention to the limits of the "hybridity" lens, both for analytical and politico-moral reasons. Analytically, identifying the hybrid nature of transboundary formations is a starting point, not an end point. A research agenda must encompass the varying ways in which different ideas and institutions combine to produce specific forms of order and authority. What counts as "innovation" is not the fact of hybridity, but the production of new forms of authority and order, and closing off of other forms.

This might seem like a call for substituting for hybridity the lens of neomedievalism – a political condition where overlapping and criss-crossing orders and authorities predominate. However, the neo-medieval lens has a tendency (as does hybridity) to celebrate innovation and variegation for their own sakes. As we have seen, many of the actors and institutions that constitute transboundary formations chronicled in this volume, whatever their goals, are supremely unaccountable to local populations: warlord-presidents, international development agencies, or multinational oil companies. For those suffering the most from unequal and violent transboundary structures, there are enormous constraints on their capacity to take their destiny in their own hands and imagine a future defined at least partly on their own terms. The organizational "innovations" they experience are more like a rope around their necks. At the same time, some chapters in this volume show how some kinds of transboundary formations become the conditions for the realization of that better future. Still, the organizational innovations that people affected by transboundary formations may fashion in response to their plight are something to be celebrated only if they provide the means to that realization. They may be looking to a time when the provision of order and authority does not have to be taken into the hands of ordinary people, to a time when things need not be so "hybridized" or suggestive of medieval political life, to a time when transboundary formations might produce the kind of authority that would be welcomed as "normalized." If this sounds like a call for a legitimate, capable, and accountable state, attribute it to our sense that in contemporary processes of globalization, and the transboundary connections they engender, the public projects associated historically with states remain critical to everyday life. This, we believe, is as true for Africa as anywhere else.

The hybridity which is indeed inherent in transboundary formations contains a wide range of political projects and engenders many political effects. Future researchers studying the relationship between transboundary forces and specific locales in Africa and elsewhere will need to discover ways of identifying the mechanisms that make these projects and effects legible and public.

References

Abba Kaka, A. 1997, "Cette fraude qui tue!" *Le Temps* 69: 8

Achu Gwan, E. 1992, "The Nigeria–Cameroon Boundary and Nigerians in Cameroon," paper submitted to the Nigeria–Cameroon Trans-border Cooperation Workshop, Nigeria, May 25–30

Adar, Korwa G. 1999, "Human Rights and Academic Freedom in Kenya's Public Universities: The Case of the Universities Academic Staff Union," *Human Rights Quarterly* 21: 179–206

Adler, Emanuel and Michael Barnett 1998, "A Framework for the Study of Security Communities," in E. Adler and M. Barnett (eds.), *Security Communities*, Cambridge: Cambridge University Press, pp. 29–66

Adler, Emanuel and Peter Haas 1992, "Conclusion: Epistemic Communities, World Order, and the Creation of a Reflective Research Program," *International Organization* 46: 367–390.

Africa Confidential 1997, "Zaire: Business at War" *Africa Confidential*, April 25: 1–3

1998a, "Angola: Protection," *Africa Confidential*, June 12: 8

1998b, "Guinea Bissau: Mane's Men," *Africa Confidential*, June 26: 3

2000, "Gems and Guns," *Africa Confidential*, April 28: 8

Africa Energy & Mining 1996, "Liberian Connection Bach," *Africa Energy & Mining*, April 10

1998a, "Angola: The Crackdown Begins," *Africa Energy & Mining*, January 28

1998b, "Banro's Congo Project Nationalized," *Africa Energy & Mining*, August 26

2000, "Border Disputes," *Africa Energy & Mining*, June 28

Africa Watch/Human Rights Watch 1991, *Kenya: Taking Liberties*, New York: Human Rights Watch

1993, *State-Sponsored Ethnic Violence in Kenya*, New York: Human Rights Watch

African Contemporary Record (1987), "Kenya: Upturn in the Economy, but Concern over Clandestine Politics," *African Contemporary Record. Annual Survey and Documents*, vol. 19, 1986/1987, edited by Colin Legum: B314–348

African Rights 1996, *Kenya Shadow Justice*, New York: African Rights

Agamben, Giorgio 1997, "The Camp as the Nomos of the Modern," in H. de Vries and S. Weber (eds.), *Violence, Identity, and Self-Determination*, Stanford: Stanford University Press, pp. 106–18.

Agnew, John 1994, "The Territorial Trap: The Geographical Assumptions of International Relations Theory," *Review of International Political Economy* 1: 53–80.

Aina, Tade Akin 1997, "Globalization and Social Policy in Africa: Issues and Research Directions," *CODESRIA Working Paper Series* 6, Dakar

Ajulu, Rok 1998, "Kenya's Democracy Experiment: The 1997 Elections," *Review of African Political Economy* 25: 275–288

Ake, Claude 1996, *Strategy for Nigeria After the Structural Adjustment Programme*, Ibadan: Development Policy Centre

Albrow, Martin 1996, *The Global Age*, Cambridge: Polity Press

Alker, Hayward and Michael J. Shapiro (eds.) 1996, *Challenging Boundaries: Global Flows, Territorial Identities*, Minneapolis: University of Minnesota Press

Alker, Hayward, Tahir Amin, Thomas Biersteker, and Takashi Inoguchi 1998, "The Dialectics of World Order," unpublished manuscript

Alter, Karen 1998, "Who are the 'Masters of the Treaty'?" European Governments and the European Court of Justice," *International Organization* 52: 121–148.

Alves, Gasparini and Belinda Cipollone (eds.) 1998, *Curbing Illicit Trafficking in Small Arms and Sensitive Technologies*, Geneva: UNIDIR

Amisi, Bertha Kadenyi 1997, *A Crisis in the Making: Conflict in the Rift Valley and Western Kenya*, Notre Dame, Indiana: The Joan B. Kroc Institute for International Peace Studies

Amnesty International 1987, *Kenya. Torture, Political Detentions and Unfair Trials*, New York: Amnesty International

  1997, *Kenya. Violations of Human Rights. Communications between Amnesty International and the Government of Kenya*, New York: Amnesty International

Anderson, Benedict 1996, "Introduction," in G. Balakrishnan (ed.), *Mapping the Nation*, London: Verso, pp. 1–16

Ansah, John-Frimpong 1991, *The Vampire State in Africa*, Trenton, NJ: Africa World Press

Anstee, Margaret Joan 1996, *Orphan of the Cold War: The Inside Story of the Collapse of the Angolan Peace Process, 1992–3*, New York: St. Martin's Press

Appadurai, Arjun 1990, "Disjuncture and Difference in the Global Cultural Economy," *Public Culture* 2: 1–24

  1996, *Modernity at Large: Cultural Dimensions of Globalization*, Minneapolis: University of Minnesota Press

Arendt, Hannah 1968, "What is Authority?" in H. Arendt, *Between Past and Future*, New York: Viking Press, pp. 91–142

Armstrong, David 1998, "Globalization and the Social State," *Review of International Studies* 24: 461–478

"Arrest and Detention in Kenya," 1987, *Index on Censorship* 16: 23–28

Arrighi, Giovanni 1994, *The Long Twentieth Century*, London: Verso

Ayers, Edward 1996, "The Expanding Shadow Economy," *World Watch* 4: 11–23

Baehr, Peter, Hilde Selbervik and Arne Tostensen 1995, "Responses to Human Rights Criticism: Kenya–Norway and Indonesia–The Netherlands," in P. Baehr, H. Hey, and J. Smith (eds.), *Human Rights in Developing Countries Yearbook 1995*, The Hague: Kluwer Law International, pp. 57–87

Bakker, Age F.P. 1996, *International Financial Institutions*, London: Longman

Balakrishnan, Gopal (ed.) 1996, *Mapping the Nation*, London: Verso

Banégas, Richard 1998, "De la guerre au maintien de la paix: le nouveau business mercenaire," *Critique Internationale* 1: 179–194

Bank of Sierra Leone 1996, "Paris Club Debt Relief Negotiation." *BSL Bulletin* 2: 42

Barikor-Wiwa, D. 1996, "The Role of Women in the Struggle for Environmental Justice in Ogoni," *Cultural Survival Quarterly* 21, 4, fall: 46–49

Baring-Gould, Sabine and Charles Bampfylde 1989, *A History of Sarawak Under Its Two White Rajahs, 1839–1908*, Oxford: Oxford University Press

Barkan, Joel D. 1992, "The Rise and Fall of the Governance Realm in Kenya," in Goran Hyden and Michael Bratton (eds.), *Governance and Politics in Africa*, Boulder: Lynne Rienner, pp. 167–192

Barnett, Michael 1992, *Confronting the Costs of War: Military Power, State, and Society in Egypt and Israel*, Princeton: Princeton University Press

Barnett, Michael and Martha Finnemore 1999, "Politics, Power, and Pathologies of International Organizations," *International Organization* 53: 699–732

Bartelson, Jens 1993, *A Genealogy of Sovereignty*, Stockholm Studies in Politics 48, University of Stockholm

Barutciski, Mikhael 1996, "The Reinforcement of Non-Admission Policies and the Subversion of UNHCR," *International Journal of Refugee Law* 8: 49–110

Bayart, Jean-François 1989a, "Les églises chrétiennes et la politique du ventre," *Politique Africaine* 35: 3–26

    1989b, *L'état en Afrique*, Paris: Fayard. (Also translated and published as Bayart 1993)

    1993, *The State in Africa: The Politics of the Belly*, New York: Longman Publishing

    1994, "L'invention paradoxale de la modernité économique," in Jean-François Bayart, *La réinvention du capitalisme*, Paris: Editions Karthala, pp. 9–43

    1997, "Le 'capital social' de l'état malfaiteur, ou les ruses de l'intelligence politique," in Jean-Francois Bayart, Stephen Ellis, and Beatrice Hibou (eds.), *La criminalisation de l'ètat en Afrique*, Brussels: Editions Complexes, pp. 55–75

    2000, "Africa in the World: A History of Extraversion," *African Affairs* 99: 217–267

Bayart, Jean-François, Stephen Ellis, and Beatrice Hibou 1997, *La criminalisation de l'état en Afrique*, Brussels: Editions Complexes. (Also translated and published as. Bayart et al. 1999)

    1999, *The Criminalization of the State in Africa*, Oxford: James Currey

Bearzi, June 1977, "Wild West Traffickers Strip Zaire of Mineral Wealth," *The Star*, Johannesburg, May 13

Beattie, Alan 2000, "Ex-IMF Chief Joins Debt Campaign," *Financial Times* August 8

Beinart, William and Colin Bundy 1987, *Hidden Struggles in Rural South Africa*, Berkeley: University of California Press

Bennafla, K. 1996, "Rapport sur les échanges transfrontaliers informels au Tchad," unpublished manuscript, Université de Paris X-Nanterre

1997, "Entre Afrique noire et monde arabe. Nouvelles tendaces des échanges 'informels' tchadiens," *Revue Tiers Monde* 152: 879–896

1998, "Mbaiboum: un marché au carrefour de frontières multiples," in J. Egg and J. Herrara (eds.), *Echanges transfrontaliers et intégration régionale en Afrique*, Nanterre: Autrepart, pp. 53–72

1999, "La fin des territoires nationaux?" *Politique Africaine* 73: 24–49

Benvenisti, Eyal 1993, *The International Law of Occupation*, Princeton: Princeton University Press

Bergquist, Charles 1986, *Coffee and Conflict in Colombia, 1886–1910*, Durham, NC: Duke University Press

Bhabha, Homi 1994, *The Location of Culture*, New York: Routledge

Biersteker, Thomas 1987, *Multinationals, the State, and Control of the Nigerian Economy*, Princeton: Princeton University Press

Birnbaum, M. 1995, *Fundamental Rights Denied: Report of the Trial of Ken Saro-Wiwa and Others*, London: Article 19

Blackburn, Robin 1988, *The Overthrow of Colonial Slavery, 1776–1848*, London: Verso

Boele, R. 1995, *Ogoni: Report of the UNPO Mission to Investigate the Solution of the Ogoni in Nigeria*, The Hague: Unrepresented Nations and Peoples Organization

Boli, John and George M. Thomas (eds.) 1999, *Constructing World Culture: International Nongovernmental Organizations since 1875*, Stanford: Stanford University Press

Boote, Anthony R. and Kamau Thugge 1997, "Debt Relief for Low-Income Countries and the HIPC Initiative," IMF Working Paper 97/24, Washington, DC

Botchwey, Kwesi 2000, "Financing for Development: Current Trends and Issues for the Future," paper presented to the United Nations Conference on Trade and Development, Bangkok, February 12

Boutros-Ghali, Boutros 1992, *An Agenda for Peace*, New York: United Nations

Bratton, Michael 1989, "Beyond the State: Civil Society and Associational Life in Africa," *World Politics* 41: 407–430

1994, "Peasant–State Relations in Postcolonial Africa: Patterns of Engagement and Disengagement," in Joel S. Migdal, Atul Kohli and Vivienne Shue (eds.), *State Power and Social Forces: Domination and Transformation in the Third World*, Cambridge: Cambridge University Press, pp. 231–254

Bratton, Michael and Nicolas van de Walle 1997, *Democratic Experiments in Africa: Regime Transitions in Comparative Perspective*, Cambridge: Cambridge University Press

Braudel, Fernand 1984, *Civilization and Capitalism. Volume III: The Perspective of the World*, New York: Harper & Row

Brenner, Neil 1997, "Global, Fragmented, Hierarchical: Henri Lefebvre's Geographies of Globalization," *Public Culture* 10: 135–168

Brian James 1997, "The New Dogs of War," *Mail on Sunday* December 7: 18

Brown, Seyom 1995, *New Forces, Old Forces and the Future of World Politics*, New York: HarperCollins

Brubaker, Rogers and Frederick Cooper 2000, "Beyond Identity," *Theory and Society* 29: 1–47

Brümmer, Stefaans 1997, "Business at War for Zaire's Wealth," *Mail & Guardian* (Johannesburg) April 15: 11

Brysk, Alison 1993, "From Above and Below: Social Movements, the International System, and Human Rights in Argentina," *Comparative Political Studies* 26: 259–285

Buell, Frederick 1994, *National Culture and the New Global System*, Baltimore: The Johns Hopkins University Press

Bull, Hedley 1979, *The Anarchical Society*, New York: Columbia University Press

Burdick, John 1993, *Looking for God in Brazil: The Progressive Catholic Church in Urban Brazil's Religious Arena*, Berkeley: University of California Press

Bureau for International Narcotics and Law Enforcement Affairs 1997, *International Narcotics Control Strategy Report 1996*, Washington, DC: US Department of State

Burley, Anne-Marie and Walter Mattli 1993, "Europe Before the Court: A Political Theory of Integration," *International Organization* 47: 41–76

Buzan, Barry 1995, "The Levels of Analysis Problem Reconsidered," in Ken Booth and Steve Smith (eds.), *International Relations Theory Today*, University Park: Pennsylvania State University Press, pp. 198–216

Callaghy, Thomas 1994, "Civil Society, Democracy, and Economic Change in Africa: A Dissenting Opinion About Resurgent Societies," in John W. Harbeson, Donald Rothchild, and Naomi Chazan (eds.), *Civil Society and the State in Africa*, Boulder: Lynne Rienner, pp. 231–253

    forthcoming, "From Reshaping to Resizing a Failing State: The Case of the Congo/Zaire," in Ian Lustick, Brendan O'Leary, and Thomas Callaghy (eds.), *Rightsizing the State*, Oxford: Oxford University Press

Callaghy, Thomas and John Ravenhill (eds.) 1993, *Hemmed In: Responses to Africa's Economic Decline*, New York: Columbia University Press

Camdessus, Michel 1999, "From the Crises of the 1990s to the New Millennium," www.imf.org/np/speeches/1999, remarks in Madrid, Spain, November 27

Camilleri, Joseph and Jim Falk (eds.) 1992, *The End of Sovereignty?*, Northampton: Elgar Publishing

Campbell, David 1996, "Political Prosaics, Transversal Politics, and the Anarchical World," in Michael J. Shapiro and Hayward Alker (eds.), *Challenging Boundaries: Global Flows, Territorial Identities*, Minneapolis: University of Minnesota Press, pp. 7–31

Campbell, James T. 1995, *Songs of Zion: The African Methodist Episcopal Church in the United States and South Africa*, Oxford: Oxford University Press

Caporaso, James 1992, "International Relations Theory and Multilateralism: The Search for Foundations," *International Organization* 46: 598–632

    1997, "Across the Great Divide: Integrating Comparative and International Politics," *International Studies Quarterly* 41: 563–592

Cardoso, Fernando Henrique and Enzo Faletto 1979, *Dependency and Development in Latin America*, Berkeley: University of California Press

Castells, Manuel 1996, *The Rise of the Network Society*, Oxford: Blackwell

1998, *End of Millennium*, Oxford: Blackwell

Chakrabarty, Dipesh 1992, "Postcoloniality and the Artifice of History: Who Speaks for 'Indian' Pasts?" *Representations* 37: 1–26

Charlick, Robert B. forthcoming, "Civil Society and Governance Reform in Africa: Reflections from the Field on the Dominant Paradigms," in Pearl T. Robinson, Catharine Newbury, and Mamadou Diouf (eds.), *Transitions in Africa: Expanding Political Space*

Chatterjee, Partha 1986, *Nationalist Thought and the Colonial World: A Derivative Discourse?*, London: Zed Press

1993, *The Nation and Its Fragments: Colonial and Postcolonial Histories*, Princeton: Princeton University Press

Chege, Michael 1998, "Responsibility and Accountability by International Institutions: Sub-Saharan Africa in the 1990s," in Francis M. Deng and Terrence Lyons (eds.), *African Reckoning: The Quest for Good Governance*, Washington, DC: The Brookings Institution Press

Chikoko 1997, "In Defence of Our Humanity," text of address by the Central Working Committee of the Chikoko Movement at a meeting with journalists in Port Harcourt, September 20

1999, "Reclaiming Our Humanity: Mission of the Chikoko Movement," issued by the Bureau of Publicity, Chikoko Movement. Reproduced in *Survival* August

Chingono, Mark 1996, *The State, Violence and Development*, Brookfield, IL: Avebury

Chopra, Jarat 1996, "The Space of Peace-Maintenance," *Political Geography* 15: 335–357

Civil Liberties Organisation 1996, *Ogoni Trials & Travails*, Lagos: Civil Liberties Organisation

Clapham, Christopher 1996, *Africa and the International System: The Politics of State Survival*, Cambridge: Cambridge University Press

Clark, A.M., E. Friedman, and K. Hochstettler 1998, "The Sovereign Limits of Global Civil Society: A Comparison of NGO Participation in UN World Conferences on the Environment, Human Rights, and Women," *World Politics* 51: 1–35

Clark, Ian 1998, "Beyond the Great Divide: Globalization and the Theory of International Relations," *Review of International Studies* 24: 379–398

Clark, John 1991, *Democratizing Development*, West Hartford: Kumarian Press

Clarke, Walter and Jeffrey Herbst (eds.) 1996, *Learning from Somalia: The Lessons of Armed Humanitarian Intervention*, Boulder: Westview Press

Clothier, P. and E. O'Connar 1996, "Pollution Warning Ignored by Shell," *Guardian*, May 13

Comaroff, Jean and John Comaroff 1991, *Of Revelation and Revolution. Volume I:* Chicago: University of Chicago Press

1994, *Ethnography and the Historical Imagination*, Boulder: Westview Press

Conklin, Alice 1997, *A Mission to Civilize: The Republican Idea of Empire in France and West Africa, 1895–1930*, Stanford: Stanford University Press

Cooper, Frederick 1980, *From Slaves to Squatters: Plantation Labor and Agriculture in Zanzibar and Coastal Kenya, 1890–1925*, New Haven: Yale University Press

1996, *Decolonization and African Society: The Labor Question in French and British Africa*, Cambridge: Cambridge University Press

1998, "Networks, Moral Discourse, and History," paper presented at the workshop on "Global Governance and International Intervention in Africa," Robert Schuman Center, European University Institute, France, March 28–29

2001, "What Is the Concept of Globalization Good For? An African Historian's Perspective." *African Affairs* 100: 189–213

forthcoming, *Africa Since 1940: The Past of the Present*, Cambridge: Cambridge University Press

Cooper, Frederick and Randall Packard (eds.) 1997, *International Development and the Social Sciences: Essays on the History and Politics of Knowledge*, Berkeley: University of California Press

Cooper Frederick, Thomas Holt, and Rebecca Scott 2000, *Beyond Slavery: Explorations of Race, Labor, and Citizenship in Post-Emancipation Societies*, Chapel Hill: University of North Carolina Press

Cooper, Frederick, Allen Isaacman, Florencia Mallon, Steve Stern, and William Roseberry 1993, *Confronting Historical Paradigms: Peasants, Labor, and the Capitalist World System in Africa and Latin America*, Madison: University of Wisconsin Press

Copson, Raymond 1999, "Africa: US Foreign Assistance," CRS Issue Brief for Congress

Coronil, Fernando 1997, *The Magical State: Nature, Money, and Modernity in Venezuela*, Chicago: University of Chicago Press

Corzine, Robert 1996, "Aid to Pave Afghan Way for Pipeline," *Financial Times* October II: 1

COSED 1999, "COSED–The Road to Self-Determination," *Survival* August

Cox, Robert 1987, *Production, Power, and World Order*, New York: Columbia University Press

Cutler, A. Claire 1999, "Locating 'Authority' in the Global Political Economy," *International Studies Quarterly* 43: 59–83

Cutler, A. Claire, Virginia Haufler, and Tony Porter (eds.) 1999, *Private Authority and International Affairs*, Albany: State University of New York Press

Czempiel, Ernst-Otto and James Rosenau (eds.) 1989, *Global Changes and Theoretical Challenges*, Lanham, MD: Lexington Books

Dahl, Robert A. 1971, *Polyarchy: Participation and Opposition*, New Haven: Yale University Press

Davis, David Brion 1975, *The Problem of Slavery in the Age of Revolution 1770–1823*, Ithaca: Cornell University Press

De Boeck, Filip 1996, "Postcolonialism, Power and Identity: Local and International Perspectives from Zaire," in Richard Werbner and Terence Ranger (eds.), *Postcolonial Identities in Africa*, London: Zed Books, pp. 75–106

1999, "Domesticating Diamonds and Dollars: Indentity, Expenditure and Sharing in Southwestern Zaire," in Peter Geschiere and Birgit Meyer (eds.), *Globalization and Identity*, Oxford: Blackwell, pp. 177–209

De Certeau, Michel 1986, *Heterologies*, trans. B. Massumi, Minneapolis: University of Minnesota Press

De Waal, Alex 1997, *Famine Crimes: Politics and the Disaster Relief Industry in Africa*, Bloomington: Indiana Unversity Press

Dean, Mitchell 1994, *Critical and Effective Histories*, New York: Routledge

Debt Relief International 1997, "HIPC Debt Strategy and Analysis Capacity-Building Programme," Programme Document, London, June, unpublished report

Deleuze, Gilles and Felix Guattari 1987, *A Thousand Plateaus: Capitalism and Schizophrenia*, Minneapolis: University of Minnesota Press

Deutsch, Karl 1968, *The Analysis of International Relations*, Upper Saddle River, NJ: Prentice-Hall

Dezalay, Yves and Bryant Garth 1996, *Dealing in Virtue: International Commercial Arbitration and the Construction of a Transnational Legal Order*, Chicago: University of Chicago Press

Dorce, F. 1996, "Cameroun: cette guerre qui cache son nom," *Jeune Afrique Economie* 229

Doyle, Michael 1986, *Empires*, Princeton: Princeton University Press

Drescher, Seymour 1987, *Capitalism and Antislavery: British Mobilization in Comparative Perspective*, Oxford: Oxford University Press

Dubois, Laurent 1999, "The Price of Liberty: Victor Hugo and the Administration of Freedom in Guadeloupe," *William and Mary Quarterly* 56: 363–392

Dunn, John 1980, *Political Obligation in its Historical Context: Essays in Political Theory*, Cambridge: Cambridge University Press

   1986, "The Politics of Representation and Good Government in Africa," in Patrick Chabal (ed.), *Political Domination in Africa: Reflections on the Limits of Power*, Cambridge: Cambridge University Press, pp. 158–174

   1994, "The Dilemma of Humanitarian Intervention," *Government and Opposition* 29: 248–261

Dyrberg, Torben Bech 1997, *The Circular Structure of Power*, London: Verso

Economist Intelligence Unit 1996, Sierra Leone: Country Survey, 1995–96, London: EIU

   1999, Country Report: Nigeria, London: EIU

Edwards, David 1989, "Mad Mullahs and Englishmen: Discourse in the Colonial Encounter," *Comparative Studies in Society and History* 30: 649–670

Egg, J. and J. Herrera (eds.) 1998, *Echanges transfrontaliers et intégration régionale en Afrique Subsaharienne*, Paris: Autrepart

Ellis, Stephen 1996, "Africa and International Corruption: The Strange Case of South Africa and Seychelles," *African Affairs* 95: 165–196

Emirbayer, Mustafa and Jeff Goodwin 1994, "Network Analysis, Culture, and the Problem of Agency," *American Journal of Sociology* 99: 1411–1454

ERA/Friends of the Earth Nigeria 1998a, *Eraction* October–December

   1998b, *Niger Delta Alert* 6, June

   1998c, *Niger Delta Alert* 9, November 1998–January 1999

   1999a, *Eraction* January

   1999b, *Niger Delta Alert* 10, February–April

Escobar, Arturo 1995, *Encountering Development: The Making and Unmaking of the Third World*, Princeton: Princeton University Press

Esparza, L. and M. Wilson (eds.) 1999, *Oil for Nothing*, US Non-Governmental Delegation Report, September 6–20

Eurodad 1998, "HIPC Update: World Bank and IMF Proposals for Debt Relief for Post-Conflict Countries," Bristing, Brussels

Evans, Peter 1979, *Dependent Development: The Alliance of Multinational, State, and Local Capital in Brazil*, Princeton: Princeton University Press

1997, "The Eclipse of the State? Reflections on Stateness in an Era of Globalization," *World Politics* 50: 62–87

Evans, Peter, Harold K. Jacobson, and Robert D. Putnam (eds.) 1995, *Double-Edged Diplomacy: International Bargaining and Domestic Politics*, Berkeley: University of California Press

Fabian, Johannes 1990, *Power and Performance: Ethnographic Explorations Through Proverbial Wisdom and Theater in Shaba, Zaire*, Madison: University of Wisconsin Press

Faes, G. 1997, "Le dernier maquis," *L'Autre Afrique* 1: 64–69

Fanon, Frantz 1966, *The Wretched of the Earth*, trans. Constance Farrington, New York: Grove Press

Fearon, James D. and David D. Laitin 1996, "Explaining Interethnic Cooperation," *American Political Science Review* 90: 715–735

Ferguson, James 1994, *The Anti-Politics Machine: "Development," Depoliticization, and Bureaucratic Domination in Lesotho*, London: University of Minnesota Press

1997, "Paradoxes of Sovereignty and Independence: 'Real' and 'Pseudo-' Nation-States and the De-politicization of Poverty," in Kirstin Hastrup and Karen Fog Olwig (eds.), *Siting Culture*, Oslo: Scandanavian University Press

Ferguson, Yale and Richard Mansbach 1996, *Polities: Authority, Identities, and Change*, Columbia, SC: University of South Carolina Press

Fick, Carolyn E. 1990, *The Making of Haiti: The Saint Domingue Revolution from Below*, Knoxville: University of Tennessee Press

Fieldhouse, David K. 1966, *The Colonial Empires: A Comparative Survey from the Eighteenth Century*, New York: Dell Publishing

Finnemore, Martha and Kathryn Sikkink 1998, "International Norm Dynamics and Political Change," *International Organization* 52: 887–917

Fisher, William 1997, "Doing Good? The Politics and Antipolitics of NGO Practices," *Annual Review of Anthropology* 26: 439–464

Fleisher, Michael L. 2000, "Sungusungu: State-sponsored Village Vigilante Groups among the Kuria of Tanzania," *Africa* 70: 209–228

Florini, Ann M. (ed.) 2000, *The Third Force: The Rise of Transnational Civil Society*, Washington, DC: Carnegie Endowment for International Peace

Forrest, Joshua Bernard 1998, "State Inversion and Nonstate Politics," in Leonardo A. Villalón and Phillip A. Huxtable (eds.), *The African State at a Critical Juncture: Between Disintegration and Reconfiguration*, Boulder: Lynne Rienner, pp. 45–56

Forsyth, Justin 1997, "Oxfam Condemns Delay on Uganda's Debt Relief: A Betrayal of the Commitment to Reduce Poor Country Debt," Oxfam International press release, April 23

Foucault, Michel 1977, *Discipline and Punish: The Birth of the Prison*, trans. A. Sheridan, New York: Vintage Books
1981, "Two Lectures," in C. Gordon (ed.), *Power/Knowledge: Selected Interviews and Other Writings 1972–1977*, New York: Routledge
1990 [1978], *The History of Sexuality. Volume I: An Introduction*, New York: Vintage Books
1991, "Governmentality," in Graham Burchell, Colin Gordon, and Peter Miller (eds.), *The Foucault Effect: Studies in Governmentality*, Chicago: University of Chicago Press, pp. 87–104
Fox, Richard and Orin Starn (eds.) 1997, *Between Resistance and Revolution*, New Brunswick: Rutgers University Press
Fraser, Nancy 1992, "Rethinking the Public Sphere: A Contribution to the Critique of Actually Existing Democracy," in Craig Calhoun (ed.), *Habermas and the Public Sphere*, Cambridge, MA: MIT Press, pp. 109–142
Fredrickson, George 1995, *Black Liberation: A Comparative History of Black Ideologies in the United States and South Africa*, Oxford: Oxford University Press
French, Howard 1996, "Yes, Things Can Get Worse in Africa," *New York Times* November 3: 92–95
Friedman, M. 1993, "Kalachnikov: trente années de rafales," *Jeune Afrique* 1701–1702
Gallagher, John and Ronald Robinson 1953, "The Imperialism of Free Trade," *The Economic History Review* 6: 1–15
Gambetta, Diego 1988a, "Can We Trust Trust?" in D. Gambetta (ed.), *Trust: Making and Breaking Cooperative Relations*, Oxford: Blackwell, pp. 213–237
(ed.) 1988b, *Trust: Making and Breaking Cooperative Relations*, Oxford: Blackwell
1997a, "Floor Discussion of 'Corruption and Development' by Susan Rose-Ackerman," in B. Pleskovic and J. Stiglitz (eds.), *Annual World Bank Conference on Development Economics 1997*, Washington, DC: The World Bank
1997b, 'Comment on "Corruption and Development," by Susan Rose-Ackerman,' in B. Pleskovic and J. Stiglitz (eds.), *Annual World Bank Conference on Development Economics 1997*, Washington, DC: The World Bank
Geffray, Christian 1990, *La cause des armes au Mozambique: antropologie d'une guerre civile*, Paris: Editions Karthala
Gellner, Ernest 1989, "Trust, Cohesion, and Social Order," in Diego Gambetta (ed.), *Trust: Making and Breaking Cooperative Relations*, Oxford: Blackwell, pp. 142–157
General Accounting Office 2000, "Developing Countries: Debt Relief for Poor Countries Faces Challenges," Report to Congressional Committees GAO/NSIAD-00-161, General Accounting Office, Washington, DC
Gerth, Hans H. and C. Wright Mills 1978, *From Max Weber: Essays in Sociology*, Oxford: Oxford University Press
Giddens, Anthony 1981, *A Critique of Contemporary Historical Materalism. Volume II: The Nation-State and Violence*, Berkeley: University of Cailfornia Press
Gifford, Paul 1994, "Some Recent Developments in African Christianity," *African Affairs* 93: 513–534

1998, *African Christianity: Its Public Role,* Bloomington: University of Indiana Press

Githongo, John 1998, "Kenya's Radical Wing Loses Political Steam," *East African* July 6–12

Glaser, Barney and Anselm L. Strauss 1967, *The Discovery of Grounded Theory: Strategies for Qualitative Research,* Chicago: Aldine

Goldstein, Judith, Miles Kahler, Robert O. Keohane, and Anne-Marie Slaughter (eds. 2000), "Legalization and World Politics," special issue of *International Organization* 54

Gordon, Chris 1997, "Mercenaries Grab Gems," *Mail & Guardian* May 9: 10

Goulet, Yves 1997, "Mixing Business with Bullets," *Jane's Intelligence Review* 9: 426–432

Gourevitch, Peter 1978, "The Second Image Reversed: The International Sources of Domestic Politics," *International Organization* 32: 881–912

Government of Uganda 1995, "A Strategy for Reducing the External Debt of Uganda," report prepared for the Consultative Group, Kampala, July 15
1996 "Uganda and the HIPC Debt Initiative," Kampala

Granovetter, Mark 1973, "The Strength of Weak Ties," *American Journal of Sociology* 78: 1360–1380

Granovetter, Mark and Richard Swedberg (eds.) 1992, *The Sociology of Economic Life,* Boulder: Westview Press

Grégoire, E. 1998, "Sahara nigérien: terre d'échanges," in J. Egg and J. Herrera (eds.), *Echanges transfrontaliers et intégration régionale en Afrique Subsaharienne,* Paris: Autrepart, pp. 91–104

Greif, Avner 1996, "Contracting, Enforcement, and Efficiency: Economics Beyond the Law," in Michael Bruno and Boris Pleskovic (eds.), *Annual World Bank Conference on Development Economics,* Washington, DC: The World Bank, pp. 239–265

Guarnizo, Luis Eduardo and Michael Peter Smith 1998, "The Locations of Transnationalism," in Michael Peter Smith and Luis Eduardo Guarnizo (eds.), *Transnationalism from Below,* New Brunswick: Transaction Publishers, pp. 3–34

Gupta, Akhil 1992, "The Song of the Nonaligned World: Transnational Identities and the Reinscription of Space in Late Capitalism," *Cultural Anthropology* 7: 63–79

Gupta, Akhil and James Ferguson 1997a, "Culture, Power, Place: Ethnography at the End of an Era," in Akhil Gupta and James Ferguson (eds.), *Culture, Power, Place: Explorations in Critical Anthropology,* Durham, NC: Duke University Press, pp. 10–32
1997b, "Discipline and Practice," in Akhil Gupta and James Ferguson (eds.), *Anthropological Locations: Boundaries and Grounds of a Field Science,* Berkeley: University of California Press, pp. 1–46

Guyer, Jane I. 1992, "Representation Without Taxation: An Essay on Democracy in Rural Nigeria, 1952–1990," *African Studies Review* 35: 41–79
1994, "The Spatial Dimensions of Civil Society in Africa: An Anthropologist Looks at Nigeria," in John W. Harbeson, Donald Rothchild, and Naomi

Chazan (eds.), *Civil Society and the State in Africa*, Boulder: Lynne Rienner, pp. 215–230

Haas, Peter M. (ed.) 1992, "Knowledge, Power, and International Policy Coordination," special issue of *International Organization* 46: 1

Hancock, Graham 1989, *Lords of Poverty: The Power, Prestige, and Corruption of the International Aid Business*, New York: Atlantic Monthly Press

Hanlon, Joseph, 1984, *Mozambique: The Revolution Under Fire*, London: Zed Books

    1991, *Mozambique: Who Calls the Shots?*, Bloomington: Indiana University Press

    1996, *Peace Without Profit*, Oxford: James Currey

Hannerz, Ulf 1996, *Transnational Connections: Culture, People, Places*, London: Routledge

Hansen, Karen 1997, *Keeping House in Lusaka*, New York: Columbia University Press

Harbeson, John W., Donald Rothchild, and Naomi Chazan (eds.), 1994, *Civil Society and the State in Africa*, Boulder: Lynne Rienner

Harding, J. 1996, "The Mercenary Business," in Jane Hindle and Alan Bennett (eds.), *London Review of Books: An Anthology*, London: Verso, pp. 3–9

Harvey, David 1989, *The Condition of Postmodernity*, Oxford: Blackwell

Haugerud, Angelique forthcoming, "The Disappearing Local? Rethinking Global/Local Connections," in Ali Mirsepassi, Amrita Basu, and Frederick Weaver (eds.),*Global/Local: Re-visioning the Area Studies Debate*, Syracuse: Syracuse University Press

Headrick, Daniel R. 1981, *The Tools of Empire: Technology and European Imperialism in the Nineteenth Century*, Oxford: Oxford University Press

Hecht, David and Maliqalim Simone 1994, *Invisible Governance: The Art of African Micropolitics*, Brooklyn: Autonomedia

Hechter, Michael 1975, *Internal Colonialism*, Berkeley: University of California Press

Hempstone, Smith 1997, *Rogue Ambassador, An African Memoir*, Tennessee: University of the South Press

Herbst, Jeffrey 1996, "Responding to State Failure in Africa," *International Security* 21: 120–44

    2000, *States and Power in Africa*, Princeton: Princeton University Press

Hibou, Beatrice 1996, *L'Afrique est-elle protectionniste? Les chemins buissonniers de la libéralisation extérieure*, Paris: Editions Karthala

    1997, "Le 'capital social' de l'état falsificateur, ou les ruses de l'intelligence économique," in Jean-François Bayart, Stephen Ellis, and Beatrice Hibou (eds.) *La criminalisation de l'état en Afrique*, Brussels: Editions Complexes, pp. 105–58

    1998, "Retrait ou redéploiement de l'état?," *Critique Internationale* 1: 151–168.

    (ed.) 1999, *La privatisation de l'état*, Paris: Editions Karthala-CERI

Hirst, Paul, and Grahame Thompson 1996, *Globalization in Question*, Cambridge: Polity Press

Hollis, Martin and Steve Smith 1990, *Explaining and Understanding International Relations*, Oxford: Oxford University Press.

Holsti, Kalevi 1996, *The State, War, and the State of War,* Cambridge: Cambridge University Press

Holt, Thomas 1990, *The Problem of Freedom: Race, Labor and Politics in Jamaica and Britain, 1832–1938,* Baltimore: The Johns Hopkins University Press

Hopkins, Anthony 1974, *An Economic History of West Africa,* New York: Columbia University Press

Howard, Rhoda E. 1991, "Repression and State Terror in Kenya 1982–1988," in Timothy P. Bushnell, Vladimir Shlapentokh, and Christopher K. Vanderpool (eds.), *State Organized Terror: The Case of Violent Internal Repression,* Boulder: Westview Press, pp. 77–98

Hudock, Ann 1996 "A Nation in Mourning," *West Africa* March 13: 337

Human Rights Watch 1999, *The Price of Oil: Corporate Responsibility and Human Rights Violations in Nigeria's Oil Producing Communities,* New York: Human Rights Watch

Human Rights Watch/Africa 1997a, *Failing the Internally Displaced: The UNDP Displaced Persons Program in Kenya,* New York: Human Rights Watch
 1997b, *Juvenile Injustice: Police Abuse and Detention of Street Children in Kenya,* New York: Human Rights Watch

Human Rights Watch Arms Project 1994, *Angola: Arms Trade and Violations of the Laws of War Since the 1992 Elections,* New York: Human Rights Watch

Huntington, Samuel 1968, *Political Order in Changing Societies,* New Haven: Yale University Press
 1991, *The Third Wave: Democratization in the Late Twentieth Century,* Norman: University of Oklahoma Press

Hurrell, Andrew and Ngaire Woods 1995, "Globalisation and Inequality," *Millennium* 24: 447–70

Hyden, Goran 1992, "Governance and the Study of Politics," in Goran Hyden and Michael Bratton (eds.), *Governance and Politics in Africa,* Boulder: Lynne Rienner, pp. 1–26
 1999, "Governance and the Reconstitution of Political Order," in Richard Joseph (ed.), *State Conflict, and Democracy in Africa,* Boulder: Lynne Rienner, pp. 179–195

ILO/JASPA 1988, *Employment in Africa: Some Critical Issues,* Geneva: ILO

IMF 1999, "Poverty Reduction Strategy Papers – Status and Next Steps," http://www.imf.org/external/np/pdr/prsp/status.htm, November 19

Indian Ocean Newsletter 1997, "Not Quite the Fifth Cavalry," *Indian Ocean Newsletter* February 8: 7

Isaacman, Allen and Barbara Isaacman 1983, *Mozambique: From Colonialism to Revolution 1900–1982,* Aldershot: Gower

Isenberg, David 1997, "Soldiers of Fortune, Ltd: A Profile of Today's Private Sector Corporate Military Firms," Center for Defense Information, Washington, DC, November, 14

Jackson, Robert 1990, *Quasi-states: Sovereignty, International Relations and the Third World,* Cambridge: Cambridge University Press
 1993, "Sub-Saharan Africa," in Robert Jackson and Alan James (eds.), *The State in a Changing World,* Oxford: Oxford University Press, pp. 136–156.

James, C.L.R. 1938, *The Black Jacobins: Toussaint L'Ouverture and the San Domingo Revolution*, New York: Vintage Books (reissued 1963)

Jane's Intellegence Review 1997, "Correction," *Jane's Intelligence Review* 9: 478

Jervis, Robert 1997, *System Effects*, Princeton: Princeton University Press

Jeter, Howard 1997, "Prepared Testimony," Special Presidential Envoy to the House International Relations Committee hearing in Libera, June 24

Jeune Afrique 1992, November 19: 28–30.

Johnson, Harry and Ted Dagne 1996, "Congress and the Somalia Crisis," in Walter Clarke and Jeffrey Herbst (eds.), *Learning from Somalia*, Boulder: Westview Press, pp. 191–204

Johnstone, Ian 1991, "Treaty Interpretation: The Authority of Interpretive Communities," *Michigan Journal of International Law* 12: 371–419

Joseph, Gilbert M. 1998, "Close Encounters: Toward a New Cultural History of US–Latin American Relations," in Gilbert M. Joseph, Catherine C. Legrand, and Ricardo D. Salvatore (eds.), *Close Encounters of Empire: Writing the Cultural History of US–Latin American Relations*, Durham, NC: Duke University Press

Joseph, Richard 1998, "Africa 1990–1997: From Abertura to Closure," *Journal of Democracy* 9: 3–17

(ed.) 1999, *State, Conflict, and Democracy in Africa*, Boulder: Lynne Rienner

Jubilee 2000 1997, http://www.oneworld.org/jubilee2000, October 31

Jubilee 2000–Zambia 2000, "Jubilee 2000–Zambia: What is the Way Forward?" http://www.jctr.org.zm/jublilee-wayf.htm

Kadende-Kaiser, Rose M. and Paul Kaiser 1998, "Identity, Citizenship, and Transnationalism: Ismailis in Tanzania and Burundians in the Diaspora," *Africa Today* 45: 461–480

Kane, Ousmane 1997, "Muslim Missionaries and African States," in Susanne Hoeber Rudolph and James Piscatori (eds.), *Transnational Religion and Fading States*, Boulder: Westview Press, pp. 47–62

Kaplan, Robert 1994, "The Coming Anarchy," *Atlantic Monthly* February: 44–76.

Kapur, Devesh, John P. Lewis and Richard Webb (eds.) 1997, *The World Bank: Its First Half Century*, Washington, DC: The Brookings Institution Press

Karimi, Joseph and Philip Ochieng 1980, *The Kenyatta Succession*, Nairobi: Transafrica

Karimu, John 1995/1996, "Government Budget and Economic and Financial Policies for the Fiscal Year," *Mimeo* June 30

Karl, Terry L. 1990, "Dilemmas of Democratization in Latin America," *Comparative Politics* 23: 1–21

Kassimir, Ronald 1998a, "Uganda: The Catholic Church and State Reconstruction," in Leonardo Villalón and Phillip Huxtable (eds.), *The African State at a Critical Juncture: Between Disintegration and Reconfiguration*, Boulder: Lynne Rienner, pp. 233–253

1998b, "The Social Power of Religious Organization and Civil Society: The Catholic Church in Uganda," *Commonwealth and Comparative Politics* 36: 54–83

1999, "The Politics of Popular Catholicism in Uganda," in Thomas Spear and Isaria N. Kimambo (eds.), *East African Expressions of Christianity*, Oxford: James Currey, pp. 248–274

Kearney, M. 1995, "The Local and the Global: The Anthropology of Globalization and Transnationalism," *Annual Review of Anthropology* 24: 546–565

Keck, Margaret E. and Kathryn Sikkink 1998, *Activists Beyond Borders: Advocacy Networks in International Politics*, Ithaca: Cornell University Press

Keen, David 1994, *The Benefits of Famine: A Political Economy of Famine and Relief in Southwestern Sudan, 1983–89*, Princeton: Princeton University Press

Kenya Human Rights Commission 1993, *The State of Human Rights in Kenya. A Year of Political Harassment*, Nairobi: Kenya Human Rights Commission
1995, *Licensed to Kill: Police Shootings In Kenya*, Nairobi: Kenya Human Rights Commission

Keohane, Robert 1987, "Theory of World Politics: Structural Realism and Beyond," in Robert Keohane (ed.), *Neorealism and Its Critics*, New York: Columbia University Press, pp. 158–203
1995, "Hobbes's Dilemma and Institutional Change in World Politics: Sovereignty in International Society," in Hans-Henrik Holm and Georg Sorensen (eds.), *Whose World Order?: Uneven Globalization and the End of the Cold War*, Boulder: Westview Press

Keohane, Robert and Helen Milner (eds.) 1996, *Internationalization and Domestic Politics*, Cambridge: Cambridge University Press

Keohane, Robert and Joseph Nye 1977, *Power and Independence*, Boston: Little, Brown

Keohane, Robert, Steve Krasner, and Peter Katzenstein 1998, "International Organization and the Study of World Politics," *International Organization* 52: 645–686

Kibwana, Kivutha 1992, *Law and the Administration of Justice in Kenya*, Nairobi: International Commission of Jurists (Kenya Section)

Kirby, John, T. Kliest, G. Frerks, W. Flikkema, and P. O'Keefe 1997, "UNHCR's Cross Border Operation in Somalia: The Value of Quick Impact Projects for Refugee Resettlement," *Journal of Refugee Studies* 10: 181–198

Klein, Martin 1997, *Slavery and French Colonial Rule*, Cambridge: Cambridge University Press

Klotz, Audie 1995, *Norms in International Politics: The Struggle against Apartheid*, Ithaca: Cornell University Press

Koroma, A.K. 1996, *Sierra Leone: Agony of a Nation*, Freetown: Afro Media

Krasner, Stephen D. (ed.) 1983, *International Regimes*, Ithaca: Cornell University Press
1995, "Power Politics, Institutions, and Transnational Relations," in Thomas Risse (ed.), *Bringing Transnational Relations Back In: Non-State Actors, Domestic Structures and International Institutions*, Cambridge: Cambridge University Press, pp. 257–279
1999, *Sovereignty: Organized Hypocrisy*, Princeton: Princeton University Press

La France Militaire et l'Afrique 1997, Brussels: Editions Complexes-GRIP

LaPalombara, Joseph 1971, "Penetration: A Crisis of Government Capacity," in Leonard Binder (ed.), *Crises and Sequences in Political Development*, Princeton: Princeton University Press, pp. 205–232

Lafargue, Jérôme 1996, *Contestations démocratiques en Afrique. Sociologie de la protestations au Kenya et en Zambie*, Paris: Editions Karthala

Last, Murray 1992, "The Power of Youth, Youth of Power: Notes on the Religions of the Young in Northern Nigeria," in H. d'Almeida-Topor, C. Coquery-Vidrovitch, O-Georg, and F. Guitard et al. (eds.), *Les jeunes en Afrique*, Paris: L'Harmattan, pp. 375–399

Latham, Robert 1997a, *The Liberal Moment*, New York: Columbia University Press

  1997b, "History, Theory, and International Order: Some Lessons from the Nineteenth Century," *Review of International Studies* 23: 419–443

  1999, "Politics in a Floating World: Toward a Critique of Global Governance," in Martin Hewson and Timothy J. Sinclair (eds.), *Approaches to Global Governance Theory*, Albany: State University of New York Press, pp. 23–53

  2000a, "The Politics and History of Responsibility Across Boundaries," *Brown Journal of World Affairs* 7: 173–184

  2000b, "Social Sovereignty," *Theory, Culture & Society* 17: 1–18

Lattimore, Owen 1962, *Studies in Frontier History*, Oxford: Oxford University Press

L'Autre Afrique 1997a, "Un billet de banque, la peut couter cher . . .," August 13–19: 66–68

  1997b, "Pauvres, inefficaces, incontrôlables . . . Que faire des armées africaines?" December 17–23: 8–19

Lawson, Tony 1997, *Economics and Reality*, New York: Routledge

Le Progrès 1997, "Armée: lumière sur la démobilisation et la réinsertion," *Le Progrès* (N'Djanena) May 13: 10–11

Legro, Jeffrey 1996, "Culture and Preferences in the International Cooperation Two-Step," *American Political Science Review* 90: 118–137

Leys, Colin 1996, *The Rise and Fall of Development Theory*, Oxford: James Currey

Licklider, Roy 1995, "The Consequences of Negotiated Settlements in Civil Wars, 1945–1993," *American Political Science Review* 89: 681–690

Lincoln, Bruce 1994, *Authority*, Chicago: University of Chicago Press

Lipschutz, Ronnie 1992, "Reconstructing World Politics: The Emergence of Global Civil Society," *Millennium* 21: 389–420.

Lipset, Seymour Martin 1962, "Introduction," in Robert Michels, *Political Parties: A Sociological Study of the Oligarchic Tendencies of Modern Democracy*, New York: The Free Press, pp. 15–39

Litfin, Karen 1994, "Framing Science: Precautionary Discourse and the Ozone Treaties," *Millennium* 24: 251–278

Lonkila, Markku 2000, "Post-Soviet Russia: A Society of Networks?" in Kangaspuro Markku (ed.), *Russia: More Different than Most?*, Helsinki: Kikimora Publications, pp. 99–112

Lonsdale, John, Stanley Booth-Clibborn, and Andrew Hake 1978, "The Emerging Pattern of Church and State Cooperation in Kenya," in E. Fasholé-Luke, Richard Gray, Adrian Hastings, and Godwin Tasie (eds.), *Christianity in Independent Africa*, Bloomington: Indiana University Press, pp. 267–284

Lopez, George and David Cortwright 1998, "Making Targets 'Smart' From Sanctions," paper delivered at the International Studies Association meetings, Minneapolis, March 18–22

Lukes, Steven 1974, *Power: A Radical View*, New York: Macmillan

MacGaffey, Janet 1991, *The Real Economy of Zaire: The Contributions of Smuggling and Other Unofficial Activities to National Wealth*, Philadelphia: University of Pennsylvania Press

McGreal, Chris and Stefaans Brümmer 1997, "DeBeers in Secret Deal with Rebels," *Mail & Guardian* April 18: 5

Maier, Karl 1996, *Angola: Promises and Lies*, Rivonia: William Waterman

Malkki, Liisa 1994, "Citizens of Humanity: Internationalism and the Imagined Community of Nations," *Diaspora* 3: 41–68.

1995, "Refugees and Exile: From 'Refugee Studies' to the National Order of Things," *Annual Review of Anthropology* 24: 495–523

1996, "Speechless Emissaries: Refugees, Humanitarianism, and Dehistoricization," *Cultural Anthropology* 11: 377–404

Mamdani, Mahmood 1996, *Citizen and Subject: Contemporary Africa and the Legacy of Late Colonialism*, Princeton: Princeton University Press

Mani, Lata 1990, "Contentious Traditions: The Debate on Sati in Colonial India," in Kumkum Sangari and Sudesh Vaid (eds.), *Recasting Women: Essays in Indian Colonial History*, New Brunswick: Rutgers University Press

Mann, Michael 1984, "The Autonomous Power of the State: Its Origins, Mechanisms and Results," *Archives Européennes de Sociologie* 25: 185–213

1986, *Sources of Social Power. Vol. I:* Cambridge: Cambridge University Press

Marchés Tropicaux 1995, "Le Liberia: une economie de guerre profitable," July 28: 1603–1606

1999, "Congo: Les combatants extravert l'exploitation du bois," September 3: 1774–1776

Martin, Guy 1995, "Continuity and Change in Franco-African Relations," *Journal of Modern African Studies* 33: 1–20

Martinez, L. 1995, "Les groupes islamistes entre guérilla et négoce. Vers une consolidation du régime algérien?," *Les Etudes du CERI* 3: 1–26

1998, *La guerre civile en Algérie*, Paris: Editions Karthala-CERI

Masquelier, Adeline 1996, "Identity, Alterity and Ambiguity in a Nigerien Community: Competing Definitions of a True Islam," in Richard Werbner and Terence Ranger (eds.), *Postcolonial Identities in Africa*, London: Zed Books, pp. 222–244

Massey, Doreen and Pat Jess (eds.) 1995, *A Place in the World: Places, Culture and Globalization*, Oxford: Oxford University Press

Mattli, Walter and Anne-Marie Slaughter 1998, "Revisiting the European Court of Justice," *International Organization* 52: 177–210

Mbembe, Achille 1992, "Provisional Notes on the Postcolony," *Africa* 62: 3–37

1993, "Epilogue: crise de légitimité, restauration autoritaire et déliquescence de l'état," in P. Geschiere and P. Konings (eds.), *Itinéraires d'accumulation au Cameroun*, Paris: ASC-Karthala, pp. 345–374

Mbembe, Achille and Janet Roitman 1995, "Figures of the Subject in Times of Crisis," *Public Culture* 7: 323–352

Mehta, Uday 1990, "Liberal Strategies of Exclusion," *Politics and Society* 18: 427–454

Meyer, John 1987, "The World Polity and the Authority of the Nation-State," in George Thomas, John W. Meyer, Francisco O. Ramirez, and John Boli (eds.), *Institutional Structure: Constituting State, Society, and the Individual*, Thousand Oaks, CA: Sage, pp. 41–70

Michels, Robert 1962, *Political Parties: A Sociological Study of the Oligarchic Tendencies of Modern Democracy*, New York: The Free Press

Miers, Suzanne and Richard Roberts (eds.) 1988, *The End of Slavery in Africa*, Madison: University of Wisconsin Press

Migdal, Joel S. 1988, *Strong Societies and Weak States: State–Society Relations and State Capabilities in the Third World*, Princeton: Princeton University Press

Millennium 1994, special issue on global civil society, 23

Minter, William 1994, *Apartheid's Contras*, London: Zed Books

Mintz, Sidney 1985, *Sweetness and Power*, New York: Penguin

Mitchell, J. Clyde 1969, *Social Networks in Urban Situations: Analysis of Personal Relationships in Central African Towns*, Manchester and New York: Manchester University Press

Mitchell, J. Clyde and Jeremy Boissevain (eds.) 1973, *Network Analysis*, The Hague: Mouton

Mitrany, David 1966, *A Working Peace System*, Chicago: Quadrangle Books

Mkandawire, Thandika 1999, "Crisis Management and the Making of 'Choiceless Democracies,'" in Richard Joseph (ed.), *State, Conflict, and Democracy in Africa*, Boulder: Lynne Rienner, pp. 119–136

Mkandawire, Thandika and Charles C. Soludo 1998, *Our Continent, Our Future: African Perspectives on Structural Adjustment*, Ottawa: International Development Research Centre

Moore, Jr., Barrington 1966, *Social Origins of Dictatorship and Democracy*, Boston: Beacon Press

Moravsik, Andrew 1993, "Introduction: Integrating International and Domestic Theories of International Bargaining," in Peter B. Evans, Harold K. Jacobson, and Robert D. Putnam (eds.), *Double-Edged Diplomacy: International Bargaining and Domestic Politics*, Berkeley: University of California Press

1997, "Taking Preferences Seriously: A Liberal Theory of International Politics," *International Organization* 51: 513–554

Moul, William 1973, "The Levels of Analysis Problem Revisited," *Canadian Journal of Political Science* 6: 494–513

Nash, Marian 1996, "Contemporary Practice of the United States Relating to International Law–Unrecognised Governments Access to US Courts," *American Journal of International Law* 90: 262–265

National Patriotic Reconstruction Assembly Government 1991, "The Legal Status of the National Patriotic Reconstruction Government as the De Facto Government of the Republic of Liberia," Gbarnga, mimeo

1992, "Memorandum of Understanding," Gbarnga, January 17

Ndegwa, Stephen N. 1996, *The Two Faces of Civil Society: NGOs and Politics in Africa*, West Hartford: Kumarian Press.
  1997, "Citizenship and Ethnicity: An Examination of Two Transition Moments in Kenyan Politics," *American Political Science Review* 91: 599–616
  1998, "The Incomplete Transition: The Constitutional and Electoral Context in Kenya," *Africa Today* 45: 193–212
N'Djamena Hebdo 1997a, "L'insécurité dans le nord Cameroun"
  1997b, "Lorsque démobilisation rime avec développement," 281: 6–7
New York Times 1997, "The New mercenaries of Africa," February 2: 14
New York Times 2000, "In the Oil Rich Niger Delta, Deep Poverty and Grim Fires," August 11: 1
Ngarngoune, S. 1997, "Alerte au Sud," *N'Djamena Hebdo* 280: 4
Ngugi, Wa Thiong'o 1993, *Moving the Centre: The Struggle for Cultural Freedoms*, London: James Currey
Niboro, I. 1997, "Shell's Racism in the Delta," *Tell* August 12: 28–31
Nordstrom, Carolyn 1995, "Contested Identities/ Essentially Contested Powers," in K. Rupesinghe (ed.), *Conflict Transformation*, London: MacMillan
  1997, *A Different Kind of War Story*, Philadelphia: University of Pennsylvania Press
  1998, "A War Dossier," *Public Culture* 10: 54–62
Noyer, Christian 1994, "Le Club de Paris et le Fonds Monétaire International," in Thierry Walrafen (ed.), *Bretton Woods: Mélange pour un cinquantenaire*, Paris: Editions le Monde, pp. 389–395
O'Brien, Robert 2000, *Contesting Global Governance: Multilateral Economic Institutions and Global Social Movements*, Cambridge: Cambridge University Press
O'Donnell, Guillermo and Philippe C. Schmitter 1986, *Transitions from Authoritarian Rule: Tentative Conclusions about Uncertain Democracies*, Baltimore: The Johns Hopkins University Press
Obi, Cyril 1997, "Globalisation and Local Resistance: The Case of the Ogoni Versus Shell," *New Political Economy* 2: 137–148
  1999, "The Crisis of Environmental Governance in the Niger Delta," *AAPS Occasional Paper* 3
"Observatoire géopolitique des drogues" 1995, *Géopolitique des drogues*, Paris: La Découverte
Oladipo, Tunde 1998, "Task Force Extortion?" *AM News* (Lagos) January 14: 2
  1999, "Alleged Looting by Marwa Administrators," *PM News* (Lagos) May 18: 1
Olarewaju, Segun 1998, "Protest Against Private Taxmen," *PM News* (Lagos) November 9: 16–17
Olowu, Dele 1999, "Local Governance, Democracy and Development," in Richard Joseph (ed.), *State, Conflict, and Democracy in Africa*, Boulder: Lynne Rienner, pp. 285–296
Onanuga, B. 1998, "The Dangerous Oil Fields," *The News* (Lagos) September 14: 13
Ong, Aihwa 1999, *Flexible Citizenship: The Cultural Logics of Transnationality*, Durham, NC: Duke University Press

Onishi, N. 1999, "Deep in the Republic of Chevron," *Sunday New York Times Magazine*, July 4

Onuf, Nicholas 1995, "Levels," *European Journal of International Relations* 1: 25–58

Oxfam International 1995, "Multilateral Debt: An End to the Crisis?" position paper, October
  1996, "Debt Relief and Poverty Reduction: New Hope for Uganda," September
  1997, "Poor Country Debt Relief: False Dawn or New Hope for Poverty Reduction?" April
  1999, "Outcome of the IMF/Work Bank September 1999 Annual Meetings: Implications for Poverty Reduction and Debt Relief," October

Pasha, Mustapha Kamal 1997, "Ibn Khaldun and World Order," in S. Gill and J. Mittelman (eds.), *Innovation and Transformation in International Studies*, Cambridge: Cambridge University Press

Perry, Donna L. 1997, "Rural Ideologies and Urban Imaginings: Wolof Immigrants in New York City," *Africa Today* 44: 229–260

Pideu, K. 1995, "Une province abandonée aux coupeurs de route," *La Nouvelle Expression (Douala)* 243: 6

Pitkin, Hannah Fenichel 1967, *The Concept of Representation*, Berkeley: University of California Press

Platt, D.C.M. 1968, "The Imperialism of Free Trade: Some Reservations," *Economic History Review* 21: 296–306

Polak, Jacques 1997, "The World Bank and IMF: A Changing Relationship," in Davesh Kapur, John P. Lewis, and Richard Webb (eds.), *The World Bank: Its First Half Century*, Washington, DC: Brookings Institution Press, pp. 473–522

Pomeranz, Kenneth 2000, *The Great Divergence: Europe, China, and the Making of the Modern World Economy*, Princeton: Princeton University Press

Powell, Walter 1990, "Neither Market nor Hierarchy: Network Forms of Organisation," *Research on Organizational Behavior* 12: 295–336

Prakash, Gyan 1990, *Bonded Histories: Geneaologies of Labor Servitude in Colonial India*, Cambridge: Cambridge University Press

Price, Richard 1998, "Reversing the Gun Sights: Transnational Civil Society Targets Land Mines," *International Organization* 52: 613–644

Przeworski, Adam and Fernando Limongi 1997, "Modernization: Theories and Facts," *World Politics* 49: 155–183

Pullella, Philip 1998, "Pope Suggests Third World Debt Relief for 2000," Reuters

Putnam, Robert D. 1988, "Diplomacy and Domestic Politics: The Logic of Two-Level Games," *International Organization* 42: 427–460

Raz, Joseph 1990a, "Introduction," in Joseph Raz (ed.), *Authority*, New York: New York University Press, pp. 1–19
  (ed.) 1990b, *Authority*, New York: New York University Press

Reeves, Ross and Michel Moulard 1993, *Postwar Strategy for Forestry Development and Environmental Management*, Monrovia: Ministry of Planning and Economic Affairs

Reno, William 1995, *Corruption and State Politics in Sierra Leone*, Cambridge: Cambridge University Press

1998, *Warlord Politics and African States*, Boulder: Lynne Rienner

Republic of Kenya 1992, "Report of the Parliamentary Select Committee to Investigate Ethnic Clashes in Western and Other Parts of Kenya," Nairobi: The National Assembly

Republic of Liberia 1993, "Memorandum on Behavior of Firestone During the Liberian Civil War," Ministry of Finance, May 6

Republic of South Africa 1998, *Commentary to Regulation of Foreign Military Assistance Act*, February 26

Reuters 1998, "Ugandan Debt Deal Seen Boosting Investor Confidence," April 9

Ribot, Jesse C. 1999, "Decentralisation, Participation and Accountability in Sahelian Forestry: Legal Instruments of Political-Administrative Control," *Africa* 69: 23–65

Rice, Susan 1997, "Remarks at African Studies Association Meeting," ASA presentation, Columbus, Ohio

Richards, Paul 1996, *Fighting for the Rain Forest: War, Youth and Resources in Sierra Leone*, Oxford: James Currey

Rieff, David 1996, *Slaughterhouse: Bosnia and the Failure of the West*, New York: Touchstone Books

Rieffel, Alexis 1985, "The Role of the Paris Club in Managing Debt Problems," *Essays in International Finance No. 161*, Princeton University

Risse, Thomas, Stephen C. Ropp, and Kathryn Sikkink (eds.) 1999, *The Power of Human Rights: International Norms and Domestic Change*, Cambridge: Cambridge University Press

Robertson, Roland 1992, *Globalization: Social Theory and Global Culture*, London: Sage

Robinson, D. 1996, *Ogoni: The Struggle Continues*, Geneva and Nairobi: World Council of Churches and All African Council of Churches

Robinson, Ronald and John Gallagher 1961, *Africa and the Victorians*, New York: Anchor Books

Roitman, Janet 1996, "Objects of the Economy and the Language of Politics in Northern Cameroon," Ph.D. dissertation, University of Pennsylvania

1998, "The Garrison-Entrepôt," *Cahiers d'Etudes Africaines* 38: 297–329

Rosenau, James N. 1969, *Linkage Politics: Essays on Convergence of National and International Systems*, New York: The Free Press

1990, *Turbulence in World Politics: A Theory of Change and Continuity*, Princeton: Princeton University Press

1992, "Governance, Order and Change in World Politics," in James N., Rosenau, and Ernst-Otto Czempiel (eds.), *Governance Without Government: Order and Change in World Politics*, Cambridge: Cambridge University Press, pp. 1–29

1997, *Along the Domestic–Foreign Frontier: Exploring Governance in a Turbulent World*, Cambridge: Cambridge University Press

Ross, Marc 1997a, "Culture and Identity in Comparative Political Analysis," in Mark Irving Lichbach and Alan S. Zuckerman (eds.), *Comparative Politics: Rationality, Culture, and Structure*, Cambridge: Cambridge University Press

1997b, *The Management of Conflict: Interpretations and Interests in Comparative Perspective*, New Haven: Yale University Press

Rothchild, Donald and Naomi Chazan (eds.) 1988, *The Precarious Balance: State and Society in Africa*, Boulder: Westview Press

Rowell, A. 1996a, *Green Backlash: Global Subversion of the Environmental Movement*, New York: Routledge

1996b "Sleeping with the Enemy," *Village Voice* January 23

Ruggie, John Gerard 1982, "International Regimes, Transactions and Change: Embedded Liberalism in the Postwar Economic Order," *International Organization* 36: 379–415

1983, "Continuity and Transformation in the World Polity: Toward a Neorealist Synthesis," *World Politics* 35: 261–285

1993, "Territoriality and Beyond: Problematizing Modernity in International Relations," *International Organization* 47: 139–174

Saccoh, Sheku 1995a, "Capital Flight in Sierra Leone," *Africa Economic Digest* February 13: 14

1995b, "Sierra Leone's Mines Evacuated," *The Mining Journal* January 27: 57

Sachs, Jeffrey, Kwesi Botchwey, Maciej Cuchra, and Sara Serban 1999, "Implementing Debt Relief for the HIPCs," Center for International Development, Harvard University, Policy Paper No. 2, August

Saluseki, Bivan 2000, "IMF Reforms Have Brought Poverty, Says Chiluba," *The Post of Zambia* February 9

Sarooshi, Daneesh 1999, *The United Nations and the Development of Collective Security: The Delegation by the UN Security Council of its Chapter VII Powers*, Oxford: Oxford University Press

Saro-Wiwa, Ken 1995, *A Month and a Day: A Detention Diary*, London: Penguin

Sassen, Saskia 1995, *Losing Control? Sovereignty in an Age of Globalization*, New York: Columbia University Press

1998a, *Globalization and Its Discontents*, London: Norton.

1998b, "The State and the New Geography of Power," paper presented at the American Anthropological Association meetings, Philadelphia

Schatzberg, Michael (ed.) 1987, *The Political Economy of Kenya*, New York: Praeger

Schmidt-Nowara, Christopher 1999, *Empire and Antislavery: Spain, Cuba, and Puerto Rico, 1833–1874*, Pittsburgh: University of Pittsburgh Press

Schmitz, Hans Peter 1999, "Transnational Human Rights Activism and Political Change in Kenya and Uganda," in Thomas Risse, Stephen C. Ropp, and Kathryn Sikkink (eds.), *The Power of Human Rights: International Norms, and Domestic Change*, Cambridge: Cambridge University Press, pp. 39–77

Schmitz, Hans Peter, and Kathryn Sikkink 2001, "Human Rights and International Relations Theory," in W. Carlsnaes, T. Risse, and B. Simmons (eds.), *Handbook of International Relations*, Thousand Oaks, CA: Sage

Schraeder, Peter, Steven Hook, and Bruce Taylor 1998, "Clarifying the Foreign Aid Puzzle: A Comparison of American, Japanese, French and Swedish Aid Flows," *World Politics* 50: 294–323

Scott, James C. 1990, *Domination and the Arts of Resistance: Hidden Transcripts*, New Haven: Yale University Press

Scott, Julius 1986, "A Common Wind: Currents of Afro-American Communication in the Age of the Haitian Revolution," Ph.D. dissertation, Duke University

Sevigny, David 1990, *The Paris Club: An Insider's View*, Ottawa: The North–South Institute

Shaw, Martin 1998, "The Historical Sociology of the Future," *Review of International Political Economy* 5: 321–336

Shearer, David 1998, *Private Armies and Military Intervention*, London: International Institute for Strategic Studies

Shils, Edward 1975, *Center and Periphery*, Chicago: University of Chicago Press

Shore, Chris and Susan Wright 1997, "Policy: A New Field of Anthropology," in Chris Shore and Susan Wright (eds.), *Anthropology of Policy: Critical Perspectives on Governance and Power*, New York: Routledge, pp. 3–41

Sikkink, Kathryn 1993, "Human Rights, Principled Issue-Networks, and Sovereignty in Latin America," *International Organization* 47: 411–441

Simmons, P.J. 1998, "Learning to Live with NGOs," *Foreign Policy* 12: 82–96

Sinclair, Timothy 1994, "Passing Judgement: Credit Rating Processes as Regulatory Mechanisms of Governance in the Emerging World Order," *Review of International Political Economy* 1: 133–160

  1999, "Bond Rating Agencies and Coordination in the Global Political Economy," in A. Claire Cutler, Virginia Haufler, and Tony Porter (eds.), *Private Authority and International Affairs*, Albany: State University of New York Press

Singer, J.D. 1961, "The Levels of Analysis Problem in International Relations," in Klaus Knorr and Sidney Verba (eds.), *The International System: Theoretical Essays*, Princeton: Princeton University Press, pp. 77–92

Sklar, Richard L. 1993, "The African Frontier for Political Science," in Robert H. Bates, V.Y. Mudimbe, and Jean O'Barr (eds.), *Africa and the Disciplines*, Chicago: University of Chicago Press, pp. 83–110

Skocpol, Theda 1979, *States and Social Revolutions: A Comparative Analysis of France, Russia and China*, Cambridge: Cambridge University Press

Skogley, S. 1997, "Complexities in Human Rights Protection: Actors and Rights Involved in the Ogoni Conflict," *Netherlands Quarterly of Human Rights* 15, 1: 51

Slaughter, Anne-Marie 1997, "The Real New World Order," *Foreign Affairs* 76: 183–197

Smith, D., D. Solinger, and S. Topik (eds.) 1999, *States and Sovereignty in the Global Economy*, New York: Routledge

Smith, Jackie, Charles Chatfield, and Ron Pagnucco (eds.) 1997, *Transnational Social Movements and Global Politics: Solidarity Beyond the State*, Syracuse: Syracuse University Press

Smith, Robert 1989, *Warfare & Diplomacy in Pre-Colonial West Africa*, Madison: University of Wisconsin Press

Soremekun, Kayode and Cyril Obi 1993, "The Changing Pattern of Private Foreign Investments in the Nigerian Oil Industry," *Africa Development* 18, 3

Soudan, F. 1996, "La guerre secrète," *Jeune Afrique* 187: 13–19

Spruyt, Hendrik 1994, *The Sovereign State and Its Competitors*, Princeton: Princeton University Press

Stallings, Barbara (ed.) 1995, *Global Change, Regional Response: The New International Context of Development*, Cambridge: Cambridge University Press

Sterling-Folker, Jennifer 1997, "Realist Environment, Liberal Process, and Domestic Level-Variables," *International Studies Quarterly* 41: 1–26

Stern, Nicholas 1997, "The World Bank as Intellectual Actor," in Davesh Kapur, John. P. Lewis, and Richard Webb (eds.), *The World Bank: Its First Half Century*, Washington, DC: Brookings Institution Press, pp. 161–274

Stoler, Ann and Frederick Cooper 1996, "Between Metropole and Colony: Rethinking a Research Agenda," in Frederick Cooper and Ann Stoler (eds.), *Tensions of Empire: Colonial Cultures in a Bourgeois World*, Berkeley: University of California Press, pp. 1–56

Stora, Benjamin 1991, *La gangrène et l'oublie: La mémoire de la guerre d'Algérie*, Paris: Editions La Découverte

Strandberg, Peter 1999, "With the Rebels in Congo," *New African* February: 18

Strange, Susan 1988, *States and Markets*, London: Pinter
    1996, *The Retreat of the State: The Diffusion of Power in the World Economy*, Cambridge: Cambridge University Press.

Strathern, Marilyn 1995, *Shifting Contexts: Transformations in Anthropological Knowledge*, New York: Routledge

Summers, Lawrence H. 1999, "Conference on Debt Relief and Poverty Reduction," Treasury News press release, July 26, at www.ustreas.gov

Swaray, John 1996, "Debt Reduction Programme," Mimeo, Governor of the Bank of Sierra Leone, April 4

Swartz, Marc J. 1968, "Introduction," in Marc J. Swartz (ed.), *Local-Level Politics: Social and Cultural Perspectives*, Chicago: Aldine Publishing, pp. 1–46

Takahashi, S. 1997, "The UNHCR Note on International Protection You Won't See," *International Journal of Refugee Law* 9: 267–273

Takaya, Bala and Sonni Gwanle, Tyoden (eds.) 1987, *The Kaduna Mafia*, Jos, Nigeria: Jos University Press

Tambiah, Stanley 1996, *Leveling Crowds*, Berkeley: University of California Press

Tarr, Byron S. 1993, "The ECOMOG Initiative in Liberia: A Liberian Perspective," *Issue* 21: 74–83

Taussig, Michael 1987, *Colonialism, Shamanism, and the Wild Man*, Chicago: University of Chicago Press

Teiga, M.B. 1997, "Une armée, certes, mais combien de divisions . . . ," *L'Autre Afrique* December 17–23: 14–15

Thomas, Daniel 2001, *The Helsinki Effect*, Princeton: Princeton University Press

Throup, David 1993, "Elections and Political Legitimacy in Kenya," *Africa* 63: 371–396

Throup, David and Charles Hornsby 1998, *Multi-Party Politics in Kenya: The Kenyatta and Moi States and the Triumph of the System in the 1992 Elections*, Oxford: James Currey

Tilly, Charles (ed.) 1975, *The Formation of National States in Western Europe*, Princeton: Princeton University Press

1990, *Coercion, Capital, and European States, AD 990–1990*, Oxford: Blackwell

Tönnies, Ferdinand 1957, *Gemeinschaft and Gesellschaft*, Ann Arbor: University of Michigan Press

Tostensen, Arne, Bård-Anders Andreassen, and Kjetil Tronvoll 1998, *Kenya's Hobbled Democracy Revisited. The 1997 General Elections in Retrospect and Prospect*, Oslo: Norwegian Institute of Human Rights

Trouillot, Michel-Rolph 1995, *The Silences of the Past: The Power and the Production of History*, Boston: Beacon Press

Tully, James 1995, *Strange Multiplicity: Constitutionalism in an Age of Diversity*, Cambridge: Cambridge University Press

Tvedt, Terje 1998, *Angels of Mercy or Development Diplomats?: NGOs and Foreign Aid*, Trenton: Africa World Press

Twaddell, William 1996, "Testimony Before the House International Relations Committee," Washington, DC, June 26

UN Commission on Human Rights 2000, "Civil and Political Rights, Including Questions of Torture and Detention," Visit of Special Rapporteur Sir Nigel Rodley to Kenya (E/CN.4/2000/9/Add.4), United Nations

United Nations Research Institute on Social Development 1995, *States of Disarray: The Social Effects of Globalization*, London: UNRISD

Uvin, Peter 1998, *Aiding Violence: The Development Enterprise in Rwanda*, West Hartford: Kumarian Press

Van de Walle, Nicolas 1999, "Globalization and African Democracy," in Richard Joseph (ed.), *State, Conflict and Democracy in Africa*, Boulder: Lynne Rienner, pp. 95–118

Van Trottenberg, Axel 1999, *World Bank Review of HIPC*, April 5, at www.worldbank.org/html/today/archives/apr5-9-99

Venter, A. J. 1997, "Angola: US Forces Guard Angolan Oilfields," *Mail & Guardian*, October 10: 10

Villalón, Leonardo A. and Phillip A. Huxtable (eds.) 1998, *The African State at a Critical Juncture: Between Disintegration and Reconfiguration*, Boulder: Lynne Rienner

Vines, Alex 1991, *Renamo: Terrorism in Mozambique*, Bloomington: Indiana University Press

Von Eschen, Penny M. 1997, *Race against Empire: Black Americans and Anticolonialism, 1937–1957*, Ithaca: Cornell University Press

Waever, Ole 1998, "Insecurity, Security, and Asecurity in the West European Non-War Community," in E. Adler and M. Barnett (eds.), *Security Communities*, Cambridge: Cambridge University Press, pp. 69–118

Walker, R.B.J. 1993, *Inside/Outside: International Relations as Political Theory*, Cambridge: Cambridge University Press

Walker, R.B.J. and S.H. Mendlovitz (eds.) 1990, *Contending Sovereignties*, Boulder: Lynne Rienner

Wallerstein, Immanuel 1974, *The Modern World-System*, New York: Academic Press

1999, "States? Sovereignty? The Dilemma of Capitalists in an Age of Transition," in D. Smith, D. Solinger, and S. Topik, *States and Sovereignty in the Global Economy*, New York: Routledge, pp. 20–33

Waltz, Kenneth 1979, *Theory of International Politics*, Reading, MA: Addison Wesley

Wapner, Paul 1995, "Politics Beyond the State: Environmental Activism and World Civic Politics," *World Politics* 47: 311–340

Watts, Michael J. 1993, "Idioms of Land and Labor: Producing Politics and Rice in Senegambia," in Thomas J. Bassett and Donald E. Crummey (eds.), *Land in African Agrarian Systems*, Madison: University of Wisconsin Press, pp. 157–193

1999, "Collective Wish Images: Geographical Imaginaries and the Crisis of National Development," in Doreen Massey, John Allen, and Philip Sarre (eds.), *Human Geography Today*, Cambridge: Polity Press, pp. 85–107

Weber, Eugene 1976, *Peasants into Frenchmen*, Stanford: Stanford University Press

Weber, Max 1978, *Economy and Society*, Berkeley: University of California Press

Wendt, Alexander 1999, *Social Theory of International Politics*, New York: Cambridge University Press

White, Harrison 1992, *Identity and Control: A Structural Theory of Social Action*, Princeton: Princeton University Press

Widner, Jennifer A. 1992, *The Rise of the One-Party-State in Kenya: From "Harambee" to "Nyayo,"* Berkeley: University of California Press

Williams, Eric 1944, *Capitalism and Slavery*, Chapel Hill: University of North Carolina Press

Williams, Marc 1996, "International Political Economy and Global Environmental Change," in J. Vogler and M. Imber (eds.), *The Environment and International Relations*, London and New York: Routledge

Wilmsen, Edwin and Patrick McAllister (eds.) 1996, *The Politics of Difference: Ethnic Premises in a World of Power*, Chicago: University of Chicago Press

Wilson, Richard (ed.) 1997, *Human Rights, Culture, and Context*, London: Pluto Press

Wonkeryor, Edward Lama 1985, *Liberia Military Dictatorship: A Fiasco "Revolution,"* Clinton, NY: Struggler's Community Press

Woods, Dwayne 1995, "Transnational Dimensions of Civil Society in Africa," unpublished MS, Purdue University

World Bank 1994, *Adjustment in Africa*, Oxford: Oxford University Press

1997a, *African Development Indicators*, Washington, DC: World Bank

1997b, *Global Development Finance 1997, 1: Analysis and Summary Tables*, Washington, DC: World Bank

1997c, "Uganda: Preliminary Document on the Initiative for HIPCs," IDA/SecM97-41, February 14

1997d, "Uganda: HIPC Debt Initiative: Final HIPC Document," IDA/R97-32, April 14

1997e, "Sierra Leone Recovery and Reintegration Project," Report No. PIC 3995, January 13

1998, "Republic of Uganda: HIPC Debt Initiative: President's Memorandum and Completion Point Document," IDA/R98-33, March 23

Wrong, Michela 1995, "Banking Thrives in Chaotic Zaire," *Financial Times* March 7: 7

Young, Crawford 1994, *The African Colonial State in Comparative Perspective*, Madison: University of Wisconsin Press

Young, Oran 1994, *International Governance: Protecting the Environment in a Stateless Society*, Ithaca: Cornell University Press

Zarate, Juan Carlos 1998, "The Emergence of a New Dog of War: Private Security Companies, International Law, and the New World Disorder," *Stanford Journal of International Law* 34: 79–119

Zartman, I. William (ed.) 1995, *Collapsed States: The Disintegration and Restoration of Legitimate Authority*, Boulder: Lynne Rienner

Zulaika, Joseba and William Douglas, 1996, *Terror and Taboo*, New York: Routledge

Zürn, Michael 1998, "The Rise of International Environmental Politics: A Review of Current Research," *World Politics* 50: 617–649

Index

Bold page numbers refer to Tables and Figures.